W9-BCA-211

Marsha McCloskey's
BLOCK Party

Marsha McCloskey's

BLOCK
Party

A Quilter's Extravaganza of 120 Rotary-Cut Block Patterns

RODALE

RODALE

WE INSPIRE AND ENABLE PEOPLE TO IMPROVE THEIR LIVES AND THE WORLD AROUND THEM

©1998 by Marsha McCloskey
Illustrations ©1998 by Mario Ferro
  and Barbara Field
Photographs ©1998 by Rodale Inc.

All rights reserved. No part of this publication may be reproduced or transmitted in any form or by any means, electronic or mechanical, including photocopy, recording, or any other information storage and retrieval system, without the written permission of the publisher, with the following exception: Rodale grants permission to photocopy patterns and quilting designs to persons making the projects for their own personal use.

The author and editors who compiled this book have tried to make all of the contents as accurate and as correct as possible. Illustrations, photographs, and text have all been carefully checked and cross-checked. However, due to the variability of materials, personal skill, and so on, neither the author nor Rodale assumes any responsibility for any injuries suffered or for damages or other losses incurred that result from the material presented herein. All instructions and diagrams should be carefully studied and clearly understood before beginning any project.

Printed in the United States of America on acid-free ∞, recycled paper ♻

Editor: **Karen Bolesta**
Cover and Interior Book Designer: **Christopher Rhoads**
Design Assistance: **Tanja L. Lipinski**
Digital Imaging Specialist: **Dale Mack**
Layout Designer: **Pat Mast**
Interior Illustrators: **Mario Ferro and Barbara Field**
Interior Photographers: **John Hamel and Mitch Mandel**
Cover Photographer: **Mitch Mandel**
Interior and Cover Photo Stylist: **Jody Olcott**
Photography Editor: **James A. Gallucci**
Copy Editor: **Erana C. Bumbardatore**
Manufacturing Coordinator: **Melinda Rizzo**
Indexer: **Nan Badgett**
Editorial Assistance: **Jodi Guiducci**

Rodale Home and Garden Books

Vice President and Editorial Director:
  Margaret J. Lydic
Managing Editor, Quilt Books: **Suzanne Nelson**
Director of Design and Production: **Michael Ward**
Associate Art Director: **Carol Angstadt**
Production Manager: **Robert V. Anderson Jr.**
Studio Manager: **Leslie M. Keefe**
Copy Director: **Dolores Plikaitis**
Book Manufacturing Manager: **Mark Krahforst**
Office Manager: **Karen Earl-Braymer**

Styled photographs were shot on location at Sears Homelife in Whitehall, Pennsylvania.

We're always happy to hear from you. For questions or comments concerning the editorial content of this book, please write to:

Rodale Inc.
Book Readers' Service
33 East Minor Street
Emmaus, PA 18098

Look for other Rodale books wherever books are sold. Or call us at (800) 848-4735.

For more information about Rodale and the books and magazines we publish, visit our Web site at:
www.rodale.com

Library of Congress Cataloging-in-Publication Data
McCloskey, Marsha.
   [Block party]
   Marsha McCloskey's block party : a quilter's extravaganza of 120 rotary-cut block patterns.
       p.   cm.
   Includes index.
   ISBN 0–87596–756–6 (hardcover)
   ISBN 1–57954–266–2 (paperback)
   1. Patchwork—Patterns. 2. Rotary cutting.
3. Patchwork quilts.   I. Title.
TT835 .M2742 1998
746.46'041—ddc211   98–25353

Distributed to the book trade by St. Martin's Press

2 4 6 8 10 9 7 5 3 1 hardcover
              8 10 9   paperback

Contents

Designing Your Own Quilt 122

Mix-and-Match Projects 140

Quiltmaking Basics 216

Introduction

When my son Matthew was about 10 years old he read a clever series of books titled *Choose Your Own Adventure*. Forerunners of today's interactive video games, these books allowed the reader to have a say in the story's outcome by offering choices at the end of each chapter. Each choice set the course for a new adventure and a different ending to the story.

In the same way, making a quilt is like setting out on a new and exciting adventure. That's why I wrote this book—I wanted you to experience the joy of "choosing your own quilting adventure." During the quiltmaking process, you make choices that define how your quilt looks and what mood it conveys. Sometimes you decide what color you want your quilt to be before you decide which setting you want to use. Or perhaps you had a great idea for a border or found a special fabric that you wanted to showcase before you decided whether you wanted to make a wallhanging or a bed-size quilt. Making a quilt is really about making decisions, regardless of where you start in the quilt-design process. It's not always easy, but it is fun, and the rewards of making a unique and personal quilt are the main reason we make quilts in the first place.

To give you all the resources you need to have a creative and satisfying quilting adventure, I start with the basics—quilt blocks. In "The Block Library" portion of this book, I provide 120 different blocks, all sized to finish at 9 inches and all suitable for rotary cutting. Collecting patchwork block designs has been a hobby for me, and over the years I've designed many of my own. To fill this Block Library, I've selected my favorite traditional blocks, plus original ones that together make a rich and versatile collection. Use this library of block designs as your creative starting point. Because the blocks are all a standard size, you can mix and match them easily within a quilt design.

Each block featured in "The Block Library" has its own page, complete with a color photograph, a rotary-cutting chart, template references, piecing diagrams, and different shading suggestions. This block collection will become a valuable resource in your quilting library and will inspire countless quilts. If you're a beginning quilter, look for blocks that have fewer pieces and easier shapes, like squares and rectangles. As you become more confident, try a block with a diagonal construction or one with lots of triangles. If you're an intermediate or advanced quilter, there are plenty of blocks to challenge your skills, including blocks with set-in seams or unusual shapes that can be cut with templates and a rotary cutter.

To give you a framework for mixing and matching blocks, I designed 15 quilt projects, all based on 9-inch blocks. You'll find these in the "Mix-and-Match Projects" section. Pick your favorite blocks, pick a project that strikes your fancy, and you're on your way to making a beautiful quilt. I've made hundreds of suggestions throughout the book to help you decide which blocks work best together.

Each of the 15 projects features different settings, lattice elements, and border treatments. If you see a project you love and absolutely want to make it just the way you see it in the book, then do it—all the instructions you need are here. But feel free to go beyond what you see and choose different blocks to come up with a quilt that is uniquely yours.

For quilters who are ready to venture further into quilt design, I've included the section called "Designing Your Own Quilt." This is an adventure guaranteed to have a happy ending, since I've provided great ideas and useful tips to help you make the best design choices possible. I take you step by step through the process and share years of quilt-making experience that I've gathered. If you've ever hesitated about designing a quilt on your own, this section makes it easy to create a unique and personal quilt.

So get ready to set out on a new and exciting quilt adventure. I've given you all the design tools you need to proceed with confidence. Browse through the blocks and settings in this book for inspiration, add in your creativity and your love of quilting, and have fun!

Using This Book

This book is divided into three basic sections: "The Block Library," "Designing Your Own Quilt," and "Mix-and-Match Projects." A small section on quiltmaking basics and an illustrated block index at the back of the book are features added for your convenience.

"The Block Library" houses a collection of 120 terrific 9-inch block patterns. Containing both traditional and original block designs, this library is an endless source of creative possibilities.

"Designing Your Own Quilt" gives you lots of easy guidelines to follow on arranging blocks together, block variations, quilt sizes, and border possibilities. Explore these design ideas and learn how simple and satisfying it is to incorporate personal touches into every quilt you make.

In "Mix-and-Match Projects," you'll find quilt designs I've already created. You get all the information you need to make a quilt like the one in the photograph at the beginning of each chapter. Or, if you prefer to create your own quilt using any of the other 120 blocks in the book, each project offers suggestions for selecting blocks that will work effectively in that setting. The directions are clearly written in a step-by-step format so that you can easily substitute the block of your choice.

The Block Library

Sewn Blocks
Each block in the collection was sewn using the piecing diagrams and cutting chart on this page. Use this color combination as inspiration for your next project.

Shading Ideas
Here's where you'll discover ways you can change the look of your block—just by changing the light, medium, and dark value placement. Some of these changes are so dramatic that you'll barely recognize it as the same block.

Clear Instructions
You'll find detailed assembly diagrams, plus pressing arrows to indicate which direction to press the seams. These diagrams break down the block into manageable units.

Cutting Charts
Each block's cutting chart gives you the details for either rotary cutting or cutting with templates. These charts tell you how many shapes to cut for one block.

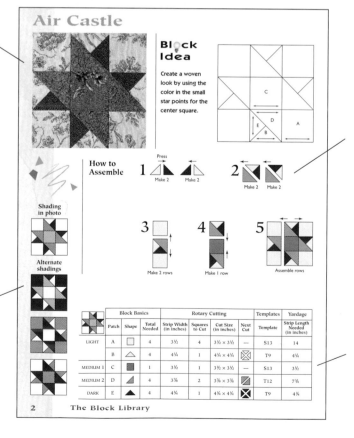

Designing Your Own Quilt

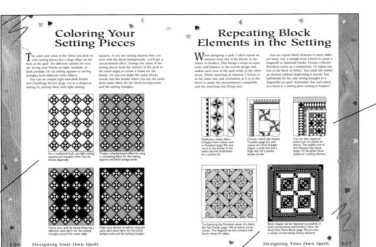

Setting Ideas

Explore the various ways you can improve your quilt without doing any extra work. Often a color or value change is all that's needed to make a big difference. You'll find many useful examples, and they're all easy to incorporate into your design.

Easy Design Variations

Discover simple ways to bring more life to your quilts. From experimenting with light and dark values in a block to adding simple design elements in your setting, these ideas can help transform a nice quilt into a show-stopper.

Lattice and Border Tips

Since a quilt top isn't finished until the last border is sewn on, these ideas help you make decisions about choosing and adding lattice, cornerstones, and borders. You'll discover hints on proportion and orientation when repeating block shapes as accents in a quilt.

Mix-and-Match Projects

Quilt Photographs

Large photographs of each quilt project allow you to clearly see all of the blocks, setting elements, and borders featured. Use these photographs to help you make block choices, plan color schemes, and decide on light and dark value placement.

Complete Directions

These instructions take you step-by-step through each quilt project and allow you to use the block or blocks of your choice. The diagrams show you the details of how the quilt is constructed and quilted.

Fabric Requirements

Look here for a complete listing of the fabric and supplies needed for this project. The fabric for each block is listed separately, so you can easily substitute your favorite block for the ones shown in the photograph.

The Block Library

The Block Library contains 120 different patterns for 9-inch quilt blocks. Because each block finishes at 9 inches, you can use them interchangeably in the projects on pages 140–215. The block collection includes both well-loved traditional blocks and original block designs that I've created over the years, ranging from super-simple to challenging. Presented in alphabetical order, each quilt block is featured on its own page with cutting, assembly, and light-, medium-, and dark-value placement information.

Page at a Glance

Color Photograph

This sewn block, made of fabrics from my stash, shows one possible color combination. Each block was made using the measurements and assembly instructions here, so you can be confident of the directions.

Shading in Photo

This shows where the light-, medium-, and dark-value fabrics are placed in the photographed block.

Alternate Shadings

See how the block design can change when you rearrange the light, medium, and dark values, then assign your own fabric colors to each value. You can photocopy these diagrams and try them in each project's Basic Setting Diagram to help you decide on a block for your quilt—just reduce or enlarge them to fit.

Block Idea

This is where you'll find useful ideas for effective color combinations, tips on fabric selection, ways to change the value placement, or possible settings for each featured block.

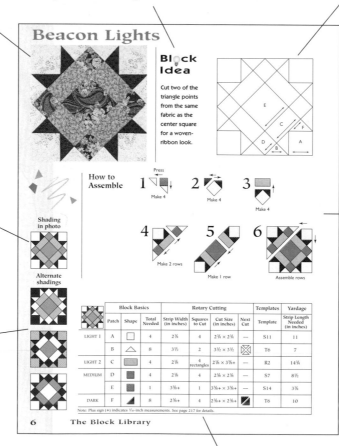

Line Drawing

A black-and-white line drawing illustrates the shapes used in the block. The letters help you identify fabric values in the cutting chart below. Grain line arrows are also given for each shape.

How to Assemble

Step-by-step color diagrams show you how to sew the block. Follow the numbered steps to build the block in the easiest way possible (the colors in the diagrams match the block in the photograph). The labels tell how many to make of each unit or row, and arrows indicate the direction—either left, right, or open—to press each seam after it's sewn.

Cutting Chart

The cutting chart gives you all the information you'll need to cut the patches for the block shown in the color photograph. You'll find more details about the cutting chart on the opposite page.

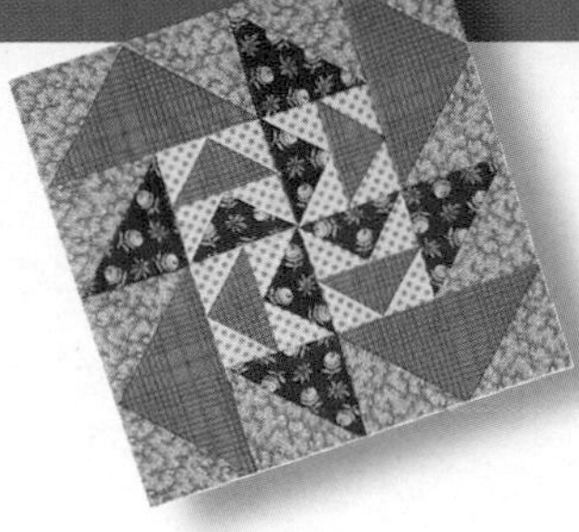

Cutting Chart at a Glance

Block Basics

"Block Basics" contains information about the block you're making. "Patch" refers to the letters in the line drawing, so you know which patch you're cutting. "Shape" identifies the shape of the patch, and "Total Needed" tells how many of that patch are needed to make one block.

Rotary Cutting

The dimensions for rotary-cut patches include a ¼-inch seam allowance. The columns in this section include: "Strip Width" (how wide to cut the strip on the fabric's crosswise grain), "Squares to Cut" (how many squares, or rectangles, you'll need to cut from that strip), "Cut Size" (what size square or rectangle to cut from the strip), and "Next Cut" (how to subcut the squares or rectangles into other shapes). If there are written instructions here, follow them carefully. When templates are mentioned, turn to page 220 to combine templates with rotary cutting for unusual shapes.

Templates

This column identifies a template number for each shape. Quilters who prefer using templates can skip the rotary-cutting portion of this chart and go straight to this column. Templates can be found on pages 226–239. Quilters who rotary cut will also find the templates useful for checking the accuracy of rotary-cut pieces.

	Block Basics			Rotary Cutting				Templates	Yardage
	Patch	Shape	Total Needed	Strip Width (in inches)	Squares to Cut	Cut Size (in inches)	Next Cut	Template	Strip Length Needed (in inches)
LIGHT 1	A	▢	4	2¾	4	2¾ × 2¾	—	S11	11
	B	 △	8	3½	2	3½ × 3½	 ⊠	T6	7
LIGHT 2	C	 ▭	4	2⅛	4 rectangles	2⅛ × 3⅝+	—	R2	14¾
MEDIUM	D	◼	4	2⅛	4	2⅛ × 2⅛	—	S7	8½
	E	◼	1	3⅝+	1	3⅝+ × 3⅝+	—	S14	3¾
DARK	F	◣	8	2⅜+	4	2⅜+ × 2⅜+	 ◩	T6	10

Note: Plus sign (+) indicates ¹/₁₆-inch measurements. See page 217 for details.

Fabric Value

Fabrics are identified here by value and represent the light, medium, and dark fabric placements as shown in the color photograph and the "Shading in photo" diagram.

Plus Measurements

This plus sign (+) indicates a rotary-cutting dimension of ¹/₁₆ inch. This measurement falls halfway between the ⅛-inch measurement-markings on most rotary rulers. See page 217 for details on cutting these ¹/₁₆-inch measurements.

Yardage

This column tells you the length of the fabric strip you'll need to make *one block*. (The width of the strip you'll need is listed under "Strip Width.") If you are making several blocks, multiply the strip length by the number of blocks you are making to get the total strip length you'll need.

If the total strip length needed is over 40 inches, divide by 40 to figure the number of strips you'll need in order to cut patches for your quilt. (Always round up to the nearest whole number.) Then, multiply the number of strips by the strip width to figure the total yardage (in inches) that you'll need.

Air Castle

Create a woven look by using the color in the small star points for the center square.

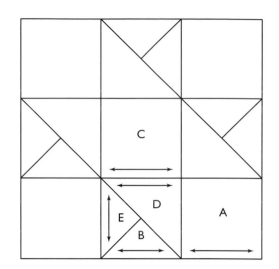

How to Assemble

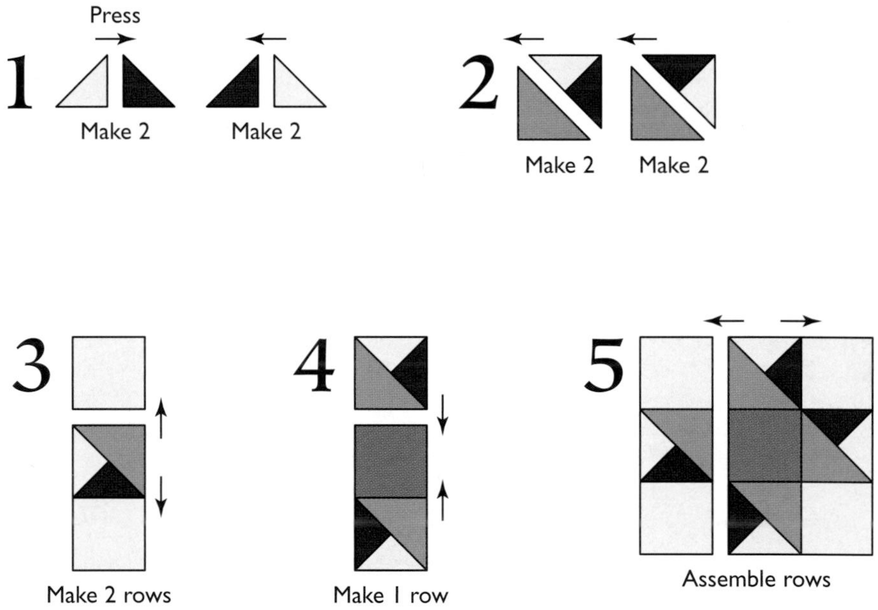

Press

1 Make 2   Make 2

2 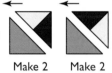 Make 2   Make 2

3 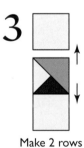 Make 2 rows

4 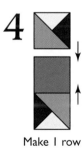 Make 1 row

5 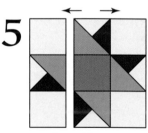 Assemble rows

Shading in photo

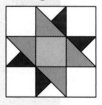

Alternate shadings

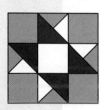

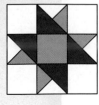

	Block Basics			**Rotary Cutting**				**Templates**	**Yardage**
	Patch	Shape	Total Needed	Strip Width (in inches)	Squares to Cut	Cut Size (in inches)	Next Cut	Template	Strip Length Needed (in inches)
LIGHT	A	☐	4	3½	4	3½ × 3½	—	S13	14
	B	△	4	4¼	1	4¼ × 4¼	⊠	T9	4¼
MEDIUM 1	C	◼	1	3½	1	3½ × 3½	—	S13	3½
MEDIUM 2	D	◸	4	3⅞	2	3⅞ × 3⅞	◿	T12	7¾
DARK	E	▲	4	4¼	1	4¼ × 4¼	⊠	T9	4¼

Antique Star

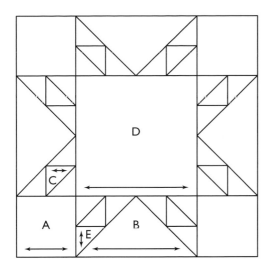

Block Idea

Change the center square and the small medium-value triangles to a light fabric for a more airy look.

How to Assemble

1 Press
Make 8

2
Make 8

3
Make 4

4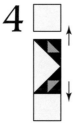
Make 2 rows

5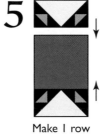
Make 1 row

6
Assemble rows

Shading in photo

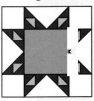

Alternate shadings

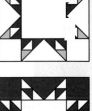

		Block Basics			Rotary Cutting				Templates	Yardage
	Patch	Shape	Total Needed	Strip Width (in inches)	Squares to Cut	Cut Size (in inches)	Next Cut	Template	Strip Length Needed (in inches)
LIGHT	A	□	4	2¾	4	2¾ × 2¾	—	S11	11
	B	△	4	5¾	1	5¾ × 5¾	⊠	T13	5¾
MEDIUM 1	C	◢	8	2	4	2 × 2	◩	T2	8
MEDIUM 2	D	■	1	5	1	5 × 5	—	S16	5
DARK	E	◣	24	2	12	2 × 2	◩	T2	24

Art Square

Block Idea

Use this as an alternate block with a 4 x 4-grid star.

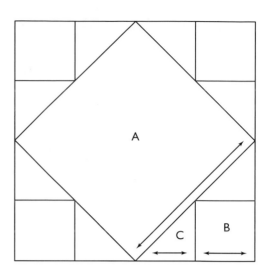

How to Assemble

1 Press ← Make 4

2 Join

3 Join

Shading in photo

Alternate shadings

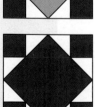

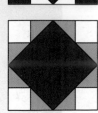

		Block Basics			Rotary Cutting				Templates	Yardage
	Patch	Shape	Total Needed	Strip Width (in inches)	Squares to Cut	Cut Size (in inches)	Next Cut	Template	Strip Length Needed (in inches)	
LIGHT	A	▢	1	$6\frac{7}{8}$	1	$6\frac{7}{8} \times 6\frac{7}{8}$	—	S17	$6\frac{7}{8}$
MEDIUM	B	▧	4	$2\frac{3}{4}$	4	$2\frac{3}{4} \times 2\frac{3}{4}$	—	S11	11
DARK	C	◣	8	$3\frac{1}{8}$	4	$3\frac{1}{8} \times 3\frac{1}{8}$	◺	T10	$12\frac{1}{2}$

Aunt Vina's Favorite

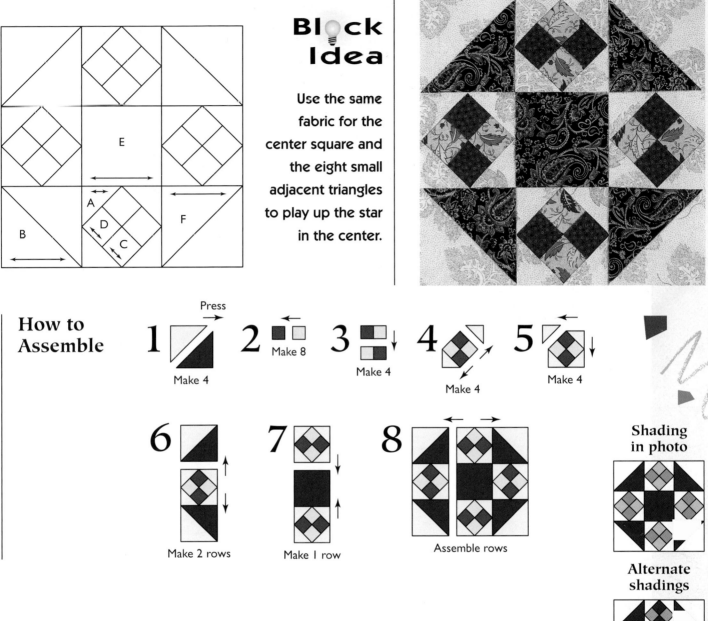

Block Idea

Use the same fabric for the center square and the eight small adjacent triangles to play up the star in the center.

How to Assemble

1 Make 4

Press

2 Make 8

3 Make 4

4 Make 4

5 Make 4

6 Make 2 rows

7 Make 1 row

8 Assemble rows

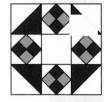

Shading in photo

Alternate shadings

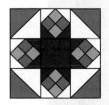

|  | Block Basics | | | Rotary Cutting | | | | Templates | Yardage |
	Patch	Shape	Total Needed	Strip Width (in inches)	Squares to Cut	Cut Size (in inches)	Next Cut	Template	Strip Length Needed (in inches)
LIGHT	A	◿	16	2⅜	8	2⅜ × 2⅜	◹	T5	19
	B	◺	4	3⅞	2	3⅞ × 3⅞	◹	T12	7¾
MEDIUM	C	▢	8	1½+	8	1½+ × 1½+	—	S2	12½
DARK 1	D	▪	8	1½+	8	1½+ × 1½+	—	S2	12½
DARK 2	E	▪	1	3½	1	3½ × 3½	—	S13	3½
	F	◢	4	3⅞	2	3⅞ × 3⅞	◤	T12	7¾

Note: Plus sign (+) indicates ¹⁄₁₆-inch measurements. See page 217 for details.

Beacon Lights

Block Idea

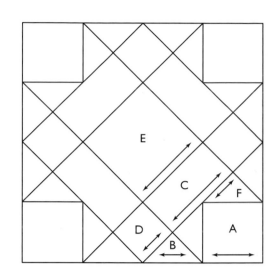

Cut two of the triangle points from the same fabric as the center square for a woven-ribbon look.

How to Assemble

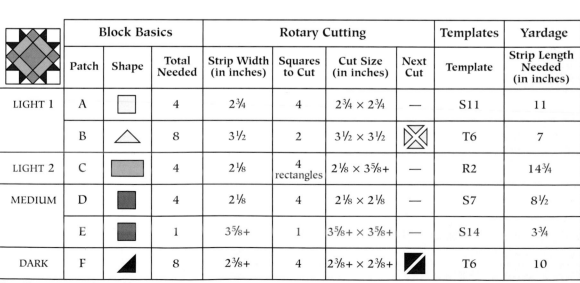

Shading in photo

Alternate shadings

		Block Basics			Rotary Cutting			Templates	Yardage
	Patch	Shape	Total Needed	Strip Width (in inches)	Squares to Cut	Cut Size (in inches)	Next Cut	Template	Strip Length Needed (in inches)
LIGHT 1	A	☐	4	$2\frac{3}{4}$	4	$2\frac{3}{4} \times 2\frac{3}{4}$	—	S11	11
	B	△	8	$3\frac{1}{2}$	2	$3\frac{1}{2} \times 3\frac{1}{2}$	⊠	T6	7
LIGHT 2	C	▭	4	$2\frac{1}{8}$	4 rectangles	$2\frac{1}{8} \times 3\frac{5}{8}+$	—	R2	$14\frac{3}{4}$
MEDIUM	D	▪	4	$2\frac{1}{8}$	4	$2\frac{1}{8} \times 2\frac{1}{8}$	—	S7	$8\frac{1}{2}$
	E	▪	1	$3\frac{5}{8}+$	1	$3\frac{5}{8}+ \times 3\frac{5}{8}+$	—	S14	$3\frac{3}{4}$
DARK	F	◤	8	$2\frac{3}{8}+$	4	$2\frac{3}{8}+ \times 2\frac{3}{8}+$	◪	T6	10

Note: Plus sign (+) indicates $\frac{1}{16}$-inch measurements. See page 217 for details.

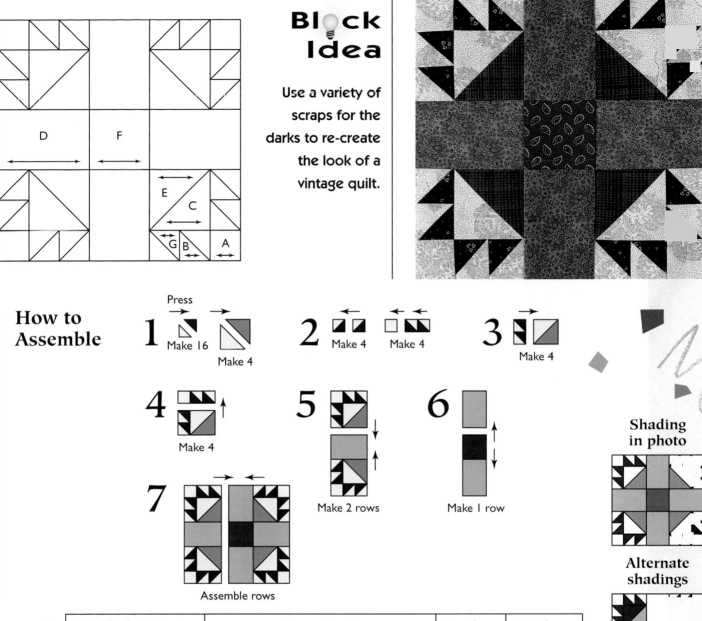

Bear's Paw

Block Idea

Use a variety of scraps for the darks to re-create the look of a vintage quilt.

How to Assemble

1 Press
Make 16
Make 4

2 Make 4   Make 4

3 Make 4

4 Make 4

5 Make 2 rows

6 Make 1 row

7 Assemble rows

Shading in photo

Alternate shadings

	Block Basics			Rotary Cutting				Templates	Yardage
	Patch	Shape	Total Needed	Strip Width (in inches)	Squares to Cut	Cut Size (in inches)	Next Cut	Template	Strip Length Needed (in inches)
LIGHT	A		4	1⅝	4	1⅝ × 1⅝	—	S3	6½
	B		16	2	8	2 × 2		T2	16
	C		4	3⅛	2	3⅛ × 3⅛		T10	6¼
MEDIUM 1	D		4	2¾	4 rectangles	2¾ × 3⅞	—	R3	15½
MEDIUM 2	E		4	3⅛	2	3⅛ × 3⅛		T10	6¼
DARK 1	F		1	2¾	1	2¾ × 2¾	—	S11	2¾
DARK 2	G		16	2	8	2 × 2		T2	16

Berkeley

Bl💡ck Idea

Set this block on point for a totally different look.

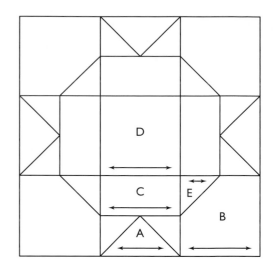

How to Assemble

 Press

1 Make 4

2 Make 4

3 Make 4

4 Make 2 rows

5 Make 1 row

6 Assemble rows

Shading in photo

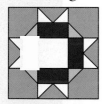

Alternate shadings

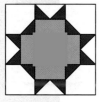

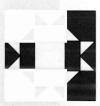

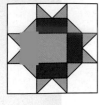

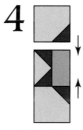

	Block Basics			Rotary Cutting				Templates	Yardage
	Patch	Shape	Total Needed	Strip Width (in inches)	Squares to Cut	Cut Size (in inches)	Next Cut	Template	Strip Length Needed (in inches)
LIGHT	A	▲	4	4¼	1	4¼ × 4¼	⊠	T9	4¼
	B	⬠	4	3½	4	3½ × 3½	Use template X2	14
MEDIUM	C	▭	4	2	4 rectangles	2 × 3½	—	R1	14
DARK	D	■	1	3½	1	3½ × 3½	—	S13	3½
	E	◣	12	2⅜	6	2⅜ × 2⅜	◪	T5	14¼

Big T

Block Idea

Use a medium for the rectangles, then switch the light and dark in the corner squares to create a star.

Block diagram (labels): D, A, B, E, C, F

How to Assemble

1 Make 4 — Press

2 Make 4

3 Make 4

4 Make 2 rows

5 Make 1 row

6 Assemble rows

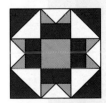
Shading in photo

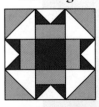
Alternate shadings

	Block Basics			Rotary Cutting				Templates	Yardage
	Patch	Shape	Total Needed	Strip Width (in inches)	Squares to Cut	Cut Size (in inches)	Next Cut	Template	Strip Length Needed (in inches)
LIGHT	A	▭	4	2	4 rectangles	$2 \times 3\frac{1}{2}$	—	R1	14
	B	△	4	$4\frac{1}{4}$	1	$4\frac{1}{4} \times 4\frac{1}{4}$	⊠	T9	$4\frac{1}{4}$
	C	◺	4	$3\frac{7}{8}$	2	$3\frac{7}{8} \times 3\frac{7}{8}$	◩	T12	$7\frac{3}{4}$
MEDIUM	D	▪	1	$3\frac{1}{2}$	1	$3\frac{1}{2} \times 3\frac{1}{2}$	—	S13	$3\frac{1}{2}$
	E	◿	4	$3\frac{7}{8}$	2	$3\frac{7}{8} \times 3\frac{7}{8}$	◩	T12	$7\frac{3}{4}$
DARK	F	◢	8	$2\frac{3}{8}$	4	$2\frac{3}{8} \times 2\frac{3}{8}$	◪	T5	$9\frac{1}{2}$

Birds in the Air

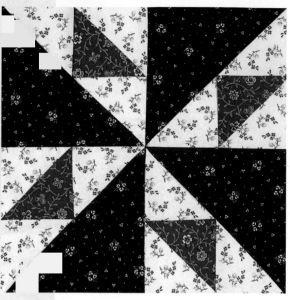

Block Idea

To create a small pinwheel, use a fourth color for the light triangles in the center.

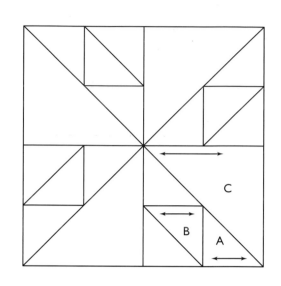

How to Assemble

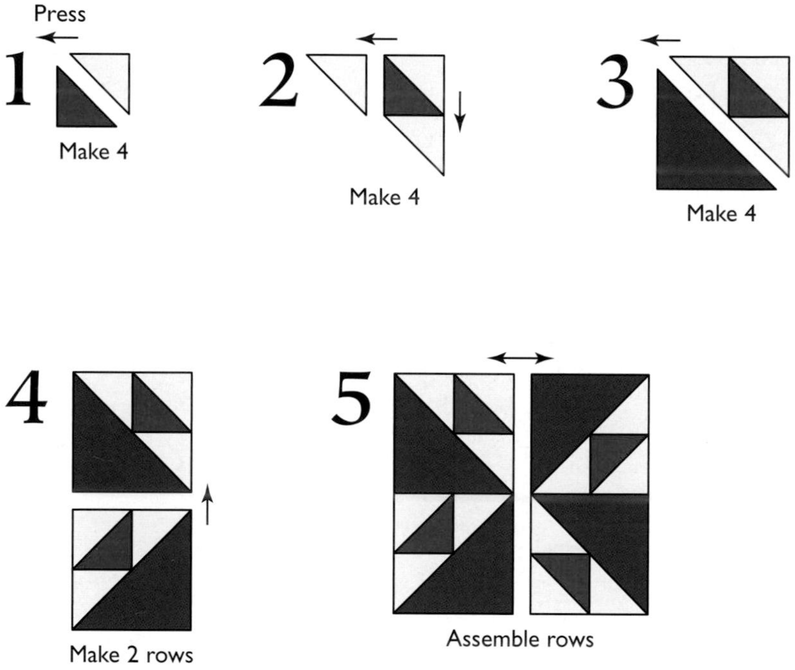

Press

1
Make 4

2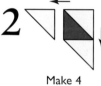
Make 4

3
Make 4

4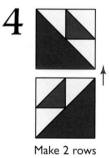
Make 2 rows

5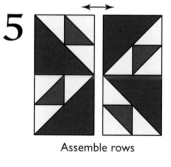
Assemble rows

Shading in photo

Alternate shadings

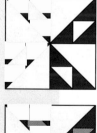

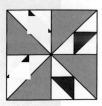

	Block Basics			Rotary Cutting				Templates	Yardage
	Patch	Shape	Total Needed	Strip Width (in inches)	Squares to Cut	Cut Size (in inches)	Next Cut	Template	Strip Length Needed (in inches)
LIGHT	A	◿	12	3⅛	6	3⅛ × 3⅛	◿	T10	18¾
MEDIUM	B	◣	4	3⅛	2	3⅛ × 3⅛	◲	T10	6¼
DARK	C	◼	4	5⅜	2	5⅜ × 5⅜	◲	T15	10¾

Blazing Star

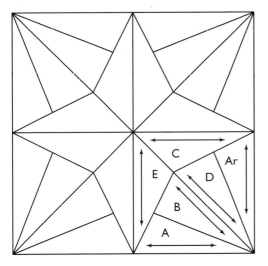

Block Idea

Use a single color for the "top" star, then use a second color for the star points in the background.

How to Assemble

1
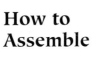
Press
Make 4   Make 4

2
Make 4   Make 4

3

Make 4

4
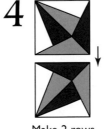
Make 2 rows

5
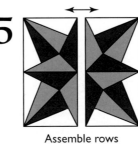
Assemble rows

Shading in photo

Alternate shadings

	Block Basics			**Rotary Cutting**				**Templates**	**Yardage**
	Patch	Shape	Total Needed	Strip Width (in inches)	Squares to Cut	Cut Size (in inches)	Next Cut	Template	Strip Length Needed (in inches)
LIGHT	A		4	—	—	Use template TT1			—
	Ar		4	—	—	Use template TT1r			—
MEDIUM	B		4	—	—	Use template TT2			—
	C		4	—	—	Use template TT3r			—
DARK	D		4	—	—	Use template TT2r			—
	E		4	—	—	Use template TT3			—

Broken Star

Block Idea

Use a different color for the points on the outer edge to create a star within a star.

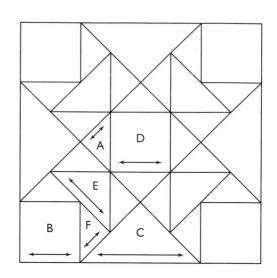

How to Assemble

1 Press → Make 4

2 Make 4

3 Make 4

4 Make 2 rows

5 Join

6 Join

7 Make 1 row

8 Assemble rows

Shading in photo

Alternate shadings

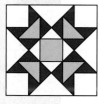

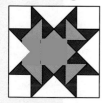

		Block Basics			Rotary Cutting			Templates	Yardage
	Patch	Shape	Total Needed	Strip Width (in inches)	Squares to Cut	Cut Size (in inches)	Next Cut	Template	Strip Length Needed (in inches)
LIGHT	A	◿	4	$2\frac{3}{8}+$	2	$2\frac{3}{8}+ \times 2\frac{3}{8}+$	◹	T6	$4\frac{7}{8}$
	B	☐	4	$2\frac{3}{4}$	4	$2\frac{3}{4} \times 2\frac{3}{4}$	—	S11	11
	C	△	4	$5\frac{3}{4}$	1	$5\frac{3}{4} \times 5\frac{3}{4}$	⊠	T13	$5\frac{3}{4}$
MEDIUM	D	■	1	$2\frac{3}{4}$	1	$2\frac{3}{4} \times 2\frac{3}{4}$	—	S11	$2\frac{3}{4}$
	E	▲	4	$4\frac{3}{8}+$	1	$4\frac{3}{8}+ \times 4\frac{3}{8}+$	⊠	T10	$4\frac{3}{8}+$
DARK	F	◣	16	$2\frac{3}{8}+$	8	$2\frac{3}{8}+ \times 2\frac{3}{8}+$	◤	T6	$19\frac{1}{2}$

Note: Plus sign (+) indicates $\frac{1}{16}$-inch measurements. See page 217 for details.

By Chance

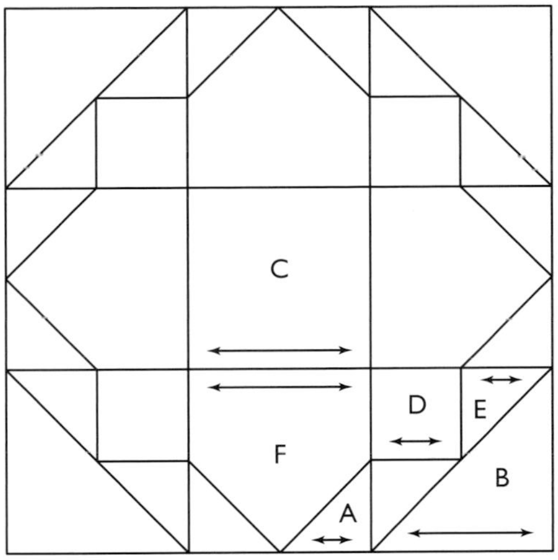

Block Idea

Use plaid flannel fabrics to transform this into a handsome homespun block.

How to Assemble

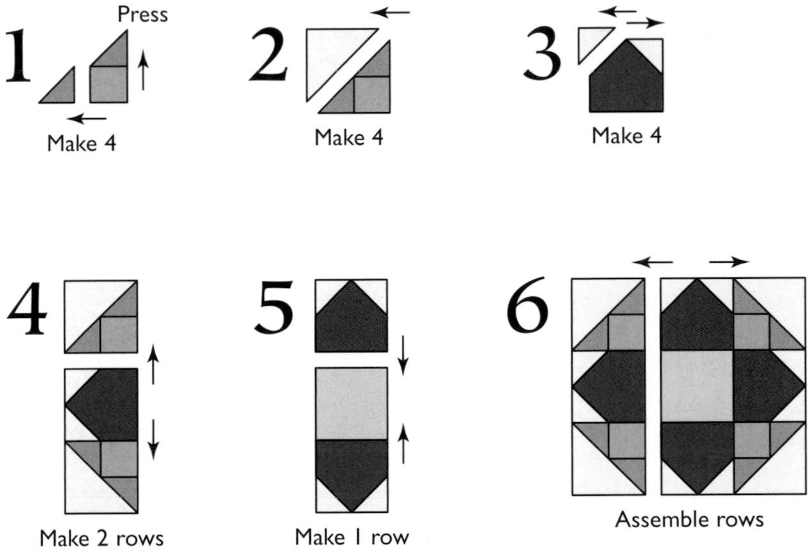

1 Press
Make 4

2 Make 4

3 Make 4

4 Make 2 rows

5 Make 1 row

6 Assemble rows

Shading in photo

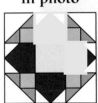

Alternate shadings

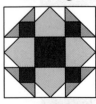

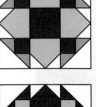

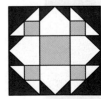

		Block Basics		Rotary Cutting				Templates	Yardage
	Patch	Shape	Total Needed	Strip Width (in inches)	Squares to Cut	Cut Size (in inches)	Next Cut	Template	Strip Length Needed (in inches)
LIGHT 1	A	◿	8	2⅜	4	2⅜ × 2⅜	◿	T5	9½
	B	◺	4	3⅞	2	3⅞ × 3⅞	◿	T12	7¾
LIGHT 2	C	▢	1	3½	1	3½ × 3½	—	S13	3½
MEDIUM 1	D	▢	4	2	4	2 × 2	—	S5	8
MEDIUM 2	E	◿	8	2⅜	4	2⅜ × 2⅜	◿	T5	9½
DARK	F	⬠	4	3½	4	3½ × 3½	⬠	Use template X2	14

Cake Stand

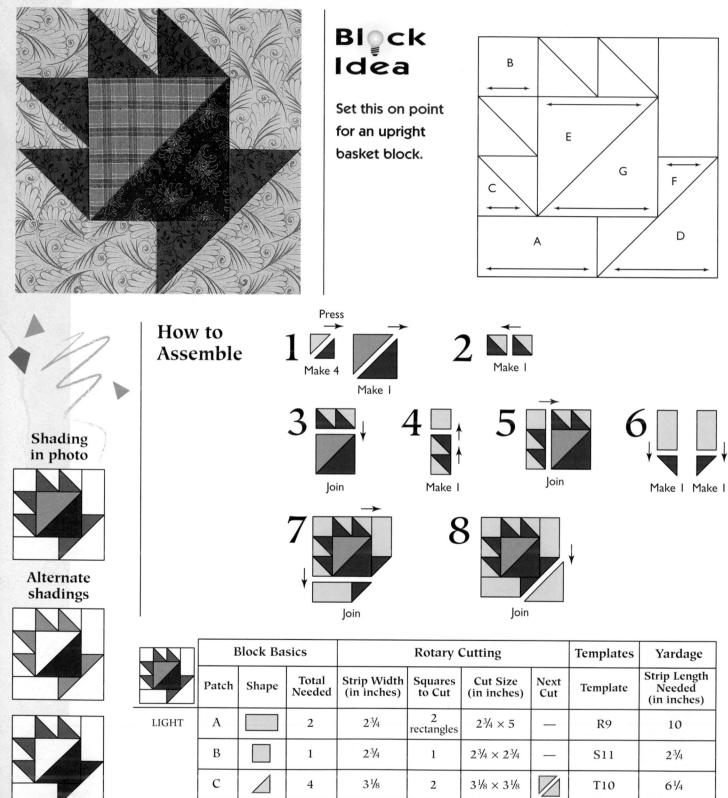

Block Idea

Set this on point for an upright basket block.

How to Assemble

1 Make 4 / Press / Make 1

2 Make 1

3 Join

4 Make 1

5 Join

6 Make 1 Make 1

7 Join

8 Join

Shading in photo

Alternate shadings

		Block Basics		**Rotary Cutting**				**Templates**	**Yardage**
	Patch	Shape	Total Needed	Strip Width (in inches)	Squares to Cut	Cut Size (in inches)	Next Cut	Template	Strip Length Needed (in inches)
LIGHT	A		2	2¾	2 rectangles	2¾ × 5	—	R9	10
	B		1	2¾	1	2¾ × 2¾	—	S11	2¾
	C		4	3⅛	2	3⅛ × 3⅛		T10	6¼
	D		1	5⅜	1	5⅜ × 5⅜		T15	5⅜
MEDIUM	E		1	5⅜	1	5⅜ × 5⅜		T15	5⅜
DARK 1	F		6	3⅛	3	3⅛ × 3⅛		T10	9⅜
DARK 2	G		1	5⅜	1	5⅜ × 5⅜		T15	5⅜

Candlelight

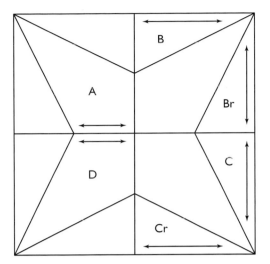

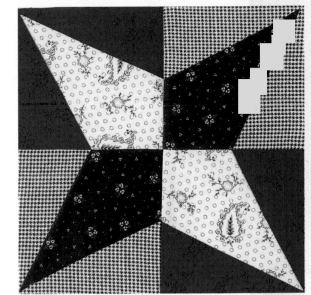

Block Idea

Use two gold prints for the star and solid black for the background to create a candlelit mood.

How to Assemble

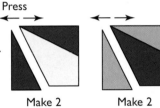

Press

1 Make 2   Make 2

2  Make 2 rows

3 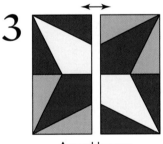 Assemble rows

Shading in photo

Alternate shadings

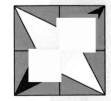

	Block Basics			Rotary Cutting				Templates	Yardage
	Patch	Shape	Total Needed	Strip Width (in inches)	Squares to Cut	Cut Size (in inches)	Next Cut	Template	Strip Length Needed (in inches)
LIGHT 1	A		2	—	—	Use template X7			—
LIGHT 2	B		2	$2\frac{7}{8}$	1 rectangle	$2\frac{7}{8} \times 5\frac{3}{1}+$		TT4	$5\frac{3}{4}+$
	Br		2	$2\frac{7}{8}$	1 rectangle	$2\frac{7}{8} \times 5\frac{3}{4}+$		TT4r	$5\frac{3}{4}+$
MEDIUM	C		2	$2\frac{7}{8}$	1 rectangle	$2\frac{7}{8} \times 5\frac{3}{4}+$		TT4	$5\frac{3}{4}+$
	Cr		2	$2\frac{7}{8}$	1 rectangle	$2\frac{7}{8} \times 5\frac{3}{4}+$		TT4r	$5\frac{3}{4}+$
DARK	D		2	—	—	Use template X7			—

Note: Plus sign (+) indicates $\frac{1}{16}$-inch measurements. See page 217 for details.

Capital T

Block Idea

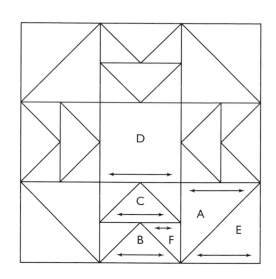

Swap the lights and darks in the four corner triangle squares to play up the T motif.

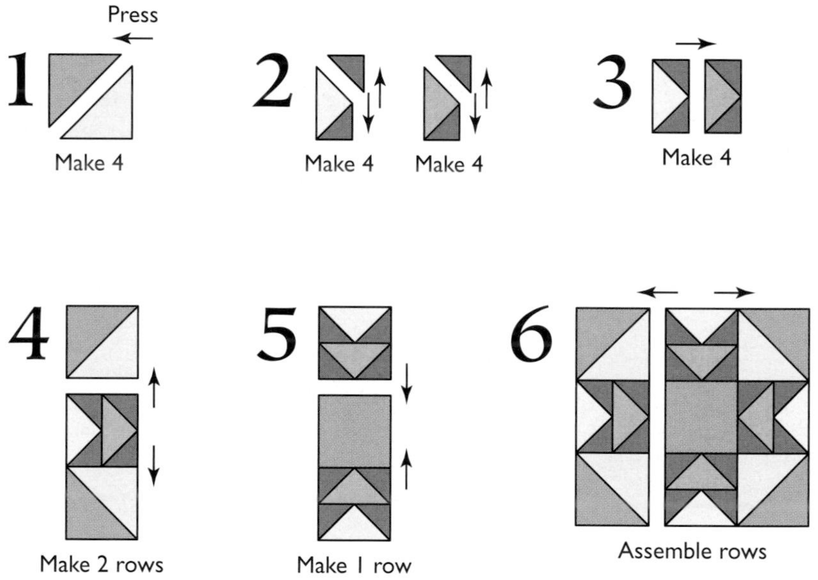

Shading in photo

Alternate shadings

How to Assemble

Press

1 Make 4

2 Make 4   Make 4

3 Make 4

4 Make 2 rows

5 Make 1 row

6 Assemble rows

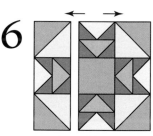

	Block Basics			**Rotary Cutting**				**Templates**	**Yardage**
	Patch	Shape	Total Needed	Strip Width (in inches)	Squares to Cut	Cut Size (in inches)	Next Cut	Template	Strip Length Needed (in inches)
LIGHT 1	A	◢	4	3⅞	2	3⅞ × 3⅞	◿	T12	7¾
LIGHT 2	B	△	4	4¼	1	4¼ × 4¼	⊠	T9	4¼
MEDIUM 1	C	△	4	4¼	1	4¼ × 4¼	⊠	T9	4¼
MEDIUM 2	D	▢	1	3½	1	3½ × 3½	—	S13	3½
	E	◢	4	3⅞	2	3⅞ × 3⅞	◿	T12	7¾
DARK	F	◣	16	2⅜	8	2⅜ × 2⅜	◿	T5	19

Castles in Spain

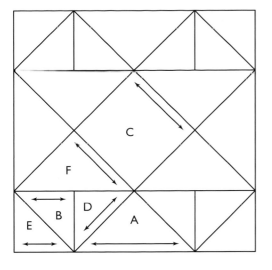

Block Idea

Make the star points a fourth color, and change the dark corner triangles to a light fabric.

How to Assemble

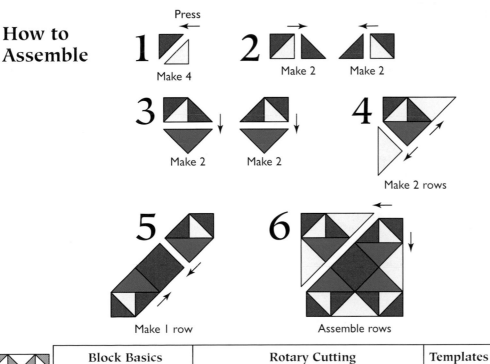

Press

1 — Make 4

2 — Make 2 — Make 2

3 — Make 2 — Make 2

4 — Make 2 rows

5 — Make 1 row

6 — Assemble rows

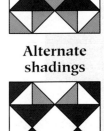

Shading in photo

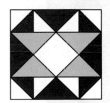

Alternate shadings

	Block Basics			Rotary Cutting				Templates	Yardage
	Patch	Shape	Total Needed	Strip Width (in inches)	Squares to Cut	Cut Size (in inches)	Next Cut	Template	Strip Length Needed (in inches)
LIGHT	A	△	4	5¾	1	5¾ × 5¾	⊠	T13	5¾
	B	◸	4	3⅛	2	3⅛ × 3⅛	◹	T10	6¼
MEDIUM	C	■	1	3⅝+	1	3⅝+ × 3⅝+	—	S14	3⅝+
	D	▲	4	4⅜+	1	4⅜+ × 4⅜+	⊠	T10	4⅜+
	E	◤	4	3⅛	2	3⅛ × 3⅛	⊠	T10	6¼
DARK	F	◤	4	4+	2	4+ × 4+	◹	T13	8⅛

Note: Plus sign (+) indicates ¹⁄₁₆-inch measurements. See page 217 for details.

Cat's Cradle

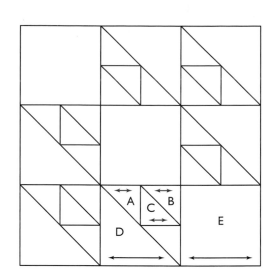

Block Idea

Use just red and white fabrics and reverse the lights and darks for a classic look.

How to Assemble

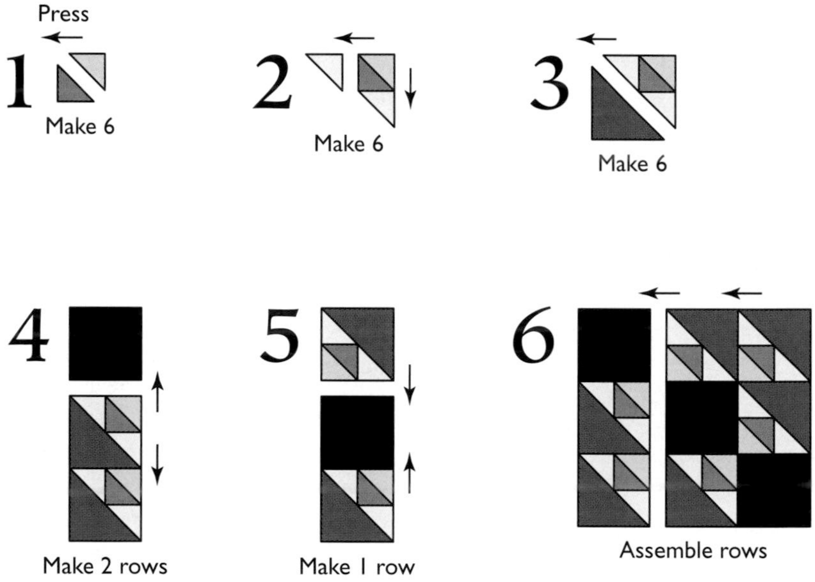

Press

1 Make 6

2 Make 6

3 Make 6

4 Make 2 rows

5 Make 1 row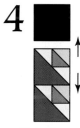

6 Assemble rows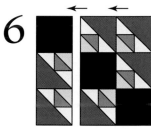

Shading in photo

Alternate shadings

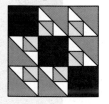

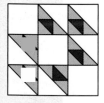

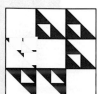

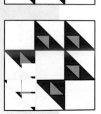

	Block Basics			**Rotary Cutting**				**Templates**	**Yardage**
	Patch	Shape	Total Needed	Strip Width (in inches)	Squares to Cut	Cut Size (in inches)	Next Cut	Template	Strip Length Needed (in inches)
LIGHT 1	A	◺	12	2⅜	6	2⅜ × 2⅜	◹	T5	14¼
LIGHT 2	B	◺	6	2⅜	3	2⅜ × 2⅜	◹	T5	7⅛
MEDIUM 1	C	◺	6	2⅜	3	2⅜ × 2⅜	◹	T5	7⅛
MEDIUM 2	D	◺	6	3⅞	3	3⅞ × 3⅞	◹	T12	11⅝
DARK	E	◼	3	3½	3	3½ × 3½	—	S13	10½

Centennial

Block Idea

Use a red, white, and blue patriotic print for the center and star points.

How to Assemble

1 Press — Make 4

2 Make 4

3 Make 2 rows

4 Make 1 row

5 Assemble rows

Shading in photo

Alternate shadings

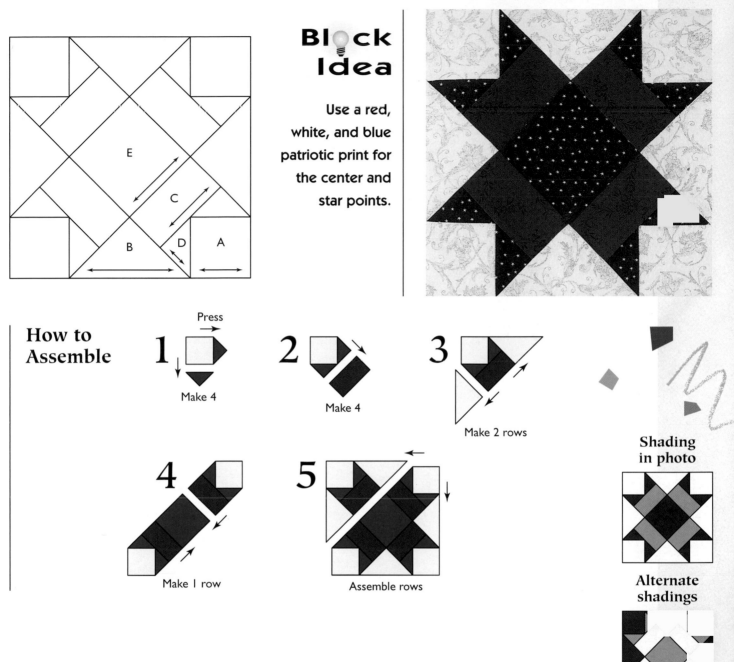

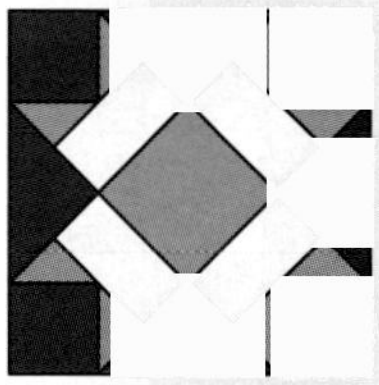

	Block Basics			Rotary Cutting				Templates	Yardage
	Patch	Shape	Total Needed	Strip Width (in inches)	Squares to Cut	Cut Size (in inches)	Next Cut	Template	Strip Length Needed (in inches)
LIGHT	A	☐	4	2¾	4	2¾ × 2¾	—	S11	11
	B	△	4	5¾	1	5¾ × 5¾	⊠	T13	5¾
MEDIUM	C	▬	4	2⅛	4 rectangles	2⅛ × 3⅝+	—	R2	14¾
DARK	D	◺	8	2⅜+	4	2⅜+ × 2⅜+	◸	T6	9¾
	E	■	1	3⅝+	1	3⅝+ × 3⅝+	—	S14	3⅝+

Note: Plus sign (+) indicates 1/16-inch measurements. See page 217 for details.

Chain of Squares

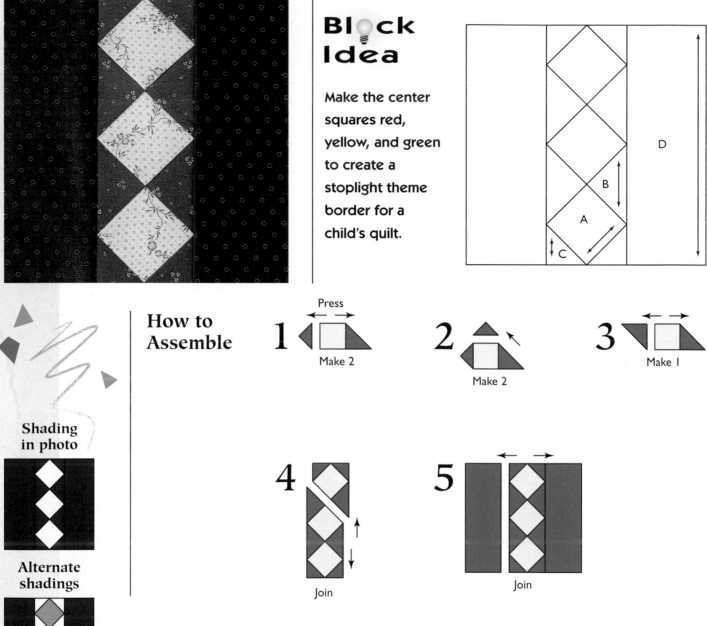

Block Idea

Make the center squares red, yellow, and green to create a stoplight theme border for a child's quilt.

How to Assemble

1 Press
Make 2

2 Make 2

3 Make 1

4 Join

5 Join

Shading in photo

Alternate shadings

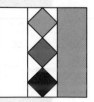

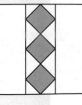

	Block Basics			**Rotary Cutting**				**Templates**	**Yardage**
	Patch	Shape	Total Needed	Strip Width (in inches)	Squares to Cut	Cut Size (in inches)	Next Cut	Template	Strip Length Needed (in inches)
LIGHT	A	☐	3	2⅝	3	2⅝ × 2⅝	—	S10	7⅞
DARK	B	▲	4	4¼	1	4¼ × 4¼	⊠	T9	4¼
	C	◣	4	2⅜	2	2⅜ × 2⅜	◩	T5	4¾
	D	▬	2	3½	2 rectangles	3½ × 9½	—	R15	19

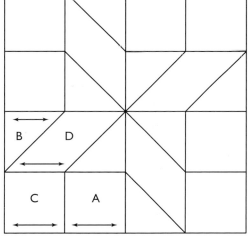

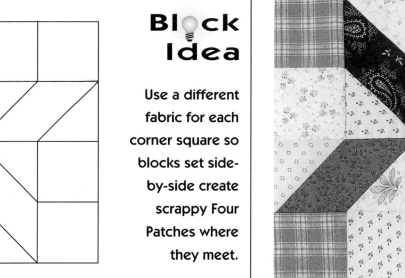

Clay's Choice

Block Idea

Use a different fabric for each corner square so blocks set side-by-side create scrappy Four Patches where they meet.

How to Assemble

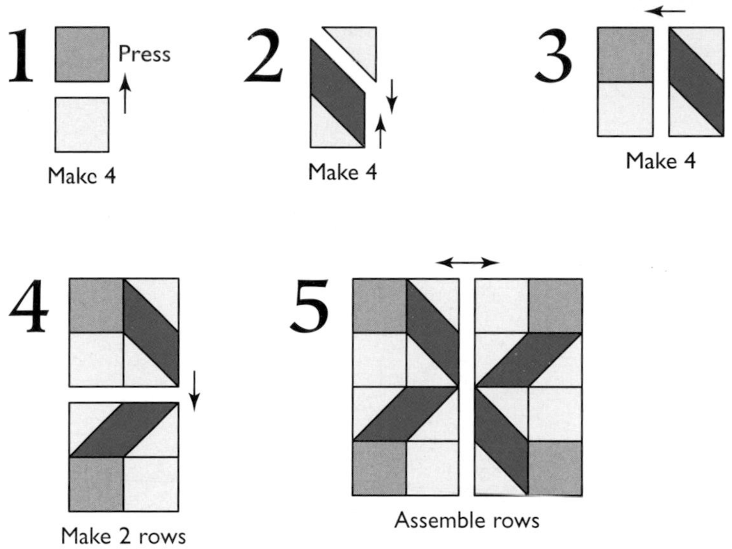

1 Press — Make 4

2 Make 4

3 Make 4

4 Make 2 rows

5 Assemble rows

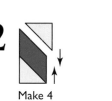

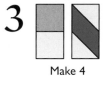

Shading in photo

Alternate shadings

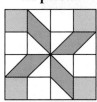

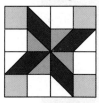

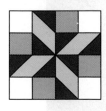

	Block Basics			Rotary Cutting				Templates	Yardage
	Patch	Shape	Total Needed	Strip Width (in inches)	Squares to Cut	Cut Size (in inches)	Next Cut	Template	Strip Length Needed (in inches)
LIGHT	A	▢	4	2¾	4	2¾ × 2¾	—	S11	11
	B	◺	8	3⅛	4	3⅛ × 3⅛	◺	T10	12½
MEDIUM	C	▢	4	2¾	4	2¾ × 2¾	—	S11	11
DARK	D	▱	4	2¾	Make a 45° angle cut at the left end of the strip, angling the ruler from bottom left to top right. Measuring from diagonal cut, make successive cuts 2⅛" apart.			D1	14¾

Combination Star

Block Idea

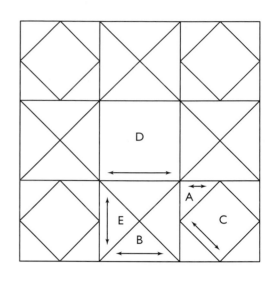

Lower the contrast between the star points and the background to create a calm, subtle block.

How to Assemble

1 Press
Make 4

2 Make 4

3 Make 8

4 Make 4

5 Make 2 rows

6 Make 1 row

7 Assemble rows

Shading in photo

Alternate shadings

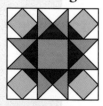

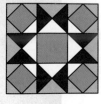

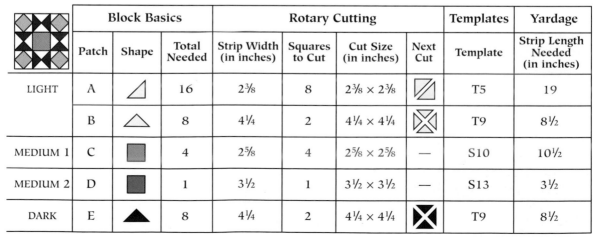

	Block Basics			Rotary Cutting				Templates	Yardage
	Patch	Shape	Total Needed	Strip Width (in inches)	Squares to Cut	Cut Size (in inches)	Next Cut	Template	Strip Length Needed (in inches)
LIGHT	A	◿	16	$2\frac{3}{8}$	8	$2\frac{3}{8} \times 2\frac{3}{8}$	◨	T5	19
	B	△	8	$4\frac{1}{4}$	2	$4\frac{1}{4} \times 4\frac{1}{4}$	⊠	T9	$8\frac{1}{2}$
MEDIUM 1	C	▢	4	$2\frac{5}{8}$	4	$2\frac{5}{8} \times 2\frac{5}{8}$	—	S10	$10\frac{1}{2}$
MEDIUM 2	D	▢	1	$3\frac{1}{2}$	1	$3\frac{1}{2} \times 3\frac{1}{2}$	—	S13	$3\frac{1}{2}$
DARK	E	▲	8	$4\frac{1}{4}$	2	$4\frac{1}{4} \times 4\frac{1}{4}$	⊠	T9	$8\frac{1}{2}$

Corn and Beans

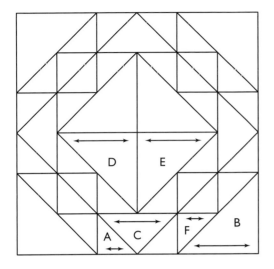

Block Idea

Try this block in the traditional colors of yellow and green on a white background.

How to Assemble

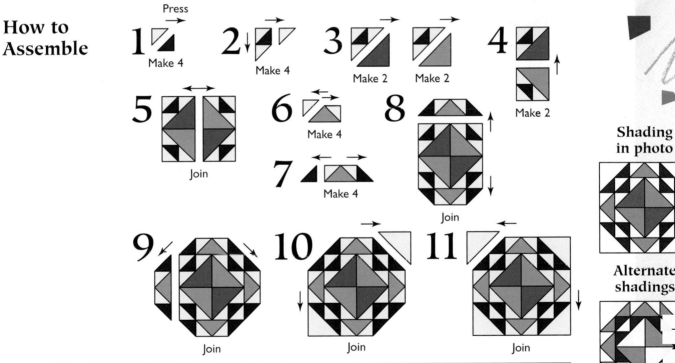

Press

1 Make 4

2 Make 4

3 Make 2 Make 2

4 Make 2

5 Join

6 Make 4

7 Make 4

8 Join

9 Join

10 Join

11 Join

Shading in photo

Alternate shadings

	Block Basics			Rotary Cutting				Templates	Yardage
	Patch	Shape	Total Needed	Strip Width (in inches)	Squares to Cut	Cut Size (in inches)	Next Cut	Template	Strip Length Needed (in inches)
LIGHT	A	◺	20	$2\frac{3}{8}$	10	$2\frac{3}{8} \times 2\frac{3}{8}$	◩	T5	$23\frac{3}{4}$
	B	◺	4	$3\frac{7}{8}$	2	$3\frac{7}{8} \times 3\frac{7}{8}$	◩	T12	$7\frac{3}{4}$
MEDIUM	C	△	4	$4\frac{1}{4}$	1	$4\frac{1}{4} \times 4\frac{1}{4}$	⧖	T9	$4\frac{1}{4}$
	D	◺	2	$3\frac{7}{8}$	1	$3\frac{7}{8} \times 3\frac{7}{8}$	◩	T12	$3\frac{7}{8}$
DARK 1	E	◺	2	$3\frac{7}{8}$	1	$3\frac{7}{8} \times 3\frac{7}{8}$	◩	T12	$3\frac{7}{8}$
DARK 2	F	◤	12	$2\frac{3}{8}$	6	$2\frac{3}{8} \times 2\frac{3}{8}$	◼	T5	$14\frac{1}{4}$

Courthouse Steps

Block Idea

Cousin to a Log Cabin, this is a great block for using up scraps.

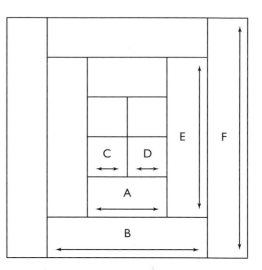

How to Assemble

1 Make 2 Press

2 Join

3 Join

4 Join

5 Join

6 Join

Shading in photo

Alternate shadings

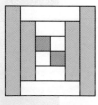

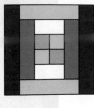

	Block Basics			Rotary Cutting				Templates	Yardage
	Patch	Shape	Total Needed	Strip Width (in inches)	Squares to Cut	Cut Size (in inches)	Next Cut	Template	Strip Length Needed (in inches)
LIGHT	A		2	2	2 rectangles	2 × 3½	—	R1	7
	B		2	2	2 rectangles	2 × 6½	—	R11	13
	C		2	2	2	2 × 2	—	S5	4
MEDIUM	D		2	2	2	2 × 2	—	S5	4
DARK	E		2	2	2 rectangles	2 × 6½	—	R11	13
	F		2	2	2 rectangles	2 × 9½	—	R13	19

Cross-Country

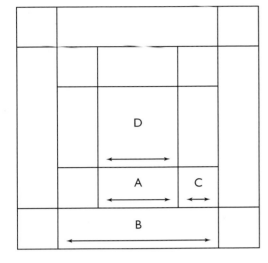

Block Idea

Use this as an alternate block to create a dynamic diagonal chain across the quilt top.

How to Assemble

1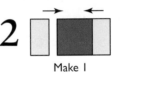
Press
Make 2   Make 2

2
Make 1

3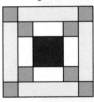
Join

4
Join

5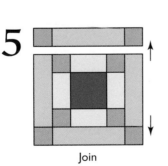
Join

Shading in photo

Alternate shadings

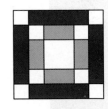

	Block Basics			Rotary Cutting				Templates	Yardage
	Patch	Shape	Total Needed	Strip Width (in inches)	Squares to Cut	Cut Size (in inches)	Next Cut	Template	Strip Length Needed (in inches)
LIGHT 1	A		4	2	4 rectangles	2 × 3½	—	R1	14
LIGHT 2	B		4	2	4 rectangles	2 × 6½	—	R11	26
MEDIUM	C		8	2	8	2 × 2	—	S5	16
DARK	D		1	3½	1	3½ × 3½	—	S13	3½

Crossroads to Jericho

Bl⊙ck Idea

Use this for a versatile alternate block in a two-block setting!

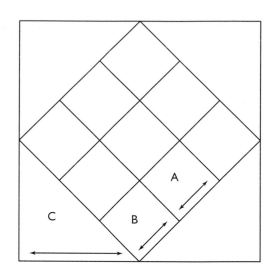

How to Assemble

1 Press
Make 2   Make 1

2 Join

3 Join

4 Join

Shading in photo

Alternate shadings

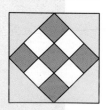

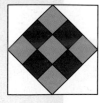

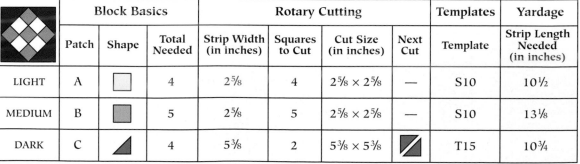

	Block Basics			Rotary Cutting				Templates	Yardage
	Patch	Shape	Total Needed	Strip Width (in inches)	Squares to Cut	Cut Size (in inches)	Next Cut	Template	Strip Length Needed (in inches)
LIGHT	A	□	4	$2\frac{5}{8}$	4	$2\frac{5}{8} \times 2\frac{5}{8}$	—	S10	$10\frac{1}{2}$
MEDIUM	B	▨	5	$2\frac{5}{8}$	5	$2\frac{5}{8} \times 2\frac{5}{8}$	—	S10	$13\frac{1}{8}$
DARK	C	◣	4	$5\frac{3}{8}$	2	$5\frac{3}{8} \times 5\frac{3}{8}$	◹	T15	$10\frac{3}{4}$

Darting Minnows

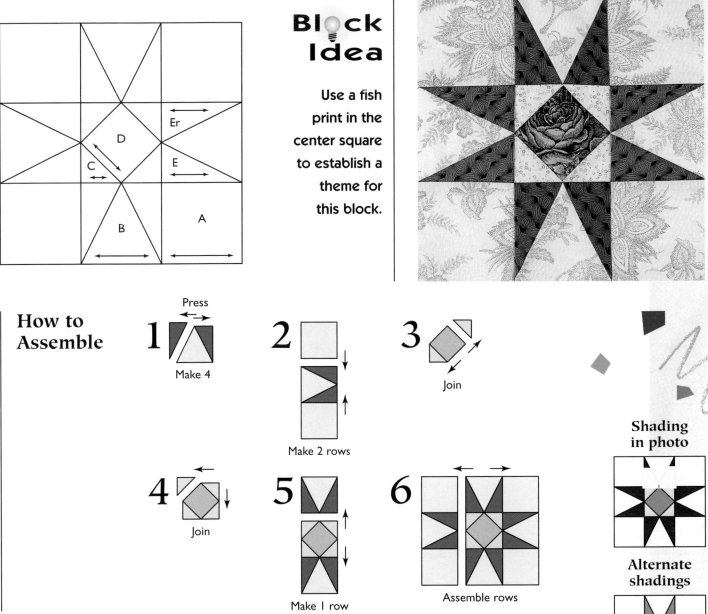

Block Idea

Use a fish print in the center square to establish a theme for this block.

How to Assemble

1 Press — Make 4

2 Make 2 rows

3 Join

4 Join

5 Make 1 row

6 Assemble rows

Shading in photo

Alternate shadings

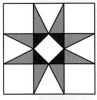

	Block Basics			Rotary Cutting				Templates	Yardage
	Patch	Shape	Total Needed	Strip Width (in inches)	Squares to Cut	Cut Size (in inches)	Next Cut	Template	Strip Length Needed (in inches)
LIGHT 1	A	▢	4	3½	4	3½ × 3½	—	S13	14
	B	△	4	—	—	Use template TT14			—
LIGHT 2	C	◺	4	2⅜	2	2⅜ × 2⅜	◹	T5	4¾
MEDIUM	D	▪	1	2⅝	1	2⅝ × 2⅝	—	S10	2⅝
DARK	E	◣	4	2⅛	2 rectangles	2⅛ × 4¼+	◥	TT13	8⅝
	Er	◢	4	2⅛	2 rectangles	2⅛ × 4¼+	◿	TT13r	8⅝

Note: Plus sign (+) indicates ¹/₁₆-inch measurements. See page 217 for details.

Dolley Madison's Star

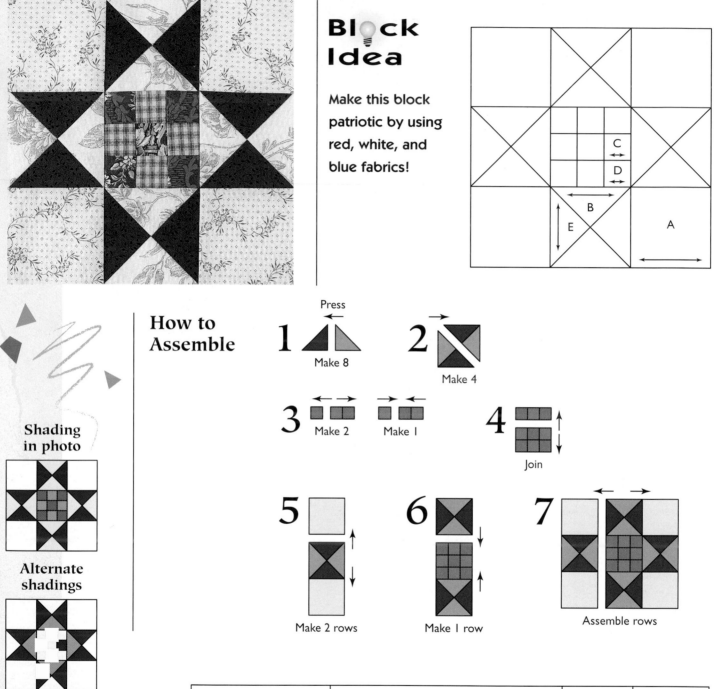

Block Idea

Make this block patriotic by using red, white, and blue fabrics!

How to Assemble

1. Make 8
Press

2. Make 4

3. Make 2   Make 1

4. Join

5. Make 2 rows

6. Make 1 row

7. Assemble rows

Shading in photo

Alternate shadings

		Block Basics		Rotary Cutting				Templates	Yardage
	Patch	Shape	Total Needed	Strip Width (in inches)	Squares to Cut	Cut Size (in inches)	Next Cut	Template	Strip Length Needed (in inches)
LIGHT 1	A		4	3½	4	3½ × 3½	—	S13	14
LIGHT 2	B		8	4¼	2	4¼ × 4¼		T9	8½
MEDIUM	C		4	1½	4	1½ × 1½	—	S1	6
DARK 1	D		5	1½	5	1½ × 1½	—	S1	7½
DARK 2	E		8	4¼	2	4¼ × 4¼		T9	8½

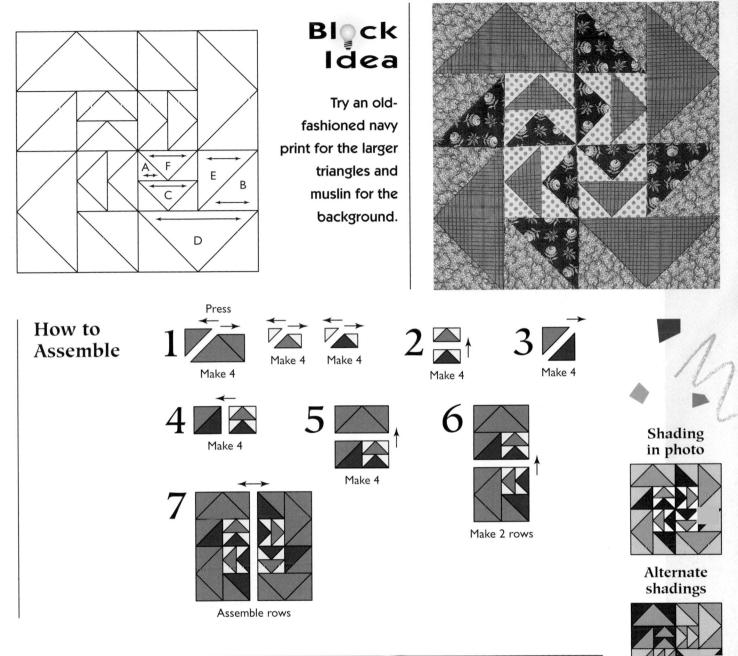

Block Idea

Try an old-fashioned navy print for the larger triangles and muslin for the background.

How to Assemble

1 Press — Make 4

Make 4   Make 4

2 Make 4

3 Make 4

4 Make 4

5 Make 4

6 Make 2 rows

7 Assemble rows

Shading in photo

Alternate shadings

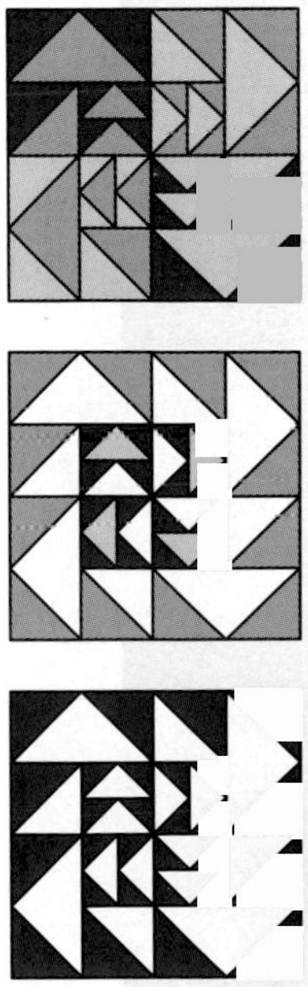

	Block Basics			Rotary Cutting				Templates	Yardage
	Patch	Shape	Total Needed	Strip Width (in inches)	Squares to Cut	Cut Size (in inches)	Next Cut	Template	Strip Length Needed (in inches)
LIGHT	A	◿	16	2	8	2 × 2	◿	T2	16
MEDIUM 1	B	◢	12	3⅛	6	3⅛ × 3⅛	◿	T10	18¾
MEDIUM 2	C	◭	4	3½	1	3½ × 3½	⊠	T6	3½
	D	◭	4	5¾	1	5¾ × 5¾	⊠	T13	5¾
DARK	E	◢	4	3⅛	2	3⅛ × 3⅛	◿	T10	6¼
	F	◭	4	3½	1	3½ × 3½	⊠	T6	3½

Double Four Patch

Bl⚲ck Idea

Use this as a simple setting block next to a more complicated block.

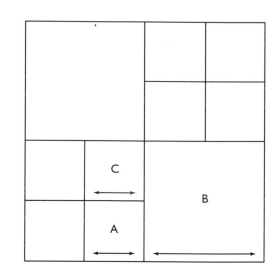

How to Assemble

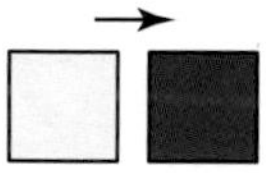

Press

1 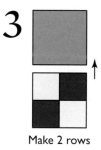 Make 4

2 Make 2

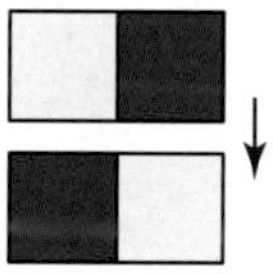

3 Make 2 rows

4 Assemble rows

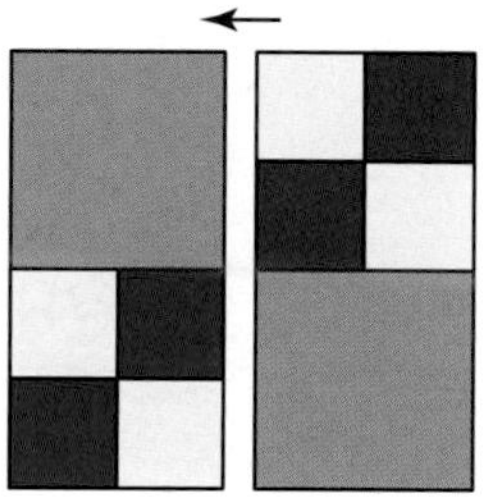

Shading in photo

Alternate shadings

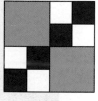

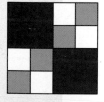

	Block Basics			**Rotary Cutting**				**Templates**	**Yardage**
	Patch	Shape	Total Needed	Strip Width (in inches)	Squares to Cut	Cut Size (in inches)	Next Cut	Template	Strip Length Needed (in inches)
LIGHT	A		4	2¾	4	2¾ × 2¾	—	S11	11
MEDIUM	B		2	5	2	5 × 5	—	S16	10
DARK	C		4	2¾	4	2¾ × 2¾	—	S11	11

Double Windmill

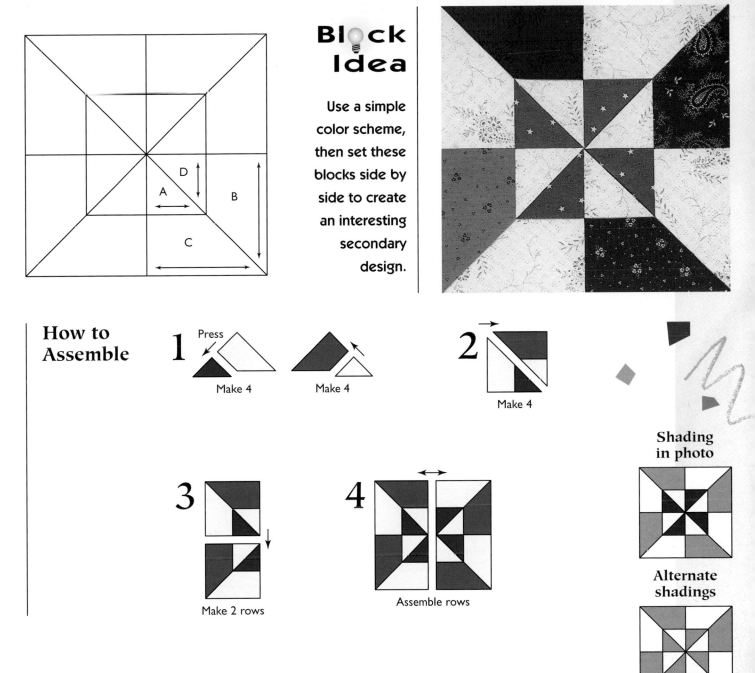

Block Idea

Use a simple color scheme, then set these blocks side by side to create an interesting secondary design.

How to Assemble

1 Press — Make 4 — Make 4

2 Make 4

3 Make 2 rows

4 Assemble rows

Shading in photo

Alternate shadings

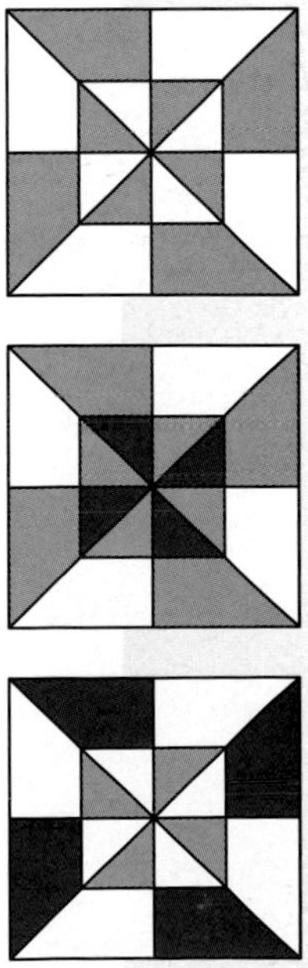

	Block Basics			**Rotary Cutting**				**Templates**	**Yardage**
	Patch	Shape	Total Needed	Strip Width (in inches)	Squares to Cut	Cut Size (in inches)	Next Cut	Template	Strip Length Needed (in inches)
LIGHT	A	◺	4	3⅛	2	3⅛ × 3⅛	◺	T10	6¼
	B	▱	4	2¾	4 rectangles	2¾ × 5⅜	Use template X8r		21½
MEDIUM	C	◢	4	2¾	4 rectangles	2¾ × 5⅜	Use template X8		21½
DARK	D	◥	4	3⅛	2	3⅛ × 3⅛	◺	T10	6¼

Double X

Block Idea

Showcase a novelty print in the large center square.

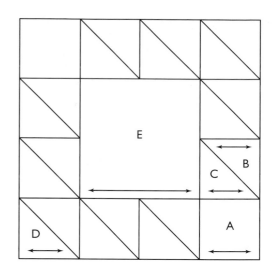

How to Assemble

1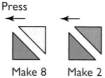
Press

Make 8   Make 2

2
Make 2   Make 2

3
Make 2 rows

4
Make 1 row

5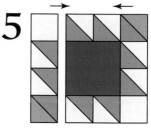
Assemble rows

Shading in photo

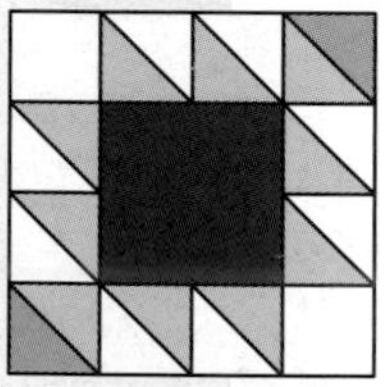

Alternate shadings

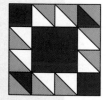

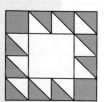

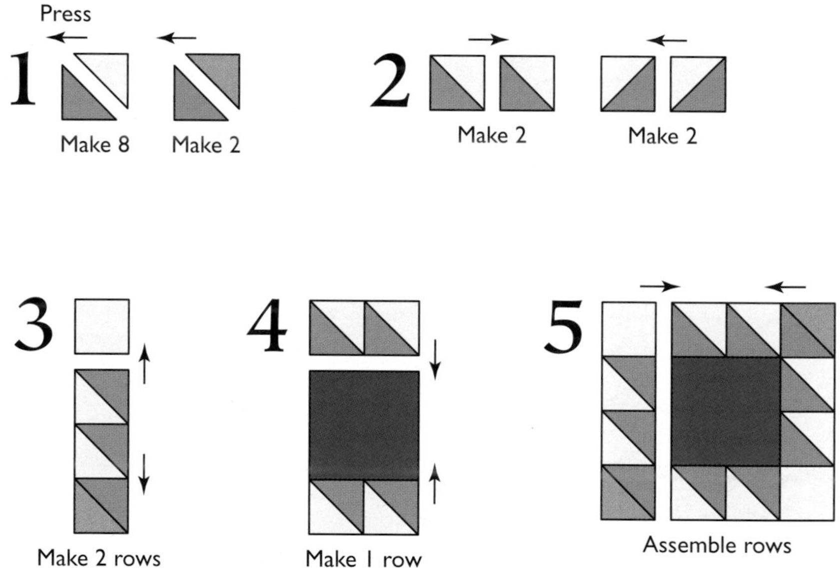

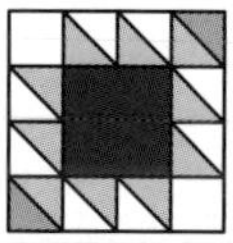	**Block Basics**			**Rotary Cutting**				**Templates**	**Yardage**
	Patch	Shape	Total Needed	Strip Width (in inches)	Squares to Cut	Cut Size (in inches)	Next Cut	Template	Strip Length Needed (in inches)
LIGHT	A	□	2	2¾	2	2¾ × 2¾	—	S11	5½
	B	◹	8	3⅛	4	3⅛ × 3⅛	◩	T10	12½
MEDIUM 1	C	◣	10	3⅛	5	3⅛ × 3⅛	◪	T10	15⅝
MEDIUM 2	D	◢	2	3⅛	1	3⅛ × 3⅛	◩	T10	3⅛
DARK	E	■	1	5	1	5 × 5	—	S16	5

Duck Paddle

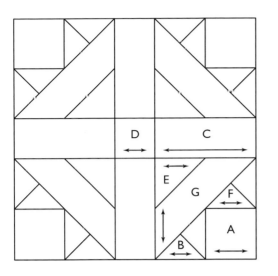

Block Idea

Use the same fabric for the rectangles in every block to create a latticed look.

How to Assemble

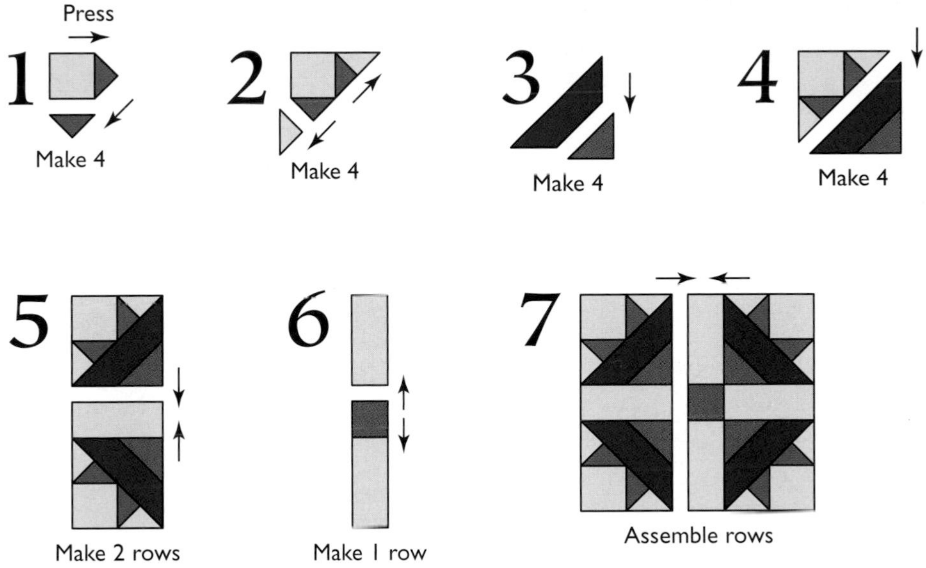

1 Press

Make 4

2

Make 4

3

Make 4

4

Make 4

5

Make 2 rows

6

Make 1 row

7

Assemble rows

Shading in photo

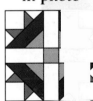

Alternate shadings

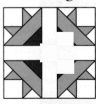

	Block Basics			**Rotary Cutting**				**Templates**	**Yardage**
	Patch	Shape	Total Needed	Strip Width (in inches)	Squares to Cut	Cut Size (in inches)	Next Cut	Template	Strip Length Needed (in inches)
LIGHT	A		4	2⅜	4	2⅜ × 2⅜	—	S8	9½
	B		8	3⅛	2	3⅛ × 3⅛		T3	6¼
	C		4	2	4 rectangles	2 × 4¼	—	R5	17
MEDIUM	D		1	2	1	2 × 2	—	S5	2
	E		4	2¾	2	2¾ × 2¾		T8	5½
DARK 1	F		8	3⅛	2	3⅛ × 3⅛		T3	6¼
DARK 2	G		4	4⅝	2	4⅝ × 4⅝	See page 219 and use template X12	9¼

Ducks and Ducklings

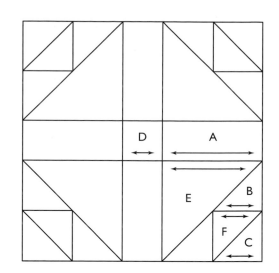

Block Idea

Make each corner unit a different color for a fun scrap quilt.

How to Assemble

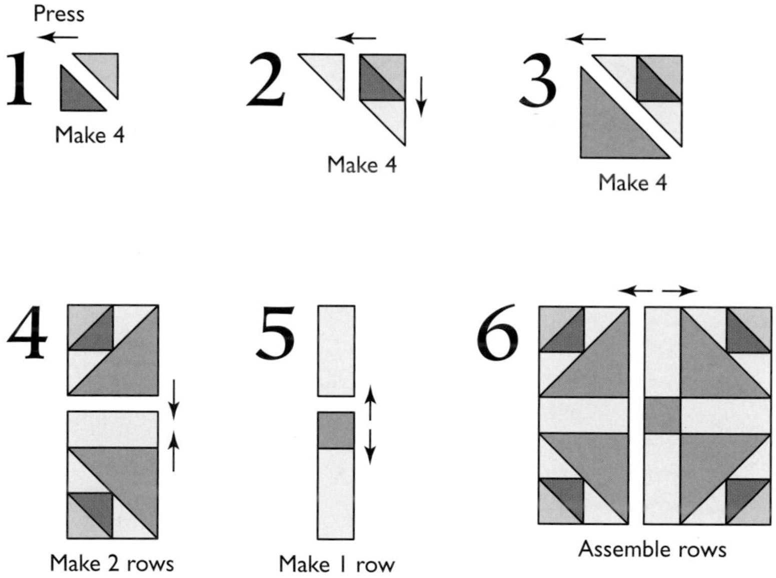

Press

1
Make 4

2
Make 4

3
Make 4

4
Make 2 rows

5
Make 1 row

6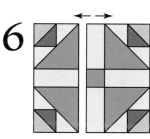
Assemble rows

Shading in photo

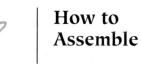

Alternate shadings

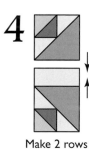

	**Block Basics**			**Rotary Cutting**				**Templates**	**Yardage**
	Patch	Shape	Total Needed	Strip Width (in inches)	Squares to Cut	Cut Size (in inches)	Next Cut	Template	Strip Length Needed (in inches)
LIGHT 1	A	▭	4	2	4 rectangles	2 × 4¼	—	R5	17
	B	◺	8	2¾	4	2¾ × 2¾	◹	T8	11
LIGHT 2	C	◣	4	2¾	2	2¾ × 2¾	◹	T8	5½
MEDIUM	D	▪	1	2	1	2 × 2	—	S5	2
	E	◣	4	4⅝	2	4⅝ × 4⅝	◹	T14	9¼
DARK	F	◢	4	2¾	2	2¾ × 2¾	◹	T8	5½

Dutchman's Puzzle

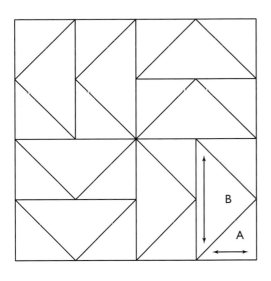

Block Idea

For a scrappy look, make each large triangle a different fabric.

B

A

How to Assemble

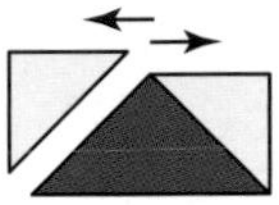

Press

1 Make 8

2 Make 4

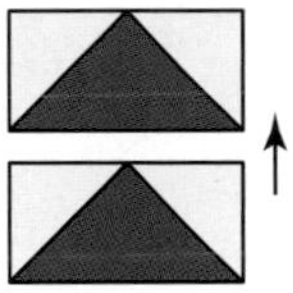

3 Make 2 rows

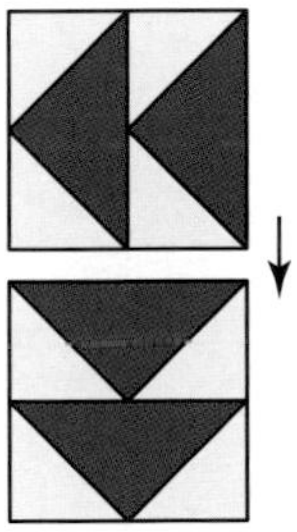

4 Assemble rows

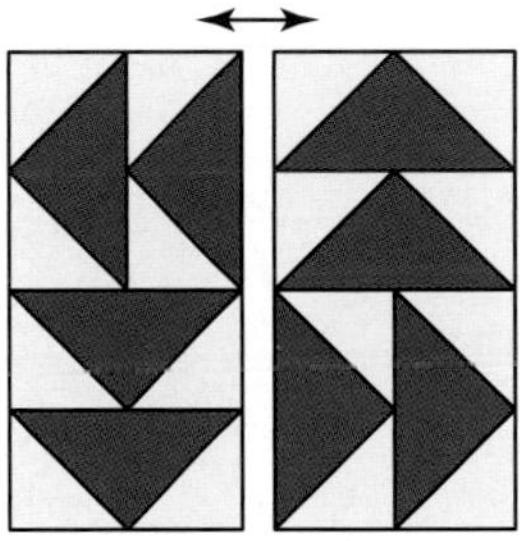

Shading in photo

Alternate shadings

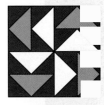

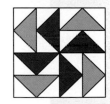

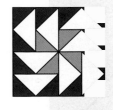

	Block Basics			Rotary Cutting				Templates	Yardage
	Patch	Shape	Total Needed	Strip Width (in inches)	Squares to Cut	Cut Size (in inches)	Next Cut	Template	Strip Length Needed (in inches)
LIGHT	A	◿	16	3⅛	8	3⅛ × 3⅛	◹	T10	25
DARK	B	▲	8	5¾	2	5¾ × 5¾	⊠	T13	11½

Eddystone Light

Bl●ck Idea

Match the large center square and the smaller squares to create a "chain" effect through each quilt block.

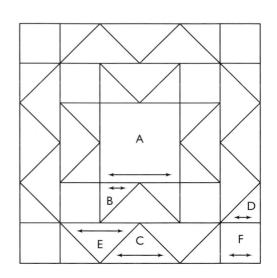

How to Assemble

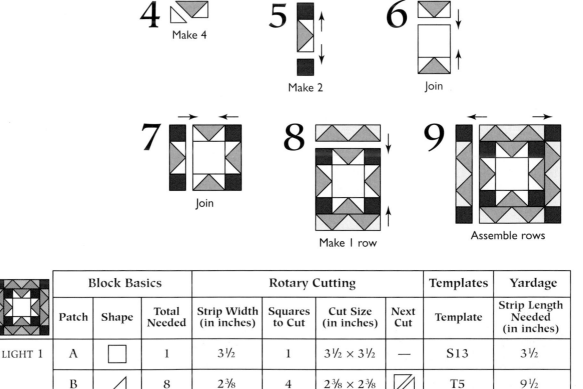

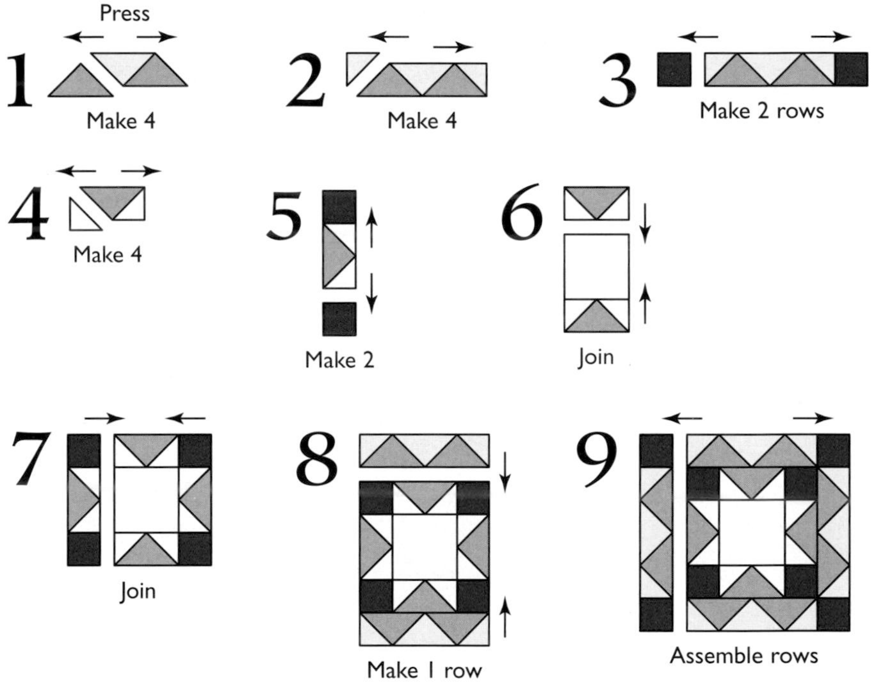

1 Make 4 — Press

2 Make 4

3 Make 2 rows

4 Make 4

5 Make 2

6 Join

7 Join

8 Make 1 row

9 Assemble rows

Shading in photo

Alternate shadings

		Block Basics		Rotary Cutting				Templates	Yardage
	Patch	Shape	Total Needed	Strip Width (in inches)	Squares to Cut	Cut Size (in inches)	Next Cut	Template	Strip Length Needed (in inches)
LIGHT 1	A	▢	1	3½	1	3½ × 3½	—	S13	3½
	B	◺	8	2⅜	4	2⅜ × 2⅜	◹	T5	9½
LIGHT 2	C	△	4	4¼	1	4¼ × 4¼	⊠	T9	4¼
	D	◹	8	2⅜	4	2⅜ × 2⅜	◹	T5	9½
MEDIUM	E	▲	12	4¼	3	4¼ × 4¼	⊠	T9	12¾
DARK	F	■	8	2	8	2 × 2	—	S5	16

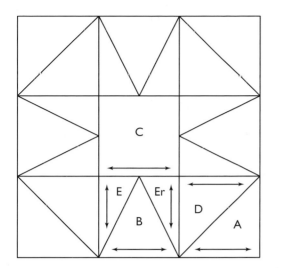

C

E   Er

B   D

A

Bl💡ck Idea

Reverse the light and dark triangles in the corner squares to emphasize the star.

How to Assemble

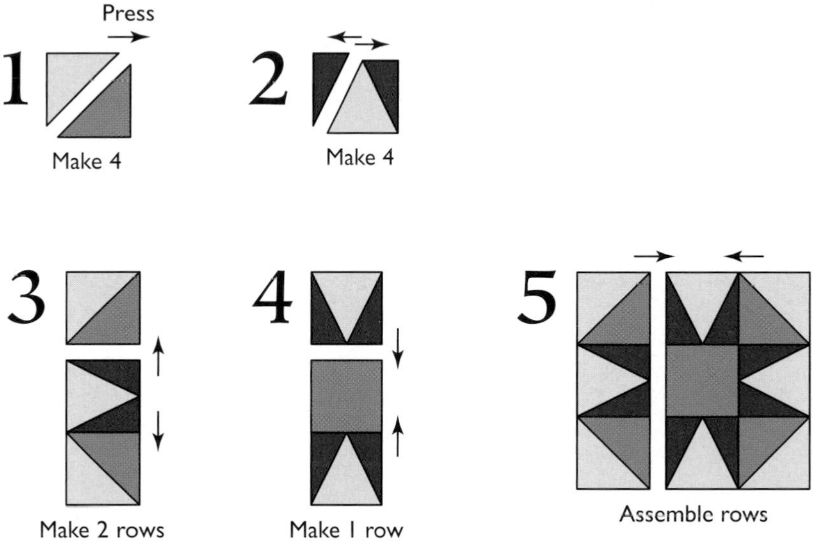

Press →

1 Make 4

2 Make 4

3 Make 2 rows

4 Make 1 row

5 Assemble rows

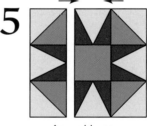

Shading in photo

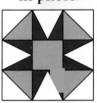

Alternate shadings

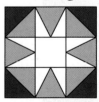

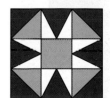

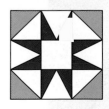

		Block Basics		Rotary Cutting				Templates	Yardage
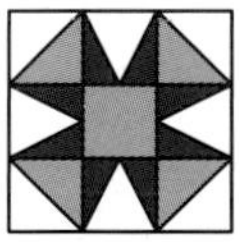	Patch	Shape	Total Needed	Strip Width (in inches)	Squares to Cut	Cut Size (in inches)	Next Cut	Template	Strip Length Needed (in inches)
LIGHT	A	◺	4	3⅞	2	3⅞ × 3⅞	◿	T12	7¾
	B	△	4	—	—	Use template TT14			—
MEDIUM	C	◼	1	3½	1	3½ × 3½	—	S13	3½
	D	◢	4	3⅞	2	3⅞ × 3⅞	◿	T12	7¾
DARK	E	◿	4	2⅛	2 rectangles	2⅛ × 4¼+	◣	TT13	8⅝
	Er	◺	4	2⅛	2 rectangles	2⅛ × 4¼+	◿	TT13r	8⅝

Note: Plus sign (+) indicates ¹/₁₆-inch measurements. See page 217 for details.

Eliza's Nine Patch

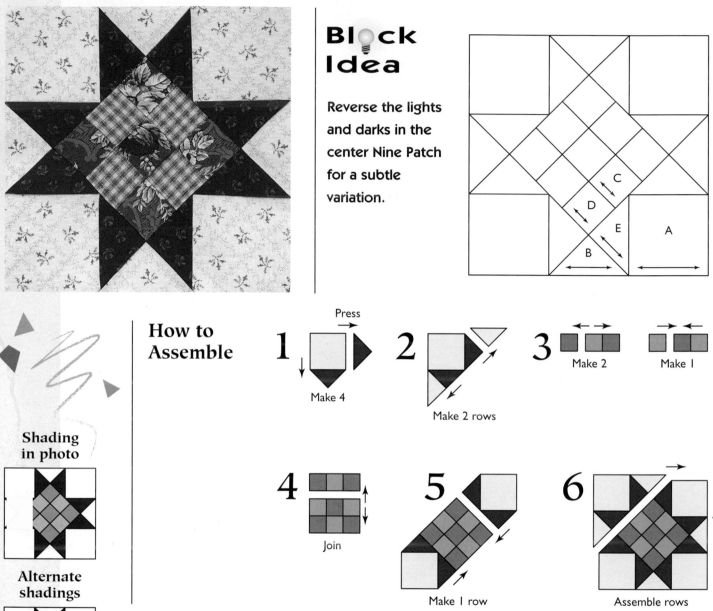

Block Idea

Reverse the lights and darks in the center Nine Patch for a subtle variation.

How to Assemble

1 Make 4 — Press

2 Make 2 rows

3 Make 2 — Make 1

4 Join

5 Make 1 row

6 Assemble rows

Shading in photo

Alternate shadings

	Block Basics			Rotary Cutting				Templates	Yardage
	Patch	Shape	Total Needed	Strip Width (in inches)	Squares to Cut	Cut Size (in inches)	Next Cut	Template	Strip Length Needed (in inches)
LIGHT 1	A	☐	4	3½	4	3½ × 3½	—	S13	14
	B	△	4	4¼	1	4¼ × 4¼	⊠	T9	4¼
LIGHT 2	C	◻	4	1⅞+	4	1⅞+ × 1⅞+	—	S4	7⅞
MEDIUM	D	◻	5	1⅞+	5	1⅞+ × 1⅞+	—	S4	9⅞
DARK	E	◥	8	3	4	3 × 3	◿	T9	12

Note: Plus sign (+) indicates ¹/₁₆-inch measurements. See page 217 for details.

Evening Star with Pinwheel

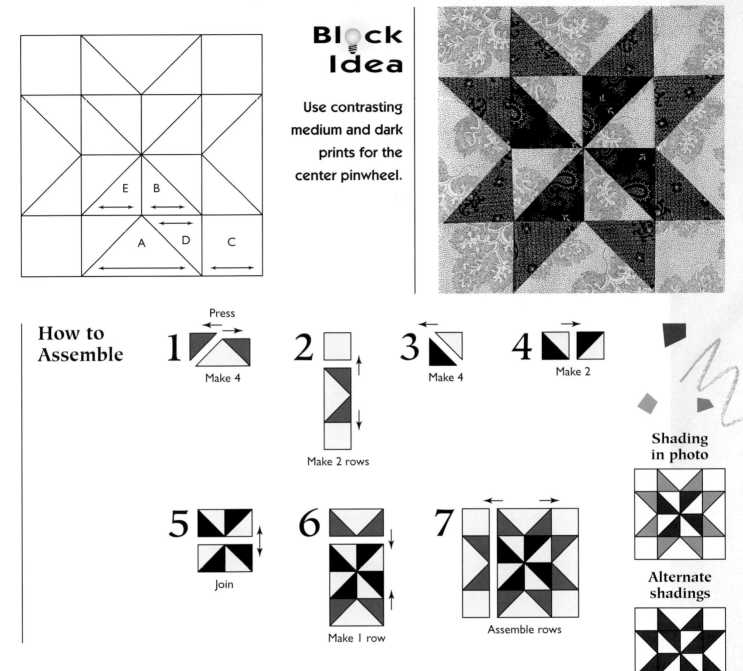

Block Idea

Use contrasting medium and dark prints for the center pinwheel.

How to Assemble

1 Press — Make 4

2 Make 2 rows

3 Make 4

4 Make 2

5 Join

6 Make 1 row

7 Assemble rows

Shading in photo

Alternate shadings

	Block Basics			Rotary Cutting				Templates	Yardage
	Patch	Shape	Total Needed	Strip Width (in inches)	Squares to Cut	Cut Size (in inches)	Next Cut	Template	Strip Length Needed (in inches)
LIGHT	A	◿	4	5¾	1	5¾ × 5¾	⊠	T13	5¾
	B	◺	4	3⅛	2	3⅛ × 3⅛	◹	T10	6¼
	C	▢	4	2¾	4	2¾ × 2¾	—	S11	11
MEDIUM	D	◢	8	3⅛	4	3⅛ × 3⅛	◢	T10	12½
DARK	E	◣	4	3⅛	2	3⅛ × 3⅛	◢	T10	6¼

Fifty-Four Forty

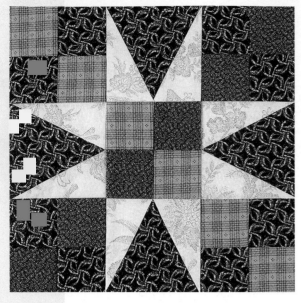

Block Idea

Swap the light and dark in this block to create a dark star on a light background.

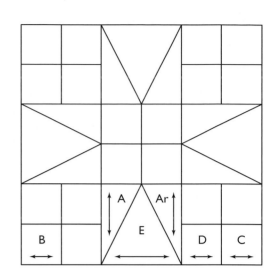

How to Assemble

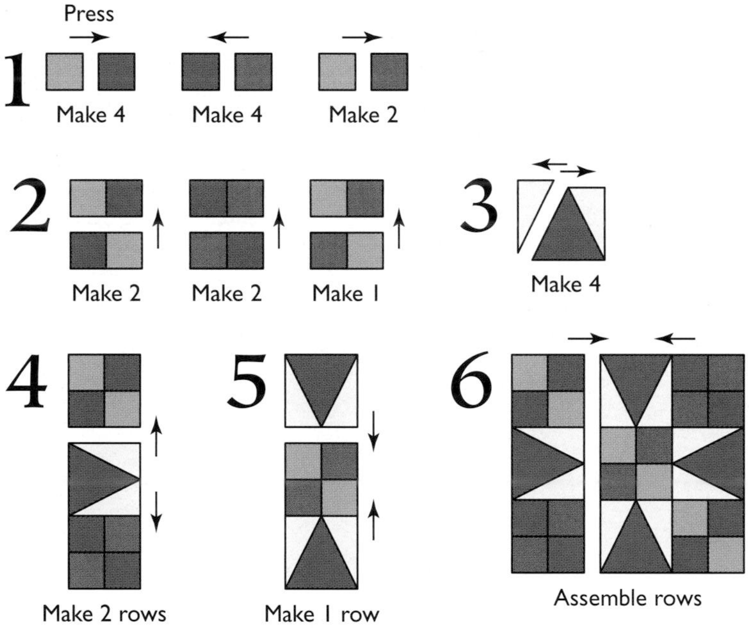

Press

1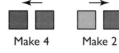
Make 4   Make 4   Make 2

2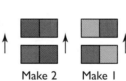
Make 2   Make 2   Make 1

3
Make 4

4
Make 2 rows

5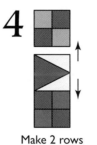
Make 1 row

6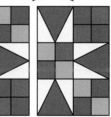
Assemble rows

Shading in photo

Alternate shadings

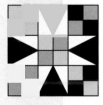

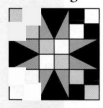

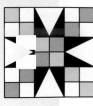

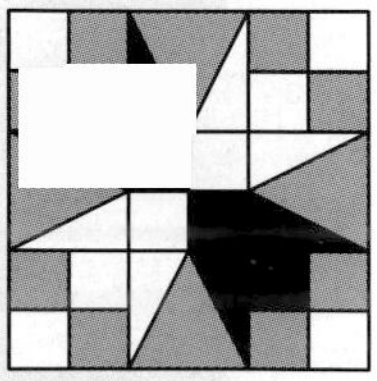

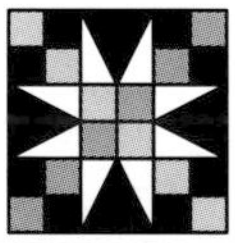	Block Basics			Rotary Cutting				Templates	Yardage
	Patch	Shape	Total Needed	Strip Width (in inches)	Squares to Cut	Cut Size (in inches)	Next Cut	Template	Strip Length Needed (in inches)
LIGHT	A	◺	4	2⅛	2 rectangles	2⅛ × 4¼+	◺	TT13	8⅝
	Ar	◸	4	2⅛	2 rectangles	2⅛ × 4¼+	◹	TT13	8⅝
MEDIUM 1	B	■	6	2	6	2 × 2	—	S5	12
MEDIUM 2	C	■	6	2	6	2 × 2	—	S5	12
DARK	D	■	8	2	8	2 × 2	—	S5	16
	E	▲	4	—	—	Use template TT14			—

Note: Plus sign (+) indicates ¹⁄₁₆-inch measurements. See page 217 for details.

Flying Geese

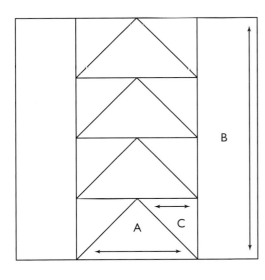

Block Idea

Line these up to make a showy (and easy!) border from blocks.

How to Assemble

1 Press

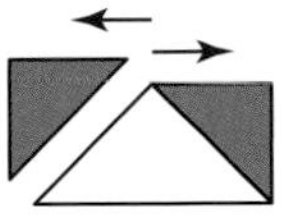

Make 4

2 Join

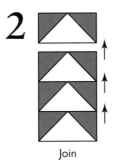

3 Join

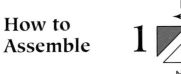

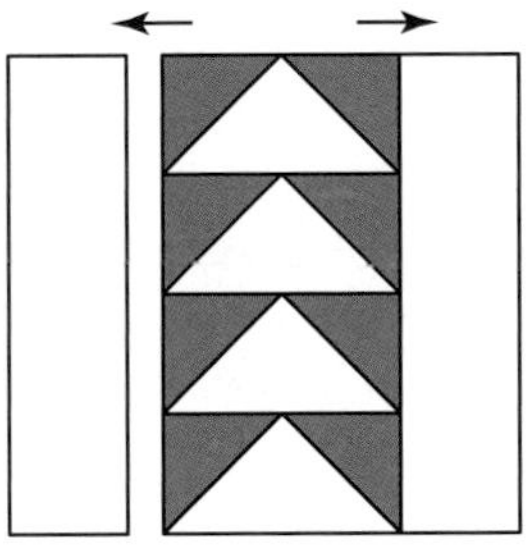

Shading in photo

Alternate shadings

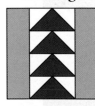

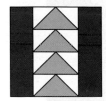

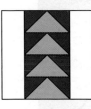

	Block Basics			Rotary Cutting				Templates	Yardage
	Patch	Shape	Total Needed	Strip Width (in inches)	Squares to Cut	Cut Size (in inches)	Next Cut	Template	Strip Length Needed (in inches)
LIGHT	A	△	4	5¾	1	5¾ × 5¾	⊠	T13	5¾
	B	▭	2	2¾	2 rectangles	2¾ × 9½	—	R14	19
DARK	C	◣	8	3⅛	4	3⅛ × 3⅛	◪	T10	12½

Flying Pinwheel

Block Idea

Use a light for the large triangles at each corner to play up the pinwheel.

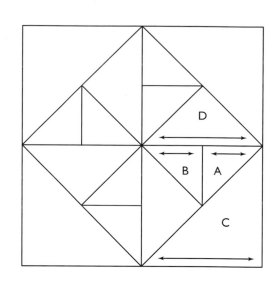

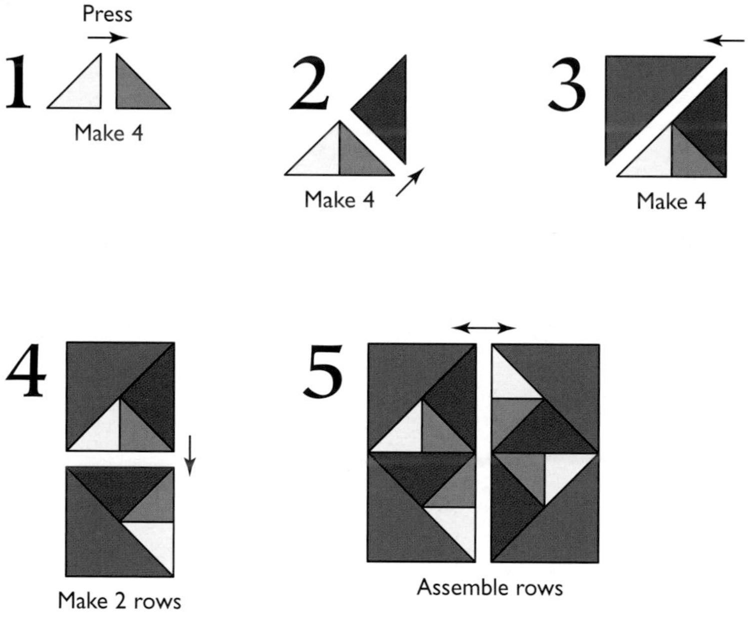

Shading in photo

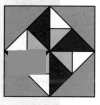

Alternate shadings

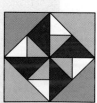

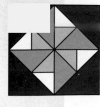

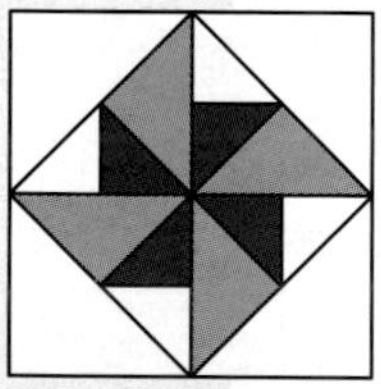

How to Assemble

1 Press → 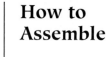 Make 4

2 Make 4

3 Make 4

4 Make 2 rows

5 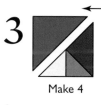 Assemble rows

		Block Basics		Rotary Cutting				Templates	Yardage
	Patch	Shape	Total Needed	Strip Width (in inches)	Squares to Cut	Cut Size (in inches)	Next Cut	Template	Strip Length Needed (in inches)
LIGHT	A		4	3⅛	2	3⅛ × 3⅛		T10	6¼
MEDIUM 1	B		4	3⅛	2	3⅛ × 3⅛		T10	6¼
MEDIUM 2	C		4	5⅜	2	5⅜ × 5⅜		T15	10¾
DARK	D		4	5¾	1	5¾ × 5¾		T13	5¾

Flying Star

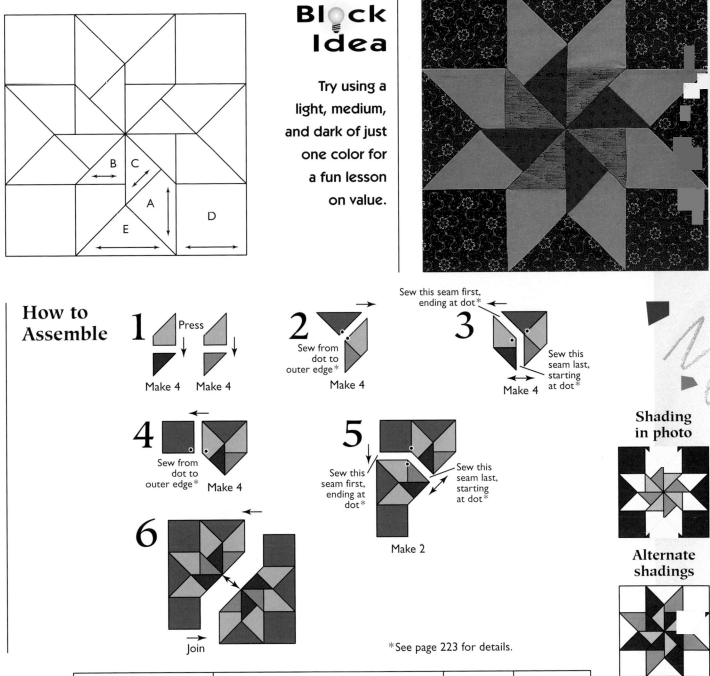

*See page 223 for details.

Block Idea

Try using a
light, medium,
and dark of just
one color for
a fun lesson
on value.

How to Assemble

1 Press — Make 4 Make 4

2 Sew from dot to outer edge* — Make 4

3 Sew this seam first, ending at dot* — Sew this seam last, starting at dot* — Make 4

4 Sew from dot to outer edge* — Make 4

5 Sew this seam first, ending at dot* — Sew this seam last, starting at dot* — Make 2

6 Join

Shading in photo

Alternate shadings

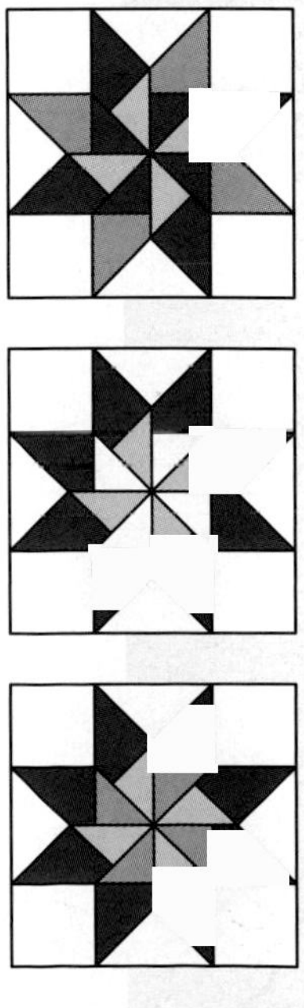

	Block Basics			Rotary Cutting				Templates	Yardage
	Patch	Shape	Total Needed	Strip Width (in inches)	Squares to Cut	Cut Size (in inches)	Next Cut	Template	Strip Length Needed (in inches)
LIGHT	A		8	—	—	Use template X9			—
MEDIUM 1	B		4	2¾	2	2¾ × 2¾		T8	5½
MEDIUM 2	C		4	2¾	2	2¾ × 2¾		T8	5½
DARK	D		4	3⅛	4	3⅛ × 3⅛	—	S12	12½
	E		4	5	1	5 × 5		T11	5

Flying X

Block Idea

Change the light fabric in the center pinwheel to a fabric with the same value as the corner squares.

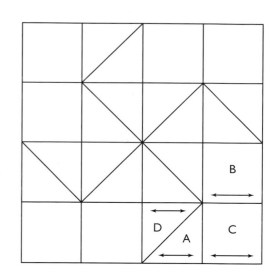

How to Assemble

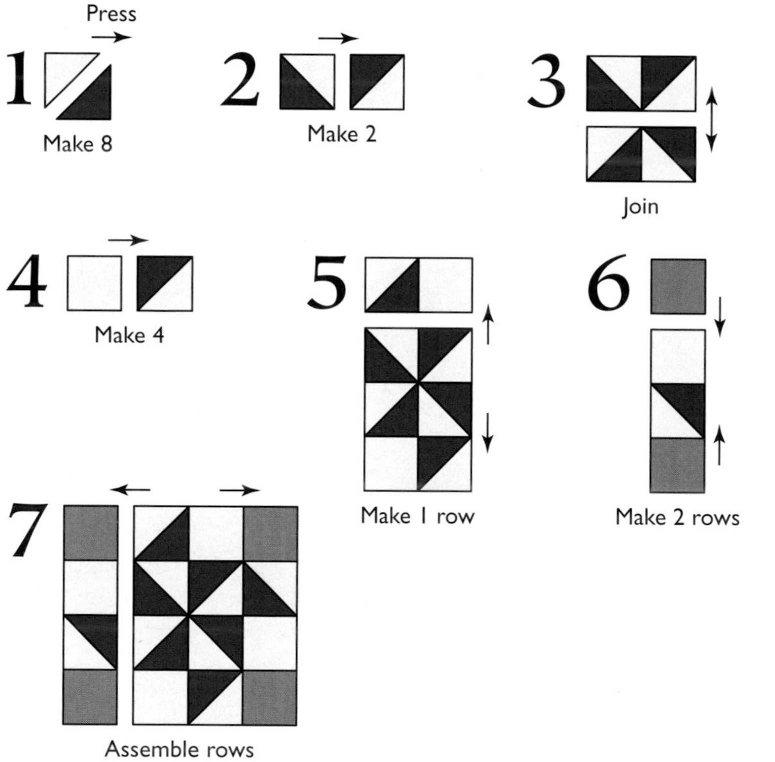

Press

1 Make 8

2 Make 2

3 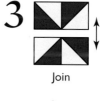 Join

4 Make 4

5 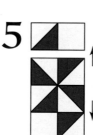 Make 1 row

6  Make 2 rows

7 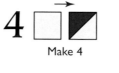 Assemble rows

Shading in photo

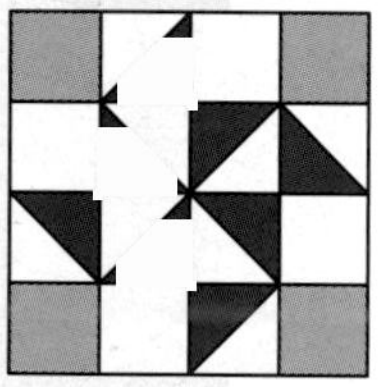

Alternate shadings

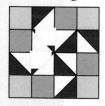
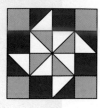

		Block Basics		Rotary Cutting				Templates	Yardage
	Patch	Shape	Total Needed	Strip Width (in inches)	Squares to Cut	Cut Size (in inches)	Next Cut	Template	Strip Length Needed (in inches)
LIGHT	A	◺	8	3⅛	4	3⅛ × 3⅛	◹	T10	12½
	B	☐	4	2¾	4	2¾ × 2¾	—	S11	11
MEDIUM	C	■	4	2¾	4	2¾ × 2¾	—	S11	11
DARK	D	◣	8	3⅛	4	3⅛ × 3⅛	◤	T10	12½

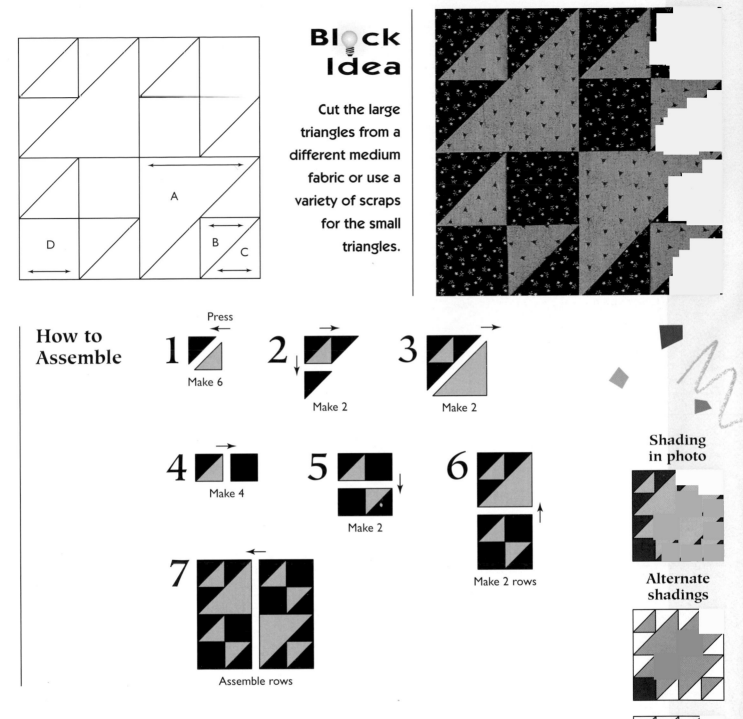

Block Idea

Cut the large triangles from a different medium fabric or use a variety of scraps for the small triangles.

How to Assemble

Press

1 Make 6

2 Make 2

3 Make 2

4 Make 4

5 Make 2

6 Make 2 rows

7 Assemble rows

Shading in photo

Alternate shadings

	Block Basics			Rotary Cutting				Templates	Yardage
	Patch	Shape	Total Needed	Strip Width (in inches)	Squares to Cut	Cut Size (in inches)	Next Cut	Template	Strip Length Needed (in inches)
MEDIUM	A		2	$5\frac{3}{8}$	1	$5\frac{3}{8} \times 5\frac{3}{8}$		T15	$5\frac{3}{8}$
	B		6	$3\frac{1}{8}$	3	$3\frac{1}{8} \times 3\frac{1}{8}$		T10	$9\frac{3}{8}$
DARK	C		10	$3\frac{1}{8}$	5	$3\frac{1}{8} \times 3\frac{1}{8}$		T10	$15\frac{5}{8}$
	D		4	$2\frac{3}{4}$	4	$2\frac{3}{4} \times 2\frac{3}{4}$	—	S11	11

Free Trade

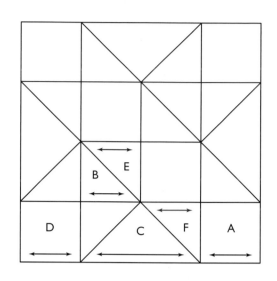

Block Idea

Lessen the diagonal effect by using the same fabric for each background patch.

B E

D C F A

How to Assemble

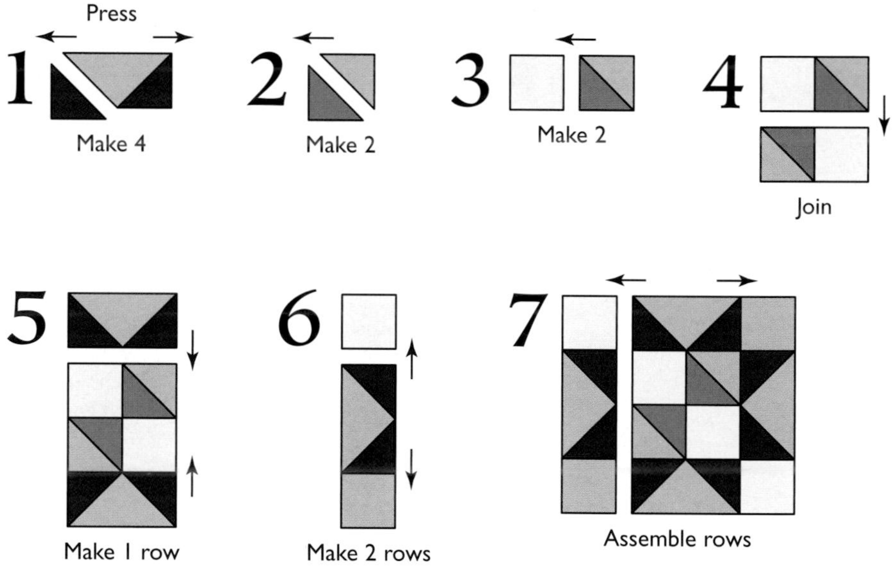

Press

1 Make 4

2 Make 2

3 Make 2

4 Join

5 Make 1 row

6 Make 2 rows

7 Assemble rows

Shading in photo

Alternate shadings

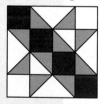

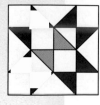

	**Block Basics**			**Rotary Cutting**				**Templates**	**Yardage**
	Patch	Shape	Total Needed	Strip Width (in inches)	Squares to Cut	Cut Size (in inches)	Next Cut	Template	Strip Length Needed (in inches)
LIGHT 1	A	▢	4	2¾	4	2¾ × 2¾	—	S11	11
LIGHT 2	B	◹	2	3⅛	1	3⅛ × 3⅛	◹	T10	3⅛
	C	△	4	5¾	1	5¾ × 5¾	⊠	T13	5¾
	D	▢	2	2¾	2	2¾ × 2¾	—	S11	5½
MEDIUM	E	◸	2	3⅛	1	3⅛ × 3⅛	◹	T10	3⅛
DARK	F	◣	8	3⅛	4	3⅛ × 3⅛	�	T10	12½

Friendship Block

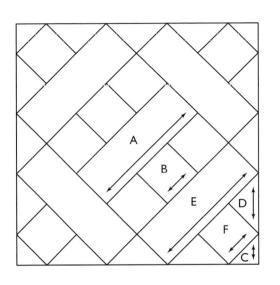

Bl🔆ck Idea

Make a memory quilt by having family members sign the light rectangles.

How to Assemble

1 Make 4 — Press

2 Make 4

3 Make 4

4 Make 2 rows

5 Make 2

6 Join

7 Make 1 row

8 Assemble rows

Shading in photo

Alternate shadings

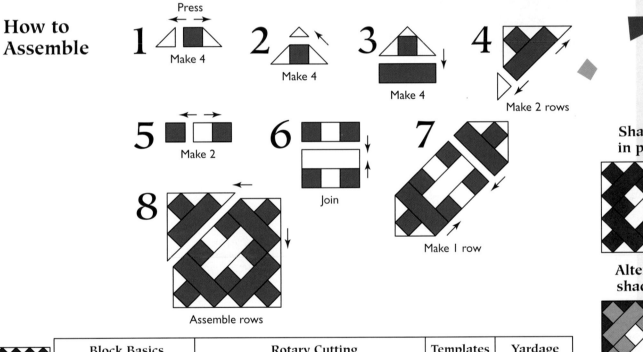

	Block Basics			Rotary Cutting				Templates	Yardage
	Patch	Shape	Total Needed	Strip Width (in inches)	Squares to Cut	Cut Size (in inches)	Next Cut	Template	Strip Length Needed (in inches)
LIGHT	A	▭	1	$2\frac{1}{8}$	1 rectangle	$2\frac{1}{8} \times 5\frac{1}{4}$	—	R10	$5\frac{1}{4}$
	B	☐	2	2+	2	2+ × 2+	—	S6	$4\frac{1}{4}$
	C	◺	4	2	2	2 × 2	◹	T2	4
	D	△	12	$3\frac{1}{2}$	3	$3\frac{1}{2} \times 3\frac{1}{2}$	⊠	T6	$10\frac{1}{2}$
DARK	E	▬	4	$2\frac{1}{8}$	4 rectangles	$2\frac{1}{8} \times 5\frac{1}{4}$	—	R10	21
	F	◼	8	2+	8	2+ × 2+	—	S6	17

Note: Plus sign (+) indicates $\frac{1}{16}$-inch measurements. See page 217 for details.

Gentleman's Fancy

Bl💡ck Idea

Use paisleys and pinstripes for a Father's Day look that can't be beat!

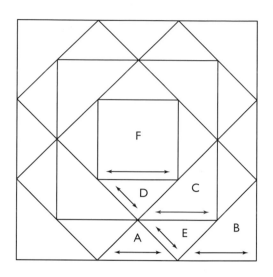

How to Assemble

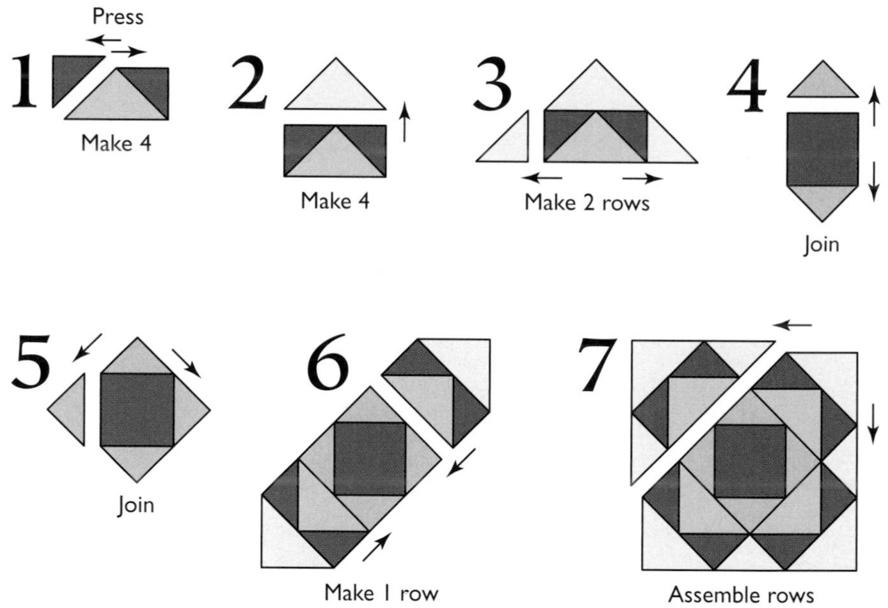

1 Press — Make 4

2 Make 4

3 Make 2 rows

4 Join

5 Join

6 Make I row

7 Assemble rows

Shading in photo

Alternate shadings

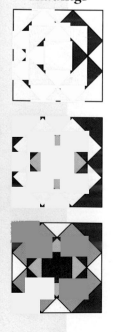

		Block Basics			Rotary Cutting				Templates	Yardage
	Patch	Shape	Total Needed	Strip Width (in inches)	Squares to Cut	Cut Size (in inches)	Next Cut		Template	Strip Length Needed (in inches)
LIGHT 1	A	△	4	4¼	1	4¼ × 4¼	⊠		T9	4¼
	B	◹	4	3⅞	2	3⅞ × 3⅞	◺		T12	7¾
LIGHT 2	C	◿	4	3⅞	2	3⅞ × 3⅞	◺		T12	7¾
MEDIUM	D	◢	4	3	2	3 × 3	◺		T9	6
DARK	E	◣	8	3	4	3 × 3	◺		T9	12
	F	◼	1	3½	1	3½ × 3½	—		S13	3½

Goose Tracks

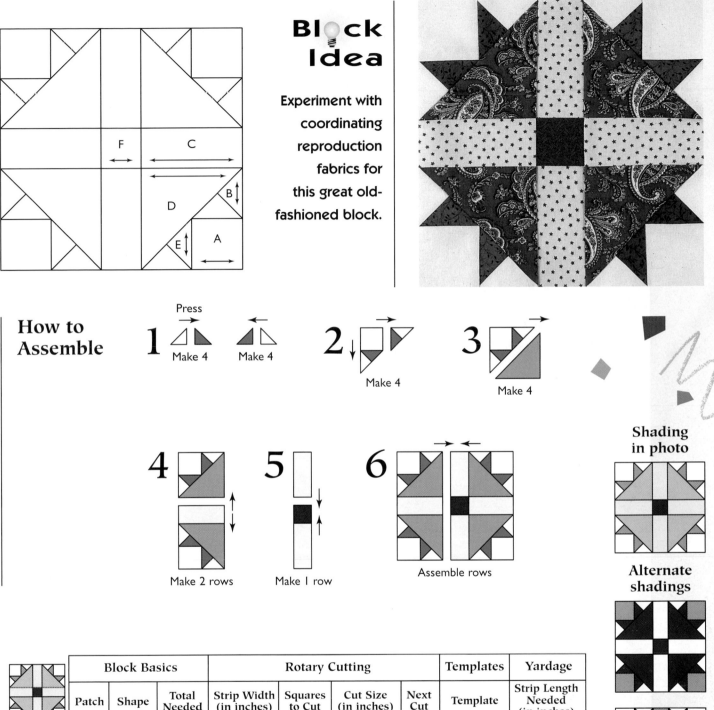

Block Idea

Experiment with coordinating reproduction fabrics for this great old-fashioned block.

How to Assemble

1 Press — Make 4 / Make 4

2 Make 4

3 Make 4

4 Make 2 rows

5 Make 1 row

6 Assemble rows

Shading in photo

Alternate shadings

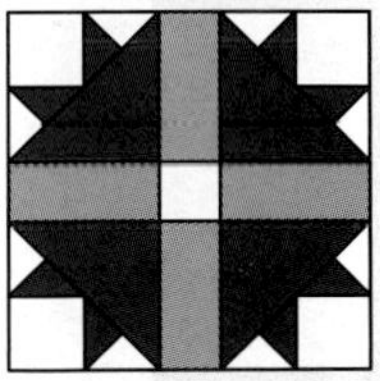

	Block Basics			Rotary Cutting				Templates	Yardage
	Patch	Shape	Total Needed	Strip Width (in inches)	Squares to Cut	Cut Size (in inches)	Next Cut	Template	Strip Length Needed (in inches)
LIGHT 1	A	▢	4	2⅜	4	2⅜ × 2⅜	—	S8	9½
	B	△	8	3⅛	2	3⅛ × 3⅛	⊠	T3	6¼
LIGHT 2	C	▭	4	2	4 rectangles	2 × 4¼	—	R5	17
MEDIUM 1	D	◺	4	4⅝	2	4⅝ × 4⅝	◩	T14	9¼
MEDIUM 2	E	▲	8	3⅛	2	3⅛ × 3⅛	⊠	T3	6¼
DARK	F	◼	1	2	1	2 × 2	—	S5	2

Grandmother's Favorite

Block Idea

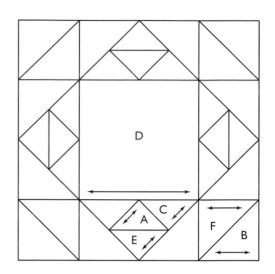

Create a 5-inch photo transfer and use it for the center square.

How to Assemble

Press

1 Make 4   Make 4

2 Make 4

3 Make 4

4 Make 2 rows

5 Make 1 row

6 Assemble rows

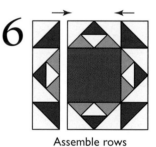

Shading in photo

Alternate shadings

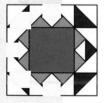

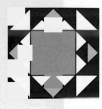

	Block Basics			Rotary Cutting				Templates	Yardage
	Patch	Shape	Total Needed	Strip Width (in inches)	Squares to Cut	Cut Size (in inches)	Next Cut	Template	Strip Length Needed (in inches)
LIGHT	A		4	$2\frac{3}{8}+$	2	$2\frac{3}{8}+ \times 2\frac{3}{8}+$		T6	5
	B		12	$3\frac{1}{8}$	6	$3\frac{1}{8} \times 3\frac{1}{8}$		T10	$18\frac{3}{4}$
MEDIUM	C		8	$2\frac{3}{8}+$	4	$2\frac{3}{8}+ \times 2\frac{3}{8}+$		T6	10
DARK 1	D		1	5	1	5×5	—	S16	5
DARK 2	E		4	$2\frac{3}{8}+$	2	$2\frac{3}{8}+ \times 2\frac{3}{8}+$		T6	5
	F		4	$3\frac{1}{8}$	2	$3\frac{1}{8} \times 3\frac{1}{8}$		T10	$6\frac{1}{4}$

Note: Plus sign (+) indicates $\frac{1}{16}$-inch measurements. See page 217 for details.

Grandmother's Pride

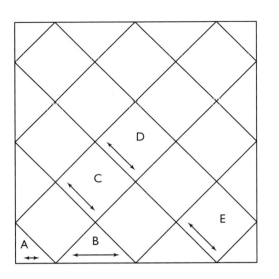

Blck Idea

This is a great block for using your special vintage fabrics.

How to Assemble

1 Press ↑ Make 4

2 Make 4

3 Make 2   Make 1

4 Join

5 Join

6 Join

Shading in photo

Alternate shadings

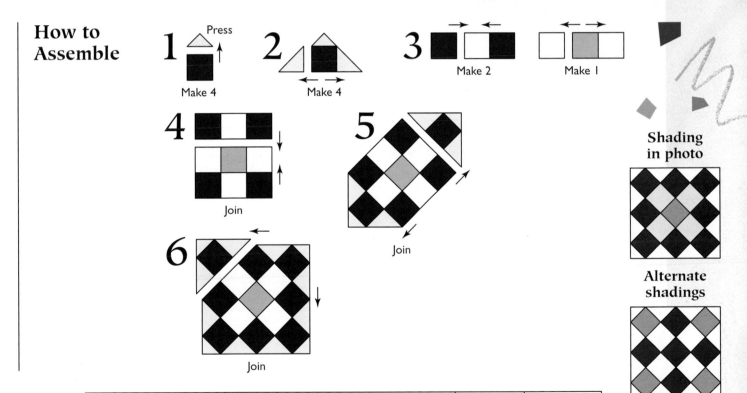

	Block Basics			Rotary Cutting				Templates	Yardage
	Patch	Shape	Total Needed	Strip Width (in inches)	Squares to Cut	Cut Size (in inches)	Next Cut	Template	Strip Length Needed (in inches)
LIGHT 1	A	◺	4	$2\frac{3}{8}$	2	$2\frac{3}{8} \times 2\frac{3}{8}$	◨	T5	$4\frac{3}{4}$
	B	△	8	$4\frac{1}{4}$	2	$4\frac{1}{4} \times 4\frac{1}{4}$	⊠	T9	$8\frac{1}{2}$
LIGHT 2	C	☐	4	$2\frac{5}{8}$	4	$2\frac{5}{8} \times 2\frac{5}{8}$	—	S10	$10\frac{1}{2}$
MEDIUM	D	▧	1	$2\frac{5}{8}$	1	$2\frac{5}{8} \times 2\frac{5}{8}$	—	S10	$2\frac{5}{8}$
DARK	E	■	8	$2\frac{5}{8}$	8	$2\frac{5}{8} \times 2\frac{5}{8}$	—	S10	21

Grape Basket

Block Idea

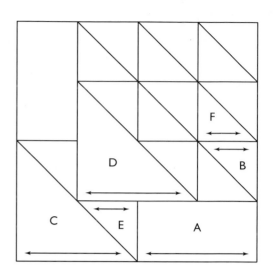

Make this block scrappy by using a variety of prints for the dark triangles.

How to Assemble

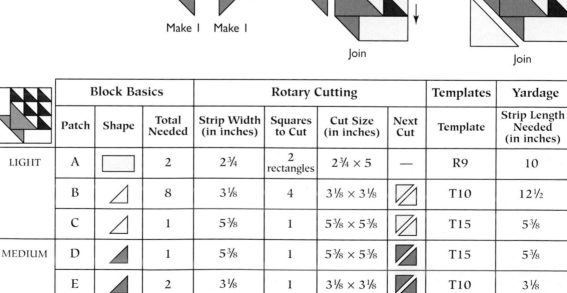

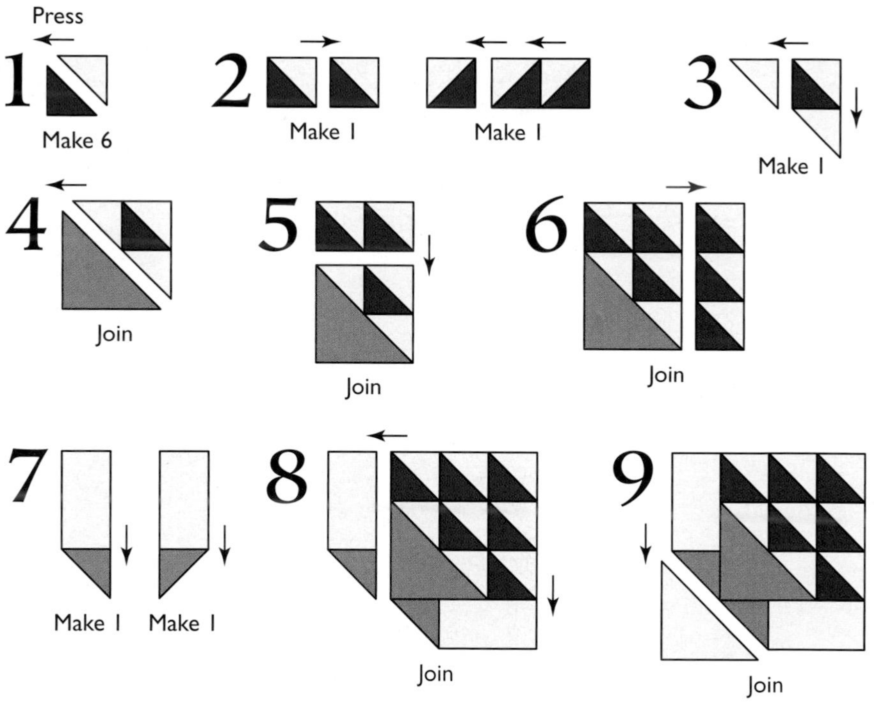

Press

1 Make 6

2 Make 1   Make 1

3 Make 1

4 Join

5 Join

6 Join

7 Make 1   Make 1

8 Join

9 Join

Shading in photo

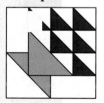

Alternate shadings

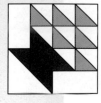

	Block Basics			Rotary Cutting				Templates	Yardage
	Patch	Shape	Total Needed	Strip Width (in inches)	Squares to Cut	Cut Size (in inches)	Next Cut	Template	Strip Length Needed (in inches)
LIGHT	A		2	2¾	2 rectangles	2¾ × 5	—	R9	10
	B		8	3⅛	4	3⅛ × 3⅛		T10	12½
	C		1	5⅜	1	5⅜ × 5⅜		T15	5⅜
MEDIUM	D		1	5⅜	1	5⅜ × 5⅜		T15	5⅜
	E		2	3⅛	1	3⅛ × 3⅛		T10	3⅛
DARK	F		6	3⅛	3	3⅛ × 3⅛		T10	9⅜

Grecian Square

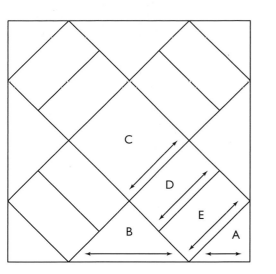

Block Idea

Reverse the lights and darks in alternate blocks.

How to Assemble

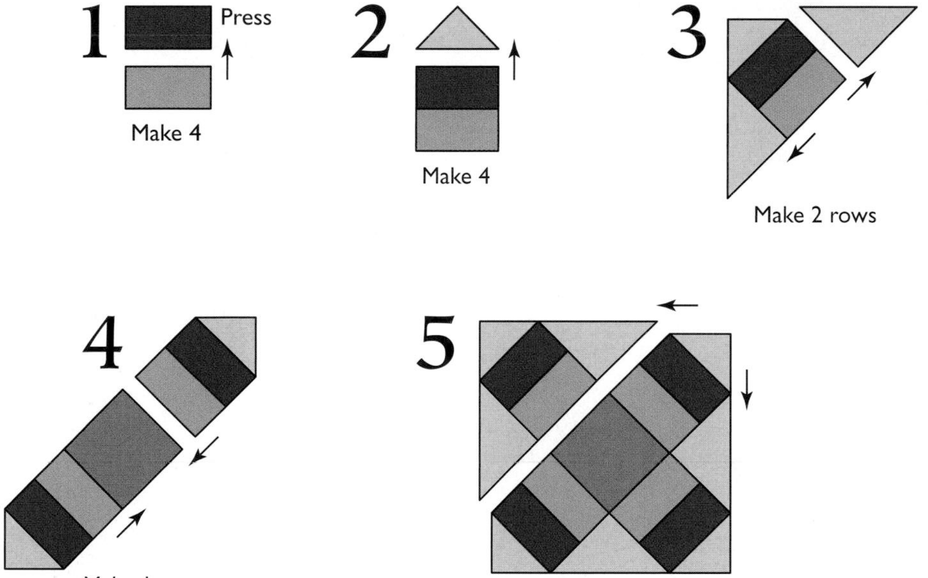

1 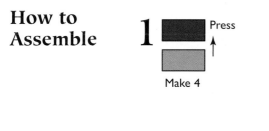 Press
Make 4

2 Make 4

3 Make 2 rows

4 Make I row

5 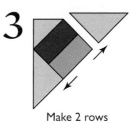 Assemble rows

Shading in photo

Alternate shadings

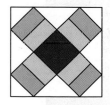

	Block Basics			**Rotary Cutting**				**Templates**	**Yardage**
	Patch	Shape	Total Needed	Strip Width (in inches)	Squares to Cut	Cut Size (in inches)	Next Cut	Template	Strip Length Needed (in inches)
LIGHT	A	◹	4	3⅛	2	3⅛ × 3⅛	◺	T10	6¼
	B	△	4	5¾	1	5¾ × 5¾	⧖	T13	5¾
MEDIUM 1	C	■	1	3⅝+	1	3⅝+ × 3⅝+	—	S14	3⅝+
MEDIUM 2	D	▬	4	2⅛	4 rectangles	2⅛ × 3⅝+	—	R2	14¾
DARK	E	▬	4	2⅛	4 rectangles	2⅛ × 3⅝+	—	R2	14¾

Note: Plus sign (+) indicates ¹⁄₁₆-inch measurements. See page 217 for details.

Handy Andy

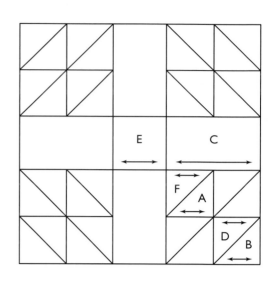

Bl💡ck Idea

Keep the center lattice the same color for each block, and set the blocks side by side.

E   C

F   A

D   B

How to Assemble

Press

 1 Make 12 Make 4

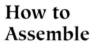 **2** Make 4 Make 4

 3 Make 4

 **4** Make 2 rows

5 Make 1 row

 6 Assemble rows

Shading in photo

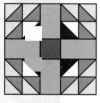

Alternate shadings

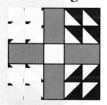

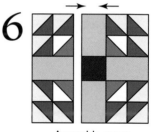

	Block Basics			Rotary Cutting				Templates	Yardage
	Patch	Shape	Total Needed	Strip Width (in inches)	Squares to Cut	Cut Size (in inches)	Next Cut	Template	Strip Length Needed (in inches)
LIGHT 1	A	◺	4	$2\frac{5}{8}$	2	$2\frac{5}{8} \times 2\frac{5}{8}$	◩	T7	$5\frac{1}{4}$
LIGHT 2	B	◿	12	$2\frac{5}{8}$	6	$2\frac{5}{8} \times 2\frac{5}{8}$	◩	T7	$15\frac{3}{4}$
MEDIUM 1	C	▭	4	$2\frac{1}{2}$	4 rectangles	$2\frac{1}{2} \times 4$	—	R4	16
MEDIUM 2	D	◣	12	$2\frac{5}{8}$	6	$2\frac{5}{8} \times 2\frac{5}{8}$	◩	T7	$15\frac{3}{4}$
DARK 1	E	■	1	$2\frac{1}{2}$	1	$2\frac{1}{2} \times 2\frac{1}{2}$	—	S9	$2\frac{1}{2}$
DARK 2	F	◣	4	$2\frac{5}{8}$	2	$2\frac{5}{8} \times 2\frac{5}{8}$	◩	T7	$5\frac{1}{4}$

Hourglass

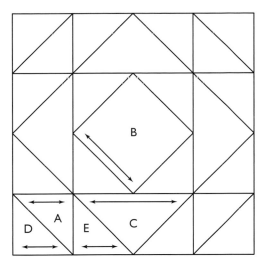

Block Idea

Select a favorite pictorial print and feature it in the block center.

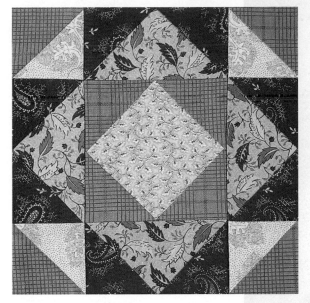

How to Assemble

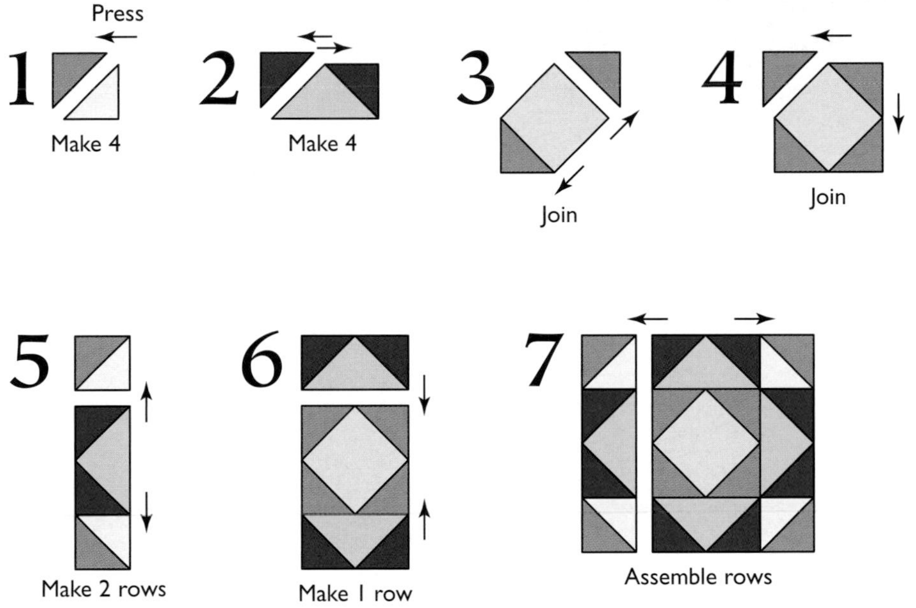

1 Make 4 — Press

2 Make 4

3 Join

4 Join

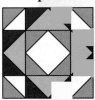

Shading in photo

5 Make 2 rows

6 Make 1 row

7 Assemble rows

Alternate shadings

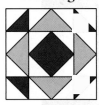

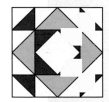

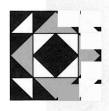

	Block Basics			Rotary Cutting				Templates	Yardage
	Patch	Shape	Total Needed	Strip Width (in inches)	Squares to Cut	Cut Size (in inches)	Next Cut	Template	Strip Length Needed (in inches)
LIGHT 1	A	◺	4	3⅛	2	3⅛ × 3⅛	◺	T10	6 1/4
LIGHT 2	B	▢	1	3⅝+	1	3⅝+ × 3⅝+	—	S14	3⅝+
MEDIUM 1	C	◿	4	5¾	1	5¾ × 5¾	⊠	T13	5¾
MEDIUM 2	D	◥	8	3⅛	4	3⅛ × 3⅛	◺	T10	12½
DARK	E	◥	8	3⅛	4	3⅛ × 3⅛	◺	T10	12½

Note: Plus sign (+) indicates ¹⁄₁₆-inch measurements. See page 217 for details.

Hovering Hawks

Set blocks side by side and play with different arrangements of the diagonals.

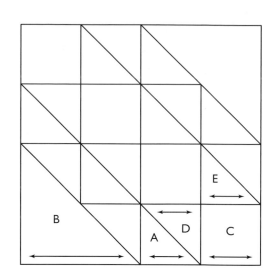

Shading in photo

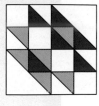

Alternate shadings

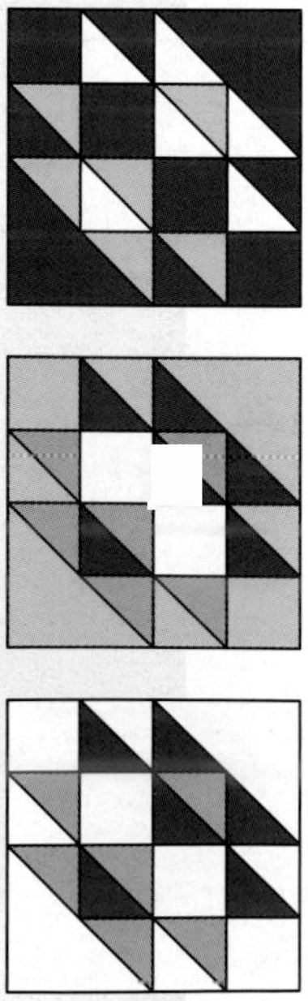

How to Assemble

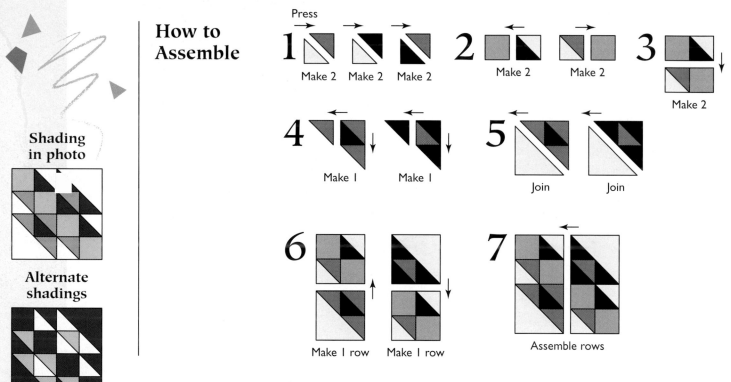

Press

1 — Make 2 Make 2 Make 2

2 — Make 2 Make 2

3 — Make 2

4 — Make 1 Make 1

5 — Join Join

6 — Make 1 row Make 1 row

7 — Assemble rows

	Block Basics			**Rotary Cutting**				**Templates**	**Yardage**
	Patch	Shape	Total Needed	Strip Width (in inches)	Squares to Cut	Cut Size (in inches)	Next Cut	Template	Strip Length Needed (in inches)
LIGHT 1	A	◺	4	3⅛	2	3⅛ × 3⅛	◹	T10	6¼
	B	◺	2	5⅜	1	5⅜ × 5⅜	◹	T15	5⅜
LIGHT 2	C	▢	4	2¾	4	2¾ × 2¾	—	S11	11
MEDIUM	D	◸	6	3⅛	3	3⅛ × 3⅛	◿	T10	9⅜
DARK	E	◣	6	3⅛	3	3⅛ × 3⅛	◿	T10	9⅜

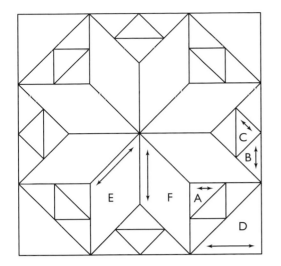

Block Idea

Emphasize the "ring" of little triangles by making them the brightest color.

How to Assemble

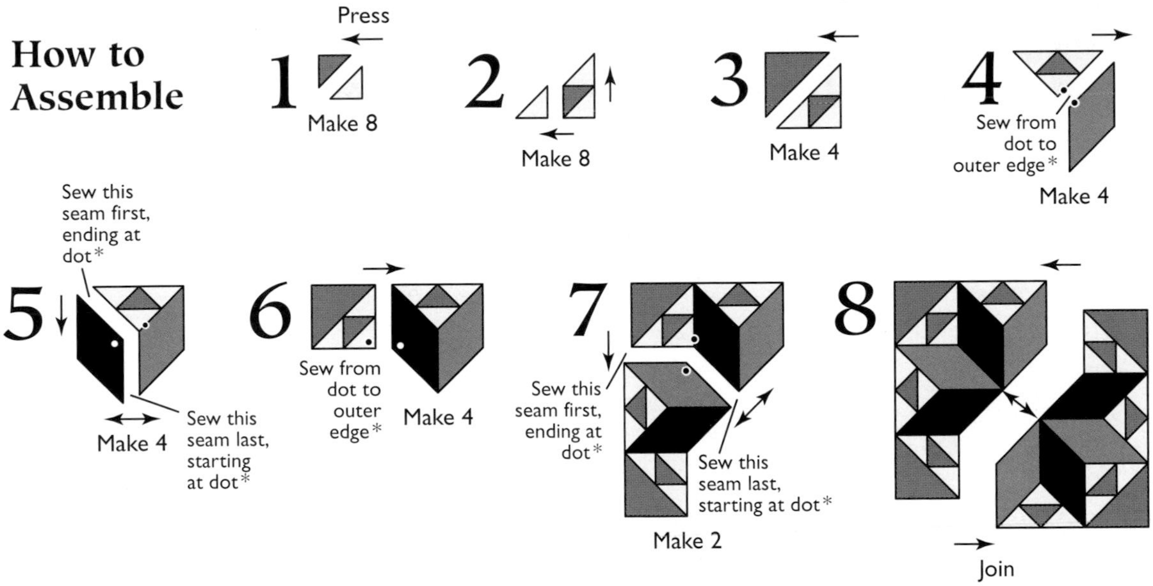

Press

1 Make 8

2 Make 8

3 Make 4

4 Sew from dot to outer edge* Make 4

5 Sew this seam first, ending at dot* Make 4 — Sew this seam last, starting at dot*

6 Sew from dot to outer edge* Make 4

7 Sew this seam first, ending at dot* — Sew this seam last, starting at dot* Make 2

8 Join

Shading in photo

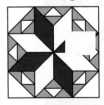

Alternate shadings

*See page 223 for details.

	Block Basics			Rotary Cutting				Templates	Yardage
	Patch	Shape	Total Needed	Strip Width (in inches)	Squares to Cut	Cut Size (in inches)	Next Cut	Template	Strip Length Needed (in inches)
LIGHT 1	A	◺	8	2⅛+	4	2⅛+ × 2⅛+		T3	8¾
	B	△	16	3⅛	4	3⅛ × 3⅛		T3	12½
LIGHT 2	C	◹	8	2⅛+	4	2⅛+ × 2⅛+		T3	8¾
	D	◸	4	3½	2	3½ × 3½		T11	7
MEDIUM	E	▱	4	2⅜	Make a 45° angle cut at one end of strip. Measuring from diagonal cut, make successive cuts 2⅜" apart.			D2	16
DARK	F	▰	4	2⅜	Make a 45° angle cut at one end of strip. Measuring from diagonal cut, make successive cuts 2⅜" apart.			D2	16

Note: Plus sign (+) indicates 1/16-inch measurements. See page 217 for details.

Jack-in-the-Pulpit

 **Block Idea**

Try a dark solid for the background with light pastels for the patches.

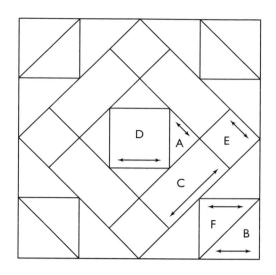

How to Assemble

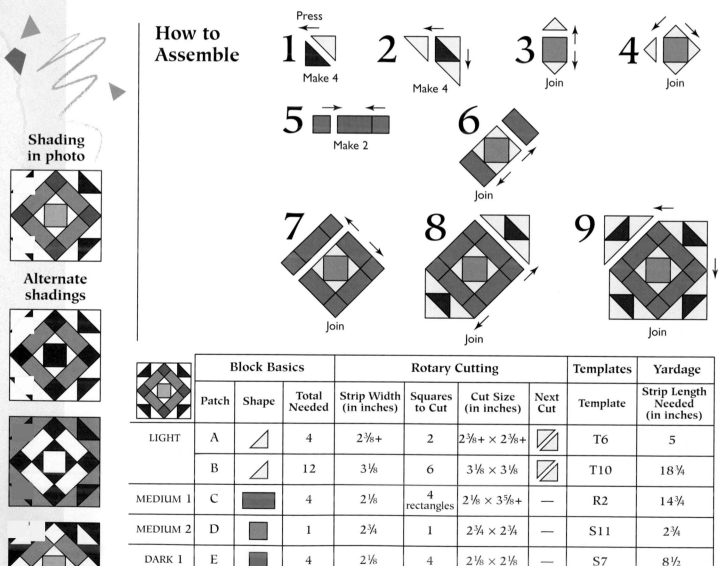

1 Make 4 — Press

2 Make 4

3 Join

4 Join

5 Make 2

6 Join

7 Join

8 Join

9 Join

Shading in photo

Alternate shadings

	Block Basics			Rotary Cutting				Templates	Yardage
	Patch	Shape	Total Needed	Strip Width (in inches)	Squares to Cut	Cut Size (in inches)	Next Cut	Template	Strip Length Needed (in inches)
LIGHT	A	◺	4	2⅜+	2	2⅜+ × 2⅜+	◿	T6	5
	B	◺	12	3⅛	6	3⅛ × 3⅛	◿	T10	18¾
MEDIUM 1	C	▭	4	2⅛	4 rectangles	2⅛ × 3⅝+	—	R2	14¾
MEDIUM 2	D	◻	1	2¾	1	2¾ × 2¾	—	S11	2¾
DARK 1	E	◻	4	2⅛	4	2⅛ × 2⅛	—	S7	8½
DARK 2	F	◣	4	3⅛	2	3⅛ × 3⅛	◣	T10	6¼

Note: Plus sign (+) indicates ¹⁄₁₆-inch measurements. See page 217 for details.

Jacob's Ladder

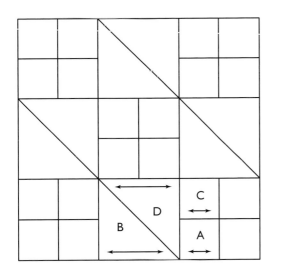

Block Idea

Repeat the Four Patch as a cornerstone when using a lattice set.

How to Assemble

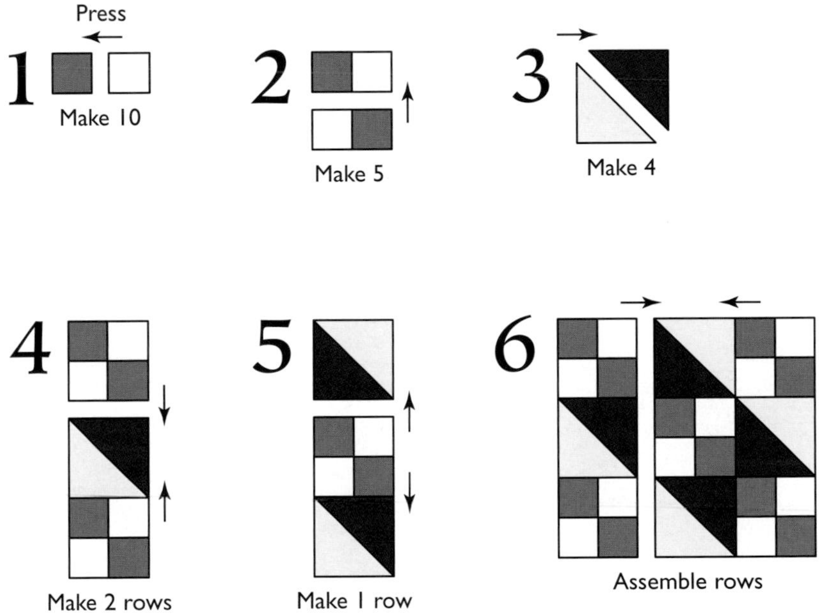

Press

1  Make 10

2 Make 5

3 Make 4

4  Make 2 rows

5 Make 1 row

6 Assemble rows

Shading in photo

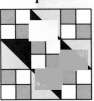

Alternate shadings

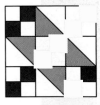

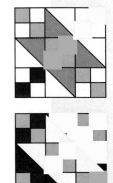

	Block Basics			Rotary Cutting				Templates	Yardage
	Patch	Shape	Total Needed	Strip Width (in inches)	Squares to Cut	Cut Size (in inches)	Next Cut	Template	Strip Length Needed (in inches)
LIGHT 1	A	☐	10	2	10	2 × 2	—	S5	20
LIGHT 2	B	◺	4	3⅞	2	3⅞ × 3⅞	◹	T12	7¾
MEDIUM	C	◼	10	2	10	2 × 2	—	S5	20
DARK	D	◣	4	3⅞	2	3⅞ × 3⅞	◤	T12	7¾

Job's Troubles

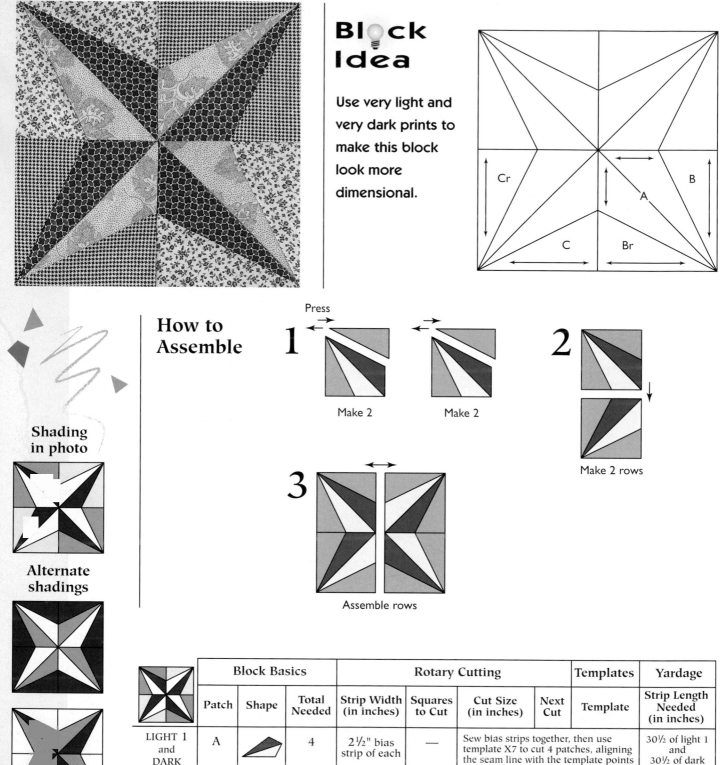

Block Idea

Use very light and very dark prints to make this block look more dimensional.

How to Assemble

1

Press

Make 2   Make 2

2

Make 2 rows

3

Assemble rows

Shading in photo

Alternate shadings

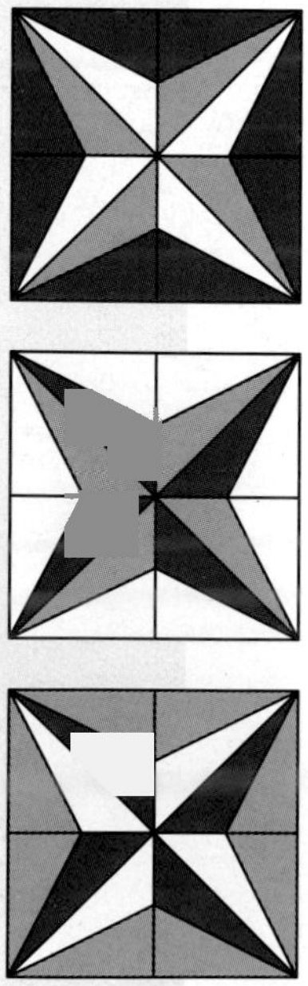

	Block Basics			Rotary Cutting				Templates	Yardage
	Patch	Shape	Total Needed	Strip Width (in inches)	Squares to Cut	Cut Size (in inches)	Next Cut	Template	Strip Length Needed (in inches)
LIGHT 1 and DARK	A		4	2½" bias strip of each	—	Sew bias strips together, then use template X7 to cut 4 patches, aligning the seam line with the template points			30½ of light 1 and 30½ of dark
LIGHT 2	B		2	2⅞	1 rectangle	2⅞ × 5¾+		TT4	5¾+
	Br		2	2⅞	1 rectangle	2⅞ × 5¾+		TT4r	5¾+
MEDIUM	C		2	2⅞	1 rectangle	2⅞ × 5¾+		TT4	5¾+
	Cr		2	2⅞	1 rectangle	2⅞ × 5¾+		TT4r	5¾+

Note: Plus sign (+) indicates ¹/₁₆-inch measurements. See page 217 for details.

Judy's Star

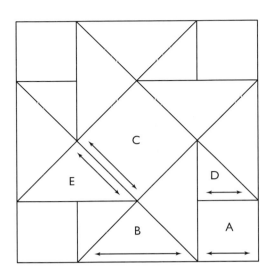

Block Idea

Make the star points scrappy for old-fashioned style.

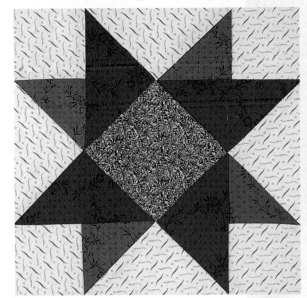

How to Assemble

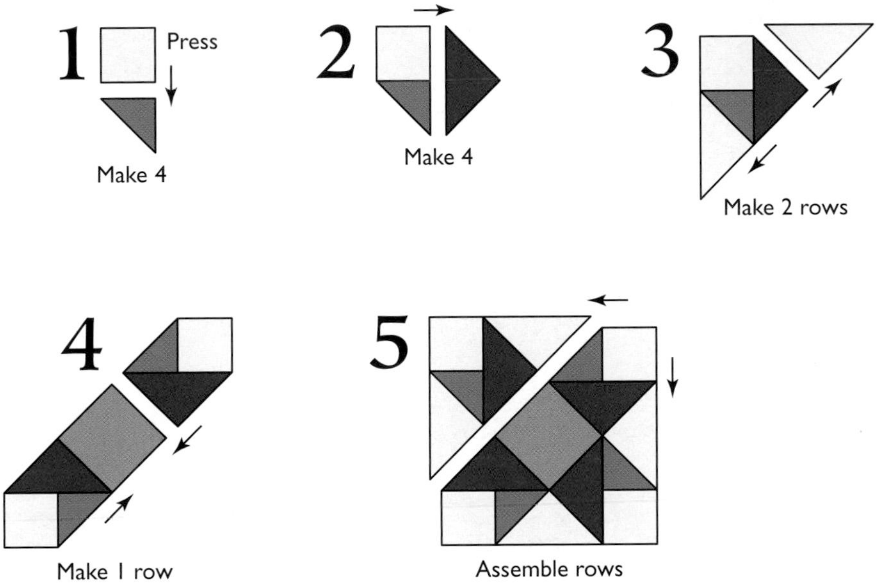

1 Press ↓ Make 4

2 Make 4

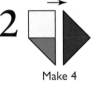

3 Make 2 rows

4 Make 1 row

5 Assemble rows

Shading in photo

Alternate shadings

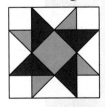

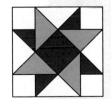

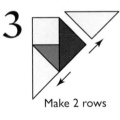

		Block Basics		Rotary Cutting				Templates	Yardage
	Patch	Shape	Total Needed	Strip Width (in inches)	Squares to Cut	Cut Size (in inches)	Next Cut	Template	Strip Length Needed (in inches)
LIGHT 1	A	▢	4	2¾	4	2¾ × 2¾	—	S11	11
	B	△	4	5¾	1	5¾ × 5¾	⊠	T13	5¾
LIGHT 2	C	▦	1	3⅝+	1	3⅝+ × 3⅝+	—	S14	3⅝+
MEDIUM	D	◣	4	3⅛	2	3⅛ × 3⅛	◿	T10	6¼
DARK	E	◣	4	4+	2	4+ × 4+	◿	T13	8⅛

Note: Plus sign (+) indicates ¹/₁₆-inch measurements. See page 217 for details.

Kaleidoscope

Bl ck Idea

Use a light fabric in the corner triangles to make the kaleidoscope float on the background.

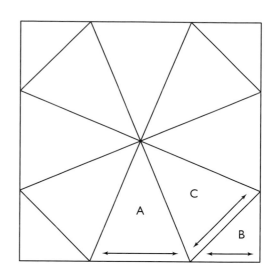

Shading in photo

Alternate shadings

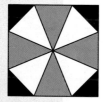

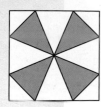

How to Assemble

1 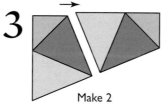 Press ↑

Make 4

2 Make 4

3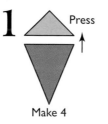

Make 2

4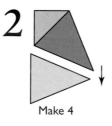

Join

	Block Basics			Rotary Cutting				Templates	Yardage
	Patch	Shape	Total Needed	Strip Width (in inches)	Squares to Cut	Cut Size (in inches)	Next Cut	Template	Strip Length Needed (in inches)
LIGHT	A	△	4	—	—	Use template TT6			—
MEDIUM	B	◺	4	3½	2	3½ × 3½	◩	T11	7
DARK	C	▲	4	—	—	Use template TT6			—

Kansas Troubles

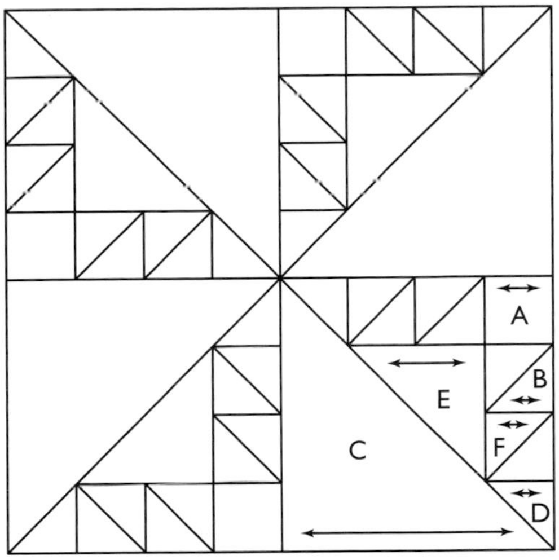

A
B
E
F
C
D

Block Idea

Make the small center pinwheel a different color.

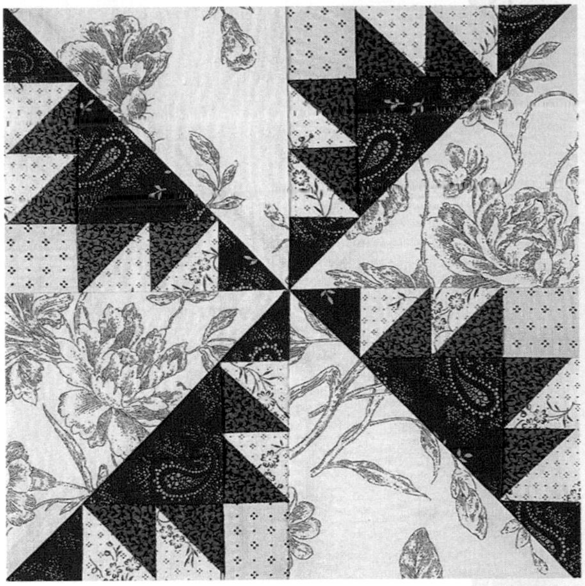

How to Assemble

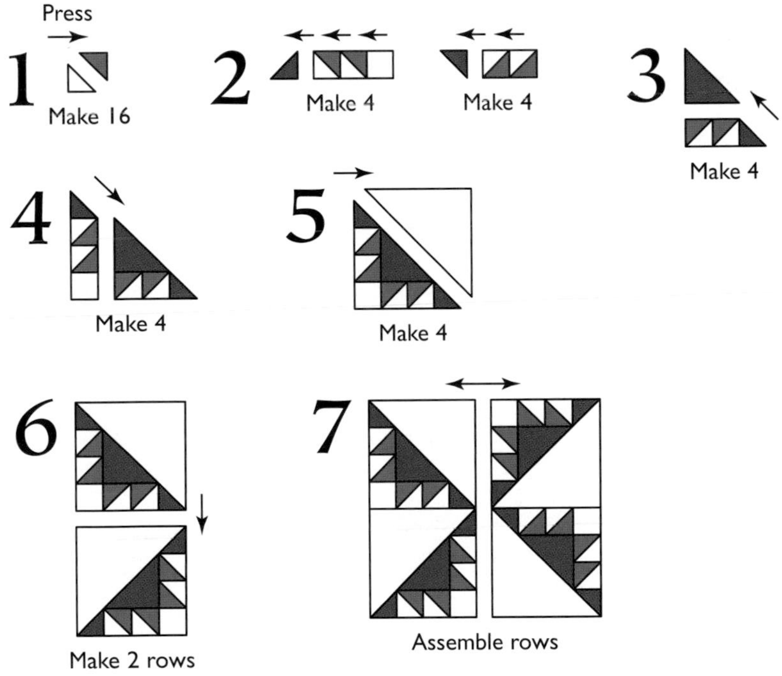

Press
1
Make 16
2
Make 4
Make 4
3
Make 4
4
Make 4
5
Make 4
6
Make 2 rows
7
Assemble rows

Shading in photo

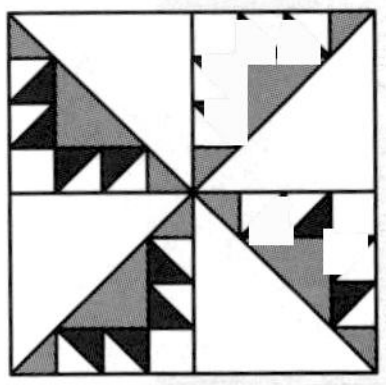

Alternate shadings

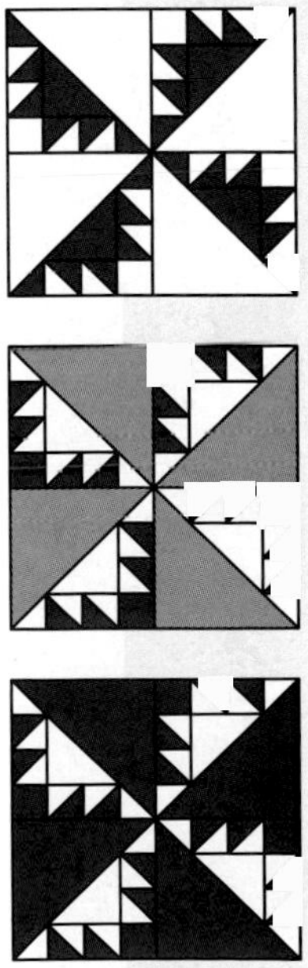

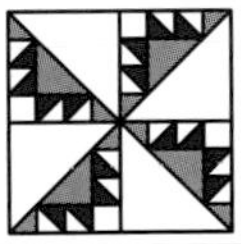

	Block Basics			Rotary Cutting				Templates	Yardage
	Patch	Shape	Total Needed	Strip Width (in inches)	Squares to Cut	Cut Size (in inches)	Next Cut	Template	Strip Length Needed (in inches)
LIGHT	A		4	1⅝	4	1⅝ × 1⅝	—	S3	6½
	B		16	2	8	2 × 2		T2	16
	C		4	5⅜	2	5⅜ × 5⅜		T15	10¾
MEDIUM	D		8	2	4	2 × 2		T2	8
	E		4	3⅛	2	3⅛ × 3⅛		T10	6¼
DARK	F		16	2	8	2 × 2		T2	16

Kayak

This makes a great two-color block—just cut patches from only light and dark fabrics.

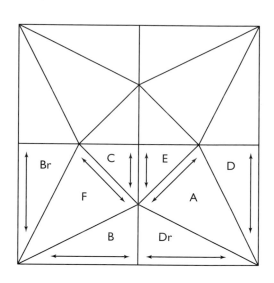

How to Assemble

1 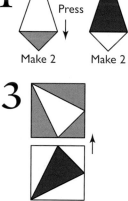 Press ↓

Make 2   Make 2

2 Make 2   Make 2

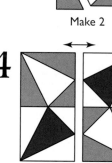

3 Make 2 rows

4 Assemble rows

Shading in photo

Alternate shadings

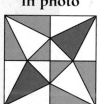

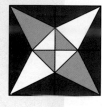

	Block Basics			**Rotary Cutting**				**Templates**	**Yardage**
	Patch	Shape	Total Needed	Strip Width (in inches)	Squares to Cut	Cut Size (in inches)	Next Cut	Template	Strip Length Needed (in inches)
LIGHT	A		2	—	—	Use template TT5			—
	B		2	$2\frac{7}{8}$	1 rectangle	$2\frac{7}{8} \times 5\frac{3}{4}+$		TT4	$5\frac{3}{4}+$
	Br		2	$2\frac{7}{8}$	1 rectangle	$2\frac{7}{8} \times 5\frac{3}{4}+$		TT4r	$5\frac{3}{4}+$
	C		2	$3\frac{1}{8}$	1	$3\frac{1}{8} \times 3\frac{1}{8}$		T10	$3\frac{1}{8}$
MEDIUM	D		2	$2\frac{7}{8}$	1 rectangle	$2\frac{7}{8} \times 5\frac{3}{4}+$		TT4	$5\frac{3}{4}+$
	Dr		2	$2\frac{7}{8}$	1 rectangle	$2\frac{7}{8} \times 5\frac{3}{4}+$		TT4r	$5\frac{3}{4}+$
	E		2	$3\frac{1}{8}$	1	$3\frac{1}{8} \times 3\frac{1}{8}$		T10	$3\frac{1}{8}$
DARK	F		2	—	—	Use template TT5			—

Note: Plus sign (+) indicates $\frac{1}{16}$-inch measurements. See page 217 for details.

Key West Beauty

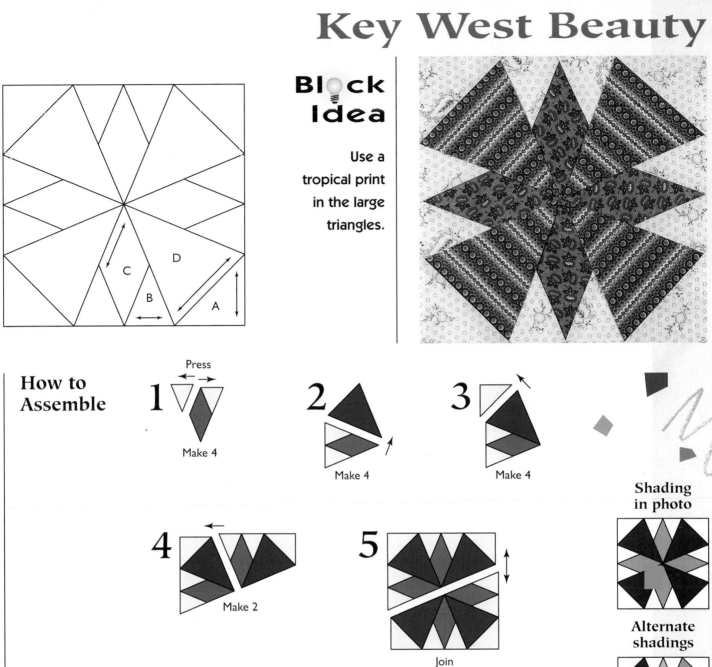

Bl☉ck Idea

Use a tropical print in the large triangles.

How to Assemble

1 Press — Make 4

2 Make 4

3 Make 4

4 Make 2

5 Join

Shading in photo

Alternate shadings

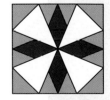

	Block Basics			Rotary Cutting				Templates	Yardage
	Patch	Shape	Total Needed	Strip Width (in inches)	Squares to Cut	Cut Size (in inches)	Next Cut	Template	Strip Length Needed (in inches)
LIGHT	A	◿	4	3½	2	3½ × 3½	◨	T11	7
	B	△	8	—	—	Use template TT7			—
MEDIUM	C	▱	4	2¼	Make a 45° angle cut at the left end of the strip, angling the ruler from bottom left to top right. Measuring from diagonal cut, make successive cuts 2¼" apart.			D3	15⅛
DARK	D	▲	4	—	—	Use template TT6			—

King's Crown

Block Idea

Change opposite corner squares to a light fabric and set blocks side by side to create Four Patches.

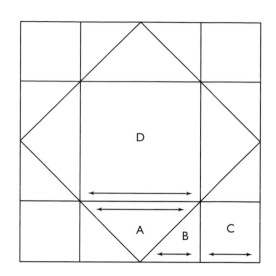

How to Assemble

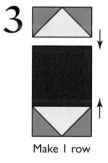

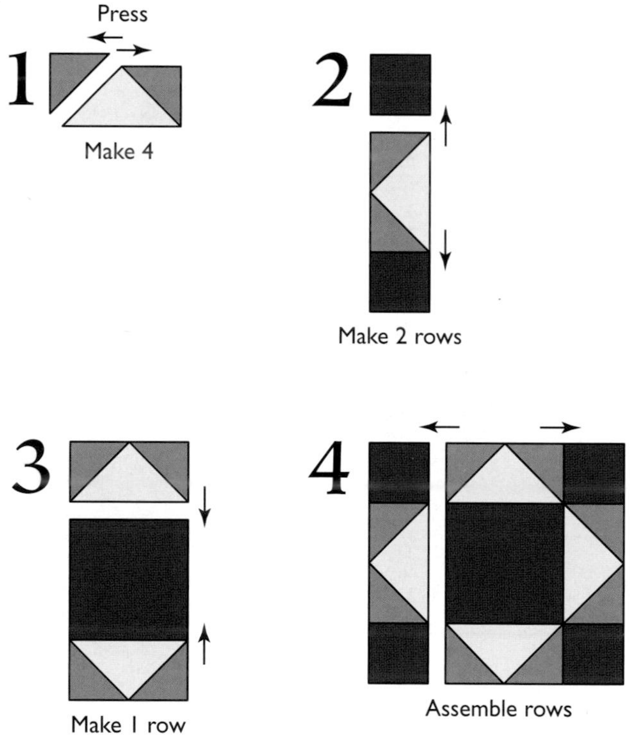

1 Press
Make 4

2 Make 2 rows

3 Make 1 row

4 Assemble rows

Shading in photo

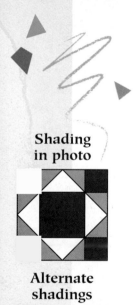

Alternate shadings

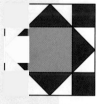

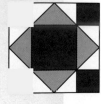

		Block Basics		Rotary Cutting				Templates	Yardage
	Patch	Shape	Total Needed	Strip Width (in inches)	Squares to Cut	Cut Size (in inches)	Next Cut	Template	Strip Length Needed (in inches)
LIGHT	A	△	4	5¾	1	5¾ × 5¾	⊠	T13	5¾
MEDIUM	B	◺	8	3⅛	4	3⅛ × 3⅛	◿	T10	12½
DARK	C	■	4	2¾	4	2¾ × 2¾	—	S11	11
	D	■	1	5	1	5 × 5	—	S16	5

LeMoyne Star

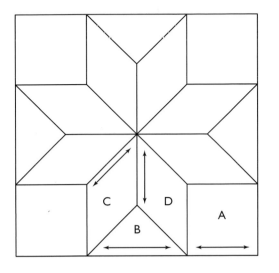

Block Idea

Try using different prints for each diamond to create a scrap quilt.

How to Assemble

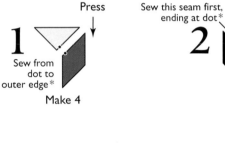

1 Press
Sew from dot to outer edge*
Make 4

2 Sew this seam first, ending at dot*
Sew this seam last, starting at dot*
Make 4

3 Sew from dot to outer edge*
Make 4

4 Sew this seam first, ending at dot*
Sew this seam last, starting at dot*
Make 2

5 Join

*See page 223 for details.

Shading in photo

Alternate shadings

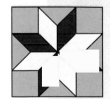

	Block Basics			Rotary Cutting				Templates	Yardage
	Patch	Shape	Total Needed	Strip Width (in inches)	Squares to Cut	Cut Size (in inches)	Next Cut	Template	Strip Length Needed (in inches)
LIGHT	A	⬜	4	3⅛	4	3⅛ × 3⅛	—	S12	12½
	B	△	4	5	1	5 × 5	⊠	T11	5
MEDIUM	C	▱	4	2⅜	Make a 45° angle cut at one end of strip. Measuring from diagonal cut, make successive cuts 2⅜" apart.			D2	16
DARK	D	▰	4	2⅜	Make a 45° angle cut at one end of strip. Measuring from diagonal cut, make successive cuts 2⅜" apart.			D2	16

Log Cabin

Block Idea

Try using two accent colors for the center triangle-square.

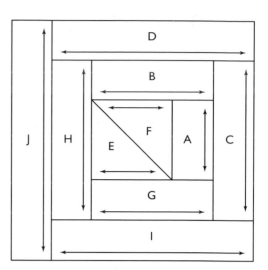

Shading in photo

Alternate shadings

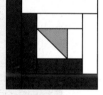

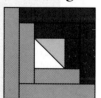

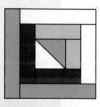

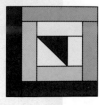

How to Assemble

1 Make 1 Press

2 Join

3 Join

4 Join

5 Join

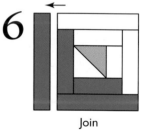

6 Join

	Block Basics			**Rotary Cutting**				**Templates**	**Yardage**
	Patch	Shape	Total Needed	Strip Width (in inches)	Squares to Cut	Cut Size (in inches)	Next Cut	Template	Strip Length Needed (in inches)
LIGHT	A		1	2	1 rectangle	$2 \times 3\frac{1}{2}$	—	R1	$3\frac{1}{2}$
	B		1	2	1 rectangle	2×5	—	R8	5
	C		1	2	1 rectangle	$2 \times 6\frac{1}{2}$	—	R11	$6\frac{1}{2}$
	D		1	2	1 rectangle	2×8	—	R12	8
	E		1	$3\frac{7}{8}$	1	$3\frac{7}{8} \times 3\frac{7}{8}$		T12	$3\frac{7}{8}$
MEDIUM	F		1	$3\frac{7}{8}$	1	$3\frac{7}{8} \times 3\frac{7}{8}$		T12	$3\frac{7}{8}$
DARK	G		1	2	1 rectangle	2×5	—	R8	5
	H		1	2	1 rectangle	$2 \times 6\frac{1}{2}$	—	R11	$6\frac{1}{2}$
	I		1	2	1 rectangle	2×8	—	R12	8
	J		1	2	1 rectangle	$2 \times 9\frac{1}{2}$	—	R13	$9\frac{1}{2}$

Log Cabin with a Chain

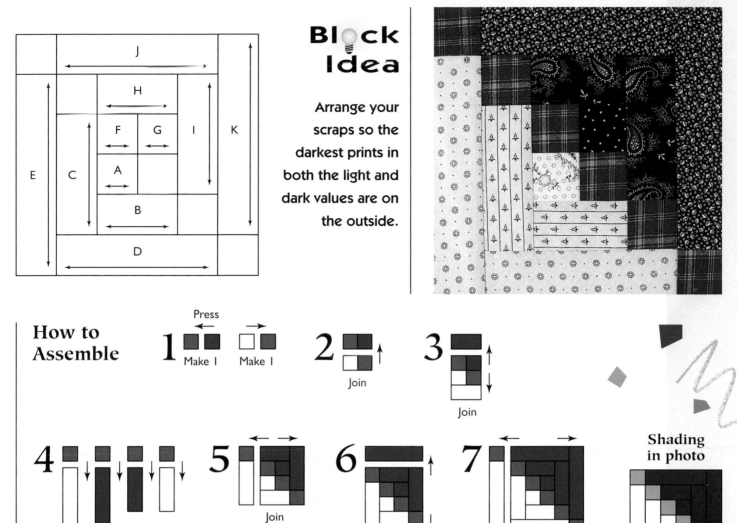

Block Idea

Arrange your scraps so the darkest prints in both the light and dark values are on the outside.

How to Assemble

Press

1 Make 1   Make 1

2 Join

3 Join

4 Make 1 of each

5 Join

6 Join

7 Join

Shading in photo

Alternate shadings

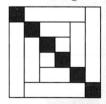

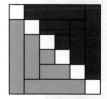

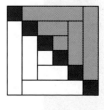

	Block Basics			Rotary Cutting				Templates	Yardage
	Patch	Shape	Total Needed	Strip Width (in inches)	Squares to Cut	Cut Size (in inches)	Next Cut	Template	Strip Length Needed (in inches)
LIGHT	A		1	2	1	2 × 2	—	S5	2
	B		1	2	1 rectangle	2 × 3½	—	R1	3½
	C		1	2	1 rectangle	2 × 5	—	R8	5
	D		1	2	1 rectangle	2 × 6½	—	R11	6½
	E		1	2	1 rectangle	2 × 8	—	R12	8
MEDIUM	F		6	2	6	2 × 2	—	S5	12
DARK	G		1	2	1	2 × 2	—	S5	2
	H		1	2	1 rectangle	2 × 3½	—	R1	3½
	I		1	2	1 rectangle	2 × 5	—	R8	5
	J		1	2	1 rectangle	2 × 6½	—	R11	6½
	K		1	2	1 rectangle	2 × 8	—	R12	8

Lost Ship

Block Idea

Use a different dark print for every other triangle square.

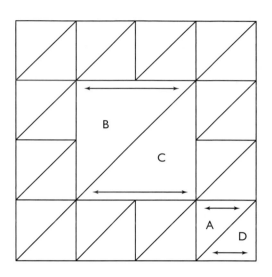

How to Assemble

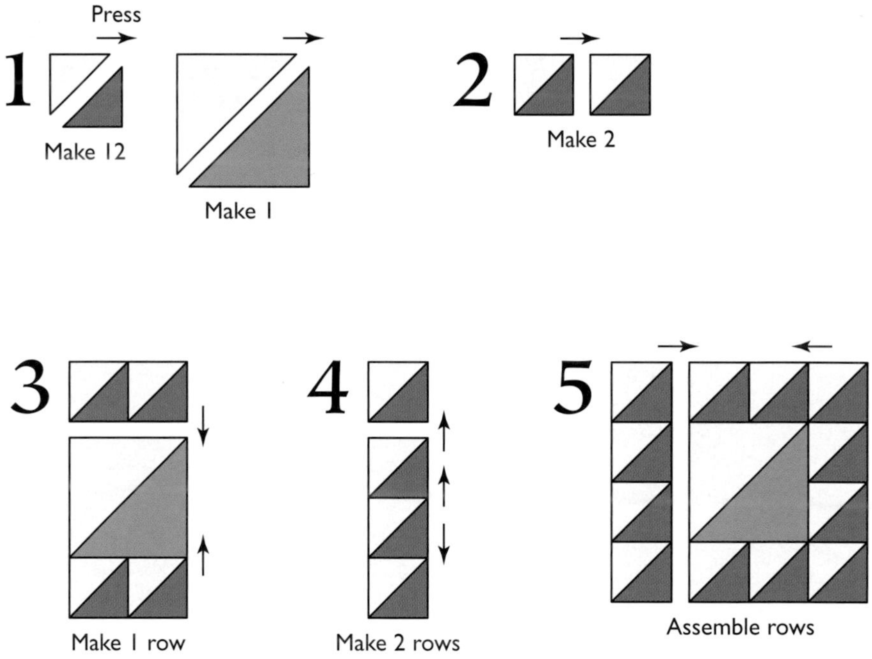

1 Make 12 / Make 1

2 Make 2

3 Make 1 row

4 Make 2 rows

5 Assemble rows

Shading in photo

Alternate shadings

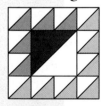

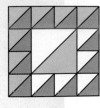

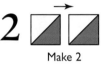

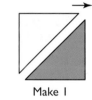

	Block Basics			Rotary Cutting				Templates	Yardage
	Patch	Shape	Total Needed	Strip Width (in inches)	Squares to Cut	Cut Size (in inches)	Next Cut	Template	Strip Length Needed (in inches)
LIGHT	A	◣	12	3⅛	6	3⅛ × 3⅛	◪	T10	18¾
	B	◣	1	5⅜	1	5⅜ × 5⅜	◪	T15	5⅜
MEDIUM	C	◣	1	5⅜	1	5⅜ × 5⅜	◪	T15	5⅜
DARK	D	◣	12	3⅛	6	3⅛ × 3⅛	◪	T10	18¾

Lucky Star

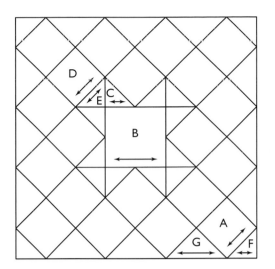

Block Idea

Use pastel hand-dyed fabric to create a softer look for this block.

How to Assemble

1 Press — Make 4

2 Make 4

3 Make 4

4 Make 4

5 Make 2 rows

6 Make 4

7 Make 2

8 Join

9 Join

10 Make 1 row

11 Assemble rows

Shading in photo

Alternate shadings

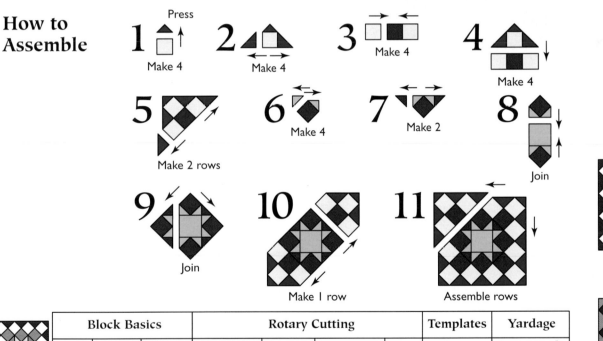

	Block Basics			Rotary Cutting				Templates	Yardage
	Patch	Shape	Total Needed	Strip Width (in inches)	Squares to Cut	Cut Size (in inches)	Next Cut	Template	Strip Length Needed (in inches)
LIGHT 1	A		12	2+	12	2+ × 2+	—	S6	24¾
LIGHT 2	B		1	2¾	1	2¾ × 2¾	—	S11	2¾
	C		8	2	4	2 × 2		T2	8
MEDIUM	D		8	2+	8	2+ × 2+	—	S6	16½
	E		4	2¾	1	2¾ × 2¾		T2	2¾
DARK	F		4	2	2	2 × 2		T2	4
	G		12	3½	3	3½ × 3½		T6	10½

Note: Plus sign (+) indicates ¹⁄₁₆-inch measurements. See page 217 for details.

Memory Lane

Block Idea

Use the same fabric for the center square and star points to emphasize the star in the center of the block.

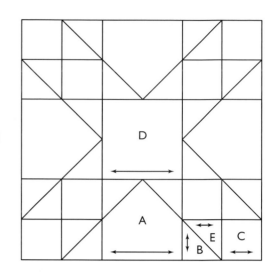

How to Assemble

Press

1 Make 8

2 Make 4

3 Make 4

4 Make 4

5 Make 2 rows

6 Make 1 row

7 Assemble rows

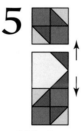
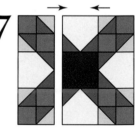

Shading in photo

Alternate shadings

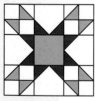

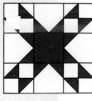

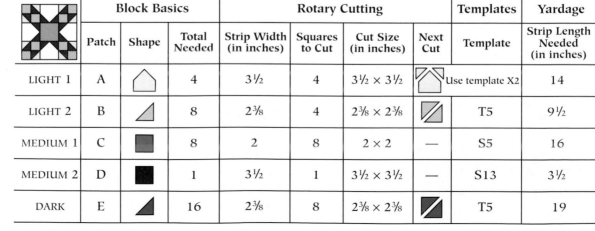

	Block Basics			Rotary Cutting				Templates	Yardage
	Patch	Shape	Total Needed	Strip Width (in inches)	Squares to Cut	Cut Size (in inches)	Next Cut	Template	Strip Length Needed (in inches)
LIGHT 1	A		4	$3\frac{1}{2}$	4	$3\frac{1}{2} \times 3\frac{1}{2}$		Use template X2	14
LIGHT 2	B		8	$2\frac{3}{8}$	4	$2\frac{3}{8} \times 2\frac{3}{8}$		T5	$9\frac{1}{2}$
MEDIUM 1	C		8	2	8	2×2	—	S5	16
MEDIUM 2	D		1	$3\frac{1}{2}$	1	$3\frac{1}{2} \times 3\frac{1}{2}$	—	S13	$3\frac{1}{2}$
DARK	E		16	$2\frac{3}{8}$	8	$2\frac{3}{8} \times 2\frac{3}{8}$		T5	19

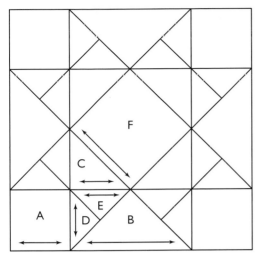

Missouri Star

Block Idea

Maintain good light-dark contrast to make the star stand out.

How to Assemble

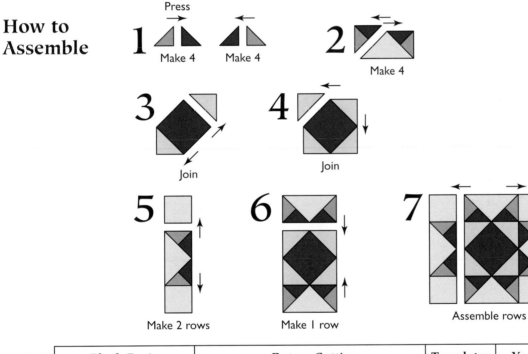

1 Press → Make 4   ← Make 4

2 Make 4

3 Join

4 Join

5 Make 2 rows

6 Make 1 row

7 Assemble rows

Shading in photo

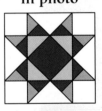

Alternate shadings

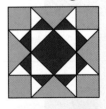

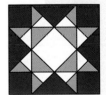

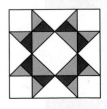

	Block Basics			Rotary Cutting				Templates	Yardage
	Patch	Shape	Total Needed	Strip Width (in inches)	Squares to Cut	Cut Size (in inches)	Next Cut	Template	Strip Length Needed (in inches)
LIGHT 1	A	□	4	2¾	4	2¾ × 2¾	—	S11	11
	B	△	4	5¾	1	5¾ × 5¾	⊠	T13	5¾
LIGHT 2	C	◿	4	3⅛	2	3⅛ × 3⅛	◩	T10	6¼
MEDIUM	D	△	8	3½	2	3½ × 3½	⊠	T6	7
DARK	E	▲	8	3½	2	3½ × 3½	⊠	T6	7
	F	■	1	3⅝+	1	3⅝+ × 3⅝+	—	S14	3⅝+

Note: Plus sign (+) indicates ¹/₁₆-inch measurements. See page 217 for details.

Mosaic

Reverse the lights and darks and have family and friends sign the light center squares.

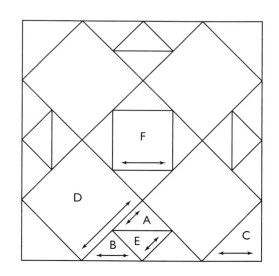

Shading in photo

Alternate shadings

How to Assemble

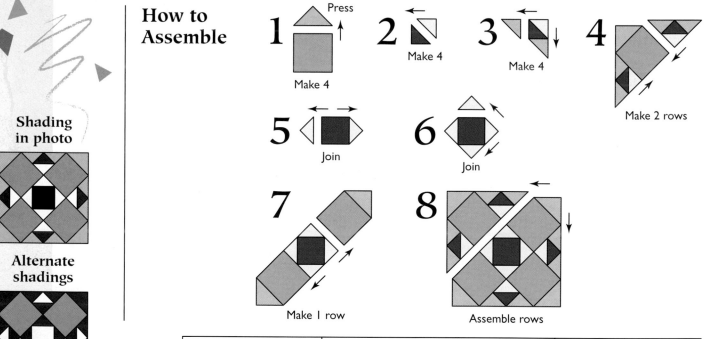

1 Make 4 — Press

2 Make 4

3 Make 4

4 Make 2 rows

5 Join

6 Join

7 Make 1 row

8 Assemble rows

	Block Basics			Rotary Cutting				Templates	Yardage
	Patch	Shape	Total Needed	Strip Width (in inches)	Squares to Cut	Cut Size (in inches)	Next Cut	Template	Strip Length Needed (in inches)
LIGHT	A	◺	8	2³⁄₈+	4	2³⁄₈+ × 2³⁄₈+	◿	T6	9¾
MEDIUM 1	B	△	8	3½	2	3½ × 3½	⊠	T6	7
	C	◺	4	3⅛	2	3⅛ × 3⅛	◿	T10	6¼
MEDIUM 2	D	▢	4	3⅝+	4	3⅝+ × 3⅝+	—	S14	14¾
DARK	E	◢	4	2³⁄₈+	2	2³⁄₈+ × 2³⁄₈+	◨	T6	4⅞
	F	◼	1	2¾	1	2¾ × 2¾	—	S11	2¾

Note: Plus sign (+) indicates ¹⁄₁₆-inch measurements. See page 217 for details.

Nonsense

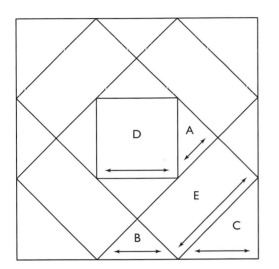

Block Idea

Try a dark background with bright Amish colors.

How to Assemble

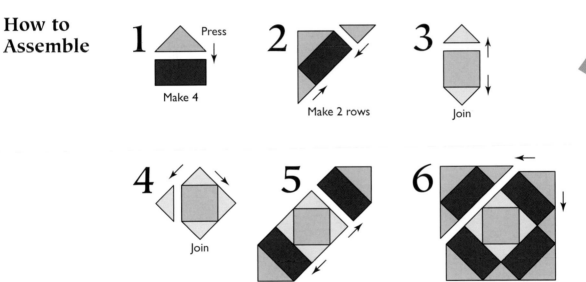

1 Press ↓ Make 4

2 Make 2 rows

3 Join

4 Join

5 Make 1 row

6 Assemble rows

Shading in photo

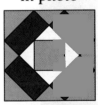

Alternate shadings

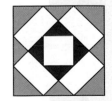

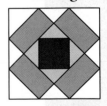

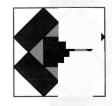

	Block Basics			Rotary Cutting				Templates	Yardage
	Patch	Shape	Total Needed	Strip Width (in inches)	Squares to Cut	Cut Size (in inches)	Next Cut	Template	Strip Length Needed (in inches)
LIGHT	A	◺	4	3	2	3 × 3	◹	T9	6
MEDIUM	B	△	4	4¼	1	4¼ × 4¼	⊠	T9	4¼
	C	◹	4	3⅞	2	3⅞ × 3⅞	◹	T12	7¾
	D	▢	1	3½	1	3½ × 3½	—	S13	3½
DARK	E	▬	4	2⅝	—	2⅝ × 4¾	—	R7	19

Ocean Waves

Block Idea

Rotate the blocks when setting them side by side to create pinwheels and quarter-square triangles where the blocks meet.

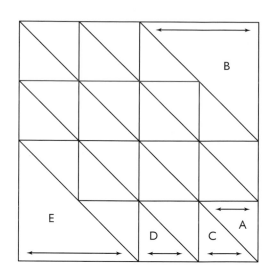

How to Assemble

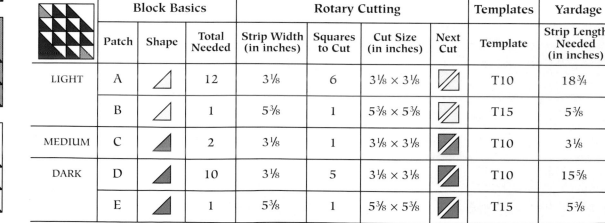

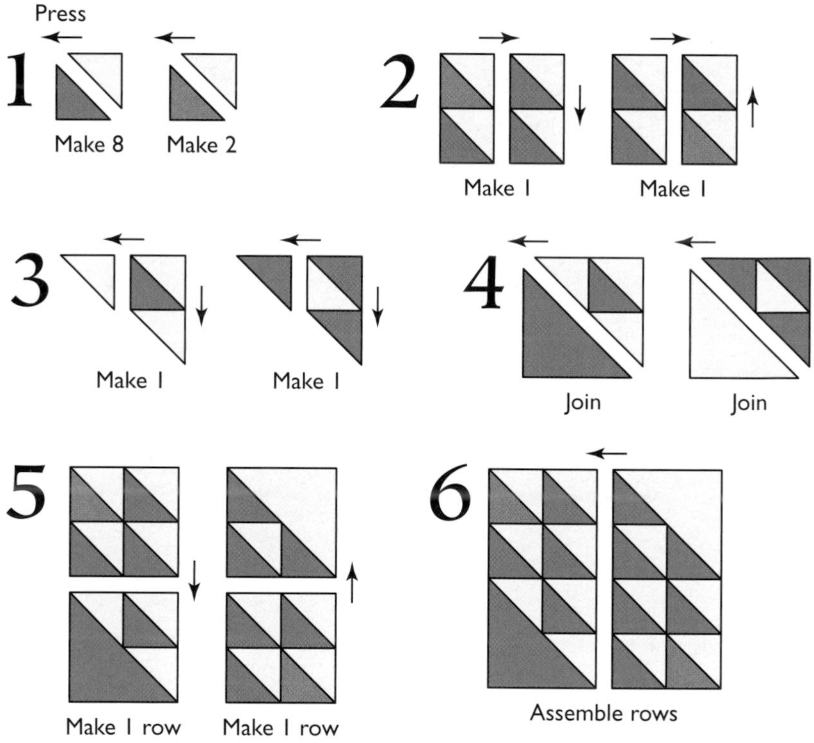

Press

1 Make 8   Make 2

2 Make 1   Make 1

3 Make 1   Make 1

4 Join   Join

5 Make 1 row   Make 1 row

6 Assemble rows

Shading in photo

Alternate shadings

	Block Basics			Rotary Cutting				Templates	Yardage
	Patch	Shape	Total Needed	Strip Width (in inches)	Squares to Cut	Cut Size (in inches)	Next Cut	Template	Strip Length Needed (in inches)
LIGHT	A	◺	12	3⅛	6	3⅛ × 3⅛	◫	T10	18¾
	B	◺	1	5⅜	1	5⅜ × 5⅜	◫	T15	5⅜
MEDIUM	C	◢	2	3⅛	1	3⅛ × 3⅛	◩	T10	3⅛
DARK	D	◢	10	3⅛	5	3⅛ × 3⅛	◩	T10	15⅝
	E	◢	1	5⅜	1	5⅜ × 5⅜	◩	T15	5⅜

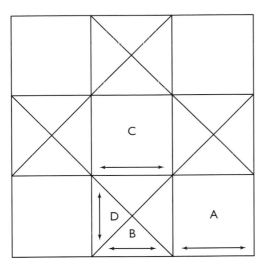

Use a large-scale print in the star and a small-scale print in the background.

How to Assemble

Press →

1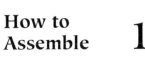
Make 8

2
Make 4

3
Make 2 rows

4
Make 1 row

5
Assemble rows

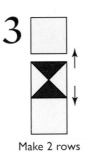

Shading in photo
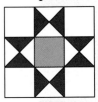

Alternate shadings
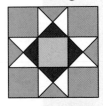

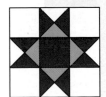

	Block Basics			Rotary Cutting				Templates	Yardage
	Patch	Shape	Total Needed	Strip Width (in inches)	Squares to Cut	Cut Size (in inches)	Next Cut	Template	Strip Length Needed (in inches)
LIGHT	A	▢	4	3½	4	3½ × 3½	—	S13	14
	B	△	8	4¼	2	4¼ × 4¼	⊠	T9	8½
MEDIUM	C	▩	1	3½	1	3½ × 3½	—	S13	3½
DARK	D	▲	8	4¼	2	4¼ × 4¼	⊠	T9	8½

Ohio Trail

Block Idea

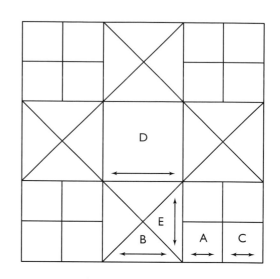

Use the Four Patches as cornerstones in lattice to continue the diagonal chain of squares.

How to Assemble

Press

1 Make 8

2 Make 4

3   Make 8

4   Make 4

5 Make 2 rows

6 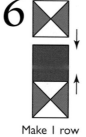 Make 1 row

7 Assemble rows

Shading in photo

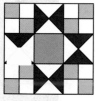

Alternate shadings

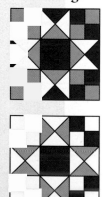

	Block Basics			Rotary Cutting				Templates	Yardage
	Patch	Shape	Total Needed	Strip Width (in inches)	Squares to Cut	Cut Size (in inches)	Next Cut	Template	Strip Length Needed (in inches)
LIGHT	A	▢	8	2	8	2 × 2	—	S5	16
	B	△	8	4¼	2	4¼ × 4¼	⊠	T9	8½
MEDIUM 1	C	◼	8	2	8	2 × 2	—	S5	16
MEDIUM 2	D	◼	1	3½	1	3½ × 3½	—	S13	3½
DARK	E	◣	8	4¼	2	4¼ × 4¼	⊠	T9	8½

One More Block

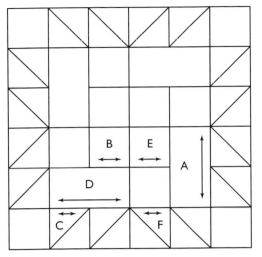

Block Idea

Use a different background fabric in each quarter block for a scrappy look.

How to Assemble

1  Press
Make 16

2 Make 4   Make 2   Make 2

3 Make 4

4 Make 2   Make 2

5  Make 2   Make 2

6 Make 2   Make 2

7 Make 2 rows

8 Assemble rows

Shading in photo

Alternate shadings

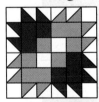

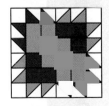

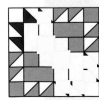

	Block Basics			Rotary Cutting				Templates	Yardage
	Patch	Shape	Total Needed	Strip Width (in inches)	Squares to Cut	Cut Size (in inches)	Next Cut	Template	Strip Length Needed (in inches)
LIGHT	A		2	2	2 rectangles	$2 \times 3\frac{1}{2}$	—	R1	7
	B		6	2	6	2×2	—	S5	12
	C		16	$2\frac{3}{8}$	8	$2\frac{3}{8} \times 2\frac{3}{8}$		T5	19
DARK	D		2	2	2 rectangles	$2 \times 3\frac{1}{2}$	—	R1	7
	E		6	2	6	2×2	—	S5	12
	F		16	$2\frac{3}{8}$	8	$2\frac{3}{8} \times 2\frac{3}{8}$		T5	19

Peaceful Hours

"Float" the star by cutting alternate blocks of the same value fabric as this block's background.

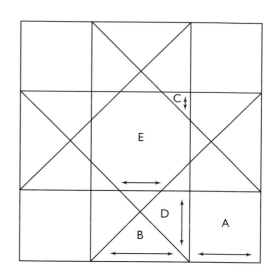

How to Assemble

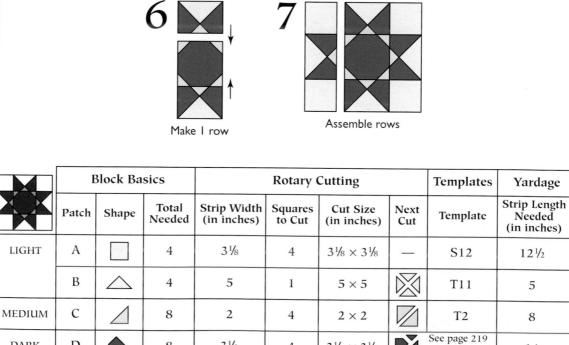

Shading in photo

Alternate shadings

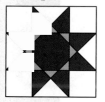

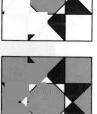

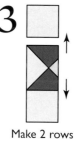

		Block Basics		Rotary Cutting				Templates	Yardage
	Patch	Shape	Total Needed	Strip Width (in inches)	Squares to Cut	Cut Size (in inches)	Next Cut	Template	Strip Length Needed (in inches)
LIGHT	A	☐	4	3⅛	4	3⅛ × 3⅛	—	S12	12½
	B	△	4	5	1	5 × 5	⊠	T11	5
MEDIUM	C	◺	8	2	4	2 × 2	◹	T2	8
DARK	D	⬠	8	3½	4	3½ × 3½	⊠	See page 219 or use template X3	14
	E	⬡	1	4¼	1	4¼ × 4¼	⬡	See page 219 and use template X4	4¼

Perpetual Motion

Use this easy block for projects that need to be made in a hurry.

How to Assemble

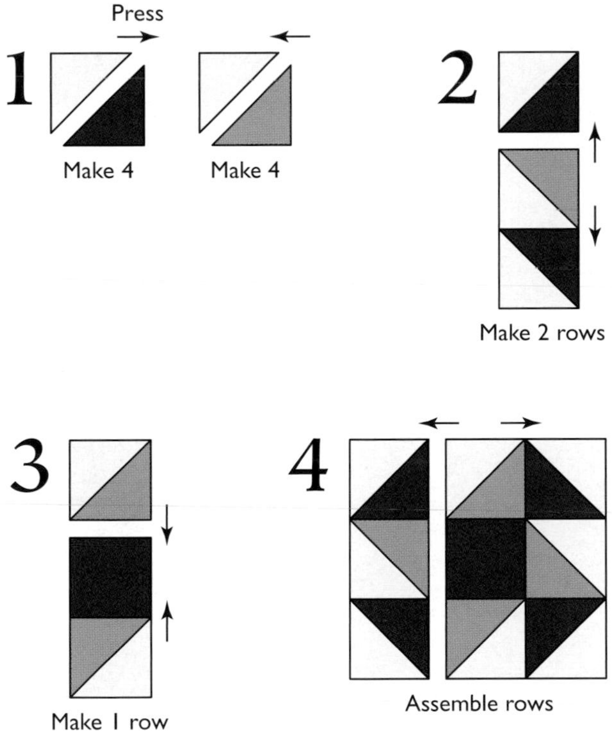

Press

 1

Make 4   Make 4

2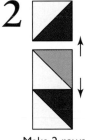

Make 2 rows

3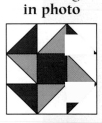

Make 1 row

4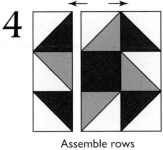

Assemble rows

Shading in photo

Alternate shadings

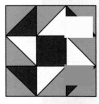

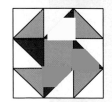

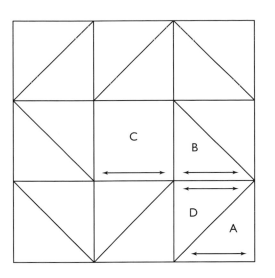

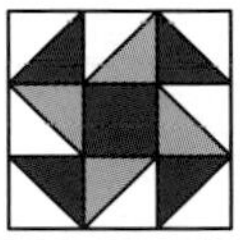

	Block Basics			Rotary Cutting				Templates	Yardage
	Patch	Shape	Total Needed	Strip Width (in inches)	Squares to Cut	Cut Size (in inches)	Next Cut	Template	Strip Length Needed (in inches)
LIGHT	A	◺	8	3⅞	4	3⅞ × 3⅞	◿	T12	15½
MEDIUM	B	◢	4	3⅞	2	3⅞ × 3⅞	◪	T12	7¾
DARK	C	■	1	3½	1	3½ × 3½	—	S13	3½
	D	◣	4	3⅞	2	3⅞ × 3⅞	◥	T12	7¾

inwheel

Block Idea

Make each large triangle a different color for a scrappy look.

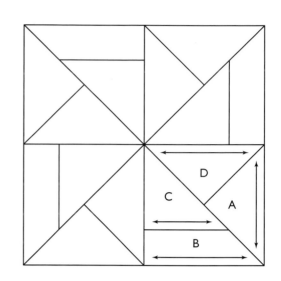

How to Assemble

1 Make 4 — Press

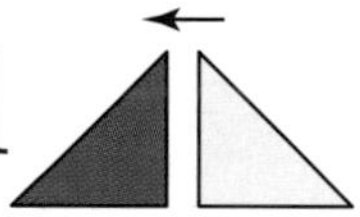

2 Make 4

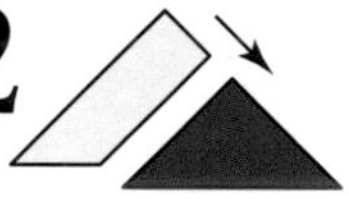

3 Make 4

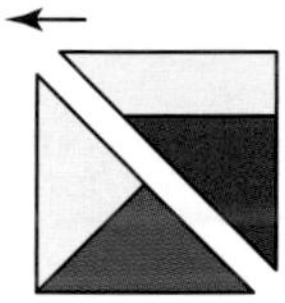

4 Make 2 rows

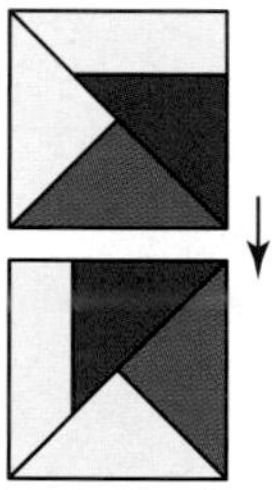

5 Assemble rows

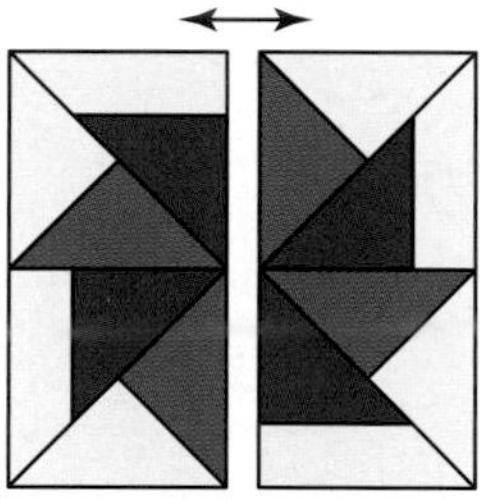

Shading in photo

Alternate shadings

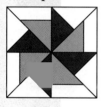

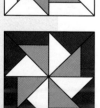

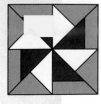

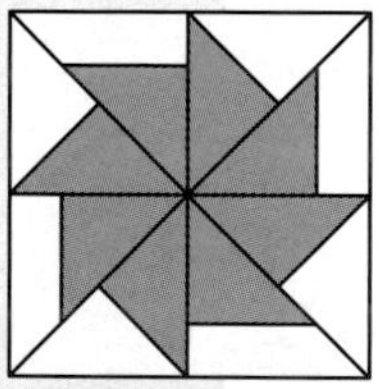

	Block Basics			Rotary Cutting				Templates	Yardage
	Patch	Shape	Total Needed	Strip Width (in inches)	Squares to Cut	Cut Size (in inches)	Next Cut	Template	Strip Length Needed (in inches)
LIGHT	A	 △	4	5¾	1	5¾ × 5¾	 ⊠	T13	5¾
	B	 ▱	4	—	—	Use template X11			—
MEDIUM	C	◣	4	4+	2	4+ × 4+	 ◪	T13	8⅛
DARK	D	 △	4	5¾	1	5¾ × 5¾	 ⊠	T13	5¾

Note: Plus sign (+) indicates 1/16-inch measurements. See page 217 for details.

Pinwheel Mosaic

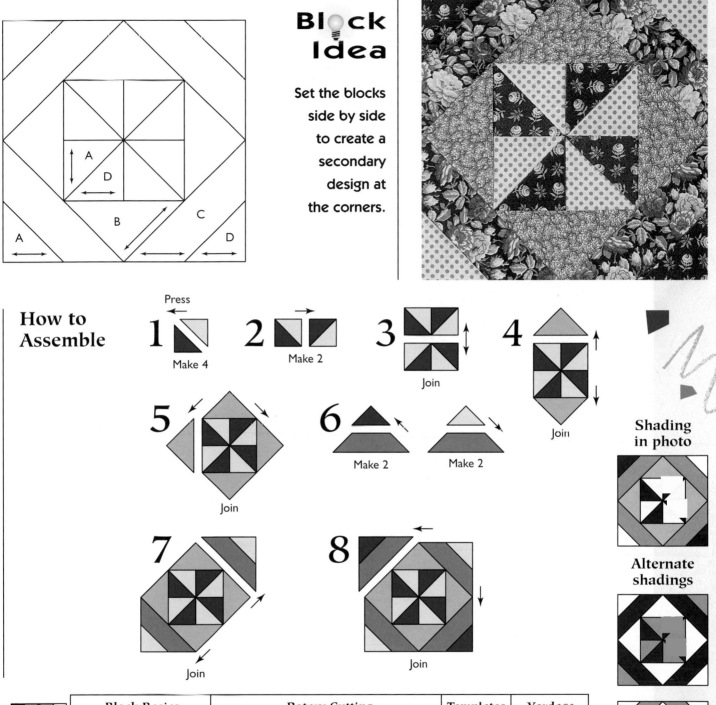

Block Idea

Set the blocks side by side to create a secondary design at the corners.

How to Assemble

Press

1 Make 4

2 Make 2

3 Join

4 Join

5 Join

6 Make 2   Make 2

7 Join

8 Join

Shading in photo

Alternate shadings

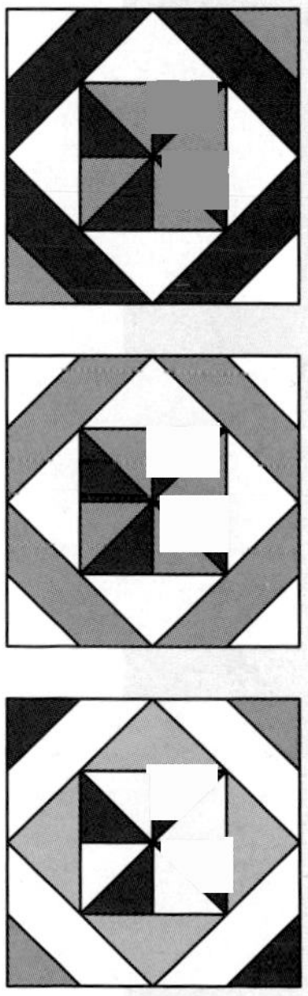

	Block Basics			Rotary Cutting				Templates	Yardage
	Patch	Shape	Total Needed	Strip Width (in inches)	Squares to Cut	Cut Size (in inches)	Next Cut	Template	Strip Length Needed (in inches)
LIGHT 1	A		6	3⅛	3	3⅛ × 3⅛		T10	9⅜
LIGHT 2	B		4	4+	2	4+ × 4+		T13	8⅛
MEDIUM	C		4	5⅜	2	5⅜ × 5⅜		See page 219 and use template X6	10¾
DARK	D		6	3⅛	3	3⅛ × 3⅛		T10	9⅜

Note: Plus sign (+) indicates ¹⁄₁₆-inch measurements. See page 217 for details.

Prairie Queen

Block Idea

Use a large-scale plaid for the dark fabric and a small-scale plaid for the medium fabric.

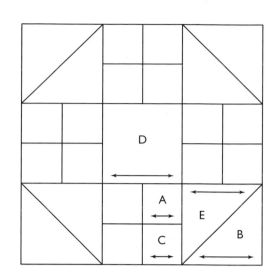

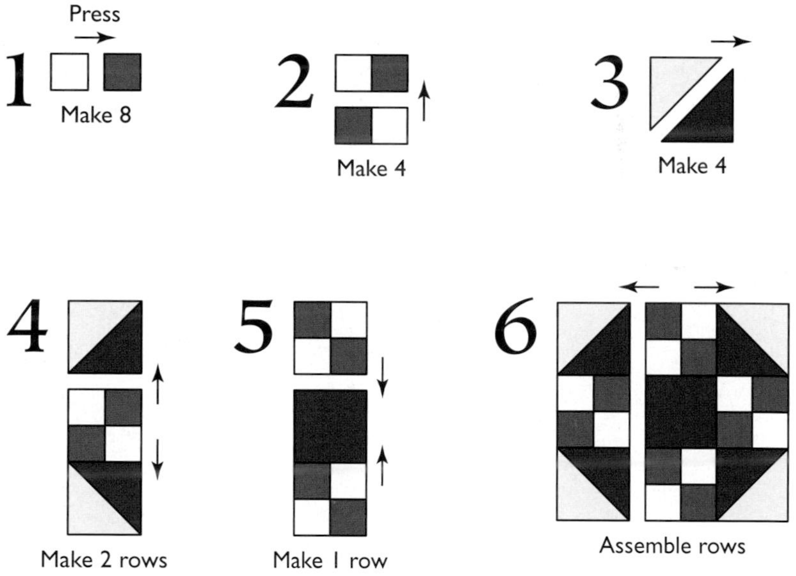

Shading in photo

Alternate shadings

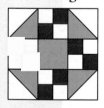

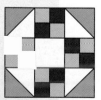

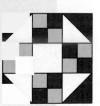

How to Assemble

Press

1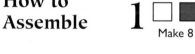
Make 8

2
Make 4

3
Make 4

4
Make 2 rows

5
Make 1 row

6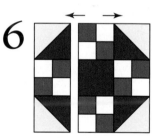
Assemble rows

	Block Basics			Rotary Cutting				Templates	Yardage
	Patch	Shape	Total Needed	Strip Width (in inches)	Squares to Cut	Cut Size (in inches)	Next Cut	Template	Strip Length Needed (in inches)
LIGHT 1	A	☐	8	2	8	2 × 2	—	S5	16
LIGHT 2	B	◺	4	3⅞	2	3⅞ × 3⅞	◩	T12	7¾
MEDIUM	C	◼	8	2	8	2 × 2	—	S5	16
DARK	D	◼	1	3½	1	3½ × 3½	—	S13	3½
	E	◣	4	3⅞	2	3⅞ × 3⅞	◥	T12	7¾

Puss in the Corner

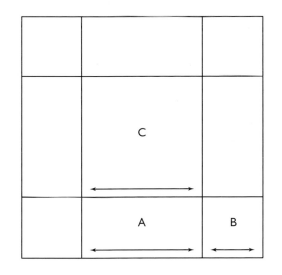

Block Idea

This makes a great alternate block to use with a fancy one.

How to Assemble

1 Press

Make 2 rows

2

Make 1 row

3 Assemble rows

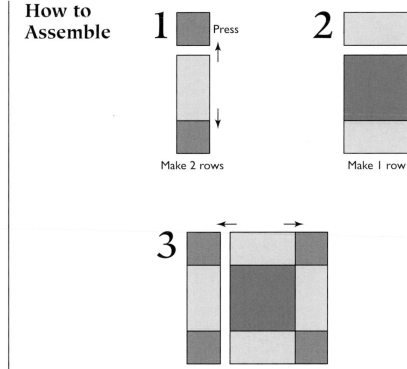

Shading in photo

Alternate shadings

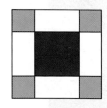

	Block Basics			Rotary Cutting				Templates	Yardage
	Patch	Shape	Total Needed	Strip Width (in inches)	Squares to Cut	Cut Size (in inches)	Next Cut	Template	Strip Length Needed (in inches)
LIGHT	A		4	2¾	4 rectangles	2¾ × 5	—	R9	20
DARK 1	B		4	2¾	4	2¾ × 2¾	—	S11	11
DARK 2	C		1	5	1	5 × 5	—	S16	5

Quail's Nest

Block Idea

Use scraps for these blocks, then alternate them with setting squares in a diagonal set.

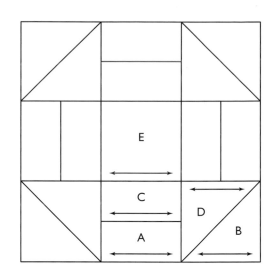

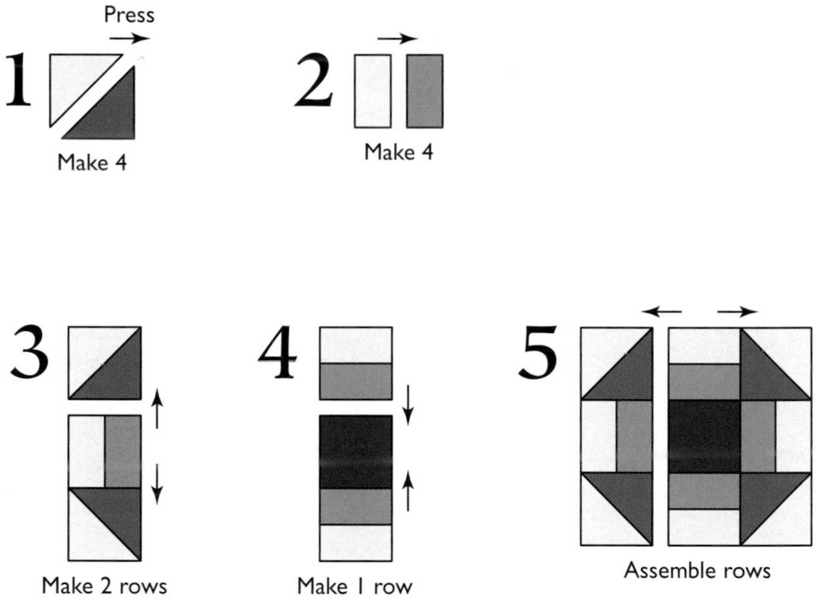

Shading in photo

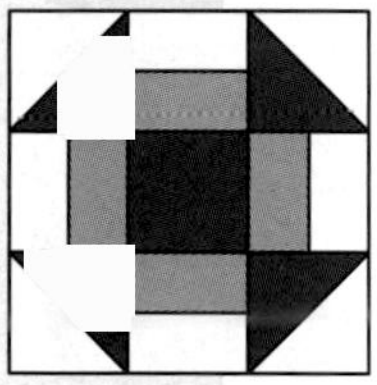

Alternate shadings

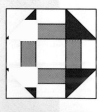

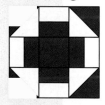

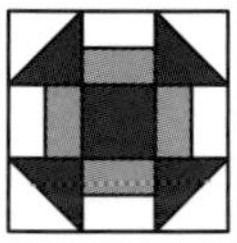

How to Assemble

Press

1 Make 4

2 Make 4

3 Make 2 rows

4 Make 1 row

5 Assemble rows

	Block Basics			Rotary Cutting				Templates	Yardage
	Patch	Shape	Total Needed	Strip Width (in inches)	Squares to Cut	Cut Size (in inches)	Next Cut	Template	Strip Length Needed (in inches)
LIGHT	A	▭	4	2	4 rectangles	2 × 3½	—	R1	14
	B	◺	4	3⅞	2	3⅞ × 3⅞	◹	T12	7¾
MEDIUM	C	▭	4	2	4 rectangles	2 × 3½	—	R1	14
DARK 1	D	◺	4	3⅞	2	3⅞ × 3⅞	◸	T12	7¾
DARK 2	E	■	1	3½	1	3½ × 3½	—	S13	3½

Rambler

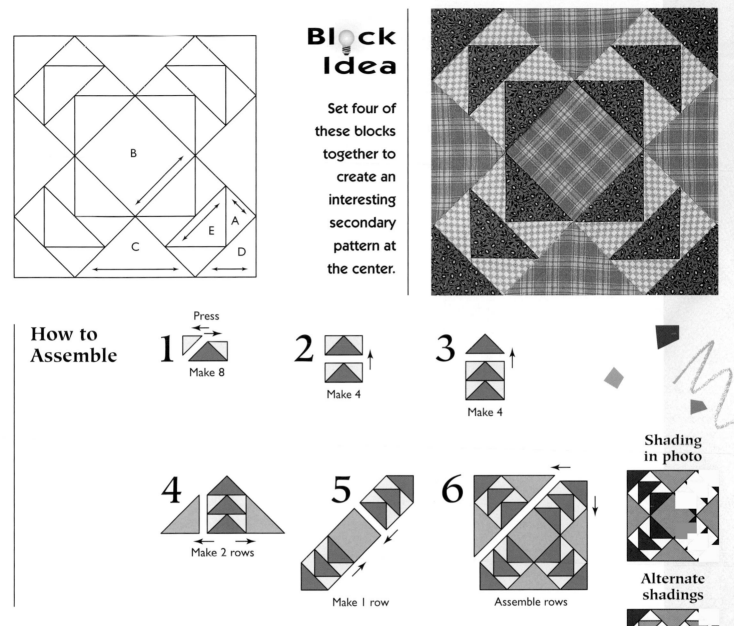

Block Idea

Set four of these blocks together to create an interesting secondary pattern at the center.

How to Assemble

1 Make 8 — Press

2 Make 4

3 Make 4

4 Make 2 rows

5 Make 1 row

6 Assemble rows

Shading in photo

Alternate shadings

	Block Basics			Rotary Cutting				Templates	Yardage
	Patch	Shape	Total Needed	Strip Width (in inches)	Squares to Cut	Cut Size (in inches)	Next Cut	Template	Strip Length Needed (in inches)
LIGHT	A		16	$2\frac{3}{8}+$	8	$2\frac{3}{8}+ \times 2\frac{3}{8}+$		T6	$19\frac{1}{2}$
MEDIUM	B		1	$3\frac{5}{8}+$	1	$3\frac{5}{8}+ \times 3\frac{5}{8}+$	—	S14	$3\frac{5}{8}+$
	C		4	$5\frac{3}{4}$	1	$5\frac{3}{4} \times 5\frac{3}{4}$		T13	$5\frac{3}{4}$
DARK	D		4	$3\frac{1}{8}$	2	$3\frac{1}{8} \times 3\frac{1}{8}$		T10	$6\frac{1}{4}$
	E		8	$4\frac{3}{8}+$	2	$4\frac{3}{8}+ \times 4\frac{3}{8}+$		T10	$8\frac{7}{8}$

Note: Plus sign (+) indicates $\frac{1}{16}$-inch measurements. See page 217 for details.

Review

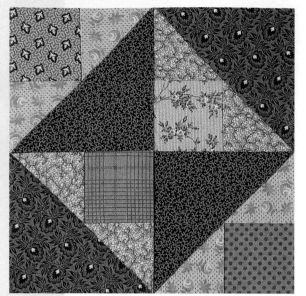

Bl⚲ck Idea

Use one quarter of the block to create a simple, yet appealing quilt border.

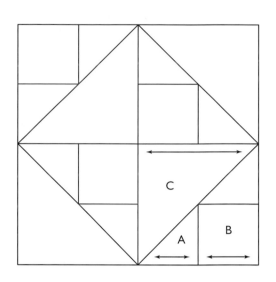

How to Assemble

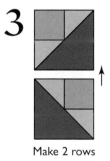

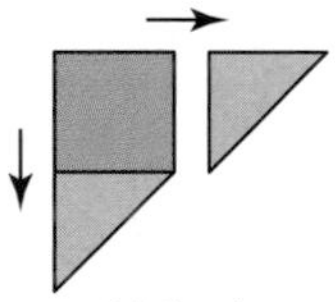

Press

1 Make 4

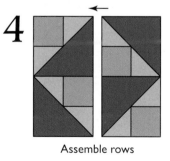

2 Make 4

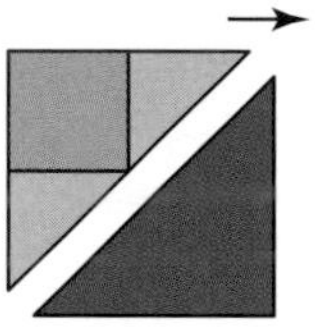

3 Make 2 rows

4 Assemble rows

Shading in photo

Alternate shadings

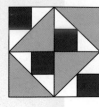

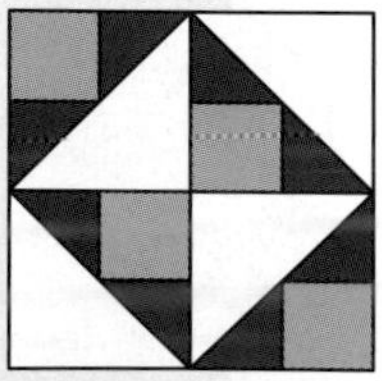

	Block Basics			Rotary Cutting				Templates	Yardage
	Patch	Shape	Total Needed	Strip Width (in inches)	Squares to Cut	Cut Size (in inches)	Next Cut	Template	Strip Length Needed (in inches)
LIGHT	A	◺	8	3⅛	4	3⅛ × 3⅛	◹	T10	12½
MEDIUM	B	▢	4	2¾	4	2¾ × 2¾	—	S11	11
DARK	C	◣	4	5⅜	2	5⅜ × 5⅜	◹	T15	10¾

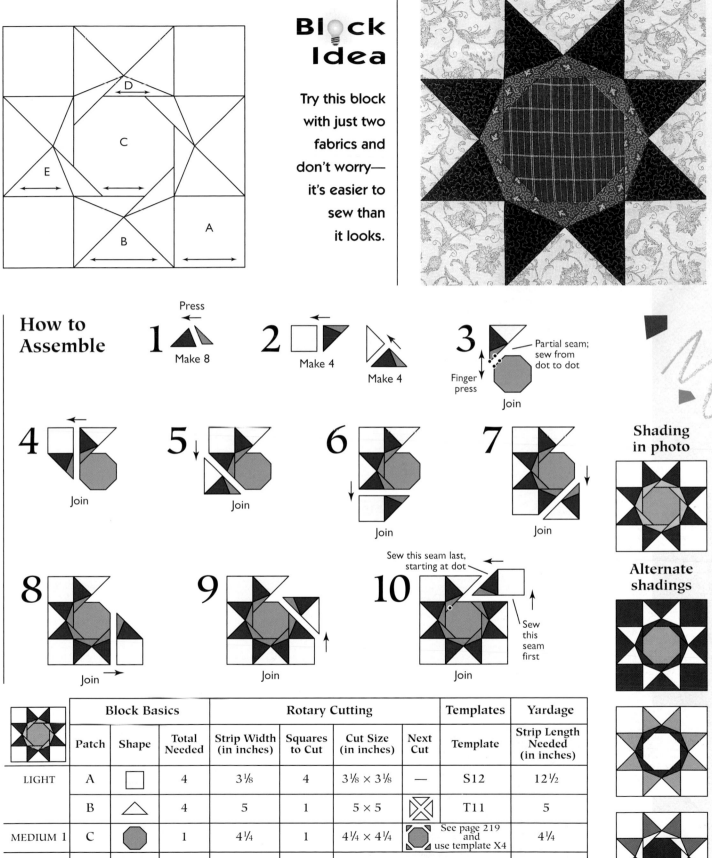

Ringed Star

Block Idea

Try this block with just two fabrics and don't worry—it's easier to sew than it looks.

How to Assemble

1 Press → Make 8

2 ← Make 4 Make 4

3 Partial seam; sew from dot to dot. Finger press. Join

4 Join

5 Join

6 Join

7 Join

Shading in photo

8 Join →

9 Join

10 Sew this seam last, starting at dot. Join. Sew this seam first

Alternate shadings

	Block Basics			**Rotary Cutting**				**Templates**	**Yardage**
	Patch	Shape	Total Needed	Strip Width (in inches)	Squares to Cut	Cut Size (in inches)	Next Cut	Template	Strip Length Needed (in inches)
LIGHT	A	☐	4	3⅛	4	3⅛ × 3⅛	—	S12	12½
	B	△	4	5	1	5 × 5	⊠	T11	5
MEDIUM 1	C	⬠	1	4¼	1	4¼ × 4¼	⬡	See page 219 and use template X4	4¼
MEDIUM 2	D	▱	8	—	—	Use template TT8			—
DARK	E	◤	8	—	—	Use template TT9			—

Rising Star

Block Idea

Use the small center star by itself as a cornerstone in lattice strips.

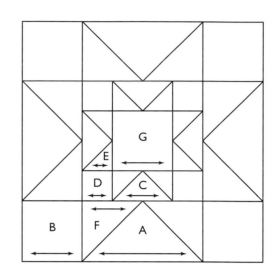

How to Assemble

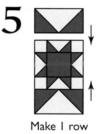

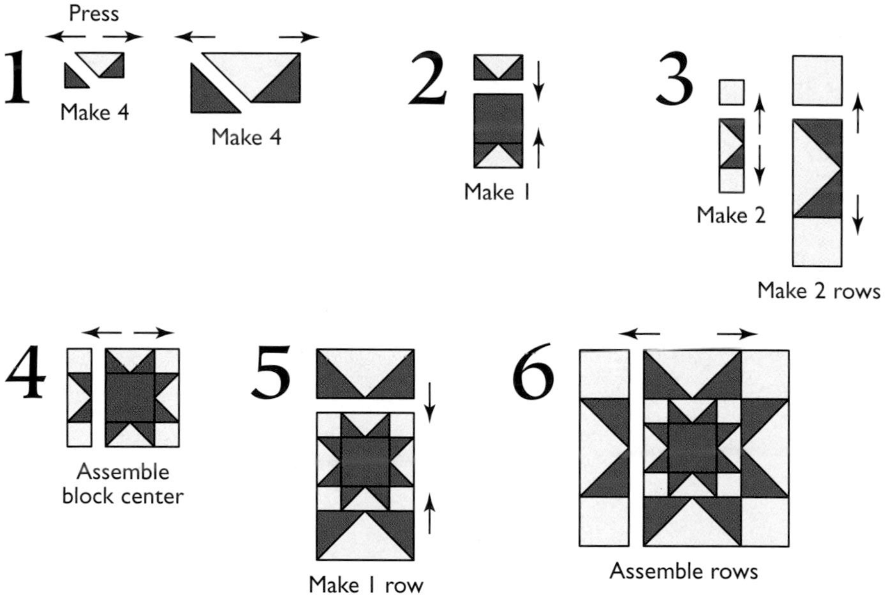

1 Make 4 / Press / Make 4

2 Make 1

3 Make 2 / Make 2 rows

4 Assemble block center

5 Make 1 row

6 Assemble rows

Shading in photo

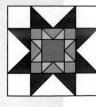
Alternate shadings

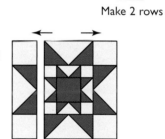

	Block Basics			Rotary Cutting				Templates	Yardage
	Patch	Shape	Total Needed	Strip Width (in inches)	Squares to Cut	Cut Size (in inches)	Next Cut	Template	Strip Length Needed (in inches)
LIGHT	A	△	4	5¾	1	5¾ × 5¾	⊠	T13	5¾
	B	□	4	2¾	4	2¾ × 2¾	—	S11	11
	C	△	4	3½	1	3½ × 3½	⊠	T6	3½
	D	□	4	1⅝	4	1⅝ × 1⅝	—	S3	6½
DARK	E	◣	8	2	4	2 × 2	◹	T2	8
	F	◢	8	3⅛	4	3⅛ × 3⅛	◹	T10	12½
	G	■	1	2¾	1	2¾ × 2¾	—	S11	2¾

Road Home

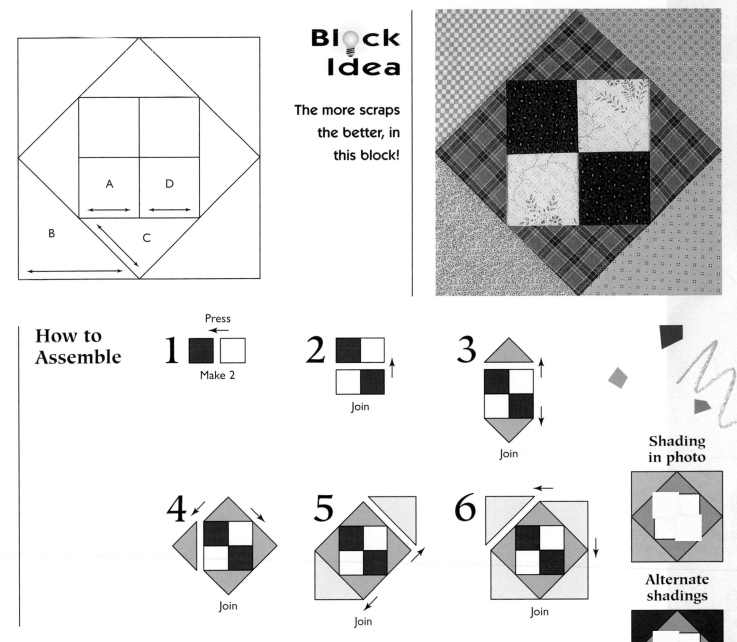

Block Idea

The more scraps the better, in this block!

How to Assemble

1 Make 2 — Press

2 Join

3 Join

4 Join

5 Join

6 Join

Shading in photo

Alternate shadings

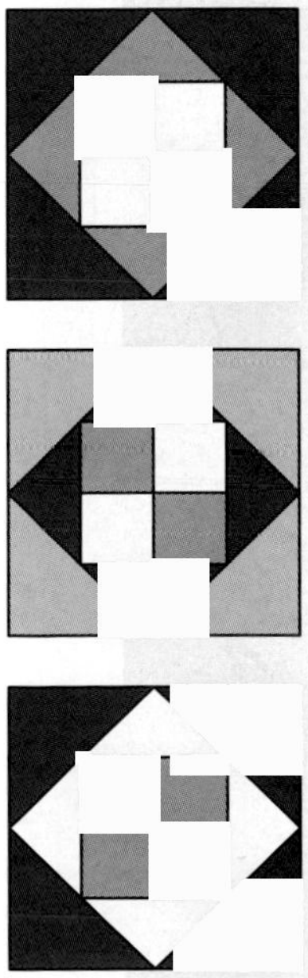

	Block Basics			Rotary Cutting				Templates	Yardage
	Patch	Shape	Total Needed	Strip Width (in inches)	Squares to Cut	Cut Size (in inches)	Next Cut	Template	Strip Length Needed (in inches)
LIGHT 1	A		2	2¾	2	2¾ × 2¾	—	S11	5½
LIGHT 2	B		4	5⅜	2	5⅜ × 5⅜		T15	10¾
MEDIUM	C		4	4+	2	4+ × 4+		T13	8⅛
DARK	D		2	2¾	2	2¾ × 2¾	—	S11	5½

Note: Plus sign (+) indicates ¹/₁₆-inch measurements. See page 217 for details.

Robbing Peter to Pay Paul

Bl⊙ck Idea

Make each of the dark outside triangles a different color.

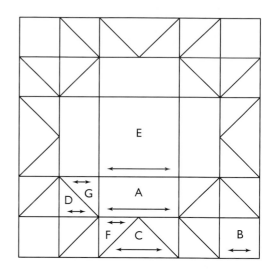

Shading in photo

Alternate shadings

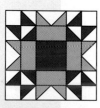

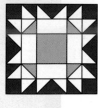

How to Assemble

Press
1 Make 12

2 Make 4

3 Make 4

4 Make 4

5 Make 4

6 Make 4

7 Make 2 rows

8 Make 1 row

9 Assemble rows

	Block Basics			Rotary Cutting				Templates	Yardage
	Patch	Shape	Total Needed	Strip Width (in inches)	Squares to Cut	Cut Size (in inches)	Next Cut	Template	Strip Length Needed (in inches)
LIGHT 1	A	▭	4	2	4 rectangles	$2 \times 3\frac{1}{2}$	—	R1	14
	B	▢	4	2	4	2×2	—	S5	8
	C	△	4	$4\frac{1}{4}$	1	$4\frac{1}{4} \times 4\frac{1}{4}$	⊠	T9	$4\frac{1}{4}$
LIGHT 2	D	◺	12	$2\frac{3}{8}$	6	$2\frac{3}{8} \times 2\frac{3}{8}$	◹	T5	$14\frac{1}{4}$
DARK 1	E	◼	1	$3\frac{1}{2}$	1	$3\frac{1}{2} \times 3\frac{1}{2}$	—	S13	$3\frac{1}{2}$
	F	◺	8	$2\frac{3}{8}$	4	$2\frac{3}{8} \times 2\frac{3}{8}$	◪	T5	$9\frac{1}{2}$
DARK 2	G	◺	12	$2\frac{3}{8}$	6	$2\frac{3}{8} \times 2\frac{3}{8}$	◪	T5	$14\frac{1}{4}$

Rolling Stone

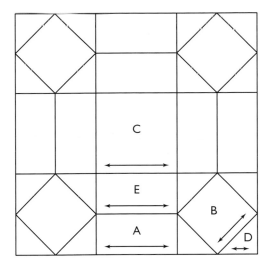

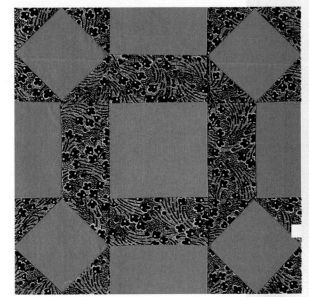

Block Idea

Alternate two bright colors in the outer squares and rectangles, and feature a punchy, large-scale print in the center.

How to Assemble

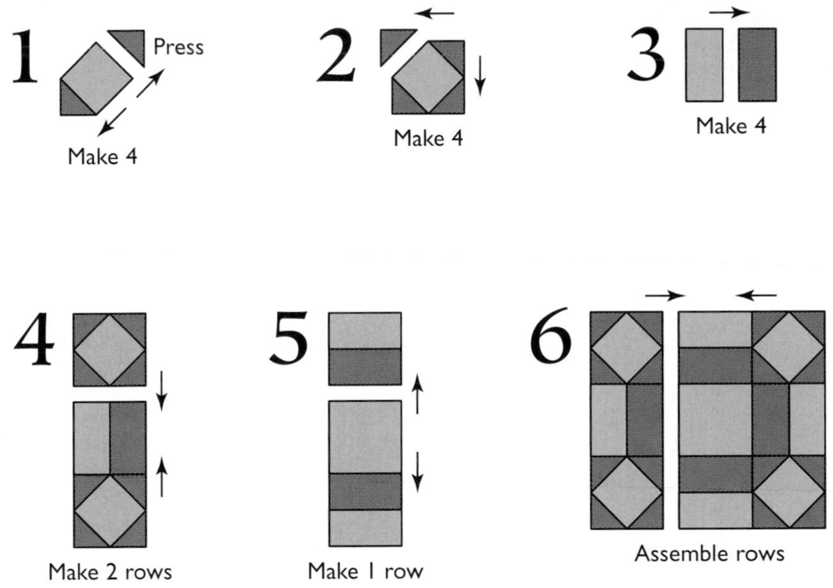

1 Press — Make 4

2 Make 4

3 Make 4

4 Make 2 rows

5 Make 1 row

6 Assemble rows

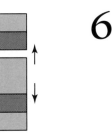

Shading in photo

Alternate shadings

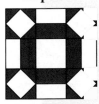

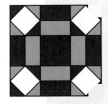

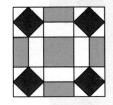

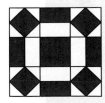

	Block Basics			Rotary Cutting				Templates	Yardage
	Patch	Shape	Total Needed	Strip Width (in inches)	Squares to Cut	Cut Size (in inches)	Next Cut	Template	Strip Length Needed (in inches)
LIGHT	A		4	2	4 rectangles	2 × 3½	—	R1	14
	B		4	2⅝	4	2⅝ × 2⅝	—	S10	10½
	C		1	3½	1	3½ × 3½	—	S13	3½
DARK	D		16	2⅜	8	2⅜ × 2⅜		T5	19
	E		4	2	4 rectangles	2 × 3½	—	R1	14

Rosebud

Block Idea

Make a dramatic statement by using black in the background and jeweltones or primaries for the focus colors.

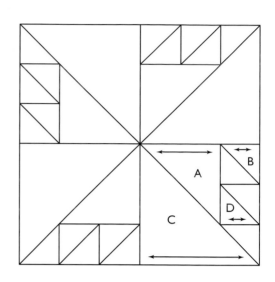

How to Assemble

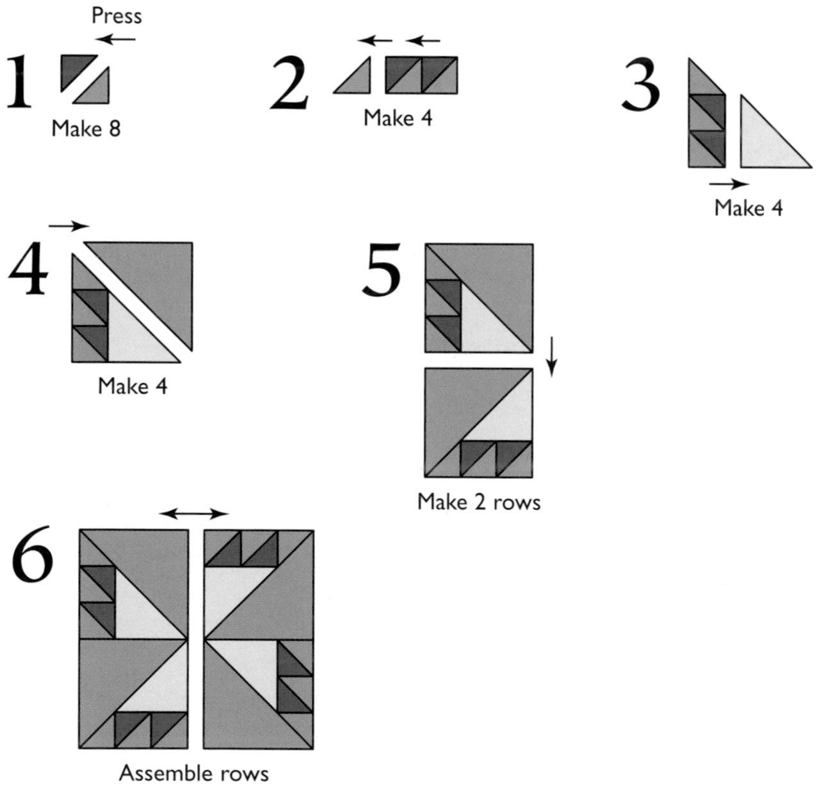

1 Press ← — Make 8

2 Make 4

3 Make 4

4 Make 4

5 Make 2 rows

6 Assemble rows

Shading in photo

Alternate shadings

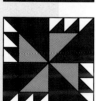
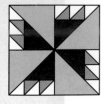

	Block Basics			Rotary Cutting				Templates	Yardage
	Patch	Shape	Total Needed	Strip Width (in inches)	Squares to Cut	Cut Size (in inches)	Next Cut	Template	Strip Length Needed (in inches)
LIGHT	A	◺	4	3⅞	2	3⅞ × 3⅞	◿	T12	7¾
MEDIUM	B	◺	12	2⅜	6	2⅜ × 2⅜	◿	T5	14¼
	C	◺	4	5⅜	2	5⅜ × 5⅜	◿	T15	10¾
DARK	D	◢	8	2⅜	4	2⅜ × 2⅜	◿	T5	9½

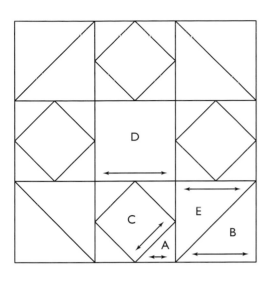

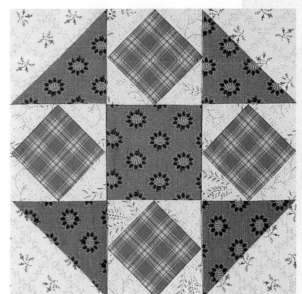

Block Idea

Create a center star by switching the fabric values in this block.

How to Assemble

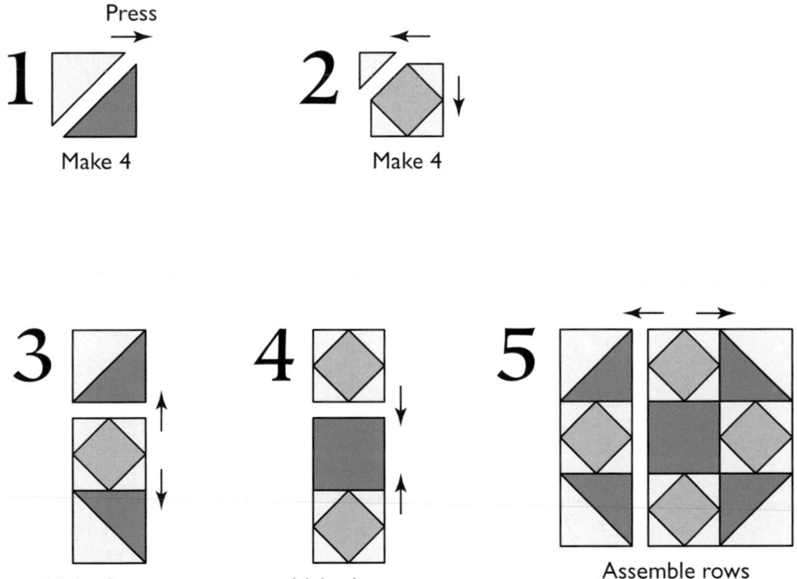

1 Press → Make 4

2 Make 4

3 Make 2 rows

4 Make 1 row

5 Assemble rows

Shading in photo

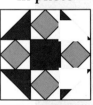

Alternate shadings

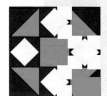

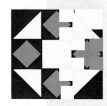

	Block Basics			Rotary Cutting				Templates	Yardage
	Patch	Shape	Total Needed	Strip Width (in inches)	Squares to Cut	Cut Size (in inches)	Next Cut	Template	Strip Length Needed (in inches)
LIGHT	A	◿	16	2⅜	8	2⅜ × 2⅜	◿	T5	19
	B	◺	4	3⅞	2	3⅞ × 3⅞	◿	T12	7¾
MEDIUM	C	◻	4	2⅝	4	2⅝ × 2⅝	—	S10	10½
DARK	D	◼	1	3½	1	3½ × 3½	—	S13	3½
	E	◣	4	3⅞	2	3⅞ × 3⅞	◿	T12	7¾

Sawtooth Star

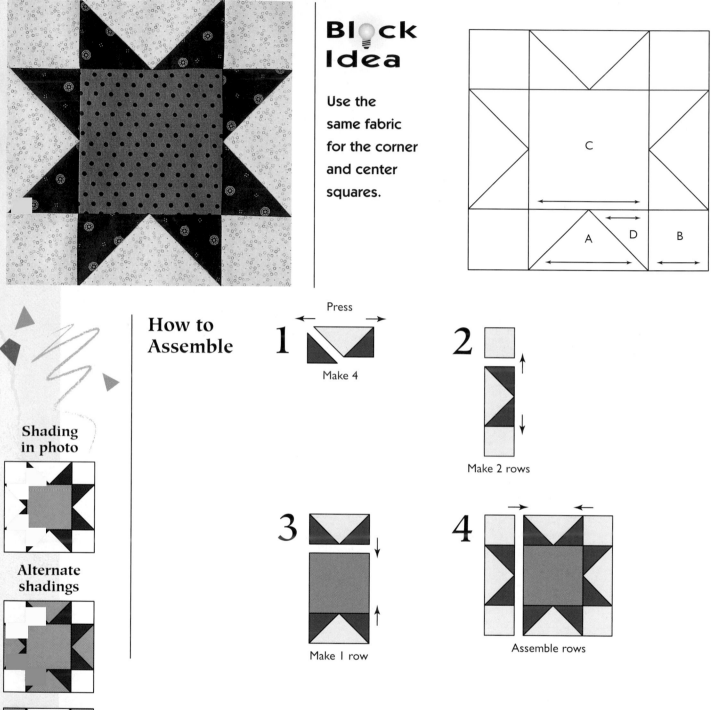

Block Idea

Use the same fabric for the corner and center squares.

How to Assemble

1 Press
Make 4

2 Make 2 rows

3 Make 1 row

4 Assemble rows

Shading in photo

Alternate shadings

		Block Basics			Rotary Cutting				Templates	Yardage
	Patch	Shape	Total Needed	Strip Width (in inches)	Squares to Cut	Cut Size (in inches)	Next Cut		Template	Strip Length Needed (in inches)
LIGHT	A	△	4	5¾	1	5¾ × 5¾	⊠		T13	5¾
	B	☐	4	2¾	4	2¾ × 2¾	—		S11	11
MEDIUM	C	◼	1	5	1	5 × 5	—		S16	5
DARK	D	◢	8	3⅛	4	3⅛ × 3⅛	◿		T10	12½

Scrap Basket

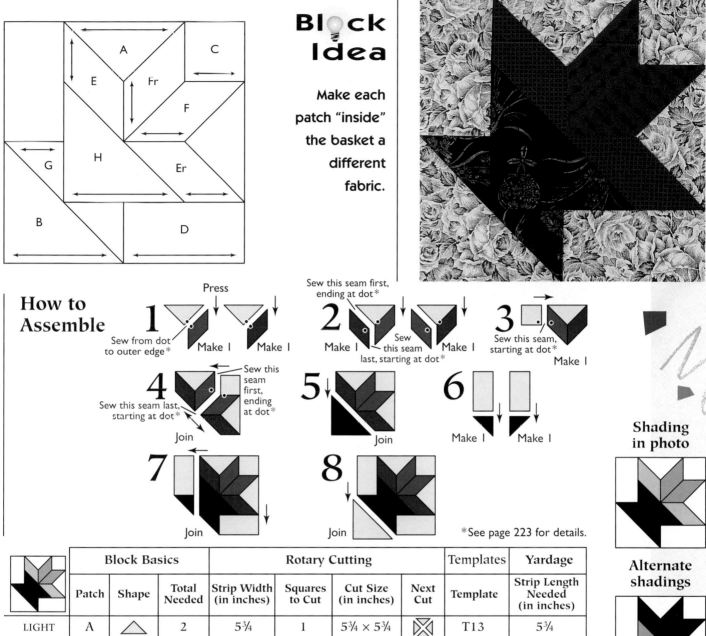

Block Idea

Make each patch "inside" the basket a different fabric.

How to Assemble

1 Sew from dot to outer edge* — Press — Make 1 — Make 1

2 Sew this seam first, ending at dot* — Make 1 — Sew this seam last, starting at dot* — Make 1

3 Sew this seam, starting at dot* — Make 1

4 Sew this seam first, ending at dot* — Sew this seam last, starting at dot* — Join

5 Join

6 Make 1 — Make 1

7 Join

8 Join

*See page 223 for details.

Shading in photo

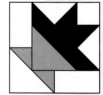

Alternate shadings

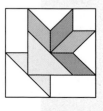

		Block Basics		Rotary Cutting				Templates	Yardage
	Patch	Shape	Total Needed	Strip Width (in inches)	Squares to Cut	Cut Size (in inches)	Next Cut	Template	Strip Length Needed (in inches)
LIGHT	A	◺	2	5¾	1	5¾ × 5¾	⊠	T13	5¾
	B	◺	1	5⅜	1	5⅜ × 5⅜	◪	T15	5⅜
	C	▢	1	2¾	1	2¾ × 2¾	—	S11	2¾
	D	▭	2	2¾	2 rectangles	2¾ × 5	—	R9	10
MEDIUM 1	E	▰	1	2¾	Make a 45° angle cut at the left end of the strip, angling the ruler from bottom left to top right. Measuring from diagonal cut, make successive cuts 2⅛" apart.			D1	5¾
	Er	▰	1	2¾	Make a 45° angle cut at the left end of the strip, angling the ruler from top left to bottom right. Measuring from diagonal cut, make successive cuts 2⅛" apart.			D1r	5¾
MEDIUM 2	F	▰	1	2¾	See E			D1	5¾
	Fr	▰	1	2¾	See Er			D1r	5¾
DARK	G	◪	2	3⅛	1	3⅛ × 3⅛	◩	T10	3⅛
	H	◪	1	5⅜	1	5⅜ × 5⅜	◩	T15	5⅜

Shoofly

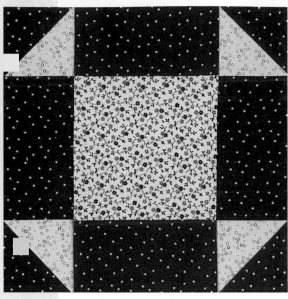

Block Idea

Use a favorite theme fabric in the large center square.

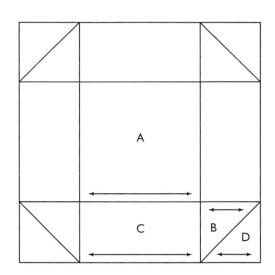

How to Assemble

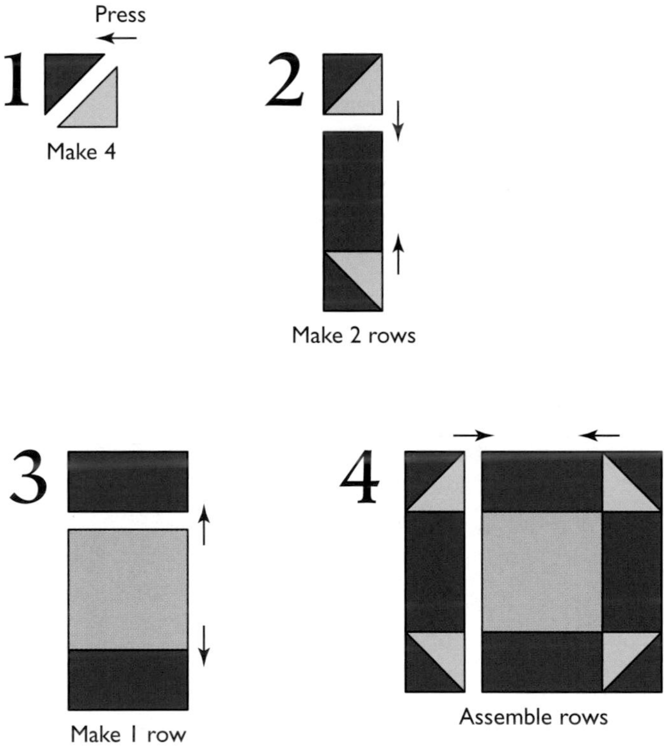

Press

1 Make 4

2 Make 2 rows

3 Make 1 row

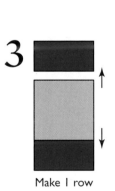

4 Assemble rows

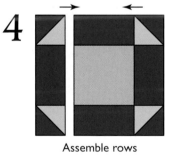

Shading in photo

Alternate shadings

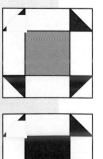

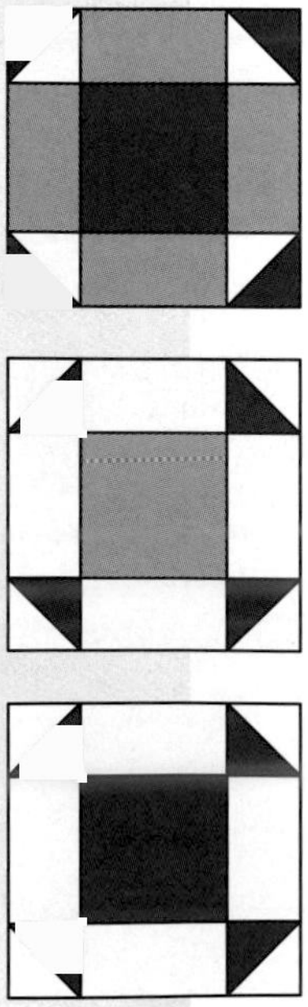

	Block Basics			Rotary Cutting				Templates	Yardage
	Patch	Shape	Total Needed	Strip Width (in inches)	Squares to Cut	Cut Size (in inches)	Next Cut	Template	Strip Length Needed (in inches)
LIGHT 1	A	▢	1	5	1	5 × 5	—	S16	5
LIGHT 2	B	◺	4	3⅛	2	3⅛ × 3⅛	◺	T10	6¼
DARK	C	▬	4	2¾	4 rectangles	2¾ × 5	—	R9	20
	D	◹	4	3⅛	2	3⅛ × 3⅛	◺	T10	6¼

Snowflake

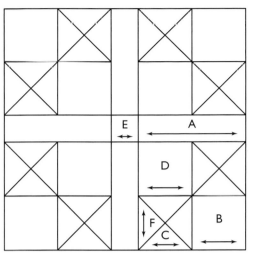

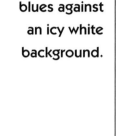

Bl💡ck Idea

Use cool blues against an icy white background.

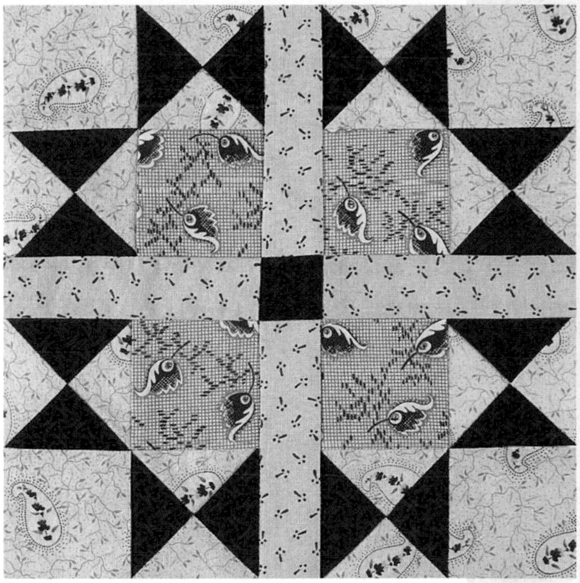

How to Assemble

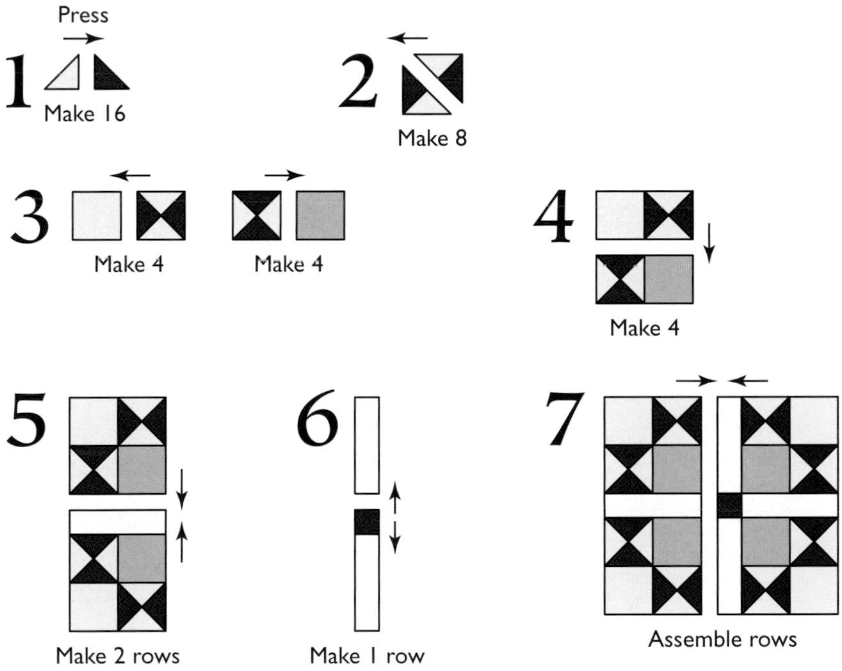

1 Press → Make 16

2 Make 8

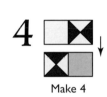

3 Make 4   Make 4

4 Make 4

5 Make 2 rows

6 Make 1 row

7 Assemble rows

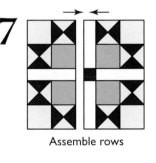

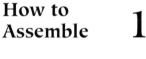

Shading in photo

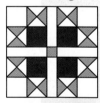

Alternate shadings

	Block Basics			Rotary Cutting				Templates	Yardage
	Patch	Shape	Total Needed	Strip Width (in inches)	Squares to Cut	Cut Size (in inches)	Next Cut	Template	Strip Length Needed (in inches)
LIGHT 1	A	▭	4	1½	4 rectangles	1½ × 4½	—	R6	18
LIGHT 2	B	◻	4	2½	4	2½ × 2½	—	S9	10
	C	△	16	3¼	4	3¼ × 3¼	⊠	T4	13
MEDIUM	D	◼	4	2½	4	2½ × 2½	—	S9	10
DARK	E	◼	1	1½	1	1½ × 1½	—	S1	1½
	F	▲	16	3¼	4	3¼ × 3¼	⊠	T4	13

Spider Web

Block Idea

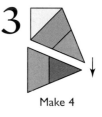

Use scraps in two different values for a dynamic look.

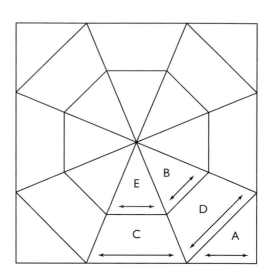

Shading in photo

Alternate shadings

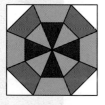

How to Assemble

1 Press — Make 4 / Make 4

2 Make 4

3 Make 4

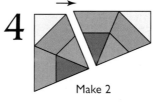

4 Make 2

5 Join

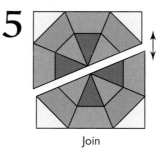

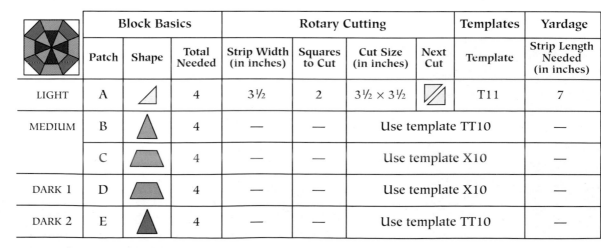

		Block Basics			Rotary Cutting				Templates	Yardage
	Patch	Shape	Total Needed	Strip Width (in inches)	Squares to Cut	Cut Size (in inches)	Next Cut	Template	Strip Length Needed (in inches)
LIGHT	A		4	3½	2	3½ × 3½		T11	7
MEDIUM	B		4	—	—	Use template TT10			—
	C		4	—	—	Use template X10			—
DARK 1	D		4	—	—	Use template X10			—
DARK 2	E		4	—	—	Use template TT10			—

Spinning Star

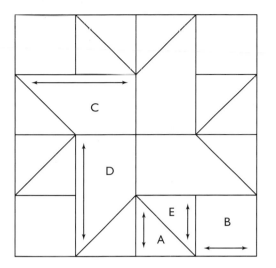

Block Idea

Make the darks in each quarter block a different flower color to create the look of four tulips set together.

How to Assemble

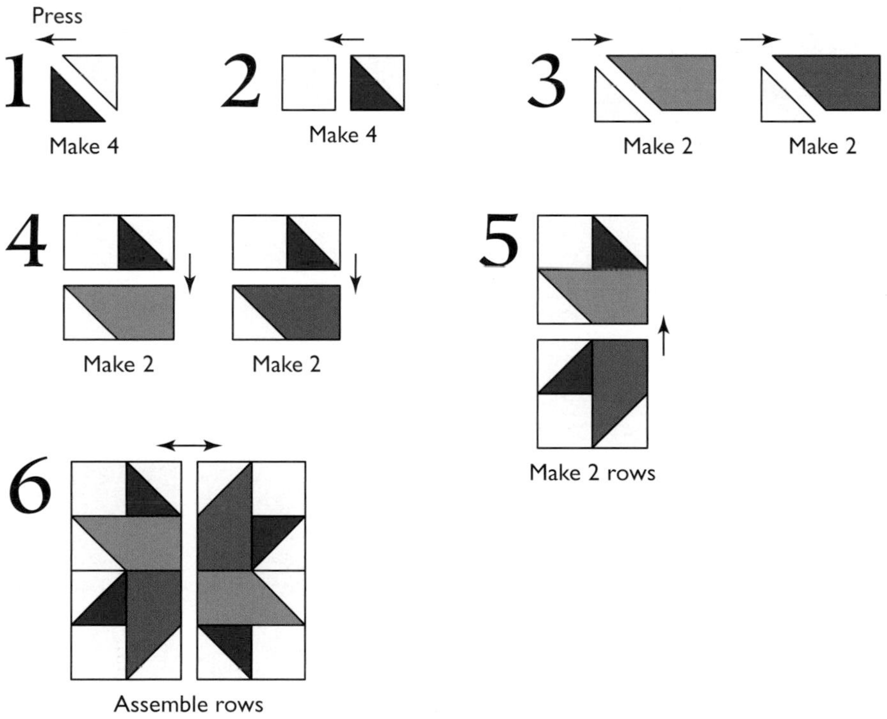

1 Press
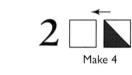
Make 4

2
Make 4

3
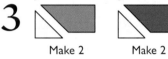
Make 2   Make 2

4
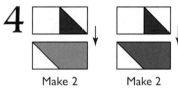
Make 2   Make 2

5
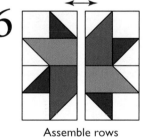
Make 2 rows

6
Assemble rows

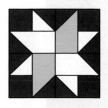

Shading in photo

Alternate shadings

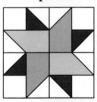

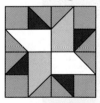

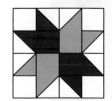

	Block Basics			Rotary Cutting				Templates	Yardage
	Patch	Shape	Total Needed	Strip Width (in inches)	Squares to Cut	Cut Size (in inches)	Next Cut	Template	Strip Length Needed (in inches)
LIGHT	A	◺	8	3⅛	4	3⅛ × 3⅛	◹	T10	12½
	B	▢	4	2¾	4	2¾ × 2¾	—	S11	11
MEDIUM 1	C	⬠	2	2¾	2 rectangles	2¾ × 5⅜	Use template X8	10¾
MEDIUM 2	D	⬠	2	2¾	2 rectangles	2¾ × 5⅜	Use template X8	10¾
DARK	E	◢	4	3⅛	2	3⅛ × 3⅛	◣	T10	6¼

Spools

Bl💡ck Idea

Use striped prints to mimic the look of thread wrapped around a spool, being sure to plan ahead when cutting so the stripes all run in the same direction.

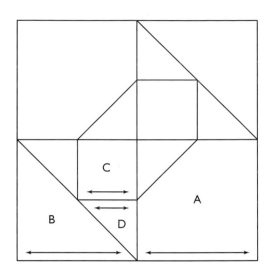

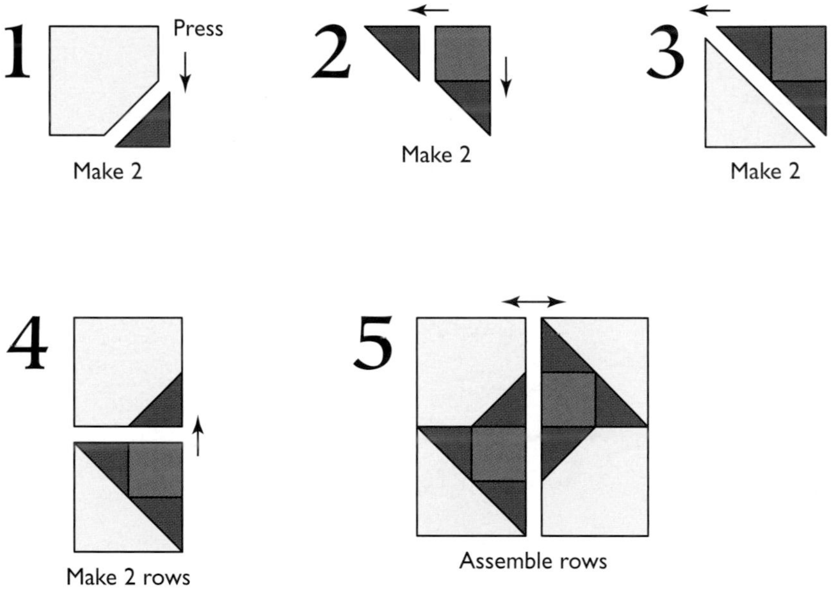

Shading in photo

Alternate shadings

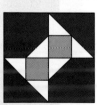

How to Assemble

1 Press ↓

Make 2

2 Make 2

3 Make 2

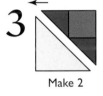

4 Make 2 rows

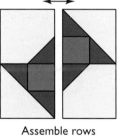

5 Assemble rows

	Block Basics			Rotary Cutting				Templates	Yardage
	Patch	Shape	Total Needed	Strip Width (in inches)	Squares to Cut	Cut Size (in inches)	Next Cut	Template	Strip Length Needed (in inches)
LIGHT	A		2	5	2	5 × 5		Use template X5	10
	B		2	5⅜	1	5⅜ × 5⅜		T15	5⅜
MEDIUM	C		2	2¾	2	2¾ × 2¾	—	S11	5½
DARK	D		6	3⅛	3	3⅛ × 3⅛		T10	9⅜

Square within a Square

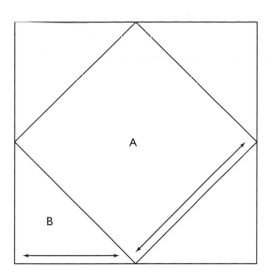

Bl☉ck Idea

Use this simple yet effective block as a setting square.

How to Assemble

1

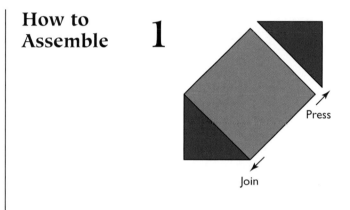

Press

Join

2

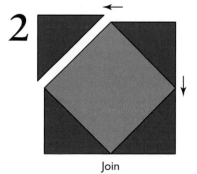

Join

Shading in photo

Alternate shadings

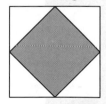

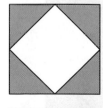

	Block Basics			Rotary Cutting				Templates	Yardage
	Patch	Shape	Total Needed	Strip Width (in inches)	Squares to Cut	Cut Size (in inches)	Next Cut	Template	Strip Length Needed (in inches)
MEDIUM	A	◻	1	$6\frac{7}{8}$	1	$6\frac{7}{8} \times 6\frac{7}{8}$	—	S17	$6\frac{7}{8}$
DARK	B	◣	4	$5\frac{3}{8}$	2	$5\frac{3}{8} \times 5\frac{3}{8}$	◺	T15	$10\frac{3}{4}$

Star Puzzle

Bl🔆ck Idea

Use traditional blue and white for the darks and lights.

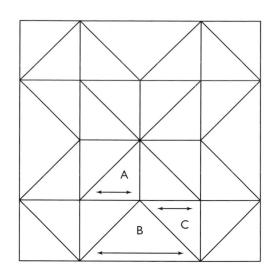

A

B   C

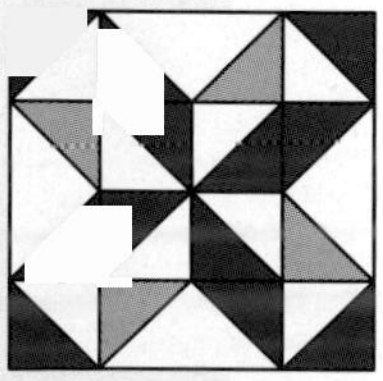

How to Assemble

Press

1 Make 8

2 Make 2

3 Join

4 Make 4

5 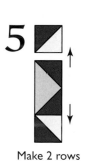 Make 2 rows

6 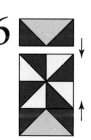 Make 1 row

7 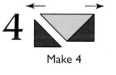 Assemble rows

Shading in photo

Alternate shadings

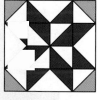

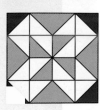

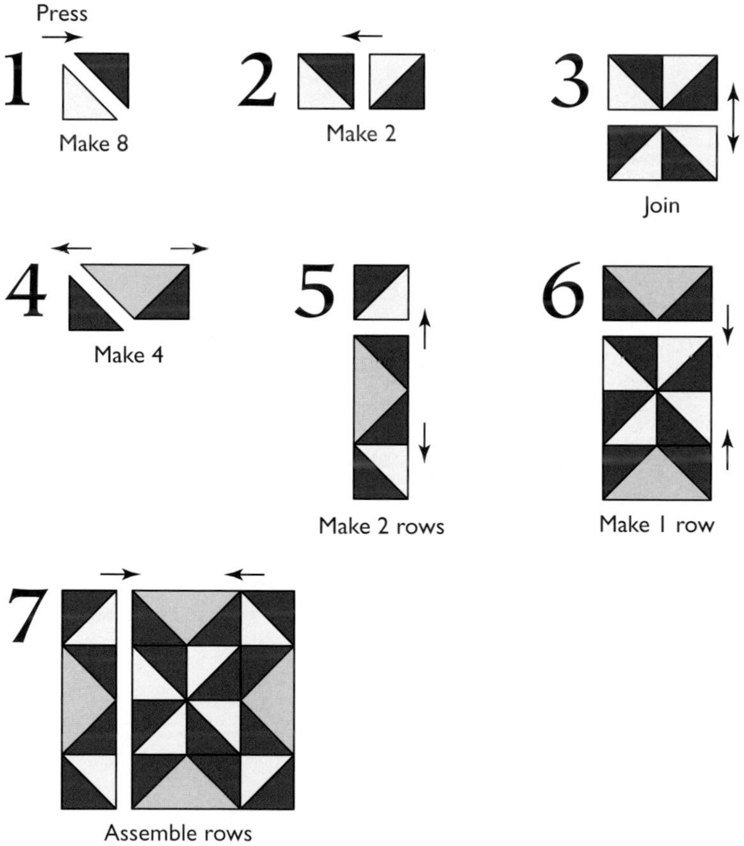

	Block Basics			Rotary Cutting				Templates	Yardage
	Patch	Shape	Total Needed	Strip Width (in inches)	Squares to Cut	Cut Size (in inches)	Next Cut	Template	Strip Length Needed (in inches)
LIGHT 1	A	◺	8	3⅛	4	3⅛ × 3⅛	◺	T10	12½
LIGHT 2	B	△	4	5¾	1	5¾ × 5¾	⊠	T13	5¾
DARK	C	◣	16	3⅛	8	3⅛ × 3⅛	◥	T10	25

Star Stairway

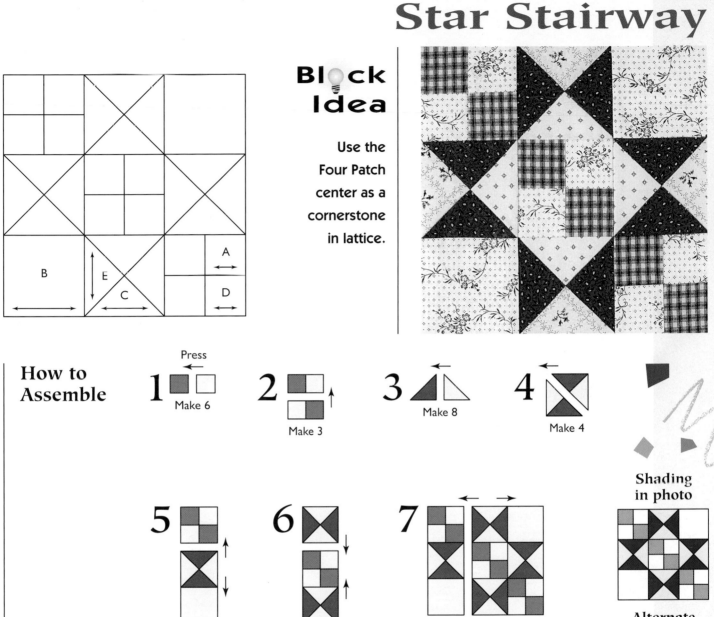

Block Idea

Use the Four Patch center as a cornerstone in lattice.

How to Assemble

1 Make 6 — Press ←

2 Make 3 — ↑

3 Make 8 — ←

4 Make 4 — ←

5 Make 2 rows

6 Make 1 row

7 Assemble rows — ← →

Shading in photo

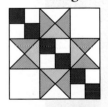

Alternate shadings

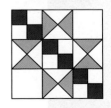

	Block Basics			Rotary Cutting				Templates	Yardage
	Patch	Shape	Total Needed	Strip Width (in inches)	Squares to Cut	Cut Size (in inches)	Next Cut	Template	Strip Length Needed (in inches)
LIGHT 1	A	☐	6	2	6	2 × 2	—	S5	12
	B	☐	2	3½	2	3½ × 3½	—	S13	7
LIGHT 2	C	△	8	4¼	2	4¼ × 4¼	⊠	T9	8½
MEDIUM	D	■	6	2	6	2 × 2	—	S5	12
DARK	E	▲	8	4¼	2	4¼ × 4¼	⊠	T9	8½

Star Tile

Block Idea

Cut the band around the star from a very light or a very dark fabric to make the star shine bright.

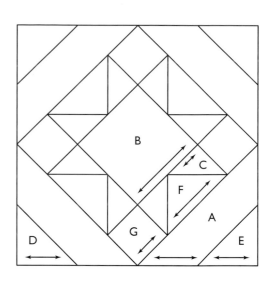

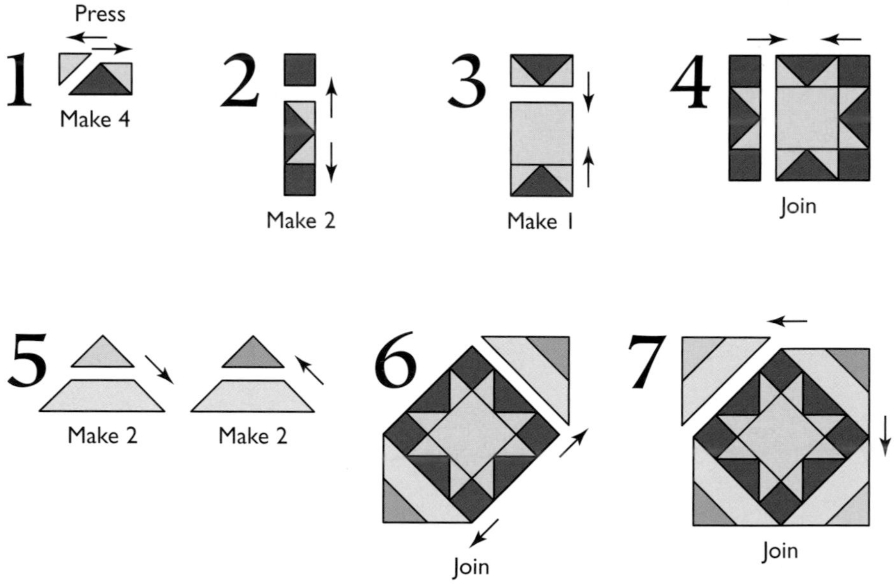

Shading in photo

Alternate shadings

How to Assemble

1 Press · Make 4

2 Make 2

3 Make 1

4 Join

5 Make 2 · Make 2

6 Join

7 Join

	Block Basics			Rotary Cutting				Templates	Yardage
	Patch	Shape	Total Needed	Strip Width (in inches)	Squares to Cut	Cut Size (in inches)	Next Cut	Template	Strip Length Needed (in inches)
LIGHT 1	A	trapezoid	4	5⅜	2	5⅜ × 5⅜	triangle	See page 219 and use template X6	10¾
LIGHT 2	B	square	1	3⅝+	1	3⅝+ × 3⅝+	—	S14	3⅝+
	C	triangle	8	2⅜+	4	2⅜+ × 2⅜+	triangle	T6	9¾
MEDIUM 1	D	triangle	2	3⅛	1	3⅛ × 3⅛	triangle	T10	3⅛
MEDIUM 2	E	triangle	2	3⅛	1	3⅛ × 3⅛	triangle	T10	3⅛
DARK	F	triangle	4	4⅜+	1	4⅜+ × 4⅜+	X	T10	4⅜+
	G	square	4	2+	4	2+ × 2+	—	S6	8½

Note: Plus sign (+) indicates ¹⁄₁₆-inch measurements. See page 217 for details.

Stepping Stones

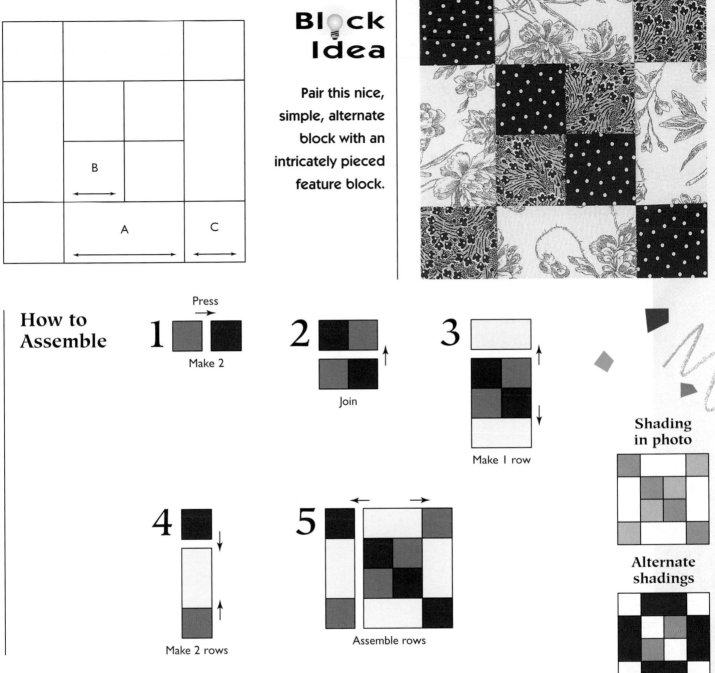

Block Idea

Pair this nice, simple, alternate block with an intricately pieced feature block.

How to Assemble

1 Make 2 — Press →

2 Join

3 Make 1 row

4 Make 2 rows

5 Assemble rows

Shading in photo

Alternate shadings

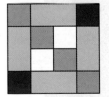

	Block Basics			Rotary Cutting				Templates	Yardage
	Patch	Shape	Total Needed	Strip Width (in inches)	Squares to Cut	Cut Size (in inches)	Next Cut	Template	Strip Length Needed (in inches)
LIGHT	A		4	2¾	4 rectangles	2¾ × 5	—	R9	20
MEDIUM	B		4	2¾	4	2¾ × 2¾	—	S11	11
DARK	C		4	2¾	4	2¾ × 2¾	—	S11	11

Swamp Patch

Block Idea

Lighten the corner triangles, and set this block on point.

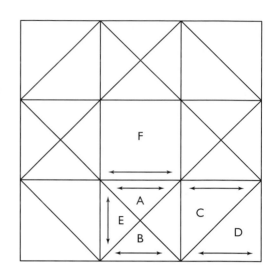

How to Assemble

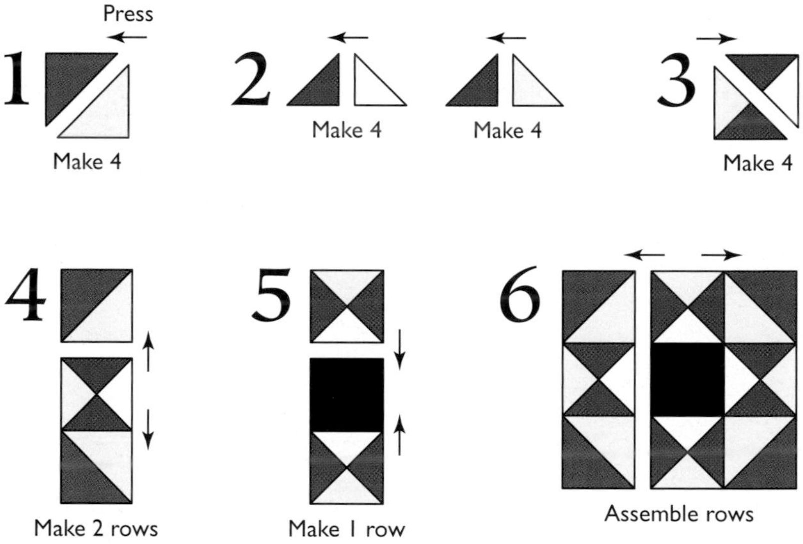

Press

1
Make 4

2
Make 4   Make 4

3
Make 4

4
Make 2 rows

5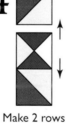
Make 1 row

6
Assemble rows

Shading in photo

Alternate shadings

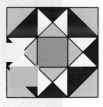

	Block Basics			Rotary Cutting				Templates	Yardage
	Patch	Shape	Total Needed	Strip Width (in inches)	Squares to Cut	Cut Size (in inches)	Next Cut	Template	Strip Length Needed (in inches)
LIGHT 1	A	△	4	4¼	1	4¼ × 4¼	⊠	T9	4¼
LIGHT 2	B	△	4	4¼	1	4¼ × 4¼	⊠	T9	4¼
	C	◺	4	3⅞	2	3⅞ × 3⅞	◩	T12	7¾
MEDIUM	D	◣	4	3⅞	2	3⅞ × 3⅞	◩	T12	7¾
DARK 1	E	▲	8	4¼	2	4¼ × 4¼	⊠	T9	8½
DARK 2	F	■	1	3½	1	3½ × 3½	—	S13	3½

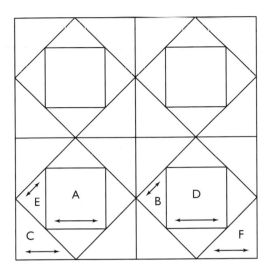

This and That

Bl💡ck Idea

Use black for the dark and bright colors for the light.

How to Assemble

1 Press — Make 2   Make 2

2 Make 2   Make 2

3 Make 2   Make 2

4 Make 2   Make 2

5 Make 2 rows

6 Assemble rows

Shading in photo

Alternate shadings

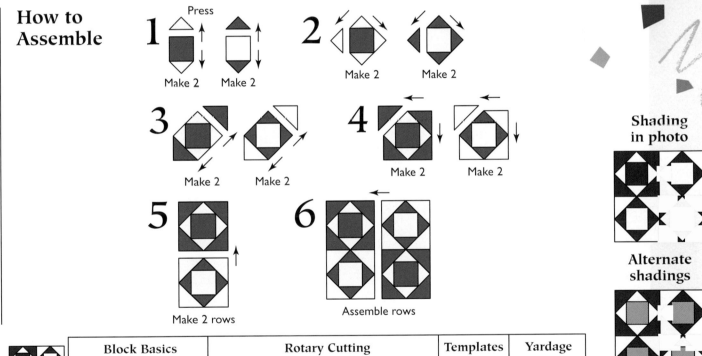

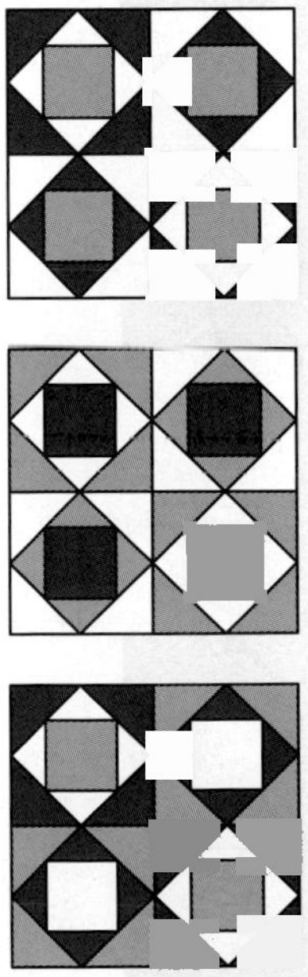

	Block Basics			Rotary Cutting				Templates	Yardage
	Patch	Shape	Total Needed	Strip Width (in inches)	Squares to Cut	Cut Size (in inches)	Next Cut	Template	Strip Length Needed (in inches)
LIGHT	A	☐	2	2¾	2	2¾ × 2¾	—	S11	5½
	B	◺	8	2⅜+	4	2⅜+ × 2⅜+	◿	T6	10
	C	◺	8	3⅛	4	3⅛ × 3⅛	◿	T10	12½
DARK	D	■	2	2¾	2	2¾ × 2¾	—	S11	5½
	E	◢	8	2⅜+	4	2⅜+ × 2⅜+	◿	T6	10
	F	◢	8	3⅛	4	3⅛ × 3⅛	◿	T10	12½

Note: Plus sign (+) indicates ¹/₁₆-inch measurements. See page 217 for details.

Turkey Tracks

Block Idea

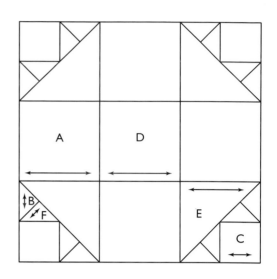

Set this block on point with plain alternate squares to create a rosebud where the corner squares meet.

How to Assemble

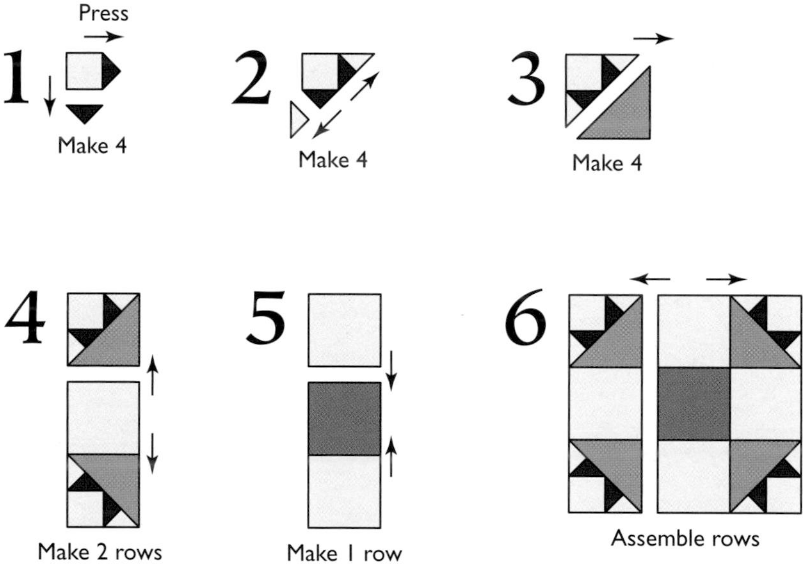

Press

1 ↓ Make 4

2 Make 4

3 Make 4

4 Make 2 rows

5 Make 1 row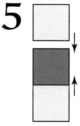

6 Assemble rows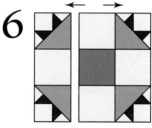

Shading in photo

Alternate shadings

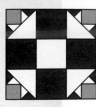

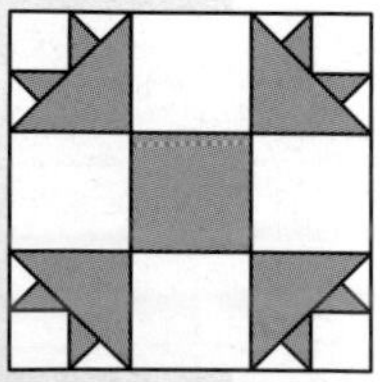

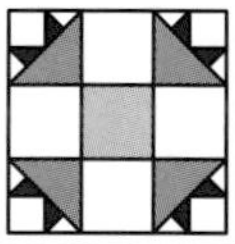	Block Basics			Rotary Cutting				Templates	Yardage
	Patch	Shape	Total Needed	Strip Width (in inches)	Squares to Cut	Cut Size (in inches)	Next Cut	Template	Strip Length Needed (in inches)
LIGHT	A	☐	4	3½	4	3½ × 3½	—	S13	14
	B	△	8	2¾	2	2¾ × 2¾	⊠	T1	5½
	C	☐	4	2	4	2 × 2	—	S5	8
MEDIUM 1	D	■	1	3½	1	3½ × 3½	—	S13	3½
MEDIUM 2	E	◢	4	3⅞	2	3⅞ × 3⅞	◩	T12	7¾
DARK	F	◣	8	1⅞+	4	1⅞+ × 1⅞+	◩	T1	7¾

Note: Plus sign (+) indicates 1/16-inch measurements. See page 217 for details.

Twinkling Star

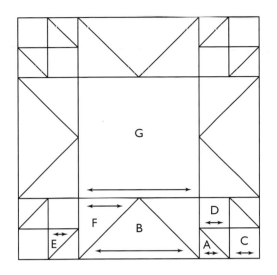

Block Idea

Set the blocks side by side to find a new star where the block corners meet.

How to Assemble

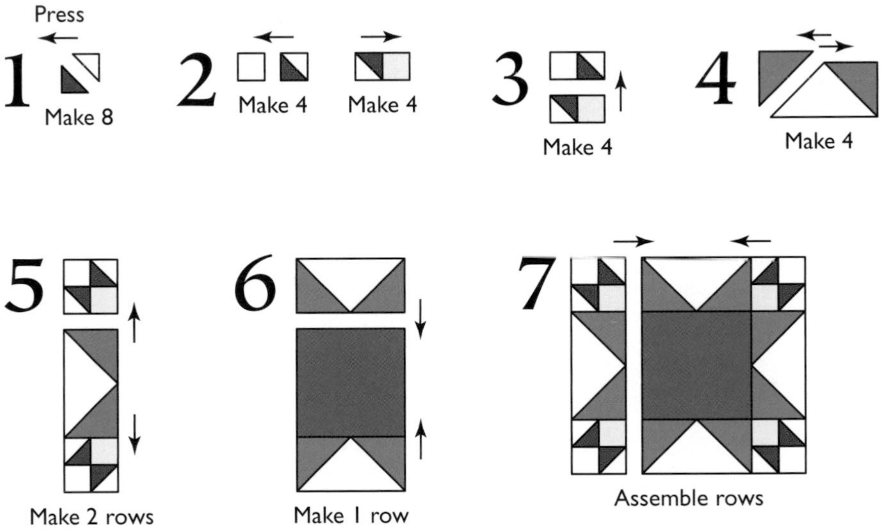

1 Press ← 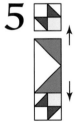 Make 8

2 Make 4   Make 4

3 Make 4

4 Make 4

5 Make 2 rows

6 Make 1 row

7 Assemble rows

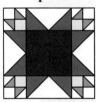
Shading in photo

Alternate shadings

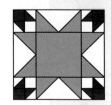

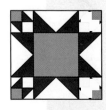

	Block Basics			Rotary Cutting				Templates	Yardage
	Patch	Shape	Total Needed	Strip Width (in inches)	Squares to Cut	Cut Size (in inches)	Next Cut	Template	Strip Length Needed (in inches)
LIGHT 1	A	◿	8	2	4	2 × 2	◿	T2	8
	B	△	4	5¾	1	5¾ × 5¾	⧓	T13	5¾
	C	▢	4	1⅝	4	1⅝ × 1⅝	—	S3	6½
LIGHT 2	D	▨	4	1⅝	4	1⅝ × 1⅝	—	S3	6½
MEDIUM	E	◢	8	2	4	2 × 2	◸	T2	8
DARK 1	F	◥	8	3⅛	4	3⅛ × 3⅛	◸	T10	12½
DARK 2	G	■	1	5	1	5 × 5	—	S16	5

Twirling Star

Block Idea

Use just two fabrics for the star points and one fabric for each point's "shadow."

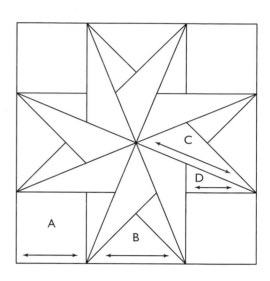

How to Assemble

1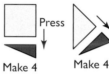
Press
Make 4   Make 4

2
Make 4   Make 4

3
Make 4

4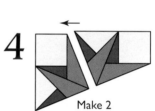
Make 2

5
Join

Shading in photo

Alternate shadings

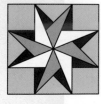

		Block Basics			Rotary Cutting				Templates	Yardage
	Patch	Shape	Total Needed	Strip Width (in inches)	Squares to Cut	Cut Size (in inches)	Next Cut	Template	Strip Length Needed (in inches)	
LIGHT	A	▢	4	3⅛	4	3⅛ × 3⅛	—	S12	12½	
	B	△	4	5	1	5 × 5	⊠	T11	5	
MEDIUM	C	◣	8	—	—	Use template TT12			—	
DARK	D	◣	8	1⅝+	4 rectangles	1⅝+ × 4⅛	◲	TT11	16½	

Note: Plus sign (+) indicates ¹/₁₆-inch measurements. See page 217 for details.

Twisting Star

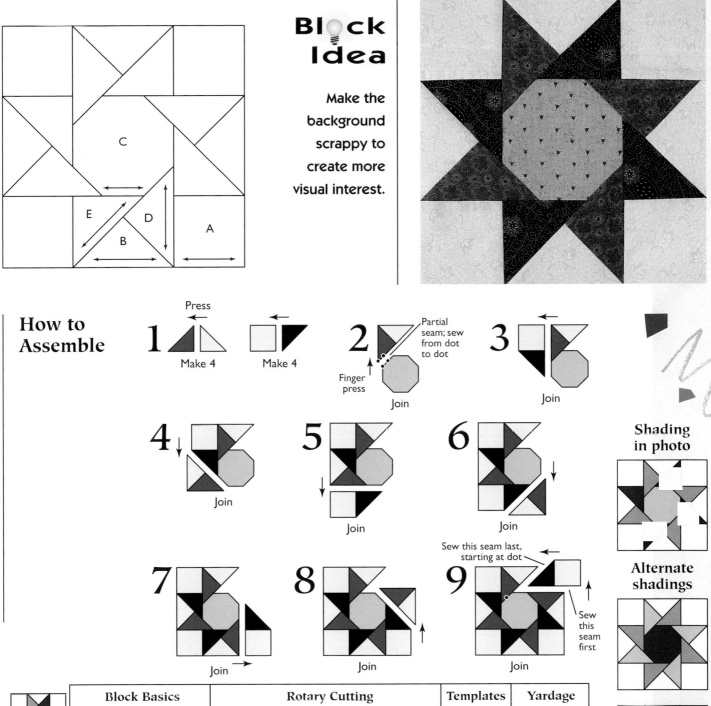

Block Idea

Make the background scrappy to create more visual interest.

How to Assemble

1 Press → Make 4   Make 4

2 Partial seam; sew from dot to dot   Finger press   Join

3 Join

4 Join

5 Join

6 Join

7 Join

8 Join

9 Sew this seam last, starting at dot   Sew this seam first   Join

Shading in photo

Alternate shadings

	Block Basics			Rotary Cutting				Templates	Yardage
	Patch	Shape	Total Needed	Strip Width (in inches)	Squares to Cut	Cut Size (in inches)	Next Cut	Template	Strip Length Needed (in inches)
LIGHT	A	▢	4	3⅛	4	3⅛ × 3⅛	—	S12	12½
	B	△	4	5	1	5 × 5	⊠	T11	5
MEDIUM 1	C	⬡	1	4¼	1	4¼ × 4¼	See page 219 and use template X4		4¼
MEDIUM 2	D	▲	4	5	1	5 × 5	⊠	T11	5
DARK	E	▲	4	5	1	5 × 5	⊠	T11	5

Variable Star

Block Idea

Combine this block with Stepping Stones to create an allover pattern that chains.

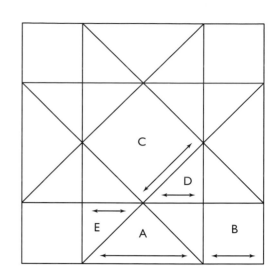

How to Assemble

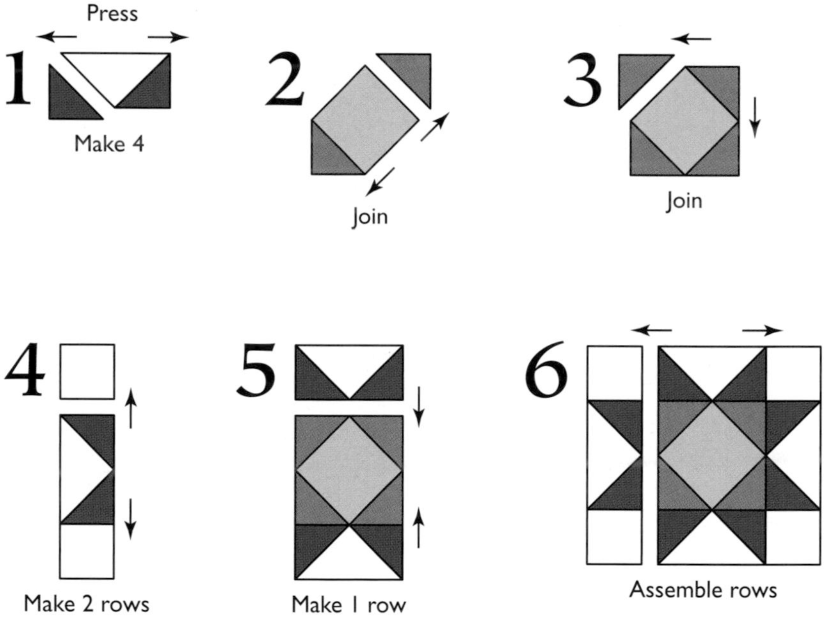

1 Press → ← Make 4

2 Join

3 Join

4 Make 2 rows

5 Make 1 row

6 Assemble rows

Shading in photo

Alternate shadings

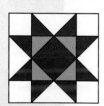

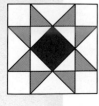

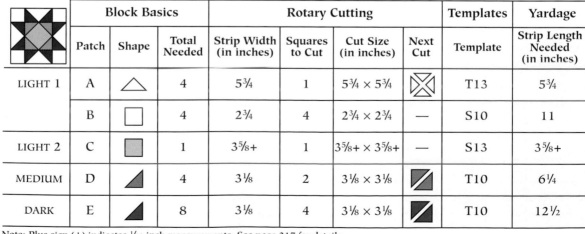

	Block Basics			Rotary Cutting				Templates	Yardage
	Patch	Shape	Total Needed	Strip Width (in inches)	Squares to Cut	Cut Size (in inches)	Next Cut	Template	Strip Length Needed (in inches)
LIGHT 1	A	△	4	5¾	1	5¾ × 5¾	⊠	T13	5¾
	B	□	4	2¾	4	2¾ × 2¾	—	S10	11
LIGHT 2	C	◻	1	3⅝+	1	3⅝+ × 3⅝+	—	S13	3⅝+
MEDIUM	D	◢	4	3⅛	2	3⅛ × 3⅛	◺	T10	6¼
DARK	E	◣	8	3⅛	4	3⅛ × 3⅛	◿	T10	12½

Note: Plus sign (+) indicates 1/16-inch measurements. See page 217 for details.

Variable Star II

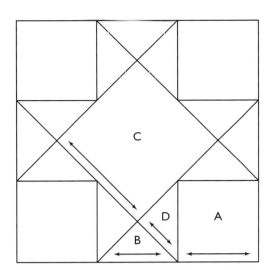

Block Idea

Make the background dark and the star points light to make this star glow.

How to Assemble

1

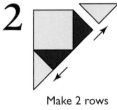

Press

Make 4

2

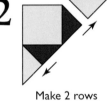

Make 2 rows

3

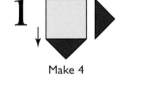

Make 1 row

4

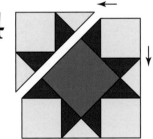

Assemble rows

Shading in photo

Alternate shadings

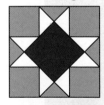

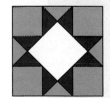

	Block Basics			**Rotary Cutting**				**Templates**	**Yardage**
	Patch	Shape	Total Needed	Strip Width (in inches)	Squares to Cut	Cut Size (in inches)	Next Cut	Template	Strip Length Needed (in inches)
LIGHT	A	☐	4	3½	4	3½ × 3½	—	S13	14
	B	△	4	4¼	1	4¼ × 4¼	⊠	T9	4¼
MEDIUM	C	◼	1	4¾	1	4¾ × 4¾	—	S15	4¾
DARK	D	◢	8	3	4	3 × 3	◺	T9	12

Water Wheel

Block Idea

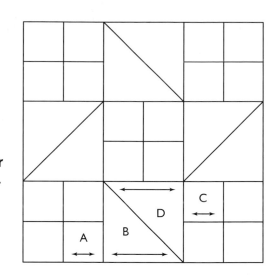

Rotate the triangle squares in half the blocks to "turn" the water wheel in the other direction.

How to Assemble

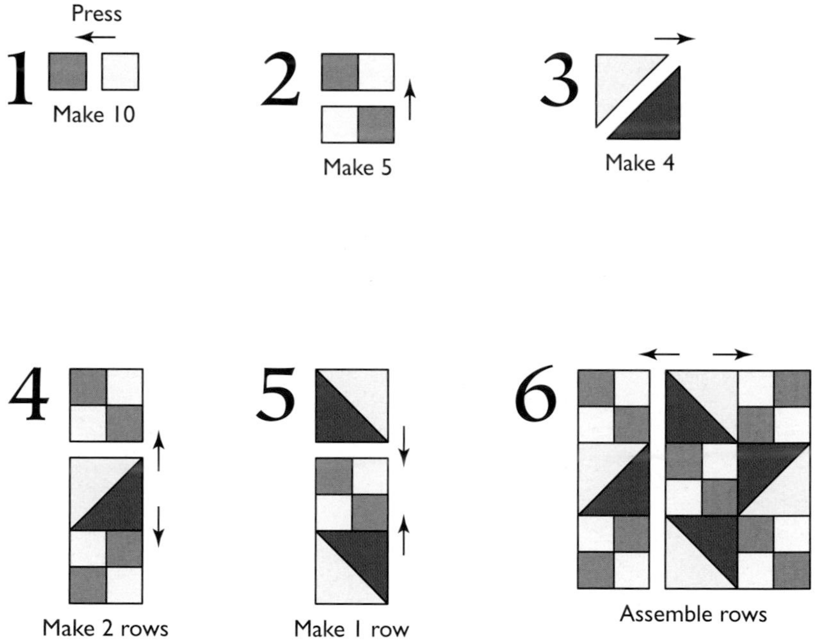

Press

1 Make 10

2 Make 5

3 Make 4

Shading in photo

Alternate shadings

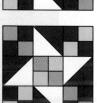

4 Make 2 rows

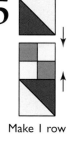

5 Make 1 row

6 Assemble rows

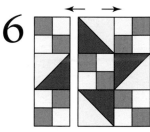

	Block Basics			Rotary Cutting				Templates	Yardage
	Patch	Shape	Total Needed	Strip Width (in inches)	Squares to Cut	Cut Size (in inches)	Next Cut	Template	Strip Length Needed (in inches)
LIGHT 1	A	☐	10	2	10	2 × 2	—	S5	20
LIGHT 2	B	◿	4	3⅞	2	3⅞ × 3⅞	◺	T12	7¾
MEDIUM	C	◼	10	2	10	2 × 2	—	S5	20
DARK	D	◣	4	3⅞	2	3⅞ × 3⅞	◩	T12	7¾

Weather Vane

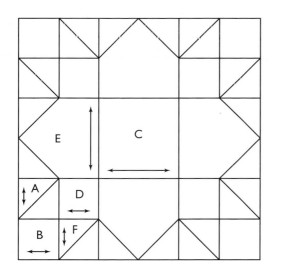

Block Idea

Try setting this block on point to see how it changes.

How to Assemble

1 Press Make 8

2 Make 4   Make 4

3 Make 4

4 Make 4

5 Make 2 rows

6 Make 1 row

7 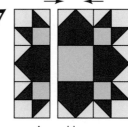 Assemble rows

Shading in photo
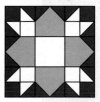

Alternate shadings
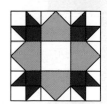

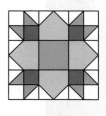

 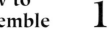

		Block Basics		Rotary Cutting				Templates	Yardage
	Patch	Shape	Total Needed	Strip Width (in inches)	Squares to Cut	Cut Size (in inches)	Next Cut	Template	Strip Length Needed (in inches)
LIGHT	A	◺	16	2³⁄₈	8	2³⁄₈ × 2³⁄₈	◩	T5	19
	B	◻	4	2	4	2 × 2	—	S5	8
MEDIUM	C	◻	1	3¹⁄₂	1	3¹⁄₂ × 3¹⁄₂	—	S13	3¹⁄₂
	D	◻	4	2	4	2 × 2	—	S5	8
DARK	E	⬠	4	3¹⁄₂	4	3¹⁄₂ × 3¹⁄₂		Use template X2	14
	F	◣	8	2³⁄₈	4	2³⁄₈ × 2³⁄₈	◩	T5	9¹⁄₂

Westland

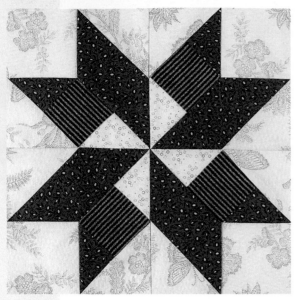

Bl🔆ck Idea

Make the small center pinwheel a different, darker contrasting color.

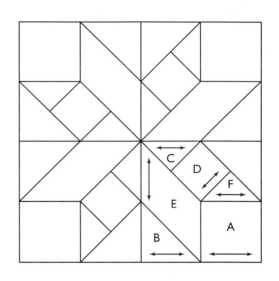

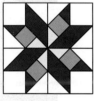

Shading in photo

Alternate shadings

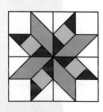

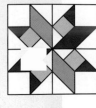

How to Assemble

1 Press ↓ Make 4

2 Make 4

3 Make 4

4 Make 4

5 Sew this seam first, ending at dot* — Make 4 — Sew this seam last, starting at dot*

6 Make 2 rows

7 Assemble rows

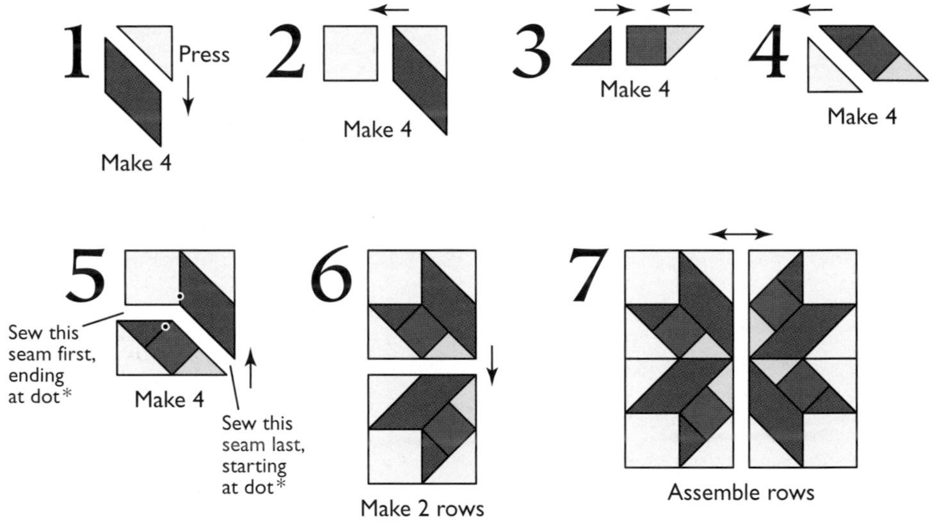

*See page 223 for details.

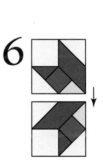

	Block Basics			**Rotary Cutting**				**Templates**	**Yardage**
	Patch	Shape	Total Needed	Strip Width (in inches)	Squares to Cut	Cut Size (in inches)	Next Cut	Template	Strip Length Needed (in inches)
LIGHT 1	A	☐	4	2¾	4	2¾ × 2¾	—	S11	11
	B	◺	8	3⅛	4	3⅛ × 3⅛	◹	T10	12½
LIGHT 2	C	△	4	3½	1	3½ × 3½	⊠	T6	3½
MEDIUM	D	◼	4	2⅛	4	2⅛ × 2⅛	—	S7	8½
DARK	E	▱	4	2¾		Make a 45° angle cut at the left end of the strip, angling the ruler from bottom left to top right. Measuring from diagonal cut, make successive cuts 2⅛" apart.		D1	14¾
	F	▲	4	3½	1	3½ × 3½	⊠	T6	3½

Whirligig

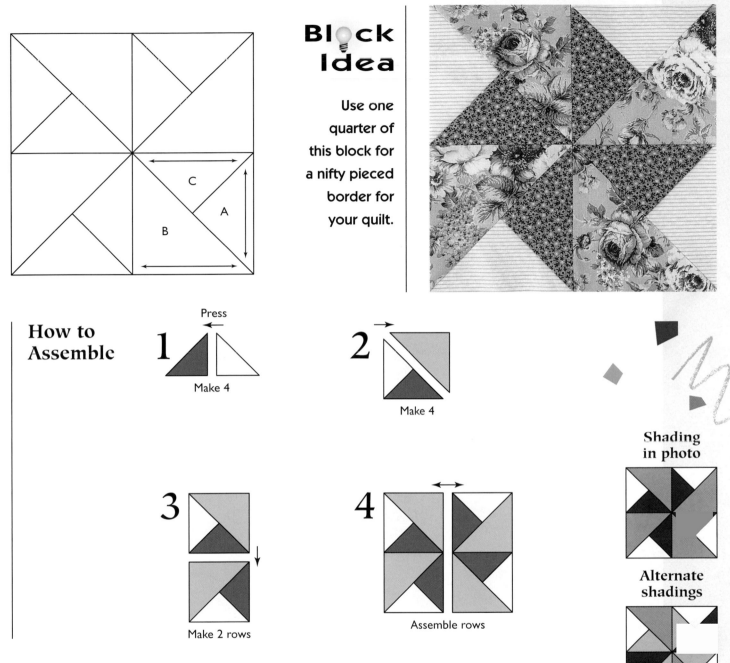

Block Idea

Use one quarter of this block for a nifty pieced border for your quilt.

How to Assemble

1 Press ←
Make 4

2 →
Make 4

3 ↓
Make 2 rows

4 ↔
Assemble rows

Shading in photo

Alternate shadings

	Block Basics			**Rotary Cutting**				**Templates**	**Yardage**
	Patch	Shape	Total Needed	Strip Width (in inches)	Squares to Cut	Cut Size (in inches)	Next Cut	Template	Strip Length Needed (in inches)
LIGHT	A	△	4	5¾	1	5¾ × 5¾	⊠	T13	5¾
MEDIUM	B	◢	4	5⅜	2	5⅜ × 5⅜	◩	T15	10¾
DARK	C	▲	4	5¾	1	5¾ × 5¾	⊠	T13	5¾

Windmill Star

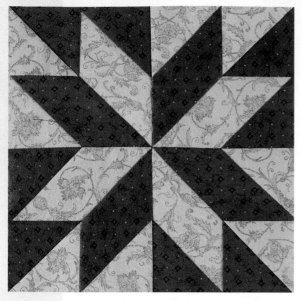

Block Idea

Pick two darks for the star and two lights for the background.

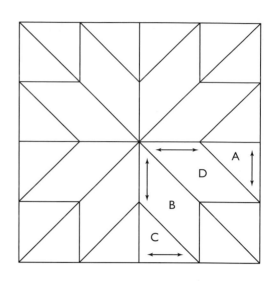

How to Assemble

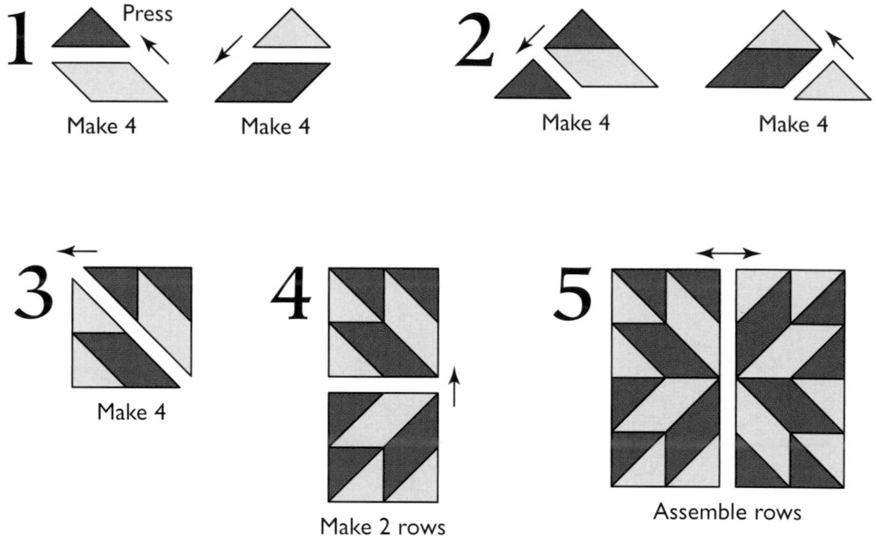

1  Press

Make 4   Make 4

2

Make 4   Make 4

3

Make 4

4 Make 2 rows

5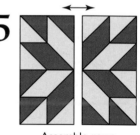

Assemble rows

Shading in photo

Alternate shadings

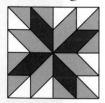

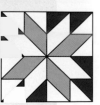

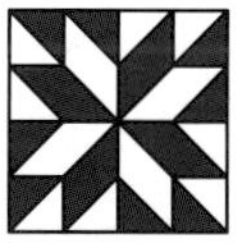

		Block Basics		Rotary Cutting				Templates	Yardage
	Patch	Shape	Total Needed	Strip Width (in inches)	Squares to Cut	Cut Size (in inches)	Next Cut	Template	Strip Length Needed (in inches)
LIGHT	A	◺	8	3⅛	4	3⅛ × 3⅛	◹	T10	12½
	B	▱	4	2¾	Make a 45° angle cut at the left end of the strip, angling the ruler from bottom left to top right. Measuring from diagonal cut, make successive cuts 2⅛" apart.			D1	14¾
DARK	C	◢	8	3⅛	4	3⅛ × 3⅛	◥	T10	12½
	D	▱	4	2¾	Make a 45° angle cut at the left end of the strip, angling the ruler from top left to bottom right. Measuring from diagonal cut, make successive cuts 2⅛" apart.			D1r	14¾

Woodland Path

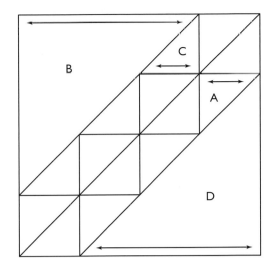

Block Idea

Set the blocks side by side with light against dark to create a pieced zigzag.

How to Assemble

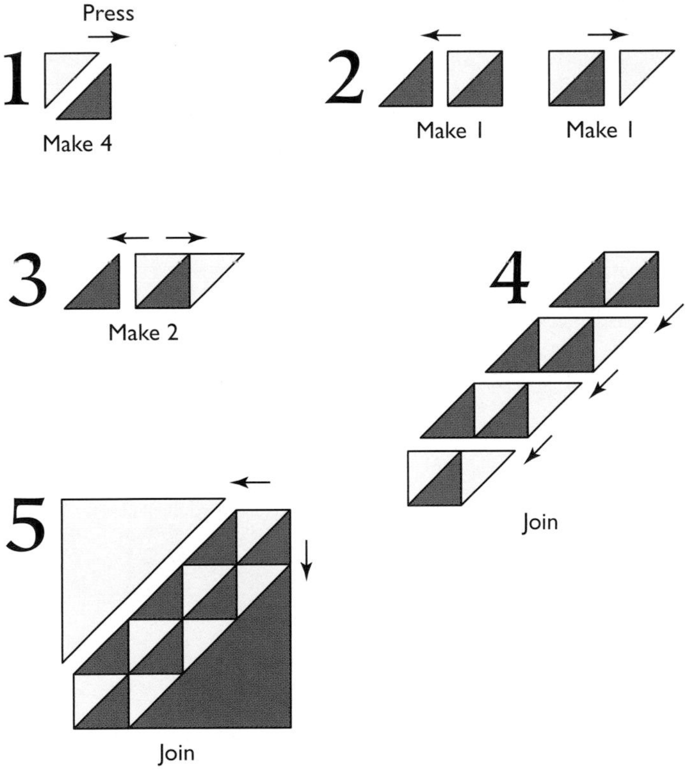

1  Press
Make 4

2
Make 1   Make 1

3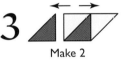
Make 2

4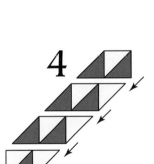
Join

5
Join

Shading in photo

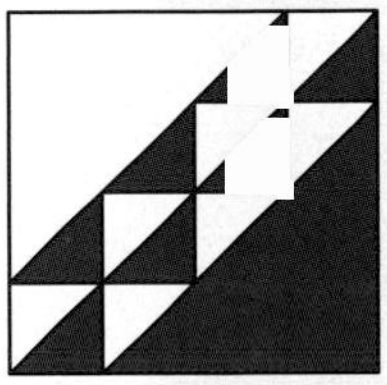

Alternate shadings

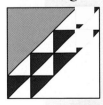

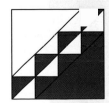

	Block Basics			**Rotary Cutting**				**Templates**	**Yardage**
	Patch	Shape	Total Needed	Strip Width (in inches)	Squares to Cut	Cut Size (in inches)	Next Cut	Template	Strip Length Needed (in inches)
LIGHT	A	◿	7	3⅛	4	3⅛ × 3⅛	◿	T10	12½
	B	◺	1	7⅝	1	7⅝ × 7⅝	◿	T16	7⅝
DARK	C	◣	7	3⅛	4	3⅛ × 3⅛	◣	T10	12½
	D	◣	1	7⅝	1	7⅝ × 7⅝	◣	T16	7⅝

Designing Your Own Quilt

Overflowing with hundreds of ideas, this chapter gives you the tools you'll need to add your own personal style to a quilt design.

With the suggestions in the pages that follow, you'll discover the fun of finding the right mix of blocks and setting elements for your quilt.

Pages at a Glance

Detailed Explanations

This section describes the various choices you can make for your quilt designs, including choosing a setting for your blocks, creating interesting block patterns, and figuring out how many blocks you'll need.

Basic Settings

These straight and diagonal settings are the ones quilters use most. You can choose to set your blocks in a straight side-by-side setting, alternate your pieced block with a plain block or another pieced block, or add lattice strips.

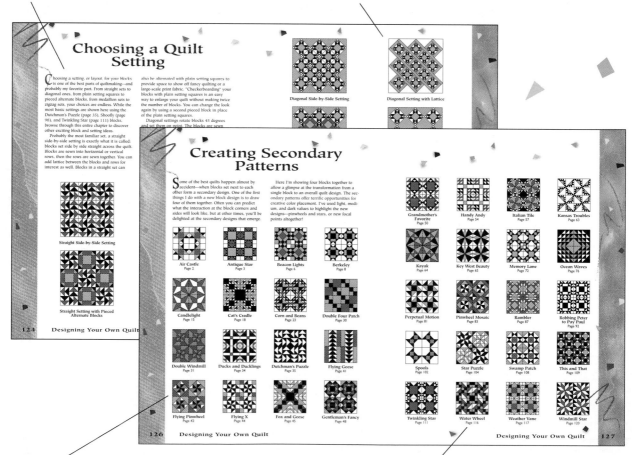

Block Ideas

Turn a simple block into a quilt full of interest. The secondary patterns that emerge when you join blocks together offer numerous opportunities for you to play up block interactions.

Page References

You'll always find a page reference for the block featured in the setting examples so you can easily turn back to "The Block Library" to see the cutting and assembly instructions for the block.

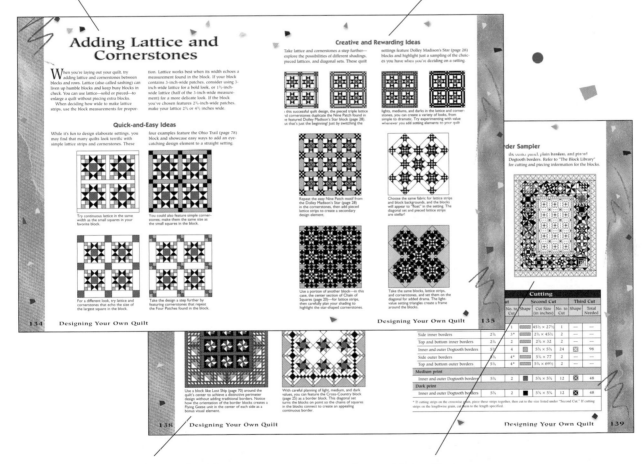

Setting Elements

All lattice is not created equal! These examples show the variety of looks you can achieve by using continuous or pieced lattice, or by adding plain or pieced cornerstones to your quilt setting.

Same Blocks, Different Looks

These sample quilt layouts highlight how easy it is to transform a nice quilt into a showstopper just by shading the lattice in light and dark values and setting the blocks and lattice in a straight or diagonal set.

Border Blocks

You'll find plenty of ideas for creative borders in this section. Forget long, plain strips of fabric—use border blocks instead for perfect-fitting borders every time.

Creative Fun

Go beyond the ordinary with this great suggestion! Piece your favorite blocks from the collection, then feature them in a border sampler. Cutting dimensions for the setting and helpful tips on choosing blocks are included here.

Choosing a Quilt Setting

Choosing a setting, or layout, for your blocks is one of the best parts of quiltmaking—and probably my favorite part. From straight sets to diagonal ones, from plain setting squares to pieced alternate blocks, from medallion sets to zigzag sets, your choices are endless. While the most basic settings are shown here using the Dutchman's Puzzle (page 35), Shoofly (page 98), and Twinkling Star (page 111) blocks, browse through this entire chapter to discover other exciting block and setting ideas.

Probably the most familiar set, a straight side-by-side setting is exactly what it is called: blocks set side by side straight across the quilt. Blocks are sewn into horizontal or vertical rows, then the rows are sewn together. You can add lattice between the blocks and rows for interest as well. Blocks in a straight set can also be alternated with plain setting squares to provide space to show off fancy quilting or a large-scale print fabric. "Checkerboarding" your blocks with plain setting squares is an easy way to enlarge your quilt without making twice the number of blocks. You can change the look again by using a second pieced block in place of the plain setting squares.

Diagonal settings rotate blocks 45 degrees and set them on point. The blocks are sewn together in diagonal rows, then the rows are sewn together. Quilts set diagonally feature side setting triangles and corner setting triangles along the outside edges to square up the quilt top. Featuring just as many design options as straight sets, blocks in a diagonal set can be used along with sashing or with plain or pieced setting blocks.

Straight Side-by-Side Setting

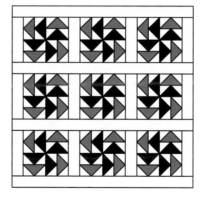

Straight Setting with Lattice

Straight Setting with Pieced Alternate Blocks

Straight Setting with Plain Setting Squares

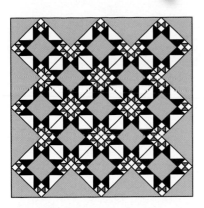

Diagonal Side-by-Side Setting

Diagonal Setting with Lattice

Diagonal Setting with Pieced Alternate Blocks

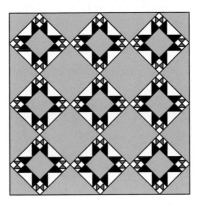

Diagonal Setting with Plain Setting Squares

Cutting Setting Triangles and Squares

For diagonally set quilts, you will need both side and corner setting triangles. The cutting dimensions below are for quilts without lattice.

Use half-square triangles to fill in the four corners of a diagonally set quilt top. (The straight grain will be on the short sides of the triangles, making the corner edges stable.) To cut the corner triangles for a quilt with 9-inch blocks, cut a 7¼-inch square, then cut it in half diagonally once. You will need to cut a total of two squares to yield four corner triangles.

Use quarter-square triangles to fill in the sides of a diagonally set quilt top. (The straight grain will be on the long side of the triangles, making the outside edges of the quilt top stable.) To cut side setting triangles for a quilt with 9-inch blocks, cut a 13⅞-inch square, then cut it in half diagonally twice (once in each direction) to yield four side setting triangles. To calculate the number of 13⅞-inch squares you'll need to cut, count the total number of side setting triangles needed, and divide by 4.

To create a checkerboard effect for your quilt, you will need to cut plain setting squares. To cut setting squares for a quilt with 9-inch blocks, cut 9½-inch squares.

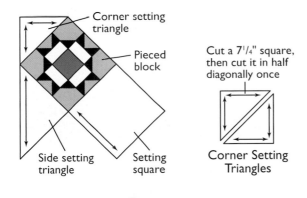

Corner setting triangle

Pieced block

Side setting triangle

Setting square

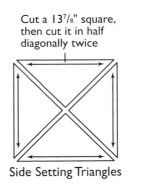

Cut a 7¼" square, then cut it in half diagonally once

Corner Setting Triangles

Cut a 13⅞" square, then cut it in half diagonally twice

Side Setting Triangles

Cut a 9½" square

Setting Squares

Creating Secondary Patterns

Some of the best quilts happen almost by accident—when blocks set next to each other form a secondary design. One of the first things I do with a new block design is to draw four of them together. Often you can predict what the interaction at the block corners and sides will look like, but at other times, you'll be delighted at the secondary designs that emerge.

Here I'm showing four blocks together to allow a glimpse at the transformation from a single block to an overall quilt design. The secondary patterns offer terrific opportunities for creative color placement. I've used light, medium, and dark values to highlight the new designs—pinwheels and stars, or new focal points altogether!

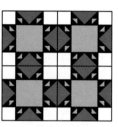

Air Castle
Page 2

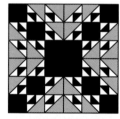

Antique Star
Page 3

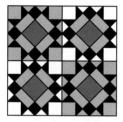

Beacon Lights
Page 6

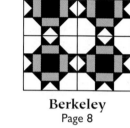

Berkeley
Page 8

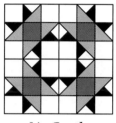

Candlelight
Page 15

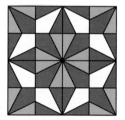

Cat's Cradle
Page 18

Corn and Beans
Page 23

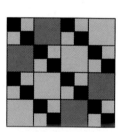

Double Four Patch
Page 30

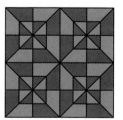

Double Windmill
Page 31

Ducks and Ducklings
Page 34

Dutchman's Puzzle
Page 35

Flying Geese
Page 41

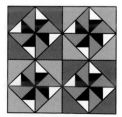

Flying Pinwheel
Page 42

Flying X
Page 44

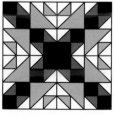

Fox and Geese
Page 45

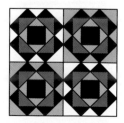

Gentleman's Fancy
Page 48

Designing Your Own Quilt

Grandmother's Favorite
Page 50

Handy Andy
Page 54

Italian Tile
Page 57

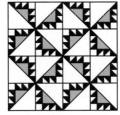

Kansas Troubles
Page 63

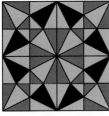

Kayak
Page 64

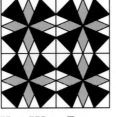

Key West Beauty
Page 65

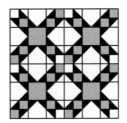

Memory Lane
Page 72

Ocean Waves
Page 76

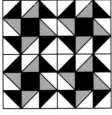

Perpetual Motion
Page 81

Pinwheel Mosaic
Page 83

Rambler
Page 87

**Robbing Peter
to Pay Paul**
Page 92

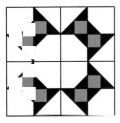

Spools
Page 102

Star Puzzle
Page 104

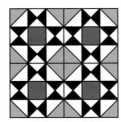

Swamp Patch
Page 108

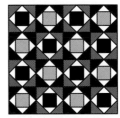

This and That
Page 109

Twinkling Star
Page 111

Water Wheel
Page 116

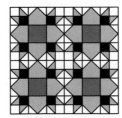

Weather Vane
Page 117

Windmill Star
Page 120

Having Fun with Asymmetrical Blocks

While most blocks in "The Block Library" are perfectly symmetrical, I've included a number of block patterns that break that mold. It's not too hard to recognize these blocks—they usually have a strong diagonal design, a clear division between light and dark (usually half light and half dark), or both.

Asymmetrical blocks can be turned and joined together in many different ways. After you make a handful of asymmetrical blocks, play with their arrangement before you sew them together. A design wall is invaluable for this. If you don't have one, clear a large space on your floor and move and turn your blocks until you find the perfect setting. Here are a few of my favorite asymmetrical blocks and settings to show you how strikingly different the same blocks can look when simply turned in a different direction.

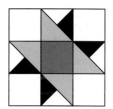
Air Castle
Page 2

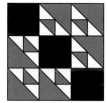
Cat's Cradle
Page 18

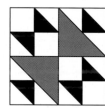
Fox and Geese
Page 45

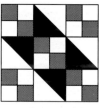
Jacob's Ladder
Page 59

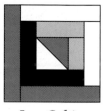
Log Cabin
Page 68

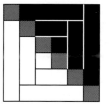
Log Cabin with a Chain
Page 69

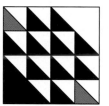
Ocean Waves
Page 76

Scrap Basket
Page 97

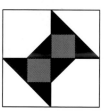
Spools
Page 102

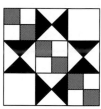
Star Stairway
Page 105

Asymmetrical Blocks

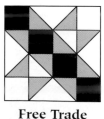
Free Trade
Page 46

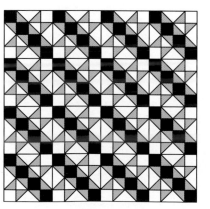

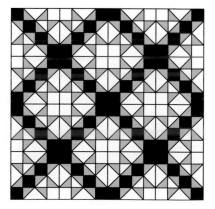

Designing Your Own Quilt

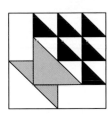

Grape Basket
Page 52

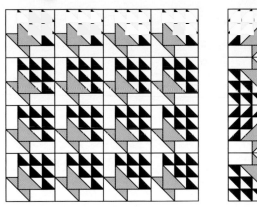

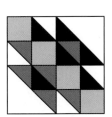

Hovering Hawks
Page 56

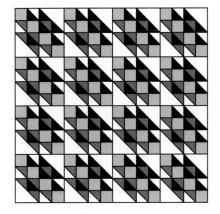

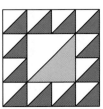

Lost Ship
Page 70

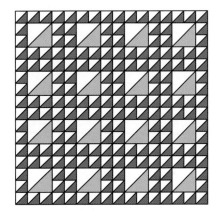

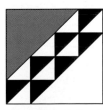

Woodland Path
Page 121

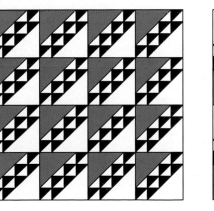

Designing Your Own Quilt

Making One Block Look Like Two

Even if you're using only one block in a side-by-side setting, you can create the illusion of a more elaborate quilt design. Make several photocopies of the block's line drawing from "The Block Library," then vary the placement of the light, medium, and dark values on each copy. I usually shade four or five samples, then arrange and rearrange them until I find two that make a statement when set side by side.

The four blocks shown here were each shaded two different ways. When set side by side, the two Free Trade blocks create an on-point star with Four Patch centers. Even though the Grecian Square blocks interact to make quarter-square triangles, it's the reversed values of the blocks themselves that make such an impact! The Jack-in-the-Pulpit blocks show how much fun you can have by simply switching light, medium, and dark values. And the two shadings of the King's Crown block work together to create a design that appears to radiate from the center, lending diagonal movement to a straight setting.

Free Trade
Page 46

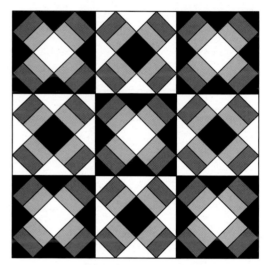

Grecian Square
Page 53

Jack-in-the-Pulpit
Page 58

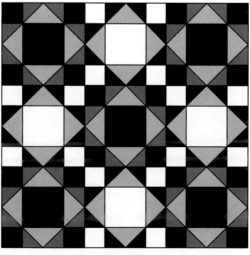

King's Crown
Page 66

Planning a Quilt's Size

Bed sizes are standardized, so it's easy to calculate the number of blocks you need for straight and diagonal settings. Since all the blocks in this book finish at 9 inches, take your desired quilt size (width and length) and divide each measurement by 9 to get the number of blocks across and down for a straight side-by-side setting. You may need to add borders to make your quilt fit perfectly.

For a diagonal setting, divide your desired quilt size (width and length) by 12.75 (the approximate diagonal measurement of a 9-inch block) to

□ Pieced block

Straight Side-by-Side

figure out the number of blocks in rows across and down. Then count the blocks that fit between the rows (called alternate blocks, even though they are often the same block pattern), and add both numbers.

The charts below offer guidelines for two quilt styles. *Comforter-size quilts* include a 12-inch drop (from the top of the mattress) on the sides and bottom of the quilt. *Coverlet-size quilts* include a 16-inch drop (from the top of the mattress) on the sides and bottom of the quilt and an extra 10 inches for a pillow tuck.

□ Pieced block   ▨ Alternate block

Diagonal Side-by-Side

Straight Side-by-Side Settings

	Comforter				Coverlet			
	Quilt Size (in inches)	Number of Blocks			Quilt Size (in inches)	Number of Blocks		
		Across	Down	Total		Across	Down	Total
Crib	30 × 45	3	5	15	36 × 54	4	6	24
Twin	63 × 87	7	9	63	71 × 101	7	11	77
Full	78 × 87	8	9	72	86 × 101	9	11	99
Queen	84 × 92	9	10	90	92 × 106	10	11	110
King	100 × 92	11	10	110	108 × 106	12	11	132

Diagonal Side-by-Side Settings

	Comforter					Coverlet				
	Quilt Size (in inches)	Number of Blocks				Quilt Size (in inches)	Number of Blocks			
		Across	Down	Alternate	Total		Across	Down	Alternate	Total
Crib	30 × 45	2	3	2	8	36 × 54	2	4	3	11
Twin	63 × 87	4	6	15	39	71 × 101	5	7	24	59
Full	78 × 87	6	6	25	61	86 × 101	6	7	30	72
Queen	84 × 92	6	7	30	72	92 × 106	7	8	42	98
King	100 × 92	7	7	36	85	108 × 106	8	8	49	113

Pairing Up Plain and Fancy

By simply alternating two different blocks, you can create interest and excitement in your quilt—without having to work too hard! Pairing a "plain" block with a "fancy" block is a sure-fire method for success. First, choose a fancy block for your quilt. Your fancy block should be complex, colorful, and the attention-getter, like the lead role in a play. Then, choose a plain block that enhances the fancy one without upstaging it, just as a supporting actor would. Plain blocks are usually very simple in both design and coloration and can be used to create an overall pattern that ties the blocks together. The plain blocks shown here are super-simple and can be paired easily with many of the fancier blocks in "The Block Library."

When you're designing two-block quilts, draw the plain and fancy blocks together on graph paper in a 4 × 4 setting (4 rows of 4 blocks each) to get an idea of what the quilt design will look like. Use a pencil to add light, medium, and dark values. If you disregard the block boundaries and seam lines when shading the blocks, you're apt to discover new, more dominant shapes and patterns.

Art Square
Page 4

Chain of Squares
Page 20

Cross-Country
Page 25

Crossroads to Jericho
Page 26

Double Four Patch
Page 30

Log Cabin with a Chain
Page 69

Puss in the Corner
Page 85

Road Home
Page 91

Shoofly
Page 98

Square within a Square
Page 103

Stepping Stones
Page 107

Woodland Path
Page 121

Plain Blocks that Enhance Fancy Ones

Woodland Path and Sawtooth Star

One strategy for choosing plain and fancy quilt blocks is to use two blocks that are built on the same grid. Because the piecing grid is the same, the seam lines in the blocks will match and will create a satisfying allover quilt design. Both the plain Woodland Path block (page 121) and fancy Sawtooth Star (page 96) blocks are based on 16-patch grids and make a terrific two-block pairing.

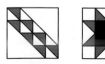

Woodland Path
Page 121

Sawtooth Star
Page 96

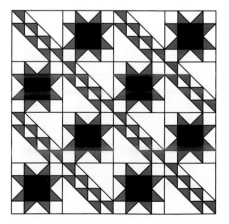

Log Cabin with a Chain and Quail's Nest

You can experiment with plain and fancy blocks by making more than one version of your fancy choice. The backgrounds of the fancier Quail's Nest (page 86) block are shaded in both light and dark values to match the natural diagonal flow of the plainer Log Cabin with a Chain (page 69) block. You actually make three blocks, one plain and two fancy, and the effect is stunning.

Log Cabin with a Chain
Page 69

Quail's Nest
Page 86

Art Square and Star Puzzle

The shading of the blocks is what gives the two-block quilt its character. Once you've done a line drawing of your layout, see if there are secondary patterns you can highlight. Here the interaction of the triangles in the plain Art Square (page 4) and fancy Star Puzzle (page 104) blocks leaves you guessing where the block seam lines are, creating a puzzle for the eyes.

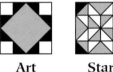

Art Square
Page 4

Star Puzzle
Page 104

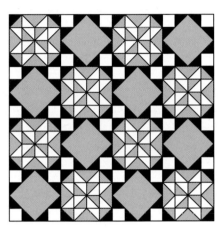

Cross-Country and By Chance

One of my favorite plain blocks is Cross-Country (page 25) because the long strip on the outside edge allows you to pair it with a variety of fancy blocks, including By Chance (page 13), without the worry of matching the seams. Even though these blocks are laid out in an easy side-by-side set, the strong double-diagonal lines of the plain Cross-Country block create an intricate-looking quilt.

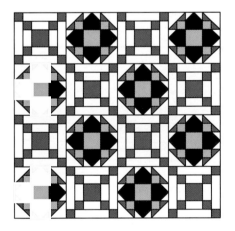

Cross-Country
Page 25

By Chance
Page 13

Square within a Square and Rising Star

Try pairing plain and fancy blocks containing the same element, even though the elements are different sizes. The outer star points in the fancy Rising Star block (page 90) are mimicked at twice the size in the plain Square within a Square block (page 103) and provide a unifying theme. In this alternating-block set, the plain and fancy blocks interact to create a secondary star pattern.

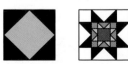

Square within a Square
Page 103

Rising Star
Page 90

Adding Lattice and Cornerstones

When you're laying out your quilt, try adding lattice and cornerstones between blocks and rows. Lattice (also called sashing) can liven up humble blocks and keep busy blocks in check. You can use lattice—solid or pieced—to enlarge a quilt without piecing extra blocks.

When deciding how wide to make lattice strips, use the block measurements for propor-tion. Lattice works best when its width echoes a measurement found in the block. If your block contains 3-inch-wide patches, consider using 3-inch-wide lattice for a bold look, or $1\frac{1}{2}$-inch-wide lattice (half of the 3-inch-wide measure-ment) for a more delicate look. If the block you've chosen features $2\frac{1}{4}$-inch-wide patches, make your lattice $2\frac{1}{4}$ or $4\frac{1}{2}$ inches wide.

Quick-and-Easy Ideas

While it's fun to design elaborate settings, you may find that many quilts look terrific with simple lattice strips and cornerstones. These four examples feature the Ohio Trail (page 78) block and showcase easy ways to add an eye-catching design element to a straight setting.

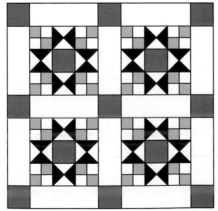

Try continuous lattice in the same width as the small squares in your favorite block.

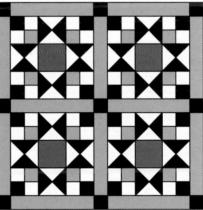

You could also feature simple corner-stones; make them the same size as the small squares in the block.

For a different look, try lattice and cornerstones that echo the size of the largest square in the block.

Take the design a step further by featuring cornerstones that repeat the Four Patches found in the block.

Creative and Rewarding Ideas

Take lattice and cornerstones a step further—explore the possibilities of different shadings, pieced lattices, and diagonal sets. These quilt settings feature Dolley Madison's Star (page 28) and highlight just a sampling of the choices you have when you're deciding on a setting.

 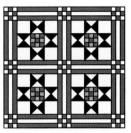

In this successful quilt design, the pieced triple lattice and cornerstones duplicate the Nine Patch found in the featured Dolley Madison's Star block (page 28). But that's just the beginning! Just by switching the

lights, mediums, and darks in the lattice and cornerstones, you can create a variety of looks, from simple to dramatic. Try experimenting with value whenever you add setting elements to your quilt.

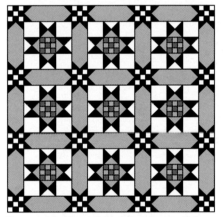

Repeat the easy Nine Patch motif from the center of Dolley Madison's Star (page 28) in the cornerstones, then add pieced lattice strips to create a secondary design element.

Choose the same fabric for lattice strips and block backgrounds, and the blocks will appear to "float" in the setting. The diagonal set and pieced lattice strips are stellar!

Use a portion of another block—in this case, the center section of Chain of Squares (page 20)—for lattice strips, then carefully plan your shading to highlight the star-shaped cornerstones.

Take the same blocks, lattice strips, and cornerstones, and set them on the diagonal for added drama. The light-value setting triangles create a frame around the blocks.

Coloring Your Setting Pieces

The color and value of the fabric you pick for your setting pieces has a huge effect on the look of the quilt. Try different options for your set, laying your blocks on light, medium, or dark yardage. Or cut setting squares or setting triangles from different-value fabrics.

You can set simple light-and-dark Ducks and Ducklings blocks (page 34) in a diagonal setting by pairing them with light setting squares. If you use setting squares that contrast with the block backgrounds, you'll get a checkerboard effect. Change the value of the setting pieces from the interior of the quilt to the outer edges to create a frame for the blocks. Or you can make the outer blocks recede into the border when you use the same dark-value fabric for the block backgrounds and the setting triangles.

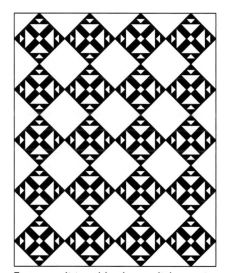

For a traditional look, use light setting squares and triangles when you set blocks diagonally.

Create a checkerboard effect by using a contrasting fabric for the setting squares and block backgrounds.

Frame your quilt by simply featuring a different value fabric for the setting triangles around the outer edge.

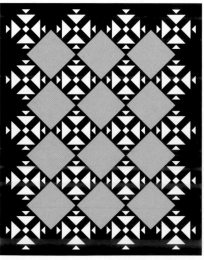

Make your blocks recede by using the same dark-value fabric for the block backgrounds and the setting triangles.

Repeating Block Elements in the Setting

When designing a quilt, I often repeat an element from one of the blocks in the lattice or borders. This brings a sense of continuity and balance to the overall design and makes each area of the quilt relate to the other areas. When repeating an element, I feature it at the same size and orientation as it is in the block to make the measurements compatible and the matching and fitting easy.

You can repeat block elements in many different ways. Use a triangle from a block to create a Dogtooth or Sawtooth border. Feature a block's Pinwheel center as a cornerstone. Or repeat one row of the block as lattice. You could also mimic an element without duplicating it exactly: Use half-blocks for the side setting triangles in a diagonally set quilt. Remember that each patch in a block is a setting piece waiting to happen!

Duplicate a shape (like a triangle) from a block such as Rosebud (page 94), and use it in the border in the same size and orientation for a perfect fit.

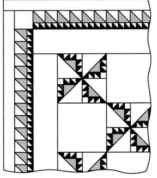

Choose a block like Kansas Troubles (page 63), and repeat two of its triangle shapes, a small one and a large one, for a pieced double border.

You can also repeat an entire row of a block for lattice. The middle row of this Missouri Star block (page 73) has great visual appeal as a setting element.

Try featuring the Pinwheel center of a block like Star Puzzle (page 104) as lattice corner-stones. This diagonal set also contains half-blocks along the edges.

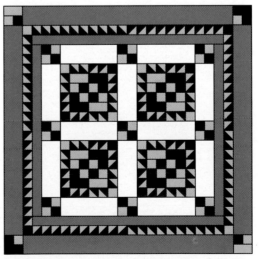

Block shapes can be repeated successfully in both cornerstones and borders. Here, the block One More Block (page 79) provides a variety of interesting setting elements.

Using Blocks as Borders

I love pieced borders because they add interest to a quilt and provide a wonderful finishing touch for the blocks. But don't think that borders always need to be pieced in strips or be long, plain strips of fabric. They don't! You can create a border by simply using pieced blocks.

Try using 9-inch blocks as borders when using 9-inch blocks in the interior because it's easy to fit them around the perimeter of the quilt. These same-size "border" blocks elimi-

nate the need for mathematical calculations (and the work involved in fitting a pieced border) because they fit right alongside other blocks. My favorite border blocks are ones that create linear movement. By rotating the blocks or setting them on point, I can create many interesting effects. The six blocks shown here are great choices for borders, but don't limit yourself to just these six. Experiment with other blocks to create unique border designs.

Chain of Squares
Page 20

Flying Geese
Page 41

Log Cabin with a Chain
Page 69

Lost Ship
Page 70

Ocean Waves
Page 76

Woodland Path
Page 121

Favorite Border Blocks

Border Block Ideas

When choosing a border block for your quilt, consider featuring one that contains the same elements found in the interior blocks, or look for a border block that complements the interior

blocks without echoing the shapes exactly. You can even repeat interior blocks in the border, changing the values and colors to give the perimeter a totally different look.

Use a block like Lost Ship (page 70) around the quilt's center to achieve a distinctive perimeter design without adding traditional borders. Notice how the orientation of the border blocks creates a Flying Geese unit in the center of each side as a bonus visual element.

With careful planning of light, medium, and dark values, you can feature the Cross-Country block (page 25) as a border block. This diagonal set turns the blocks on point so the chains of squares in the blocks connect to create an appealing continuous border.

Create a Border Sampler

It's exciting to discover the perfect border block, but did you realize that all blocks are perfect border blocks when you create a border sampler? Samplers are exciting, so start by piecing 24 of your favorite 9-inch blocks from "The Block Library." Set them end-to-end around a center panel. This large panel is designed to showcase a large-scale print, elaborate quilting skills, or both.

A sampler is just what the name implies—a sampling of different block patterns, values, and grids. Place blocks that are split diagonally in the corners of the sampler because they visually turn the corner. Here, I've used Grape Basket (page 52), Hovering Hawks (page 56), Log Cabin with a Chain (page 69), and Lost Ship (page 70). Be sure to place the Dogtooth borders on the design wall when you're experimenting with block placement. These pieced borders help to unify and contain the blocks in the sampler and often create interesting interactions in the setting.

This border sampler measures 69 × 87 inches. The cutting chart below lists the cutting dimensions for the border sampler shown, including the center panel, plain borders, and pieced Dogtooth borders. Refer to "The Block Library" for cutting and piecing information for the blocks.

Cutting							
First Cut		**Second Cut**			**Third Cut**		
Strip Width (in inches)	No. to Cut	Shape	Cut Size (in inches)	No. to Cut	Shape	Total Needed	
Light print							
Center panel	45½	1	▭	45½ × 27½	1	—	—
Side inner borders	2¾	3*	▭	2¾ × 45½	2	—	—
Top and bottom inner borders	2¾	2	▭	2¾ × 32	2	—	—
Inner and outer Dogtooth borders	5¾	4	■	5¾ × 5¾	24	⊠	96
Side outer borders	5¾	4*	▭	5¾ × 77	2	—	—
Top and bottom outer borders	5¾	4*	▭	5¾ × 69½	2	—	—
Medium print							
Inner and outer Dogtooth borders	5¾	2	■	5¾ × 5¾	12	⊠	48
Dark print							
Inner and outer Dogtooth borders	5¾	2	■	5¾ × 5¾	12	⊠	48

*If cutting strips on the crosswise grain, piece these strips together, then cut to the size listed under "Second Cut." If cutting strips on the lengthwise grain, cut them to the length specified.

Mix-and-Match Projects

This chapter is full of inspiring, do-it-yourself projects that let you mix and match blocks and settings to create a quilt design with your signature on it. Each quilt featured here is really a quilt template, or shell, that you can use as a framework for designing your own quilt.

Because this book is designed to let you make choices, the block information and setting information are presented separately in each project, allowing you to navigate easily through a project if you've decided to use different blocks than those shown in the quilt photograph.

Pages at a Glance

Color Photograph

Projects are shown in color. Small projects, like Joan's Quilt Bag, are photographed in room settings so you can see how fun it is to use these projects. Large quilts are shown flat so you can identify the blocks and settings used.

Number of Pieced Blocks

This logo is your key to how many 9-inch blocks you'll need to make. Blocks used in the quilt setting (border blocks, for example), however, are not included in this count, so some projects may require you to piece additional setting blocks.

Choosing Blocks to Use

Look here for suggestions on choosing blocks that will work in this project, and learn why blocks work in different settings. You'll not only find numerous blocks to try, but you'll also learn the reasons behind the suggestions.

Setting Success

Here you'll discover the unique features of the quilt setting and its construction methods, plus a discussion of special elements—like pieced setting blocks—that add interest to the project.

Project Basics

Here are the nuts and bolts of each project—the finished project size, the number of blocks needed, and details about the setting pieces and borders.

Fabric and Supplies

These are the fabrics and supplies used in the project. Yardage is given separately for blocks and setting pieces, so substituting a different block is a snap. All yardage is based on 40-inch-wide fabric.

Cutting

In this section you'll find cutting information for the blocks and the setting pieces. All dimensions include a ¼-inch seam allowance, and all strips are cut on the crosswise grain, unless otherwise indicated.

Assembly Diagram

Here you'll find the assembly sequence for joining the blocks, setting pieces, and borders. The block rows and borders are exploded from the diagram to help you visualize the various units used in the quilt.

Idea Box

These tips and techniques highlight quiltmaking shortcuts, setting suggestions, and special ways to give the quilt project personal style.

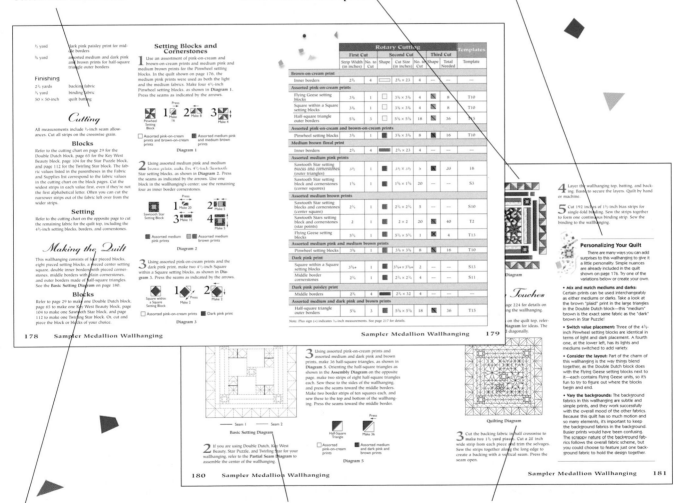

Making the Quilt

These are start-to-finish directions and detailed illustrations so you can successfully complete the project. If you're new to quiltmaking, refer to "Quiltmaking Basics" on page 216 for details on basic construction methods.

Basic Setting Diagram

This diagram is shown with plain squares so you can easily imagine what other blocks might look like in this setting. To road test your favorite blocks in the quilt design, photocopy the black-and-white line drawings from "The Block Library," enlarging or reducing them to fit the plain squares.

Quilting Diagram

This illustration shows how the quilt in the photograph was quilted. The quilting designs shown in this diagram were designed specifically to fit all of the 9-inch blocks used in the book, and they can be used interchangeably from project to project.

Patchwork Pillows

— Setting Success —

This setting is very simple, so quilters wanting a quick project should take notice. Start by piecing your favorite 9-inch block, then add wide, straight borders to create a frame that's really easy to sew. Make the pillow smaller or larger in a snap— just add or subtract borders to change the finished size.

1 choosing **blocks** to use

pieced block

The pillows shown feature the Cake Stand (page 14) and Road Home (page 91) blocks. Almost any block pattern in this book can be used for these pillows. Choose simple blocks with large pieces to balance the wide, plain borders. Air Castle, Judy's Star, Nonsense, or Sawtooth Star would be good choices. Use a dramatic large-scale print for the borders to give the pillow style.

 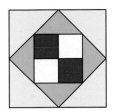

Cake Stand   **Road Home**

Project Basics

Finished Pillow: 16 inches square
Finished Block: 9 inches
Number of Blocks: 1 per pillow
Setting Highlights: Straight set and simple border

Fabric and Supplies

Cake Stand Block

¼ yard	light gold print (light)
¼ yard	medium gold print (medium)
⅛ yard	dark brown print (dark 1)
¼ yard	dark rust print (dark 2)

Road Home Block

⅛ yard	cream print (light 1)
¼ yard	assorted light yellow prints (light 2)
¼ yard	medium gold plaid (medium)
⅛ yard	dark brown print (dark)

Setting (for each pillow)

| ¼ yard | large-scale gold floral for inner borders |
| ¼ yard | dark brown or green print for outer borders |

Finishing (for each pillow)

18-inch square	quilt batting
⅝ yard	muslin for lining
2 yards	¼-inch-diameter covered upholstery piping
⅝ yard	fabric for pillow back
16-inch	square pillow form

Cutting

All measurements include ¼-inch seam allowances. Cut all strips on the crosswise grain.

Blocks

Refer to the cutting chart on page 14 for the Cake Stand block or page 91 for the Road Home block. The fabric values listed in the parentheses in the Fabric and Supplies list correspond to the fabric values in the cutting chart on the block page. Cut the widest strips in each value first, even if they're not the first alphabetical letter. Often you can cut the narrower strips out of the fabric left over from the wider strips.

Setting

Refer to the cutting chart on page 144 to cut the remaining fabric for the pillow borders and back.

Making the Pillow

The pillow front consists of one pieced block and simple borders.

Blocks

Refer to page 14 to make one Cake Stand block or page 91 to make one Road Home block. Or, cut and piece the block of your choice.

Borders

1 Referring to the **Borders Diagram** on page 144, sew one inner border A to the top and bottom of the block, pressing the seams toward the border. Sew one inner border B to each side of the block, pressing the seams toward the borders.

2 Sew borders C and D to the block in the same manner.

Cutting					
	First Cut		**Second Cut**		
	Strip Width (in inches)	No. to Cut	Shape	Cut Size (in inches)	No. to Cut
Gold floral					
Inner border A	2½	1	▭	2½ × 9½	2
Inner border B	2½	1	▭	2½ × 13½	2
Dark brown or green print					
Outer border C	2	1	▭	2 × 13½	2
Outer border D	2	1	▭	2 × 16½	2
Muslin					
Lining	18	1	▢	18 × 18	2

Borders Diagram

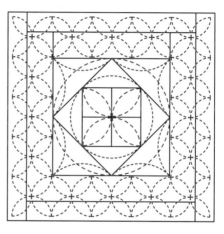

Road Home Quilting Diagram

Finishing Touches

1 Read "Finishing" on page 224 for details on quilting the pillow.

2 Mark quilting designs, referring to **Cake Stand Quilting Diagram** and **Road Home Quilting Diagram**.

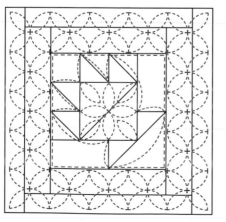

Cake Stand Quilting Diagram

3 Layer the pillow-front, batting, and one muslin lining piece to create a quilt sandwich. Baste to secure the layers. Quilt by hand or machine. Do not trim the batting and lining yet. You will trim any excess fabric after the pillow is assembled.

4 Using a zipper foot and a ¼-inch seam allowance, sew the piping to the right side of the pillow-front as follows: Place one end of the piping in the middle of one side of the pillow-front, matching raw edges of the pillow-front fabric and the piping. If upholstery piping is used, work with the chain-stitched side up. Backtack 1 inch from the piping end, then continue sewing on top of the piping stitches to the first corner. At each corner, clip the seam allowance on the piping to create a graceful curve, then continue sewing around the corner, as shown in **Diagram 1** on the opposite page.

Wendy's Gift Bags

— Setting Success —

Start a family tradition of recycled gift wrapping with the prettiest packaging possible. These gift bags feature a single quilt block and easy-to-cut rectangular pieces, making assembly a snap. The large gift bag is ideal for a shirt box, and the medium gift bag holds a square box perfectly. You can adapt this bag to fit any size gift just by changing the size of the center panels and vertical strips.

1 choosing **blocks** to use

pieced block These gift bags feature the Kansas Troubles (page 63) and Twinkling Star (page 111) blocks. Refer to the **Gift Bag Diagram** on page 150 to see the setting used in the gift bags. Blocks with an airy feel work best in this setting, so your best bet is to feature blocks that have action in the center and an open look around the edges. Any Star block would look great, especially if you're making the bag for a holiday gift. Try Blazing Star, Eddystone Light, Flying Star, or Italian Tile. The Friendship block would also add a special touch to the handmade gift bag; use a permanent pen to add a heartfelt sentiment to the center rectangle to personalize the gift. Or, use Double X, Gentleman's Fancy, Log Cabin with a Chain, or Nonsense for a handsome gift bag that's just perfect for a man on your gift list. Try matching the names of the blocks with the people receiving the gifts: Use Cat's Cradle for a cat lover; Grandmother's Pride or Grandmother's Favorite for Grandma; Courthouse Steps for a lawyer; Darting Minnows for a fisherman; Rosebud for a gardener; Woodland Path for a hiker; Ocean Waves or Beacon Lights for a sailor; or Free Trade for a businessman.

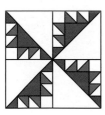 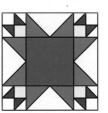

Kansas Troubles   **Twinkling Star**

Project Basics

Finished Size: 16 × 25½ inches (large) or
   16 × 20¼ inches (medium)
Finished Block: 9 inches
Number of Blocks: 1 per bag
Setting Highlights: One block set straight with lattice strips and side panels, an easy lining, and ribbon closure

Fabric and Supplies

Kansas Troubles Block

¼ yard	light cream print (light)
⅛ yard	medium red print (medium)
⅛ yard	dark green print (dark)

Twinkling Star Block

¼ yard	very light off-white print (light 1)
⅛ yard	off-white print (light 2)
⅛ yard	medium red print (medium)
⅛ yard	dark green print (dark 1)
¼ yard	very dark green print (dark 2)

Setting (for the large gift bag)

⅛ yard	medium red print 1
¼ yard	medium red print 2
⅜ yard	dark green print 1
¼ yard	dark green print 2

Setting (for the medium gift bag)

⅛ yard	medium green print 1
¼ yard	medium green print 2
⅜ yard	dark red print 1
¼ yard	dark red print 2

Finishing (for each bag)

1 yard	lining fabric
1 yard	¾-inch-wide grosgrain ribbon

Cutting

All measurements include ¼-inch seam allowances. Cut all strips on the crosswise grain.

Blocks

Refer to the cutting chart on page 63 for the Kansas Troubles block or page 111 for the Twinkling Star block. The fabric values listed in the parentheses in the Fabric and Supplies list

| | Cutting | | | | |
| | **First Cut** | | **Second Cut** | | |
	Strip Width (in inches)	No. to Cut	Shape	Cut Size (in inches)	No. to Cut
Large Gift Bag					
Medium red print 1					
Lattice strip A	2	1	▬	$2 \times 9\frac{1}{2}$	2
Medium red print 2					
Lattice strip D	2	3*	▬	$2 \times 51\frac{1}{2}$	2
Dark green print 1					
Center panel B	$9\frac{1}{2}$	1	▬	$9\frac{1}{2} \times 11\frac{3}{4}$	1
Center panel C	$9\frac{1}{2}$†	1	▬	$9\frac{1}{2} \times 28\frac{1}{4}$	1
Dark green print 2					
Side panel E	$2\frac{1}{2}$	3*	▬	$2\frac{1}{2} \times 51\frac{1}{2}$	2
Lining fabric					
Lining	$16\frac{1}{2}$	2	▭	$16\frac{1}{2} \times 26$	2
Medium Gift Bag					
Medium green print 1					
Lattice strip F	2	1	▬	$2 \times 9\frac{1}{2}$	2
Medium green print 2					
Lattice strip I	2	3‡	▭	2×41	2
Dark red print 1					
Center panel G	$9\frac{1}{2}$	1	▬	$9\frac{1}{2} \times 7\frac{1}{2}$	1
Center panel H	$9\frac{1}{2}$†	1	▬	$9\frac{1}{2} \times 22$	1
Dark red print 2					
Side panel J	$2\frac{1}{2}$	3‡	▬	$2\frac{1}{2} \times 41$	2
Lining fabric					
Lining	$16\frac{1}{2}$	2	▭	$16\frac{1}{2} \times 20\frac{3}{4}$	2

*Piece these strips together, then cut two $51\frac{1}{2}$-inch-long pieces.

†Cut this strip from the remaining width of fabric after cutting the Center Panel B or G.

‡Piece these strips together, then cut two 41-inch-long pieces.

correspond to the fabric values in the cutting chart on the block pages.

Setting

Refer to the cutting chart above to cut the remaining fabric for the gift bag.

Making the Gift Bag

Each gift bag features one pieced block, wide center panels, lattice strips, and side panels. The bag is lined, then finished with a ribbon tie. See the **Gift Bag Diagram** on page 150.

Wendy's Gift Bags 149

Blocks

Refer to page 63 to make one Kansas Troubles block for the large gift bag or page 111 to make one Twinkling Star block for the medium gift bag. Or, cut and piece the block or blocks of your choice.

Assembly

1 If you have selected a block other than Kansas Troubles or Twinkling Star for the large or medium gift bag, refer to the **Gift Bag Diagram** for the layout of the lattice strips and center and side panels. See Steps 2 through 8 to assemble the gift bag.

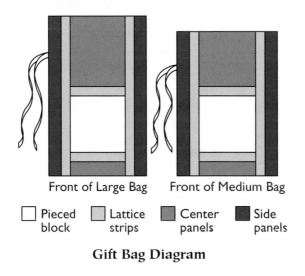

Front of Large Bag   Front of Medium Bag

☐ Pieced   ☐ Lattice   ☐ Center   ☐ Side
  block   strips   panels   panels

Gift Bag Diagram

> ## Accurate and Easy
>
> If you find it necessary to sew over pins when piecing blocks, sew slowly to reduce your chances of hitting the pins with your needle. And use thin pins, like silk pins, because they won't distort seam allowances.

2 If you are using Kansas Troubles for the large gift bag or Twinkling Star for the medium gift bag, refer to the **Assembly Diagram** to assemble the bag. For the large gift bag, sew lattice strip A to the top and bottom of the pieced block. Press the seams toward the lattice strips. For the medium gift bag, sew lattice strip F to the top and bottom of the pieced block. Press the seams toward the lattice strips.

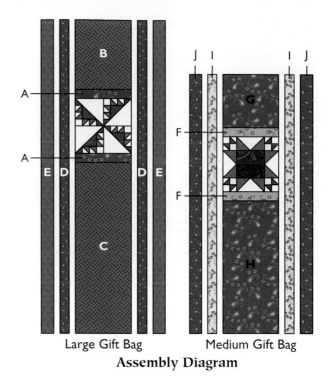

Large Gift Bag   Medium Gift Bag
Assembly Diagram

3 For the large gift bag, sew center panel B to the top of the pieced center panel and center panel C to the bottom to complete the pieced center panel. See the **Assembly Diagram**, above. Press the seams toward panels B and C. For the medium gift bag, sew center panel G to the top of the pieced center panel and center panel H to the bottom to complete the pieced center panel, as shown in the diagram. Press the seams toward panels G and H.

4 For the large gift bag, sew one lattice strip D to each side of the pieced center panel, as shown in the the **Assembly Diagram**, above. Press the seams toward D. Repeat for side panel E, pressing the seams toward D. For the medium gift bag, sew one lattice strip I to the sides of the pieced center panel. Press the seams toward I. Repeat for side panel J, pressing the seams toward I.

5 Fold the gift bag in half with right sides together so the fold is at the bottom of the bag. Sew along both side edges using a ¼-inch seam allowance. Leave the top edge open. Do not turn right side out.

6 For the lining, place two lining pieces with right sides together, and sew around three sides using a ¼-inch seam allowance, as shown in the **Lining Diagram** on the opposite page. Leave the top edge open. Turn the lining right side out.

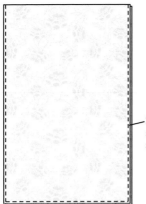

Sew along three sides using a ¼" seam allowance

Lining Diagram

Finishing Touches

Fold the ribbon in half. Place the ribbon fold on a side seam about one-quarter of the way down the gift bag. Working from the outside of the gift bag, sew the ribbon to the bag, using a very small stitch length and stitching in the ditch, as shown in the **Ribbon Diagram**. Cut the ribbon ends on the diagonal.

Place the ribbon on a side seam and sew it to the bag, stitching in the ditch

7 Insert the lining inside the gift bag, then sew the top edges together using a ¼-inch seam allowance. Leave a 3- to 4-inch opening.

8 Turn the gift bag right side out, tucking the lining inside. Topstitch ⅛ inch from the top edge.

Ribbon Diagram

Making a Small Gift Bag

This small gift bag is just the right size for a CD. It features the 4½-inch center of the Rising Star block (page 90) and is constructed in the same manner as the large and medium gift bags.

First, choose a block that has an interesting 4½-inch pieced center. Good choices include Double Dutch, Flying X, Free Trade, Rising Star, and Variable Star. Turn to the page where your chosen block is featured, then cut and piece the patches for just the block center.

For the bag, you will need about ⅜ yard total of assorted red print fabric and ⅜ yard of lining fabric. You'll also need a 1-yard length of ⅜-inch-wide grosgrain ribbon. Cut one 5 × 6½-inch piece for center panel A, one 5 × 13½-inch piece for center panel B, and two 2½ × 24-inch strips for side panel C. Cut a 9 × 24½-inch piece for the lining.

Referring to the **Small Gift Bag Assembly Diagram,** sew center panel A to the top of the block and center panel B to the bottom of the block. Press the

seams toward the panels. Sew one side panel C to each side of the center panel, then press the seams toward the lattice strips.

Follow Steps 5 through 8 on the opposite page and above to finish and line the small gift bag. Sew the ribbon to the bag about 3 inches from the top edge.

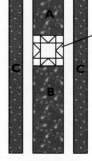

Use any 4½" block center here

Small Gift Bag Assembly Diagram

Joan's Quilt Bag

— Setting Success —

This stylish quilt storage bag features two blocks set on point, setting triangles, and simple lattice strips, all extra-fancy touches for a very practical storage bag. The quick lining, easy-to-sew casing, and drawstring closure work together to keep light and dust from damaging your precious quilts.

2 choosing **blocks** to use

pieced blocks

This quilt bag features the Weather Vane block shown on page 117. Refer to the **Basic Setting Diagram** on page 154 to see the setting used in the quilt bag. Naturally, the best block to use for this quilt bag would be the block used for the quilt you're storing inside! However, if you're making this as a gift or don't have a particular quilt in mind, try any number of blocks that look good set on point for the center panel. Choose Darting Minnows, Duck Paddle, Peaceful Hours, Scrap Basket, or Snowflake. To create a quilt bag that shows off your piecing skills, look for blocks that contain unusual shapes or a large number of patches, like Flying Star, Italian Tile, or Twirling Star. Or, if you've made a quilt as a gift, present it in a quilt bag that features the Friendship Block. Add a heartfelt sentiment to the center of the block for a special remembrance.

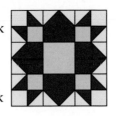

Weather Vane

Project Basics

Finished Size: 22 × 33 inches
Finished Block: 9 inches
Number of Blocks: 2
Setting Highlights: Two blocks set diagonally, framed with lattice strips and side panels, then made into a lined quilt bag with drawstring closure

Fabric and Supplies

Weather Vane Blocks

¼ yard	light cream print (light)
⅛ yard	medium maroon plaid or print (medium)
⅛ yard	dark maroon print (dark)

Setting

1 yard	light large-scale floral print for quilt bag
½ yard	medium maroon-on-cream print for setting triangles
⅜ yard	dark maroon print for lattice

Finishing

1⅜ yards	lining fabric
4 yards	twisted cord for drawstring
⅛ yard	maroon print for drawstring yo-yos

Cutting

All measurements include ¼-inch seam allowances. Cut all strips on the crosswise grain, unless otherwise indicated.

Blocks

Refer to the cutting chart on page 117 for the Weather Vane block. The fabric values listed in the parentheses in the Fabric and Supplies list correspond to the fabric values in the cutting chart on the block page. Cut the widest strips in each value first, even if they're not the first alphabetical letter. Often you can cut the narrower strips out of the fabric left over from the wider strips.

Setting

Refer to the cutting chart on page 154 to cut the remaining fabric for the quilt bag.

Making the Bag

The bag front consists of two pieced blocks, setting triangles, lattice strips, and side panels. The bag back features center and side panels and lattice strips. The bag is lined, then finished with a drawstring casing. See the **Basic Setting Diagram** on page 154.

Blocks

Refer to page 117 to make two Weather Vane blocks. Or, cut and piece the block or blocks of your choice.

Quilt Bag Front

1 If you have selected a block or blocks other than Weather Vane, refer to the **Basic Setting Diagram** on page 154 to assemble the pieced center panel. Sew the pieced blocks and setting triangles together in diagonal rows, pressing the seams toward the setting pieces. Sew the rows together.

				Cutting			
	First Cut		**Second Cut**			**Third Cut**	
	Strip Width (in inches)	No. to Cut	Shape	Cut Size (in inches)	No. to Cut	Shape	Total Needed
Light large-scale floral print							
Lattice strip A	2*	2	▭	2 × 13¼	2	—	—
Lattice strip B	3½*	4	▭	3½ × 32	4	—	—
Center back panel C	13¼*	1	▭	13¼ × 32	1	—	—
Casing strip	3½*	2	▭	3½ × 24¼	2	—	—
Medium maroon-on-cream print							
Side setting triangles	13⅞	1	☐	13⅞ × 13⅞	1	⊠	2
Corner setting triangles	7¼†	1	☐	7¼ × 7¼	2	◲	4
Dark maroon print							
Lattice strip D	2	1	▬	2 × 13¼	2	—	—
Lattice strip E	2	4	▬	2 × 32	4	—	—
Lining fabric							
Lining pieces	22¼	2	▭	22¼ × 32	2	—	—

*Cut from lengthwise grain.
†Cut this strip from the remaining width of fabric after cutting the side setting triangles.

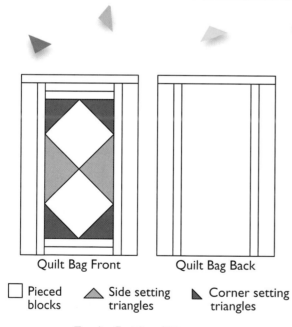

Pieced blocks
Side setting triangles
Corner setting triangles

Basic Setting Diagram

Pieced Center Assembly Diagram

2 If you are using Weather Vane blocks for your quilt bag, refer to the **Pieced Center Assembly Diagram**, and sew the blocks and setting triangles together in diagonal rows. Press the seams toward the setting pieces, and sew the rows together.

3 Sew lattice strip D to the top and bottom of the pieced center panel, as shown in the **Front Assembly Diagram** on the opposite page. Press the seams toward the lattice strips. Sew lattice strip A to the top and bottom of the pieced center panel, pressing the seams toward lattice strip D.

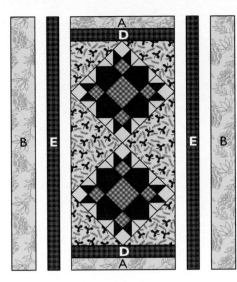

Front Assembly Diagram

4 Sew one lattice strip E to each side of the pieced center panel, as shown in the **Front Assembly Diagram**, above. Press the seams toward lattice strip E. Sew one lattice strip B to each side in the same manner. Press the seams toward lattice strip E.

Quilt Bag Back

1 Referring to the **Back Assembly Diagram**, sew one lattice strip E to each side of the center back panel C. Press the seams toward the lattice strips.

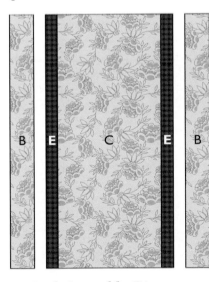

Back Assembly Diagram

2 Sew one lattice strip B to each side of the center panel, as shown in the **Back Assembly Diagram**, above. Press the seams toward lattice strip E.

Assembly

1 With the right sides of the quilt bag front and back together, sew around the sides and bottom of the bag using a ¼-inch seam allowance and leaving the top of the bag open. Turn the bag right side out.

2 For the lining, place two lining pieces with right sides together and sew around the sides and bottom in the same way you did in Step 1. Leave the lining top open. Do not turn right side out.

3 Insert the lining inside the quilt bag, matching side seams, corners, and the top edge. Set the bag aside.

4 On each casing strip, turn under ½ inch, then another ½ inch on each short end, and hem to create a finished edge. Hemmed strips should measure 22¼ inches long. On one long edge of each casing strip, press under ¼ inch, as shown in **Diagram 1**.

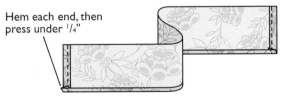

Hem each end, then press under ¼"

Diagram 1

5 With right sides together, match the unpressed edge of the casing strip to the top edge of the bag front and lining, then sew the strip to the bag using a ¼-inch seam allowance, as shown in **Diagram 2**. Fold the casing strip to the inside of the bag, stretching it slightly to extend beyond the side seam of the bag. Sewing from the outside of the bag, topstitch in the ditch where you added the casing strip, catching the folded-under edge of the casing as you sew, as shown in **Diagram 3** on page 156. Sew the casing strip to the bag back in the same manner.

Sew the casing strip to the bag front and front lining using ¼" seam allowance

¼"

Diagram 2

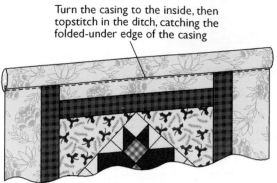

Turn the casing to the inside, then topstitch in the ditch, catching the folded-under edge of the casing

Diagram 3

6 To add extra strength to the area where the casing strips meet, tack together the bottom ³/₈ inch of the casing strips with a machine satin stitch (closely spaced zigzag stitch), working from the outside of the quilt bag. See **Diagram 4**.

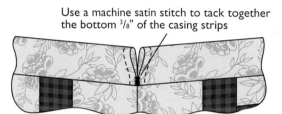

Use a machine satin stitch to tack together the bottom ³/₈" of the casing strips

Diagram 4

7 Make boxed corners by turning up 2 inches of each bottom corner along the side seam line. Tack down the corner by stitching in the ditch, as shown in **Diagram 5**.

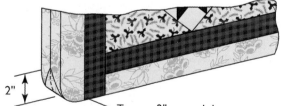

2"

Turn up 2" on each bottom corner, then tack down by stitching in the ditch

Diagram 5

Finishing Touches

1 Cut the twisted cord into two 2-yard lengths. Attach a large safety pin to the end of one length, then insert it into the front casing. Referring to **Diagram 6**, feed the cord through both the front and back casings, ending on the same side of the bag where you started. Starting on the other side of the bag, feed the remaining

cord through the front and back casing, exiting at the starting point. Tie each cord's ends together about 1 inch from the casing edge.

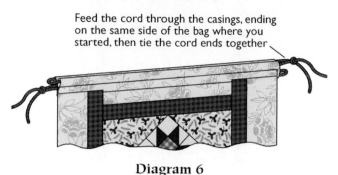

Feed the cord through the casings, ending on the same side of the bag where you started, then tie the cord ends together

Diagram 6

2 To make yo-yos for the drawstring ends, use the **Yo-Yo Template** to trace and cut four yo-yo circles. Turn under a ¼-inch hem all around each circle. Make running stitches by hand close to the fold, making the stitches about ¼ inch long and ¼ inch apart, as shown in **Diagram 7**. Pull up the gathering stitches, then tuck 1 inch of the twisted cord into the yo-yo. Pull the thread tightly, then sew through the yo-yo and the cord to secure.

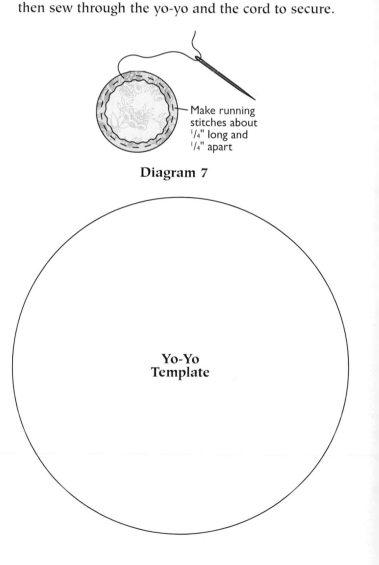

Make running stitches about ¼" long and ¼" apart

Diagram 7

Yo-Yo Template

Three-Block Table Runner

— *Setting Success* —

On-point blocks add a touch of flair to this quick-and-easy table runner. Ideal for beginners assembling their first diagonal setting, this project features three blocks and three simple rows—and only one seam to line up in each row!

Three-Block
Table Runner

3

pieced
blocks

choosing **blocks** to use

This table runner features the Air Castle (page 2), Ohio Star (page 77), and Turkey Tracks (page 110) blocks. Refer to the **Basic Setting Diagram** on the opposite page to see the setting used in the table runner. Blocks often look much different set diagonally than when they are set straight, so turn each block you've selected on point to see if the "new" look that emerges is one that fits with the mood you're trying to create. If you would like a table runner that features three of the same block, try Grape Basket or Scrap Basket. If you'd like to feature a sampler, look for blocks with good center interest and similar structure. The trio Peaceful Hours, Ringed Star, and Twisting Star are all based on the LeMoyne Star and have an octagon in the center, so they would look great together. Or, use a 16-patch star as your inspiration and choose Missouri Star, Rising Star, and Westland.

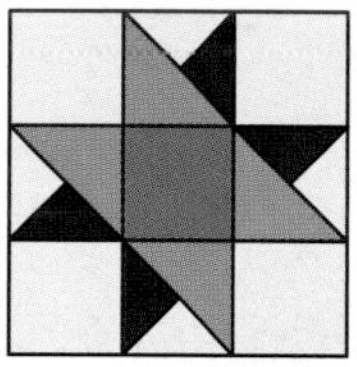

Air Castle    Ohio Star    Turkey Tracks

Project Basics

Finished Size: 21¼ × 46¾ inches
Finished Block: 9 inches
Number of Blocks: 3
Setting Highlights: Diagonal set with side and corner setting triangles and wide borders

Fabric and Supplies

Air Castle Block

¼ yard	light cream print (light)
⅛ yard	medium tan print (medium 1)
⅛ yard	medium green print (medium 2)
¼ yard	dark fuchsia print (dark)

Ohio Star Block

¼ yard	light cream print (light)
⅛ yard	medium tan print (medium)
¼ yard	dark fuchsia print (dark)

Turkey Tracks Block

⅛ yard	light cream print (light)
⅛ yard	medium tan print (medium 1)
⅛ yard	medium green print (medium 2)
⅛ yard	dark fuchsia print (dark)

Setting

| ½ yard | medium tan print for setting triangles |
| ½ yard | light cream print for borders |

Finishing

1½ yards	backing fabric
½ yard	binding fabric
25 × 50-inch	quilt batting

Cutting

All measurements include ¼-inch seam allowances. Cut all strips on the crosswise grain.

Blocks

Refer to the cutting charts on pages 2, 77, and 110 for the Air Castle, Ohio Star, and Turkey Tracks blocks. The fabric values listed in the parentheses in the Fabric and Supplies list correspond to the fabric values in the cutting charts on the block pages. Cut the widest strips in each value first, even if they're not the first alphabetical letter. Often you can cut the narrower strips out of the fabric left over from the wider strips.

Setting

Refer to the cutting chart on the opposite page to cut the setting triangles and borders for the table runner.

158   **Three-Block Table Runner**

Cutting						
First Cut		**Second Cut**			**Third Cut**	
Strip Width (in inches)	No. to Cut	Shape	Cut Size (in inches)	No. to Cut	Shape	Total Needed
Medium tan print						
Side setting triangles	$13\frac{7}{8}$	1	▩	$13\frac{7}{8} \times 13\frac{7}{8}$	1	⊠	4
Corner setting triangles	$7\frac{1}{4}^{*}$	1	▩	$7\frac{1}{4} \times 7\frac{1}{4}$	2	◨	4
Light cream print						
Side borders	$4\frac{1}{2}$	2	▭	$4\frac{1}{2} \times 38\frac{3}{4}$	2	—	—
Top and bottom borders	$4\frac{1}{2}$	1	▭	$4\frac{1}{2} \times 21\frac{1}{4}$	2	—	—

*Cut this strip from the remaining width of fabric after cutting the side setting triangles.

Making the Runner

This table runner consists of three pieced blocks and setting triangles. A border completes the quilt top. See the **Basic Setting Diagram** below.

Blocks

Refer to page 2 to make one Air Castle block, page 77 to make one Ohio Star block, and page 110 to make one Turkey Tracks block. Or, cut and piece the block or blocks of your choice.

Assembly

1 If you have selected a block or blocks other than Air Castle, Ohio Star, and Turkey Tracks, refer to the **Basic Setting Diagram** to assemble the table runner. Sew the pieced blocks and side and corner setting triangles together in diagonal rows, pressing the seams toward the setting pieces. Sew the rows together.

2 If you are using the Air Castle, Ohio Star, and Turkey Tracks blocks for your table topper, refer to the **Assembly Diagram** to lay out the rows. Sew the pieced blocks and side and corner setting triangles together in diagonal rows, pressing the seams toward the setting pieces. Sew the rows together.

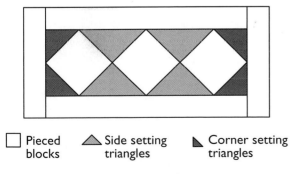

☐ Pieced blocks   △ Side setting triangles   ◣ Corner setting triangles

Basic Setting Diagram

Assembly Diagram

Borders

1 Referring to the **Assembly Diagram** on page 159, sew the side borders to the table runner. Press the seams toward the borders.

2 Sew the top and bottom borders to the table runner. Press the seams toward the borders.

Finishing Touches

1 Read "Finishing" on page 224 for details on assembling and finishing the table runner.

2 Mark quilting designs on the quilt top, referring to the **Quilting Diagram** for ideas.

Quilting Diagram

3 Cut a 25 × 50-inch piece for the backing. Layer the table runner top, batting, and backing. Baste to secure the layers. Quilt by hand or machine.

4 Cut 146 inches of 1½-inch bias strips for single-fold binding. Sew the strips together to form one continuous binding strip. Sew the binding to the table runner.

ACCURATE and Easy

This is a great first project if you've decided to try machine quilting. Use a size 80/12 needle if you are using cotton or cotton-covered polyester thread. If you plan to quilt in the ditch around the setting triangles and blocks, a walking (or even-feed) foot makes the process much easier. This specialty foot helps feed the layers of the quilt through the machine more evenly. If you would like to add curved lines of machine quilting, use an embroidery (or darning) foot. These are usually made of metal or plastic, and the bottom of the foot is an open circle that lets you view the sewing area. Use the embroidery foot with the feed dogs of the machine lowered or covered.

Four-Block Sampler

— Setting Success —

In this setting, the hard work's been done for you—all you need to add to the design is four terrific blocks. The center and corner setting blocks contain jumbo patches that create a secondary, yet serene, focal point. The triangles in the Sawtooth borders and cornerstones act as unifiers; they duplicate the shapes found in the setting blocks and can mimic triangles in blocks you've selected, as well.

4

pieced blocks

choosing **blocks** to use

This wallhanging features four star designs; Antique Star (page 3), Broken Star (page 12), Evening Star with Pinwheel (page 39), and LeMoyne Star (page 67) blocks. It also features pieced alternate squares for center and corner setting blocks that form a large Shoo Fly design. The directions for these blocks are given in this project. The larger design formed by the setting blocks ties the sampling of stars together. Refer to the **Basic Setting Diagram** on page 164 to see the setting used in the quilt.

This is a basic nine-block setting, and it presents all sorts of possibilities for combining two sets of blocks—four of one design and five of another. For instance, instead of four pieced design blocks and five setting blocks, as shown, the positions could be reversed and five pieced blocks and four alternate blocks could be used. See pages 132 and 133 for suggestions for two-block combinations.

Try five Eddystone Light blocks with four Cross-Country blocks, five Stepping Stones blocks with four Road Home blocks, or five Sawtooth Star blocks with four Star Tile blocks. If you want to duplicate the sampler feel of this setting, select four of your favorite blocks, then combine them with either Art Square or Candlelight—both are good alternate blocks.

Antique Star    Broken Star   Evening Star   LeMoyne Star
with Pinwheel

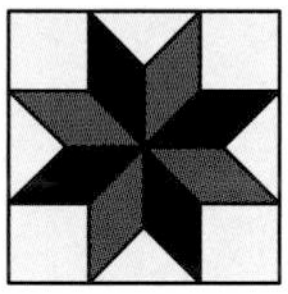

Project Basics

Finished Size: 41 × 41 inches
Finished Block: 9 inches
Number of Blocks: 4
Setting Highlights: Straight set with pieced setting
   blocks, inner Sawtooth borders, and wide outer
   borders with pieced cornerstones

Fabric and Supplies

Antique Star Block

¼ yard	black-on-white print (light)
⅛ yard	medium gray print 1 (medium 1)
¼ yard	medium gray print 2 (medium 2)
⅛ yard	black print (dark)

Broken Star Block

¼ yard	black-on-white print (light)
¼ yard	medium gray print (medium)
⅛ yard	black print (dark)

Evening Star with Pinwheel Block

¼ yard	black-on-white print (light)
⅛ yard	medium gray print (medium)
⅛ yard	black print (dark)

LeMoyne Star Block

¼ yard	black-on-white print (light)
⅛ yard	medium gray print (medium)
⅛ yard	black print (dark)

Setting

¾ yard	black-on-white print for setting blocks, Sawtooth borders, and cornerstones
⅞ yard	medium gray large-scale plaid for setting blocks and outer borders
¼ yard	medium gray houndstooth check for setting blocks
⅛ yard	medium gray print for cornerstones
½ yard	black print for Sawtooth borders, Flying Geese units, and cornerstones

Finishing

2½ yards	backing fabric
½ yard	binding fabric
45 × 45-inch	quilt batting

Cutting							
First Cut		**Second Cut**			**Third Cut**		
Strip Width (in inches)	No. to Cut	Shape	Cut Size (in inches)	No. to Cut	Shape	Total Needed	
Black-on-white print							
Setting blocks	$9\frac{7}{8}$	1	☐	$9\frac{7}{8} \times 9\frac{7}{8}$	2	◺	4
Sawtooth borders*	$3\frac{1}{8}$	3	☐	$3\frac{1}{8} \times 3\frac{1}{8}$	26	◺	52
Cornerstones	$3\frac{5}{8}$†	1	☐	$3\frac{5}{8} \times 3\frac{5}{8}$	4	—	—
Medium gray large-scale plaid							
Setting blocks	$5\frac{3}{8}$	1	☐	$5\frac{3}{8} \times 5\frac{3}{8}$	2	◺	4
Setting blocks	5‡	1	☐	5×5	4	—	—
Outer borders	5	4	▭	5×32	4	—	—
Medium gray houndstooth check							
Setting blocks	$5\frac{3}{8}$	1	☐	$5\frac{3}{8} \times 5\frac{3}{8}$	2	◺	4
Setting blocks	5‡	1	☐	5×5	2	—	—
Medium gray print							
Cornerstones	$3\frac{1}{8}$	1	■	$3\frac{1}{8} \times 3\frac{1}{8}$	2	◣	4
Black print							
Sawtooth borders*	$3\frac{1}{8}$	2	■	$3\frac{1}{8} \times 3\frac{1}{8}$	22	◥	44
Cornerstones	$3\frac{1}{8}$	1	■	$3\frac{1}{8} \times 3\frac{1}{8}$	6	◥	12
Flying Geese units	$5\frac{3}{4}$	1	■	$5\frac{3}{4} \times 5\frac{3}{4}$	1	✕	4

*See "Making Half-Square Triangles Using Bias-Strip Piecing" on page 175 for cutting information if you prefer to make half-square triangles using the bias strip piecing method.

†Cut this strip from the remaining width of fabric after cutting the patches for the setting block.

‡Cut this strip from the remaining width of fabric after cutting the patches for the setting blocks from the $5\frac{3}{8}$-inch strip.

Cutting

All measurements include ¼-inch seam allowance. Cut all strips across the crosswise grain.

Blocks

Refer to the cutting chart on page 3 for the Antique Star block, page 12 for the Broken Star block, page 39 for the Evening Star with Pinwheel block, and page 67 for the LeMoyne Star block. The fabric values listed in the parentheses in the Fabric and Supplies list correspond to the fabric values in the cutting chart on each of the block pages. Cut the widest strips in each value first, even if they're not the first alphabetical letter. Often you can cut the narrower strips out of the fabric left over from the wider strip.

Setting

Refer to the cutting chart above to cut the remaining fabric for the wallhanging.

Making the Quilt

This quilt consists of four pieced blocks, five pieced setting blocks, inner Sawtooth borders, and wide outer borders with pieced cornerstones. See the **Basic Setting Diagram** on page 164.

Blocks

Refer to page 3 to make one Antique Star block, page 12 to make one Broken Star block, page 39 to make one Evening Star with Pinwheel block, and page 67 to make one LeMoyne Star block. Or, cut and piece the block or blocks of your choice.

Setting Blocks

1 Make the center setting block, referring to **Diagram 1**. Press the seams as indicated by the arrows.

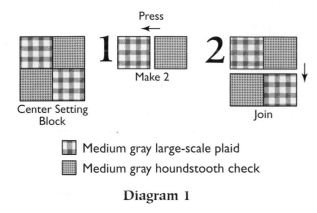

Press

1 Make 2

2 Join

Center Setting Block

■ Medium gray large-scale plaid
■ Medium gray houndstooth check

Diagram 1

2 Referring to **Diagram 2**, make two corner setting blocks in each fabric combination for a total of four corner setting blocks. Press the seams as indicated by the arrows.

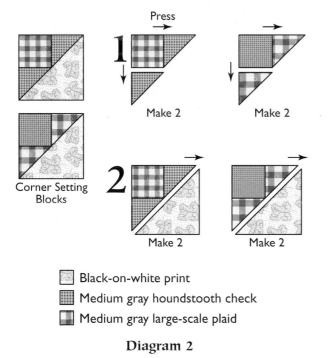

Press

1 Make 2   Make 2

Corner Setting Blocks

2 Make 2   Make 2

■ Black-on-white print
■ Medium gray houndstooth check
■ Medium gray large-scale plaid

Diagram 2

Assembly

1 If you have selected a block or blocks other than Antique Star, Broken Star, Evening Star with Pinwheel, or LeMoyne Star, refer to the **Basic Setting Diagram** to assemble the wallhanging. Sew the pieced blocks and pieced setting blocks together in horizontal rows, pressing the seams toward the setting blocks. Sew the rows together.

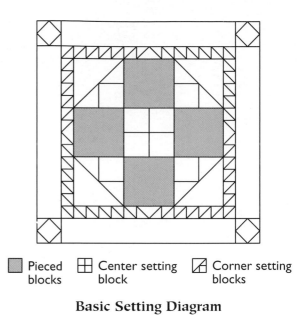

■ Pieced blocks   ⊞ Center setting block   ⧄ Corner setting blocks

Basic Setting Diagram

2 If you are using Antique Star, Broken Star, Evening Star with Pinwheel, and LeMoyne Star, refer to the **Assembly Diagram** and sew the blocks and setting blocks together in horizontal rows, pressing the seams toward the setting blocks. Sew the rows together.

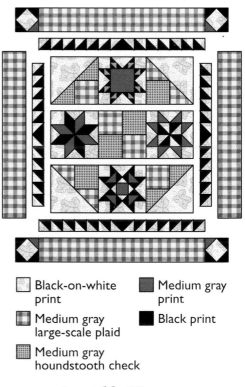

■ Black-on-white print   ■ Medium gray print
■ Medium gray large-scale plaid   ■ Black print
■ Medium gray houndstooth check

Assembly Diagram

Borders

1 For the Sawtooth borders, refer to **Diagram 3** on the opposite page to make 44 half-square

triangle units and four Flying Geese units. Press the seams as indicated by the arrows.

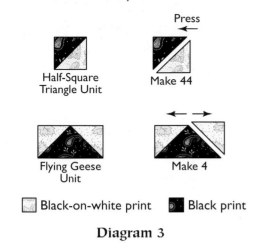

Press

Half-Square Triangle Unit

Make 44

Flying Geese Unit

Make 4

▨ Black-on-white print   ◼ Black print

Diagram 3

2 Sew the half-square triangle units and Flying Geese units into rows, as shown in **Diagram 4**. Each side border contains 10 half-square triangle units and 1 Flying Geese unit. The top and bottom borders each have 12 half-square triangle units and 1 Flying Geese unit. Referring to the **Assembly Diagram** on the opposite page, sew the side borders, then the top and bottom borders, to the wallhanging.

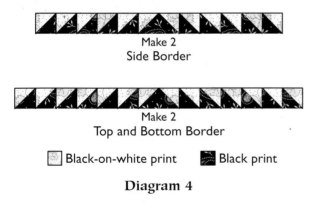

Make 2
Side Border

Make 2
Top and Bottom Border

▨ Black-on-white print   ▨ Black print

Diagram 4

3 Make four cornerstones, as shown in **Diagram 5**. Press the seams as indicated by the arrows.

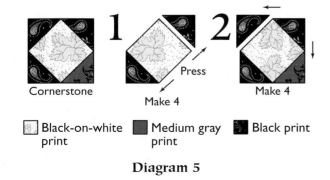

Cornerstone

1

Press

Make 4

2

Make 4

▨ Black-on-white print   ◼ Medium gray print   ◼ Black print

Diagram 5

4 Referring to the **Assembly Diagram** on the opposite page, sew one outer border to each side of the wallhanging. Sew one cornerstone to each end of the remaining two outer borders. Sew these to the top and bottom of the wallhanging.

Finishing Touches

1 Read "Finishing" on page 224 for details on assembling and finishing the wallhanging.

2 Mark quilting designs on the quilt top, referring to the **Quilting Diagram** for ideas. The pieced blocks were quilted with a continuous heart design. The block perimeters, Sawtooth borders, and cornerstones were also quilted in the ditch.

Quilting Diagram

3 Cut the backing fabric in half crosswise to make two 45 × 40-inch pieces. Cut one 23-inch-wide strip from each length and trim the selvages. Sew these lengths together along one long edge to create a backing with a vertical seam. Press the seam open.

4 Layer the wallhanging top, batting, and backing. Baste to secure the layers. Quilt by hand or machine.

5 Cut 174 inches of 1½-inch bias strips for single-fold binding. Sew the strips together to form one continuous binding strip. Sew the binding to the quilt top.

Tipped Pinwheel Wallhanging

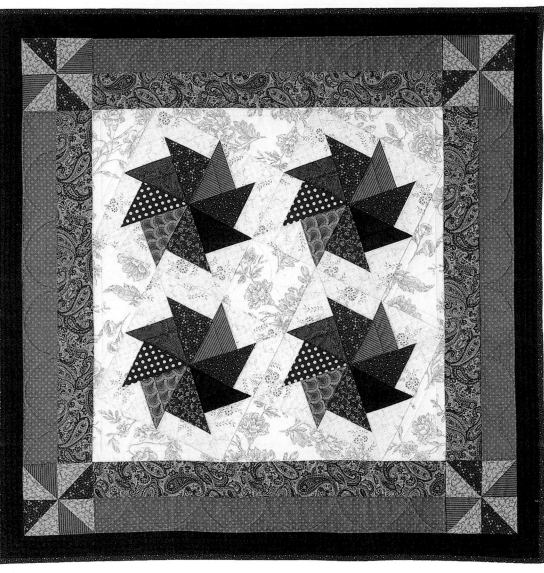

— Setting Success —

Add interest to a simple set by tipping quilt blocks at a gentle angle. The slight tip sets the blocks in motion and turns an ordinary layout into an extraordinary one. Use long triangles to "square" the outer edges and a simple square for the center. The pinwheel cornerstones and triple borders keep up the high energy level and create visual interest in this dynamic setting.

4 choosing blocks to use

pieced blocks

This wallhanging features the Pinwheel block (page 82). Refer to the **Basic Setting Diagram** on page 168 to see the setting used in the wallhanging. When picking a block to use in this setting, remember that the blocks aren't quite on point—they're just slightly tipped. So rotate the blocks you're considering, and see how they look. Good choices for a tipped set are symmetrical blocks with a definite center patch or pivot point, like Blazing Star, Flying Star, Kansas Troubles, LeMoyne Star, Twirling Star, and Whirligig. Also, keep the pieced cornerstones in mind when you're making your block choice. The spinning motion of the cornerstones can be used to choose a theme for your wallhanging. Other good choices would be the Missouri Star (use the full block in the tipped set, then repeat the 4½-inch Square-within-a-Square center of the same block for the cornerstones), or use the Broken Star, Sawtooth Star, or Spinning Star as the block in the tipped set and the 4½-inch Sawtooth Star center of the Rising Star block as the cornerstones. Or try four different blocks with a similar theme.

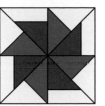

Pinwheel

Project Basics

Finished Size: 35½ × 35½ inches
Finished Block: 9 inches
Number of Blocks: 4
Setting Highlights: Tipped set with a setting square and setting triangles, double inner border with pinwheel cornerstones, and narrow outer borders

Fabric and Supplies

Pinwheel Blocks

⅜ yard	cream print (light)
¼ yard	assorted medium blue prints (medium)
¼ yard	assorted dark red prints (dark)

Setting

½ yard	cream print for setting square and triangles
½ yard	medium brown print 1 for inner border 1
½ yard	medium brown print 2 for inner border 2
⅛ yard	light brown print for pinwheel cornerstones
⅛ yard	medium blue print for cornerstones
⅛ yard	dark red print for cornerstones
⅜ yard	dark blue print for outer border

Finishing

1¼ yards	backing fabric
½ yard	binding fabric
40 × 40-inch	quilt batting

Cutting

All measurements include ¼-inch seam allowances. Cut all strips on the crosswise grain.

Blocks

Refer to the cutting chart on page 82 for the Pinwheel block. The fabric values listed in the parentheses in the Fabric and Supplies list correspond to the fabric values in the cutting chart on the block page. Cut the widest strips in each value first, even if they're not the first alphabetical letter. Often you can cut the narrower strips out of the fabric left over from the wider strips.

Setting

Refer to the cutting chart on page 168 to cut the remaining fabric for the wallhanging.

Making the Quilt

This wallhanging consists of four pieced blocks, a setting square, and setting triangles. The two inner borders have pinwheel cornerstones; narrow outer borders complete the wallhanging. See the **Basic Setting Diagram** on page 168.

Cutting						
	First Cut		**Second Cut**		**Third Cut**	
	Strip Width (in inches)	No. to Cut	Shape	Cut Size (in inches)	Shape	Total Needed
Cream print						
Setting square	5	1	▢	5 × 5	1	—	—
Setting triangles	4⅝*	2	See Diagrams 1 and 2		8	—	—
Medium brown print 1						
Inner border 1	2¾	4	▭	2¾ × 23	4	—	—
Medium brown print 2						
Inner border 2	2¾	4	▭	2¾ × 23	4	—	—
Light brown print						
Pinwheel cornerstones	3⅛	1	▢	3⅛ × 3⅛	8	◹	16
Medium blue print						
Pinwheel cornerstones	3⅛	1	▢	3⅛ × 3⅛	4	◸	8
Dark red print						
Pinwheel cornestones	3⅛	1	▪	3⅛ × 3⅛	4	◣	8
Dark blue print						
Top and bottom outer borders	2	2	▬	2 × 35½	2	—	—
Side outer borders	2	2	▬	2 × 32	2	—	—

*Cut one of these strips from the remaining width of fabric after cutting the setting square from the 5-inch strip.

Blocks

Refer to page 82 to make four Pinwheel blocks. Or, cut and piece the block or blocks of your choice.

Assembly

1 If you have selected a block or blocks other than Pinwheel, refer to the **Basic Setting Diagram** for the layout. Sew the pieced blocks and setting pieces together as described in Steps 2 through 5.

2 The setting triangles surrounding the pieced Pinwheel blocks will finish at two different sizes, but originally they are cut the same size to keep things as simple as possible when cutting. You will trim four of the setting triangles (the ones that form the corners) *after* you've sewn them to the pieced blocks because it's easier than cutting them at an odd angle before attaching them. To

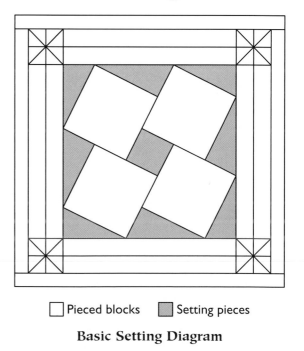

☐ Pieced blocks ▨ Setting pieces

Basic Setting Diagram

make an easy-to-use paper template for cutting the side and corner setting triangles, draw a 5⅛ × 10⅜-inch rectangle. Draw a diagonal line from top right to bottom left, as shown in **Diagram 1A**, and cut out the half-rectangle template. Tape the template to the underside of your ruler, as shown in **1B**. See page 220 for more on paper templates.

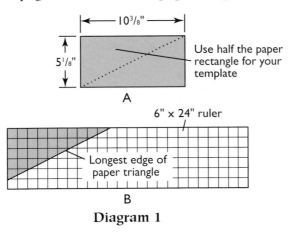

Use half the paper rectangle for your template

10⅜"

5⅛"

A

6" × 24" ruler

Longest edge of paper triangle

B

Diagram 1

3 To cut the setting triangles, place the ruler on one of the 4⅝-inch fabric strips, aligning the longest edge of the paper template with the edge of the fabric strip, as shown in **Diagram 2**. Cut the triangles from both sides of the strip, rotating the ruler for every other triangle. Cutting the triangles this way allows the stable straight grain to finish along the outside edge of the wallhanging's center. Cut a total of eight setting triangles.

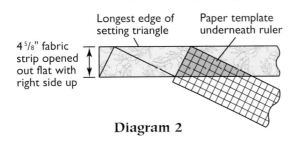

Longest edge of setting triangle

Paper template underneath ruler

4⅝" fabric strip opened out flat with right side up

Diagram 2

4 Trim the points of each setting triangle so that the longer of the two perpendicular legs (*not* the rectangle's longest edge) measures exactly 9½ inches, as shown in **Diagram 3**. By trimming the points of the setting triangles, you will be able to perfectly match up the setting triangles and the pieced blocks before sewing them together.

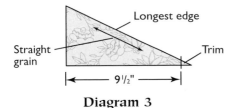

Longest edge

Straight grain

Trim

9½"

Diagram 3

5 Referring to **Diagram 4A**, sew triangles to two adjacent edges of each of the Pinwheel blocks. Be sure to orient the triangles exactly as shown in the diagram, with the longest edge away from the Pinwheel block and the shortest edge lined up evenly with the edge of the block. Seam allowances are shown in the diagram for clarity. Trim one triangle at a 90 degree angle, as shown in **4B**, leaving a ¼-inch seam allowance at the top of the block. This unit forms one-quarter of the center of the wallhanging, as shown in **4C**. Repeat for all four quarters of the wallhanging's center.

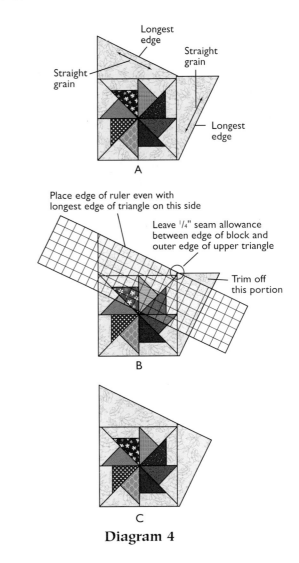

Longest edge

Straight grain

Straight grain

Longest edge

A

Place edge of ruler even with longest edge of triangle on this side

Leave ¼" seam allowance between edge of block and outer edge of upper triangle

Trim off this portion

B

C

Diagram 4

6 Lay out each quarter of the wallhanging's center and the setting square, as shown in **Diagram 5** on page 170. You will use two partial seams and three full seams to assemble the wallhanging's center. You will be sewing in numerical order as shown in the diagram. Partial seams are used in this wallhanging to avoid setting in pieces.

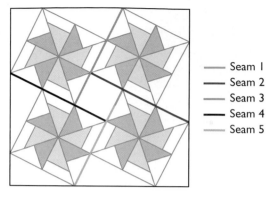

Diagram 5

Seam 1
Seam 2
Seam 3
Seam 4
Seam 5

7 To sew the partial seam that joins part of the Pinwheel block with part of the setting square (seam 1 in **Diagram 5**), begin sewing at the upper edge of the square, sew about halfway down the square's side, and backtack, as shown in the **Partial Seam Detail**.

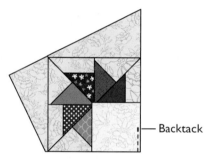

— Backtack

Partial Seam Detail

8 Sew seams 2, 3, and 4 (as shown in **Diagram 5**), sewing from inner edge to outer edge. To sew seam 5, start with a backtack, stitching over the previously sewn seam (seam 1) by a few stitches, and sew to the outer edge of the wallhanging's center.

Borders

1 Make four small pinwheels, as shown in the **Cornerstone Assembly Diagram**, using the light brown, medium blue, and dark red prints.

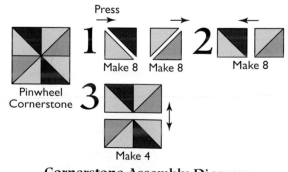

Press

Pinwheel
Cornerstone

1 Make 8 Make 8

2 Make 8

3

Make 4

Cornerstone Assembly Diagram

2 Referring to the **Assembly Diagram**, pair and sew together the two brown print border strips to make four inner borders. Sew one of these to each side of the wallhanging. Press seams toward the borders. Sew one pinwheel cornerstone to each end of the two remaining inner borders, orienting them as shown, and sew them to the top and bottom of the wallhanging. Press toward the borders.

Assembly Diagram

3 Sew one outer border to each side of the wallhanging. Press seams toward the borders. Sew the remaining outer borders to the top and bottom of the wallhanging, pressing seams toward the borders.

Finishing Touches

1 Read "Finishing" on page 224 for details on assembling and finishing the wallhanging.

2 Mark quilting designs on the wallhanging. The pieced blocks were quilted in the ditch and the center setting square was quilted in a pumpkin seed design.

3 Cut a 40-inch square of backing fabric. Layer the quilt top, batting, and backing. Baste to secure the layers. Quilt by hand or machine.

4 Cut 158 inches of 1½-inch bias strips for single-fold binding. Sew the strips together to form one continuous binding strip. Sew the binding to the wallhanging.

Bear's Paw
Wallhanging

— Setting Success —

This simple four-block grouping becomes dramatic when it is surrounded by eye-catching elements like wide lattice and triple borders. The lattice serves as an effective frame, creating four windowpanes for your favorite 9-inch blocks. Use this setting as a showcase for blocks with similar themes (like stars), or for four of the same block for a more unified look.

4

choosing blocks to use

This wallhanging features the Bear's Paw block (page 7). Refer to the **Basic Setting Diagram** on the opposite page to see the setting used in this quilt. This four-block setting is especially effec-tive when you choose a block

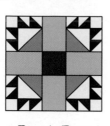

Bear's Paw

containing patches that mimic elements in the setting, such as the half-square triangles and plain large squares. If you want to highlight the bold lattice in the wallhanging, try substituting a block like Handy Andy, which features its own lattice through the middle of the block. Or if you want to play up the Sawtooth look, choose Kansas Troubles, One More Block, or Robbing Peter to Pay Paul because they contain a large number of Sawtooth points. Even though the proportions are slightly different, other blocks with center crosses and small triangles are Duck Paddle, Goose Tracks, and Snowflake.

Project Basics

Finished Size: 34¼ × 34¼
Finished Block: 9 inches
Number of Blocks: 4
Setting Highlights: Straight set, lattice and corner-stones, and triple borders

Fabric and Supplies

Bear's Paw Blocks

⅜ yard	assorted blue-on-cream or green-on-cream prints (light)
¼ yard	medium green print (medium 1)
⅜ yard	assorted medium blue prints (medium 2)
⅛ yard	dark red print (dark 1)
¼ yard	dark blue print (dark 2)

Setting

⅜ yard	dark blue stripe 1 for lattice
⅛ yard	dark red print for center corner-stone
½ yard	assorted dark blue prints* for Sawtooth borders and lattice cornerstones
¼ yard	medium green print for inner borders
½ yard	assorted blue-on-cream or green-on-cream prints* for Sawtooth borders and Sawtooth border cornerstones
1 yard	dark blue stripe 2† for outer bor-ders

Finishing

1¼ yards	backing fabric
½ yard	binding fabric
38 × 38-inch	quilt batting

*Purchase ¾ yard if you prefer to use the bias strip piecing method for sewing half-square triangles; see page 175.
†Purchase ⅜ yard if you are not using a stripe fabric.

Cutting

All measurements include ¼-inch seam allow-ances. Cut all strips on the crosswise grain unless otherwise indicated.

Blocks

Refer to the cutting chart on page 7 for the Bear's Paw block. The fabric values listed in the paren-theses in the Fabric and Supplies list correspond to the fabric values in the cutting chart on the block page. Cut the widest strips in each value first, even if they're not the first alphabetical letter. Often you can cut the narrower strips out of the fabric left over from the wider strips.

Setting

Refer to the cutting chart on the opposite page to cut the remaining fabric for the quilt top.

Cutting							
	First Cut		**Second Cut**			**Third Cut**	
	Strip Width (in inches)	No. to Cut	Shape	Cut Size (in inches)	No. to Cut	Shape	Total Needed
Dark blue stripe 1							
Lattice	$2\frac{3}{4}$*	12	▬	$2\frac{3}{4} \times 9\frac{1}{2}$	12	—	—
Dark red print							
Center cornerstone	$2\frac{3}{4}$	1	■	$2\frac{3}{4} \times 2\frac{3}{4}$	1	—	—
Dark blue prints							
Sawtooth borders†	2	3	■	2×2	48	◩	96
Lattice cornerstones	$2\frac{3}{4}$	1	■	$2\frac{3}{4} \times 2\frac{3}{4}$	12	—	—
Medium green print							
Side inner borders	$1\frac{5}{8}$	2	▬	$1\frac{5}{8} \times 25\frac{1}{4}$	2	—	—
Top and bottom inner borders	$1\frac{5}{8}$	2	▬	$1\frac{5}{8} \times 27\frac{1}{2}$	2	—	—
Blue-on-cream or green-on-cream prints							
Sawtooth borders†	2	3	☐	2×2	48	◨	96
Sawtooth border cornerstones	$1\frac{5}{8}$	1	☐	$1\frac{5}{8} \times 1\frac{5}{8}$	4	—	—
Dark blue stripe 2							
Outer borders	$2\frac{3}{4}$*	4	▬	$2\frac{3}{4} \times 29\frac{3}{4}$	4	—	—

*Cut these strips lengthwise so stripes run lengthwise in the lattice.
†See page 175 for cutting information if you prefer to make half-square triangles using the bias-strip piecing method.

Making the Quilt

This wallhanging consists of four pieced blocks, pieced lattice and plain cornerstones, and three borders, including a pieced Sawtooth border and two plain borders. See the **Basic Setting Diagram**.

Blocks

Refer to page 7 to make four Bear's Paw blocks. Or, cut and piece the block or blocks of your choice.

Assembly

1 If you have selected a block or blocks other than Bear's Paw, refer to the **Basic Setting Diagram** to assemble the wallhanging. Sew the pieced blocks, lattice, and cornerstones together in horizontal rows, pressing the seams toward the lattice strips in both the block rows and the lattice rows. Sew the rows together.

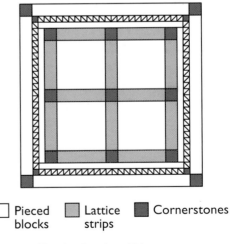

☐ Pieced blocks   ▨ Lattice strips   ■ Cornerstones

Basic Setting Diagram

2 If you are using Bear's Paw blocks for your quilt, refer to the **Assembly Diagram** on page 174 and sew the blocks, lattice, and cornerstones together in horizontal rows. Press the seams toward the lattice strips in both the block rows and the lattice rows. Sew the rows together.

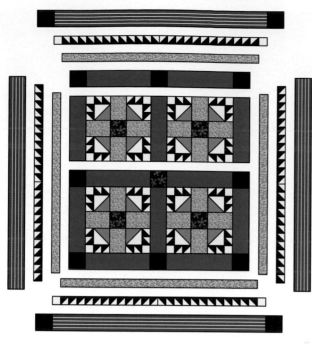

Assembly Diagram

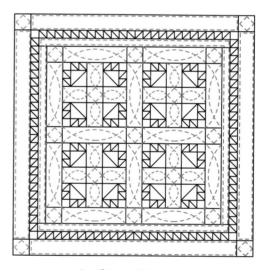

Make 2
Side Sawtooth Borders

Make 2
Top and Bottom Sawtooth Borders

Sawtooth Borders Assembly Diagram

4 Sew the side Sawtooth borders to the quilt, as shown in **Assembly Diagram**. Sew the top and bottom Sawtooth borders to the quilt, as shown. Press seams toward the inner borders. Sew the outer borders to the sides of the quilt. Sew one cornerstone to each end of the two remaining outer borders. Sew these to the top and bottom of the quilt, pressing seams toward the outer borders.

Borders

1 Referring to the **Assembly Diagram** above, sew the side inner borders to the quilt. Sew the top and bottom inner borders to the quilt. Press seams toward the borders.

2 For the Sawtooth borders, make 96 half-square triangles by sewing 2-inch dark blue print and blue-on-cream or green-on-cream print triangles together. See the **Half-Square Triangle Diagram**. Press the seams toward the dark blue triangles. Or use bias strip piecing to make half-square triangles. See "Making Half-Square Triangles Using Bias-Strip Piecing" on the opposite page. You will need to cut four 11¼-inch squares each of the dark blue print and blue-on-cream or green-on-cream print to yield enough half-square triangles.

Half-Square Triangle Diagram

3 Sew the half-square triangles together in four rows of 24 each, reversing the direction of the diagonals at the middle of each row. See the **Sawtooth Borders Assembly Diagram**. Press the seams open. Add one Sawtooth border cornerstone to each end of two border strips to make the top and bottom borders.

Finishing Touches

1 Read "Finishing" on page 224 for details on assembling and finishing the wallhanging.

2 Mark quilting designs on the quilt top, referring to the **Quilting Diagram** for ideas. The pieced blocks were also quilted in the ditch.

Quilting Diagram

3 Cut a 40-inch square of backing fabric. Layer the quilt top, batting, and backing. Baste to secure the layers. Quilt by hand or machine.

4 Cut 147 inches of 1½-inch bias strips for single-fold binding. Sew the strips together to form a continuous strip. Sew the binding to the quilt top.

Making Half-Square Triangles Using Bias-Strip Piecing

Half-square triangles can be made using the bias-strip piecing method. Bias-strip piecing means you sew bias strips together, and cut squares along the seam line.

From the assorted blue-on-cream or green-on-cream prints, cut four 11¼-inch squares. From the dark blue print, cut four 11¼-inch squares. Pair one cream print square with a dark blue print square, placing right sides together. Cut diagonally from one corner of the square to its opposite corner; this 45 degree cut establishes the bias. See the **Bias Diagram.**

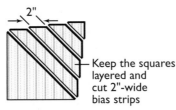

Cutting from corner to corner establishes a true 45° bias

Bias Diagram

Keeping the squares layered, measure from the first cut and cut strips 2 inches wide. Cut the whole square into bias strips, as shown in the **Strip Cutting Diagram.**

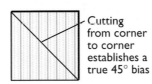

2"

Keep the squares layered and cut 2"-wide bias strips

Strip Cutting Diagram

Pick up pairs of strips; they are already right sides together and perfectly aligned. Referring to the **Sewing Diagram,** sew each pair together along the long bias edge, using a ¼-inch seam allowance. Press the seams open. There will be six strip pairs and two sets of triangles. Sew the triangles together in the same manner, then press the seams open.

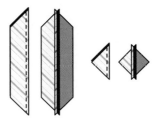

Sewing Diagram

For cutting efficiency, line up the pairs as shown in the **Strip Assembly Diagram.** Sew the longest strip pairs together first, then attach the next longest until they are all joined, keeping the bottom edges aligned. Press the seams open.

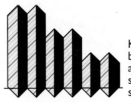

Keep the bottom edges aligned when sewing together strip pairs

Strip Assembly Diagram

Using a square ruler, place the 45 degree diagonal line of the ruler on a seam line. Cut a square a few threads larger than 1⅝ × 1⅝ inches, as shown in the **Square Cutting Diagram.** Turn the square upside down and trim it to exactly 1⅝ × 1⅝ inches.

Line up the 45° ruler line with the seam line and cut a square a bit larger than 1⅝"

Square Cutting Diagram

Referring to the **Layout Diagram,** cut additional squares in the same manner. Each strip pair assembly should yield about 29 bias-strip pieced squares, each 1⅝ × 1⅝ inches. For this project, you will need a total of 96, so you will need to make four strip pair assemblies.

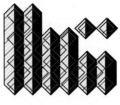

Layout Diagram

Sampler Medallion
Wallhanging

— *Setting Success* —

Traditionally, medallion quilts featured a large central motif surrounded by numerous borders and intricate cornerstones. This wallhanging charmingly adds to the tradition—a mix-and-match sampler of blocks and smaller setting blocks as its center focal point. The construction is easy because you assemble each quarter of the center sampler, then join the quarters with a center setting block.

4 pieced blocks — choosing **blocks** to use

This wallhanging features the Double Dutch (page 29), Key West Beauty (page 65), Star Puzzle (page 104), and Twirling Star blocks (page 112). It also features four different 4½-inch setting blocks (Flying Geese, Pinwheel, Sawtooth Star, and Square within a Square). The directions for these are given within this project. Refer to the **Basic Setting Diagram** on page 180 to see the setting for this wallhanging. When considering other blocks to use in this quilt setting, think about what makes these blocks work together: There are three sets of repeated motifs (Pinwheels, Flying Geese, and Stars) and a controlled color palette. The smaller setting blocks borrow shapes and patch sizes from the 9-inch blocks. To further unify the composition, the small Sawtooth Star in the center is repeated as border cornerstones. Other groups of four blocks to consider would be Missouri Star, Mosaic, Rambler, and Variable Star II, or Combination Star, Goose Tracks, Pinwheel, and Rising Star. Because each block in these four-block sets is based on a different grid, the grouping is interesting and vibrant.

| Double Dutch |  Key West Beauty |  Star Puzzle |  Twirling Star |

| Flying Geese | 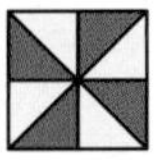 Pinwheel | 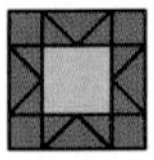 Sawtooth Star |  Square within a Square |

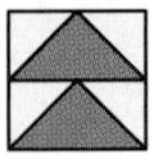

Project Basics

Finished Size: 45½ × 45½ inches
Finished Block: 9 inches
Number of Blocks: 4
Setting Highlights: Straight set with 4½-inch setting blocks to create a sampler of small and large blocks; double inner borders with pieced "setting block" cornerstones, middle borders with plain cornerstones, and half-square triangle outer borders

Fabric and Supplies

Double Dutch Block

⅛ yard	pink-on-cream print (light)
⅛ yard	medium pink print (medium 1)
¼ yard	medium brown print (medium 2)
⅛ yard	dark brown print (dark)

Key West Beauty Block

⅛ yard	pink-on-cream print (light)
⅛ yard	medium pink print (medium)
¼ yard	dark brown print (dark)

Star Puzzle Block

¼ yard	pink-on-cream print (light 1)
⅛ yard	brown-on-cream print (light 2)
⅛ yard	dark brown print (dark)

Twirling Star Block

¼ yard	pink-on-cream print (light)
⅛ yard	medium brown print (medium)
⅛ yard	dark pink print (dark)

Setting

½ yard	brown-on-cream print for inner borders
⅝ yard	pink-on-cream prints for Flying Geese and Square within a Square setting blocks, and half-square triangle outer borders
⅛ yard	assorted pink-on-cream and brown-on-cream prints for Pinwheel setting blocks
½ yard	medium brown floral print for inner borders
⅜ yard	assorted medium pink prints for Pinwheel and Sawtooth Star setting block and cornerstones
⅜ yard	assorted medium brown prints for Flying Geese, Pinwheel, and Sawtooth Star setting block and cornerstones
⅛ yard	dark pink print for Square within a Square setting blocks and middle border cornerstones

continued on next page

| ½ yard | dark pink paisley print for middle borders |
| ⅝ yard | assorted medium and dark pink and brown prints for half-square triangle outer borders |

Finishing

2¾ yards	backing fabric
¾ yard	binding fabric
50 × 50-inch	quilt batting

Cutting

All measurements include ¼-inch seam allowances. Cut all strips on the crosswise grain.

Blocks

Refer to the cutting chart on page 29 for the Double Dutch block, page 65 for the Key West Beauty block, page 104 for the Star Puzzle block, and page 112 for the Twirling Star block. The fabric values listed in the parentheses in the Fabric and Supplies list correspond to the fabric values in the cutting chart on the block pages. Cut the widest strips in each value first, even if they're not the first alphabetical letter. Often you can cut the narrower strips out of the fabric left over from the wider strips.

Setting

Refer to the cutting chart on the opposite page to cut the remaining fabric for the quilt top, including the 4½-inch setting blocks, borders, and cornerstones.

Making the Quilt

This wallhanging consists of four pieced blocks, eight pieced setting blocks, a pieced center setting square, double inner borders with pieced cornerstones, middle borders with plain cornerstones, and outer borders made of half-square triangles. See the **Basic Setting Diagram** on page 180.

Blocks

Refer to page 29 to make one Double Dutch block, page 65 to make one Key West Beauty block, page 104 to make one Sawtooth Star block, and page 112 to make one Twirling Star block. Or, cut and piece the block or blocks of your choice.

Setting Blocks and Cornerstones

1 Use an assortment of pink-on-cream and brown-on-cream prints and medium pink and medium brown prints for the Pinwheel setting blocks. In the quilt shown on page 176, the medium pink prints were used as both the light and the medium fabrics. Make four 4½-inch Pinwheel setting blocks, as shown in **Diagram 1**. Press the seams as indicated by the arrows.

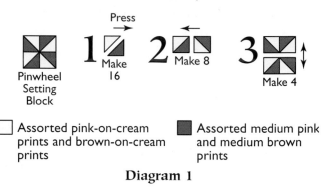

Assorted pink-on-cream prints and brown-on-cream prints

Assorted medium pink and medium brown prints

Diagram 1

2 Using assorted medium pink and medium brown prints, make five 4½-inch Sawtooth Star setting blocks, as shown in **Diagram 2**. Press the seams as indicated by the arrows. Use one block in the wallhanging's center; use the remaining four as inner border cornerstones.

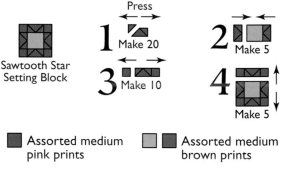

Assorted medium pink prints

Assorted medium brown prints

Diagram 2

3 Using assorted pink-on-cream prints and the dark pink print, make two 4½-inch Square within a Square setting blocks, as shown in **Diagram 3**. Press the seams as indicated by the arrows.

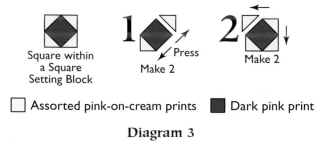

Assorted pink-on-cream prints

Dark pink print

Diagram 3

	Rotary Cutting							Templates
	First Cut		Second Cut			Third Cut		
	Strip Width (in inches)	No. to Cut	Shape	Cut Size (in inches)	No. to Cut	Shape	Total Needed	Template
Brown-on-cream print								
Inner borders	2¾	4	▭	2¾ × 23	4	—	—	—
Assorted pink-on-cream prints								
Flying Geese setting blocks	3⅛	1	◻	3⅛ × 3⅛	4	◨	8	T10
Square within a Square setting blocks	3⅛	1	◻	3⅛ × 3⅛	4	◨	8	T10
Half-square triangle outer borders	5⅜	3	◻	5⅜ × 5⅜	18	◨	36	T15
Assorted pink-on-cream and brown-on-cream prints								
Pinwheel setting blocks	3⅛	1	◼	3⅛ × 3⅛	8	◨	16	T10
Medium brown floral print								
Inner borders	2¾	4	▭	2¾ × 23	4	—	—	—
Assorted medium pink prints								
Sawtooth Star setting blocks and cornerstones (outer triangles)	3½	1	◼	3½ × 3½	5	◻	20	T6
Sawtooth Star setting block and cornerstones (corner squares)	1⅝	1	◼	1⅝ × 1⅝	20	—	—	S3
Assorted medium brown prints								
Sawtooth Star setting blocks and cornerstones (center square)	2¾	1	◼	2¾ × 2¾	5	—	—	S10
Sawtooth Stars setting block and cornerstones (star points)	2	1	◼	2 × 2	20	◨	40	T2
Flying Geese setting blocks	5¾	1	◼	5¾ × 5¾	1	◻	4	T13
Assorted medium pink and medium brown prints								
Pinwheel setting blocks	3⅛	1	◼	3⅛ × 3⅛	8	◨	16	T10
Dark pink print								
Square within a Square setting blocks	3⅝+	1	◼	3⅝+ × 3⅝+	2	—	—	S13
Middle border cornerstones	2¾	1	◼	2¾ × 2¾	4	—	—	S11
Dark pink paisley print								
Middle borders	2¾	4	▬	2¾ × 32	4	—	—	—
Assorted medium and dark pink and brown prints								
Half-square triangle outer borders	5⅜	3	◼	5⅜ × 5⅜	18	◨	36	T15

Note: Plus sign (+) indicates ¹⁄₁₆-inch measurements. See page 217 for details.

4 Using assorted pink-on-cream prints and assorted medium brown prints, make two 4½-inch Flying Geese setting blocks, as shown in **Diagram 4**. Press as indicated by the arrows.

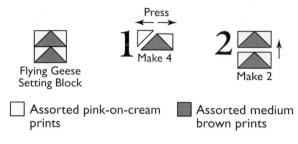

Flying Geese
Setting Block

Press
1 Make 4

2 Make 2

☐ Assorted pink-on-cream prints ☐ Assorted medium brown prints

Diagram 4

Assembly

1 If you have selected a block or blocks other than Double Dutch, Key West Beauty, Star Puzzle, and Twirling Star, refer to the **Basic Setting Diagram** to assemble the wallhanging. Referring to the diagram, sew pairs of the 4½-inch setting blocks together (seam 1), then sew each pair to a 9-inch block (seam 2). Sew the wallhanging top together using a partial seam, as shown in the **Partial Seam Diagram**.

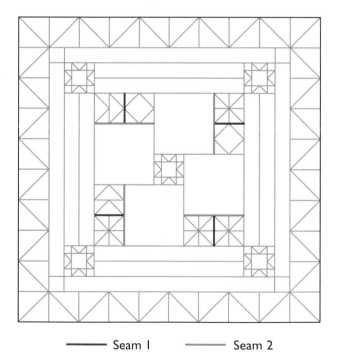

———— Seam 1   ———— Seam 2

Basic Setting Diagram

2 If you are using Double Dutch, Key West Beauty, Star Puzzle, and Twirling Star for your wallhanging, refer to the **Partial Seam Diagram** to assemble the center of the wallhanging.

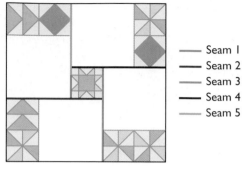

——— Seam 1
——— Seam 2
——— Seam 3
——— Seam 4
——— Seam 5

Partial Seam Diagram

Borders

1 Sew the brown-on-cream print and medium brown floral print inner border strips into pairs. Sew a pair to each side of the wallhanging with the floral print on the outside edge. Press the seams toward the borders. Sew one Sawtooth Star setting block to each end of the two remaining pairs. Sew these to the top and bottom of the wallhanging with the medium brown floral print on the outside edge. Press the seams toward the borders.

2 Sew one middle border strip to each side of the wallhanging, and press the seams toward the middle borders. Sew one middle border cornerstone to each end of the two remaining strips. Sew these to the top and bottom of the wallhanging, and press the seams toward the middle borders.

3 Using assorted pink-on-cream prints and assorted medium and dark pink and brown prints, make 36 half-square triangles, as shown in **Diagram 5**. Orienting the half-square triangles as shown in the **Assembly Diagram** on the opposite page, make two strips of eight half-square triangles each. Sew these to the sides of the wallhanging, and press the seams toward the middle borders. Make two border strips of ten squares each, and sew these to the top and bottom of the wallhanging. Press the seams toward the middle border.

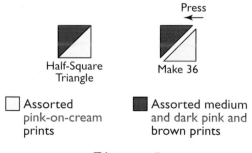

Press

Half-Square
Triangle   Make 36

☐ Assorted pink-on-cream prints ☐ Assorted medium and dark pink and brown prints

Diagram 5

Assembly Diagram

Finishing Touches

1 Read "Finishing" on page 224 for details on assembling and finishing the wallhanging.

2 Mark quilting designs on the quilt top, referring to the **Quilting Diagram** for ideas. The quilt center is crosshatched diagonally.

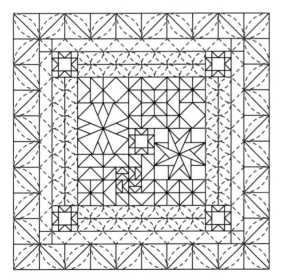

Quilting Diagram

3 Cut the backing fabric in half crosswise to make two 1⅜-yard pieces. Cut a 25-inch-wide strip from each piece and trim the selvages. Sew the strips together along the long edge to create a backing with a vertical seam. Press the seam open.

4 Layer the wallhanging top, batting, and backing. Baste to secure the layers. Quilt by hand or machine.

5 Cut 192 inches of 1½-inch bias strips for single-fold binding. Sew the strips together to form one continuous binding strip. Sew the binding to the wallhanging.

Personalizing Your Quilt

There are many ways you can add surprises to this wallhanging to give it a little personality. Simple nuances are already included in the quilt shown on page 176. Try one of the variations below or create your own.

• **Mix and match mediums and darks:** Certain prints can be used interchangeably as either mediums or darks. Take a look at the brown "plaid" print in the large triangles in the Double Dutch block—this "medium" brown is the exact same fabric as the "dark" brown in Star Puzzle!

• **Switch value placement:** Three of the 4½-inch Pinwheel setting blocks are identical in terms of light and dark placement. A fourth one, at the lower left, has its lights and mediums switched to add variety.

• **Consider the layout:** Part of the charm of this wallhanging is the way things blend together, as the Double Dutch block does with the Flying Geese setting blocks next to it—each contains Flying Geese units, so it's fun to try to figure out where the blocks begin and end.

• **Vary the backgrounds:** The background fabrics in this wallhanging are subtle and simple prints, and they work successfully with the overall mood of the other fabrics. Because this quilt has so much motion and so many elements, it's important to keep the background fabrics in the background. Busier prints would have been confusing. The scrappy nature of the background fabrics follows the overall fabric scheme, but you could choose to feature just one background fabric to hold the design together.

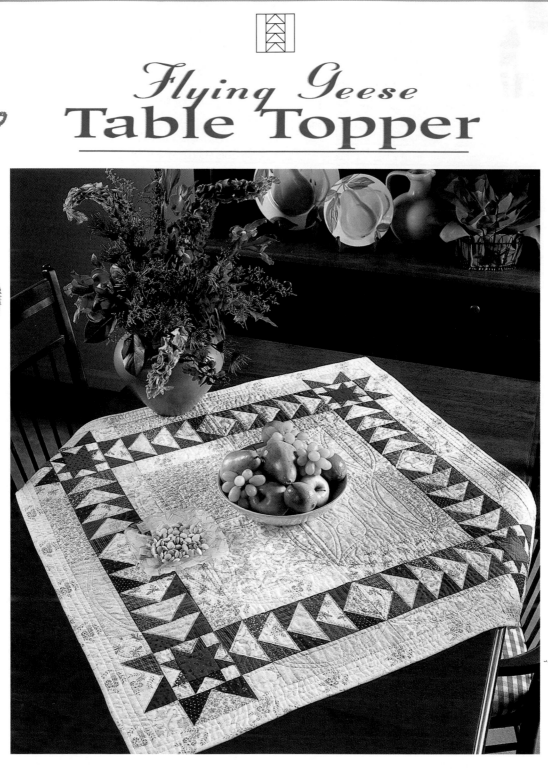

Flying Geese Table Topper

— *Setting Success* —

Blocks can be used as borders, too! This setting shows that quilt blocks can fit as well in borders as in the center of a quilt. Plus, these border blocks eliminate the need for extensive calculations because their finished size of 9 inches is the same as other blocks in this book, making them a perfect fit. Here the border blocks surround simple squares, but they also look terrific when they frame pieced blocks.

12 choosing blocks to use

pieced blocks This table topper features the Flying Geese (page 41) and Rising Star (page 90) blocks. Refer to the **Basic Setting Diagram** on page 184 to see the setting used in the quilt. Notice how the outer star points of the Rising Star block interact with the Flying Geese block to form a continuous border. Antique Star and Broken Star could pair with the Flying Geese block just as effectively.

Other border blocks create a diagonal line. These include Chain of Squares, Log Cabin with a Chain, Lost Ship, Ocean Waves, and Woodland Path. Use Rambler as a border block and you'll make a double diagonal line, or use Birds in the Air to create continuous pinwheels. When deciding whether a block works as a border block, look at the shapes that are created where the blocks meet. If something interesting appears or if it creates a new design (often referred to as a secondary pattern), that block can be used successfully as a border block.

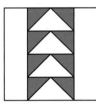 

Flying Geese   **Rising Star**

Project Basics

Finished Size: 39 × 39 inches
Finished Block: 9 inches
Number of Blocks: 8 Flying Geese, 4 Rising Star
Setting Highlights: Straight side-by-side set, blocks used as a border, and center setting squares to showcase quilting designs

Fabric and Supplies

Flying Geese Blocks

| ¾ yard | assorted white-and-purple prints (light) |
| ⅜ yard | assorted dark purple prints (dark) |

Rising Star Blocks

| ½ yard | assorted white-and-purple prints (light) |
| ½ yard | assorted dark purple prints (dark) |

Setting

| ⅜ yard | white-and-purple print 1 for setting squares* |
| 1¼ yards | white-and-purple print 2 for borders |

Finishing

2⅝ yards	backing fabric
½ yard	binding fabric
43-inch square	quilt batting

Or use four different white-and-purple prints, each measuring at least 9½ inches square.

Cutting

All measurements include ¼-inch seam allowances. Cut all fabric strips on the crosswise grain unless otherwise indicated.

Blocks

Refer to the cutting chart on page 41 for the Flying Geese block and page 90 for the Rising Star block. The fabric values listed in the parentheses in the Fabric and Supplies list correspond to the fabric values in the cutting chart on the block pages. Cut the widest strips in each value first, even if they're not the first alphabetical letter. Often you can cut the narrower strips out of fabric left over from the wider strips.

Setting

Refer to the cutting chart on page 184 to cut the remaining fabric for the quilt.

Making the Quilt

This quilt consists of 12 pieced blocks and 4 setting squares. Narrow borders complete the quilt top. See the **Basic Setting Diagram** on page 184.

Cutting					
	First Cut		**Second Cut**		
	Strip Width (in inches)	No. to Cut	Shape	Cut Size (in inches)	No. to Cut
White-and-purple prints 1					
Setting squares	9½*	1	☐	9½ × 9½	4
White-and-purple print 2					
Side borders	2†	2	▭	2 × 36½	2
Top and bottom borders	2†	2	▭	2 × 39½	2

*Or cut one 9½-inch square from four different white-and-purple prints.
†Cut lengthwise to avoid seams.

Blocks

Refer to page 41 to make eight Flying Geese blocks and page 90 to make four Rising Star blocks. Or, cut and piece the block or blocks of your choice.

Assembly

1 If you have selected blocks other than Flying Geese and Rising Star, refer to the **Basic Setting Diagram** to assemble the table topper. Sew the pieced blocks and setting squares together in horizontal rows, pressing the seams in opposite directions from row to row. Sew the rows together.

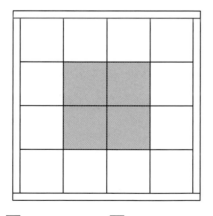

☐ Pieced blocks ■ Setting squares

Basic Setting Diagram

2 If you are using the Flying Geese and Rising Star blocks for your table topper, refer to the **Assembly Diagram** to lay out the blocks. Be sure to position the Flying Geese blocks as shown in the diagram to duplicate the interaction of the

Flying Geese units and the Rising Star points. Sew the blocks together in horizontal rows, pressing the seams in opposite directions from row to row. Sew the rows together.

Assembly Diagram

Borders

1 Referring to the **Assembly Diagram** above, sew the side borders to the quilt. Press seams toward the borders.

2 Sew the top and bottom borders to the quilt. Press seams toward the borders.

Finishing Touches

1 Read "Finishing" on page 224 for details on assembling and finishing the quilt.

2 Mark quilting designs on the quilt, referring to the **Quilting Diagram** for ideas. The pieced blocks are also quilted in the ditch.

Quilting Diagram

3 Cut the backing fabric in half crosswise to make two pieces of equal length. Cut one 22-inch-wide strip from each length and trim the selvages. Sew these lengths together along one long edge to create a backing with a vertical seam. Press the seam open.

4 Layer the quilt top, batting, and backing. Baste to secure the layers. Quilt by hand or machine.

5 Cut 166 inches of 1½-inch bias strips for single-fold binding. Sew the strips together to form one continuous binding strip. Sew the binding to the quilt top.

Making Flying Geese

Flying Geese blocks are a great way to show off accurate piecing skills. Press the seam allowances on each Flying Geese unit away from the large triangle. Notice the X that forms where the two sewing lines cross. To create nice, crisp triangle points, use this X as a sewing guide when sewing two Flying Geese units together.

Place two units right sides together, with the unit with the sewn X on the top. Sew along the edge, right through the center of the X, using a ¼-inch seam to join the two Flying Geese units, as shown in the **Sewing Diagrams.** Press the seam away from the large triangle point.

When the patches are pressed open, you'll see a perfectly precise triangle point, as shown in the **Flying Geese Diagram.**

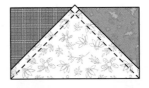
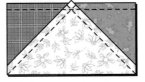

Sewing Diagrams

Flying Geese Diagram

Star Tile
Baby Quilt

— Setting Success —

Look twice! This may appear to be two different blocks set on point, but it's really just one block set straight. The interesting feature of this setting is the movement and action created solely by the blocks being set side by side. Block corners—and often edges—can form entirely new patterns when joined. The pieced inner border plays up the two-block illusion by "completing" the quarter-square triangle design.

12 choosing **blocks** to use

pieced blocks

This quilt features the Star Tile block (page 106). Refer to the **Basic Setting Diagram** on page 188 to see the setting used in this quilt. Pinwheel Mosaic is also a perfect block for this setting because the block corners interact with

Star Tile

the inner pieced border to create the same quarter-square triangles that Star Tile does.

This easy straight set with blocks placed side-by-side is great for blocks that create secondary patterns at the corners. Turn to page 126 to see line drawings for blocks drawn in sets of four. Drawing the blocks together lets you see the inter-action of the shapes where the blocks touch. It is sometimes very interesting and can spark new design ideas. Sometimes, though, nothing exciting seems to happen at all. Look for blocks that form secondary designs at the corners or edges when set side by side. Experiment with shading to emphasize the different shapes. It is even possible to "hide" where the real block begins and ends, and create totally new designs.

Double Windmill, Kansas Troubles, Whirligig, and Windmill Star form new pinwheels at the corners, while Twinkling Star forms little stars. Blocks with a square-within-a-square configura-tion, like Crossroads to Jericho and Road Home, will form quarter-square triangles at the corners if you alternate the coloring in opposite corners or alternate blocks. If using a block with square patches in the corners, like Jacob's Ladder, Ohio Trail, or Water Wheel, be sure to change the value (by using a lighter or a darker fabric) or color of the corner squares so they form Four Patches instead of large, solid-looking squares when joined.

Project Basics

Finished Size: 44 × 53 inches
Finished Block: 9 inches
Number of Blocks: 12
Setting Highlights: Straight set with pieced first border, plain second border, Sawtooth third bor-der, and plain fourth border

Fabric and Supplies

Star Tile Blocks

¼ yard *each*	four assorted light blue prints (light 1)
½ yard	light yellow floral print (light 2)
⅛ yard	medium blue plaid (medium 1)
⅛ yard	medium yellow juvenile print (medium 2)
⅝ yard	dark blue print (dark)

Setting

½ yard *each*	four assorted light blue prints for pieced first border and plain fourth border*
1¼ yards	light yellow floral print for plain second border
⅛ yard	medium blue plaid for pieced first border
⅝ yard	medium yellow juvenile print for pieced first border and third Sawtooth border
½ yard	dark blue print for third Sawtooth border

Finishing

3 yards	backing fabric
¾ yard	binding fabric
52 × 61-inch	quilt batting

½ yard each is sufficient for borders cut on the crosswise grain. If you prefer borders cut on the more stable lengthwise grain, purchase 1⅝ yards each of the four assorted light blue prints.

Cutting

All measurements include ¼-inch seam allow-ances. Cut all strips on the crosswise grain, unless otherwise indicated.

Blocks

Refer to the cutting chart on page 106 for the Star Tile block. The fabric values listed in the paren-theses in the Fabric and Supplies list correspond to the fabric values in the cutting chart on the block page. Cut the widest strips in each value first, even if they're not the first alphabetical letter. Often you can cut the narrower strips out of the fabric left over from the wider strips.

The Star Tile block in this quilt features a planned scrappy look. Each of the four trapezoids in the block (template X6) is cut from a different light blue print, then laid out in the same position in each block. If you would like to duplicate this planned look, you will need to cut 12 of template X6 from *each* of the four different light blue prints. Refer to the **Fabric Placement Diagram** to identify and lay out the fabrics for each block before sewing.

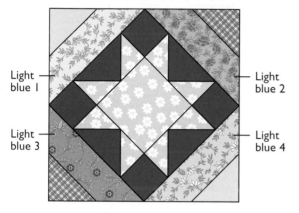

Light blue 1 — Light blue 2
Light blue 3 — Light blue 4

Fabric Placement Diagram

Setting

Refer to the cutting chart on the opposite page to cut the remaining fabric for the quilt top. There are four different light blue prints used in the plain fourth border, so follow the cutting directions carefully. Note that the borders are numbered one through four (one is the inner border, four is the outer border) and that the assorted light blue prints are also referred to by the numbers one through four in the cutting chart and step-by-step directions.

Making the Quilt

This quilt consists of 12 pieced blocks and an inner pieced border that "completes" the quilt center. There are three additional borders: a plain middle border, a Sawtooth border, and a plain but scrappy outer border. See the **Basic Setting Diagram**.

Blocks

Refer to page 106 to make 12 Star Tile blocks. Or, cut and piece the block or blocks of your choice.

Assembly

1 If you have selected a block or blocks other than Star Tile, refer to the **Basic Setting Diagram** to assemble the quilt. Sew the pieced blocks together in horizontal rows, pressing the seams in opposite directions from row to row. Sew the rows together.

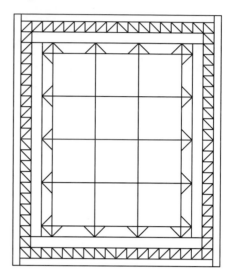

Basic Setting Diagram

2 If you are using the Star Tile blocks for your quilt, refer to the **Assembly Diagram** to lay out the quilt center, alternating the yellow and blue corner patches. Sew the pieced blocks together in horizontal rows, pressing the seams in opposite directions from row to row. Sew the rows together.

Assembly Diagram

	Cutting						
	First Cut		**Second Cut**			**Third Cut**	
	Strip Width (in inches)	No. to Cut	Shape	Cut Size (in inches)	No. to Cut	Shape	Total Needed
Assorted light blue prints*							
Border one	$2\frac{3}{4}$	5	▭	$2\frac{3}{4} \times 10\frac{1}{4}$	14	See "Accurate and Easy" on page 190	14
Border one cornerstones	$3\frac{1}{8}$	1	▢	$3\frac{1}{8} \times 3\frac{1}{8}$	2	◺	4
Border four (sides)	2	Cut 1 each from light blue 1 and light blue 4†	▭	$2 \times 53\frac{1}{2}$	1 each of light blue 1 and light blue 4	—	—
Border four (top and bottom)	2	Cut 1 each from light blue 2 and light blue 3†	▭	2×41	1 each of light blue 2 and light blue 3	—	—
Light yellow floral print							
Border two (sides)	$2\frac{3}{4}$†	2	▭	$2\frac{3}{4} \times 41$	2	—	—
Border two (top and bottom)	$2\frac{3}{4}$‡	2	▭	$2\frac{3}{4} \times 36\frac{1}{2}$	2	—	—
Medium yellow juvenile print							
Pieced first border (including cornerstones)	$3\frac{1}{8}$	1	▢	$3\frac{1}{8} \times 3\frac{1}{8}$	8	◺	16
Third Sawtooth border	$3\frac{1}{8}$	4	▢	$3\frac{1}{8} \times 3\frac{1}{8}$	38	◺	76
Medium blue plaid							
Border one (including cornerstones)	$3\frac{1}{8}$	1	▨	$3\frac{1}{8} \times 3\frac{1}{8}$	8	◺	16
Dark blue print							
Border three	$3\frac{1}{8}$	4	◼	$3\frac{1}{8} \times 3\frac{1}{8}$	38	◺	76

*Assign each light blue print a number before you begin piecing and cutting.
†If cutting strips on the crosswise grain, piece each pair of strips together, then cut to the size listed under "Second Cut." If cutting strips on the lengthwise grain, cut each strip to the size listed under "Second Cut."
‡Cut from the lengthwise grain.

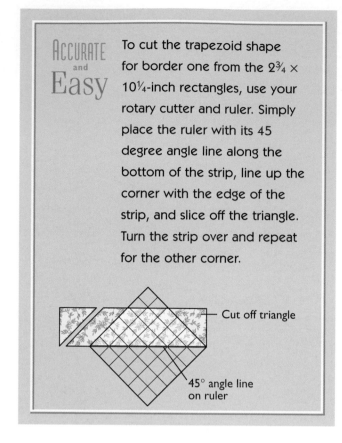

ACCURATE and Easy

To cut the trapezoid shape for border one from the 2¾ × 10¼-inch rectangles, use your rotary cutter and ruler. Simply place the ruler with its 45 degree angle line along the bottom of the strip, line up the corner with the edge of the strip, and slice off the triangle. Turn the strip over and repeat for the other corner.

← Cut off triangle

45° angle line on ruler

Borders

1 Sew together the segments and cornerstones for border one, as shown in **Border One Diagram**. Press the seams as indicated by the arrows.

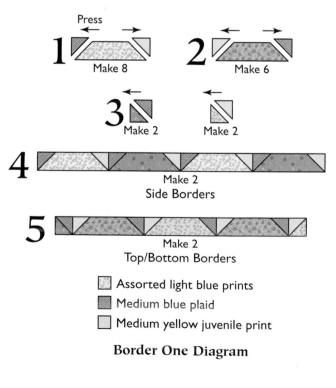

Border One Diagram

2 Sew the side borders to the quilt, and press the seams toward the border. Sew the top and bottom borders to the quilt, and press the seams toward the borders. Refer to the **Assembly Diagram** on page 188 as needed.

3 For border two, sew side border two strips to each side of the quilt. Press the seams toward border two. Sew top and bottom border two strips to the top and bottom of the quilt. Press the seams toward border two. Refer to the **Assembly Diagram** on page 188 as needed.

4 For border three, make 76 half-square triangles, as shown in **Half-Square Diagram**. Press the seams as indicated by the arrow.

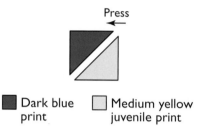

Press

■ Dark blue print   ☐ Medium yellow juvenile print

Half-Square Diagram

5 To complete border three, refer to the **Assembly Diagram** on page 188 and sew together the Sawtooth borders for the sides, using 20 half-square triangles per border. Reverse the direction of the diagonals at the middle of each border. Repeat for the top and bottom borders, using 18 half-square triangles per border, again reversing the direction of the diagonals at the middle of the border. Sew the Sawtooth borders to the sides of the quilt. Press the seams toward border two. Sew the Sawtooth borders to the top and bottom of the quilt. Press the seams toward border two.

6 For border four, sew the light blue 2 strip to the top of the quilt and the light blue 3 strip to the bottom of the quilt. Press the seams toward border four. Sew the light blue 1 strip to the left side of the quilt and the light blue 4 strip to the right side of the quilt. Press the seams toward border four.

Finishing Touches

1 Read "Finishing" on page 224 for details on assembling and finishing the quilt.

2 Mark quilting designs on the quilt top, referring to the **Quilting Diagram** for ideas.

Quilting Diagram

3 Cut the backing fabric into two 1½-yard pieces. Cut a 26-inch-wide strip from each piece, then trim the selvages. Sew the pieces together along the long edges to create a backing with a vertical seam. Press the seam open.

4 Layer the quilt top, batting, and backing. Baste to secure the layers. Quilt by hand or machine.

5 Cut 204 inches of 1½-inch bias strips for single-fold binding. Sew the strips together to form one continuous binding strip. Sew the binding to the quilt top.

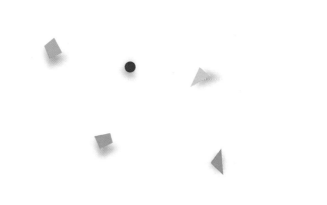

Fitting Your Sawtooth Borders

If you're ready to add your Sawtooth borders to the quilt top and you find that they're too small, don't rush to pick up your seam ripper and resew the seams with a smaller seam allowance. The Sawtooth borders contain a large number of seams, and there is a chance that you can recover the necessary width by pressing. Carefully re-press the borders, paying special attention to the seam joins. The width you need may simply be lost in the loft of the seams.

If, after pressing, your borders are still too small, check your ¼-inch seam allowances for accuracy.

Even if your seam allowance is too large by only ⅟₃₂ inch, that compounds to 1¼ inches lost in each side Sawtooth border. Careful pressing and sewing are essential when fitting a pieced border to a quilt.

Fox and Geese Quilt

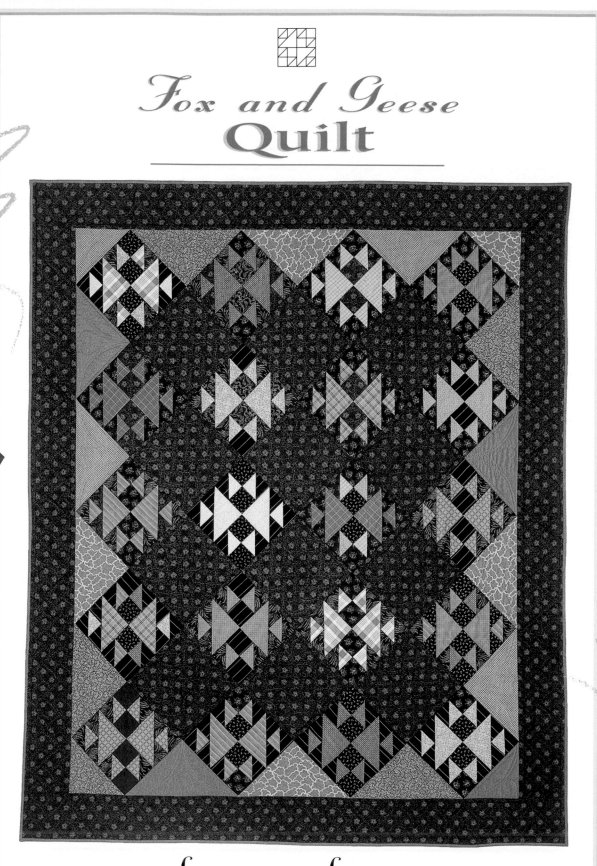

— Setting Success —

Placing blocks on point can energize a quilt. Diagonal rows go together easily since there are so few seams to match. The color you choose for the setting pieces can dramatically change the look of your quilt. Setting squares that are the same color as the background of the pieced blocks will make the designs float; setting squares and triangles made of a contrasting fabric will give a checkerboard effect.

20 choosing blocks to use

pieced blocks

This quilt features the Fox and Geese block (page 45). Refer to the **Basic Setting Diagram** to see the setting used in the quilt. When selecting a block for a diagonal set, choose one that looks great when set on point. Basket blocks are a natural choice. Also look for blocks that create linear motion across the quilt, like Birds in the Air, Cross-Country, or Ohio Trail.

Fox and Geese

Project Basics

Finished Size: 61 × 73½ inches
Finished Block: 9 inches
Number of Blocks: 20
Setting Highlights: Diagonal setting and plain setting squares; contrasting-color setting triangles create a no-hassle "frame" around quilt center

Fabric and Supplies

Fox and Geese Blocks

1 yard	assorted gold prints (medium)
1⅜ yards	assorted black prints (dark)

Setting

2 yards	black print for setting squares and border
⅞ yard	assorted olive green prints for setting triangles

Finishing

4½ yards	backing fabric
¾ yard	binding fabric
69 × 78-inch	quilt batting

Cutting

All measurements include ¼-inch seam allowances. Cut all strips on the crosswise grain.

Blocks

Refer to the cutting chart on page 45 for the Fox and Geese block. The fabric values listed in the parentheses in the Fabric and Supplies list correspond to the fabric values in the cutting chart on the block page. Cut the widest strips in each value first, even if they're not the first alphabetical letter. Often you can cut the narrower strips out of the fabric left over from the wider strips.

Setting

Refer to the cutting chart on page 194 to cut the remaining fabric for the quilt top.

Making the Quilt

This quilt consists of 20 pieced blocks, plus setting squares and triangles. See the **Basic Setting Diagram** below.

Blocks

Refer to page 45 to make 20 Fox and Geese blocks. Or, cut and piece the block or blocks of your choice.

Assembly

1 If you have selected a block or blocks other than Fox and Geese, refer to the **Basic Setting Diagram** to assemble the quilt. Sew the pieced blocks and setting pieces together in diagonal rows, pressing the seams toward the setting pieces. Sew the rows together.

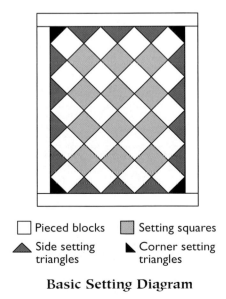

☐ Pieced blocks   ▦ Setting squares
▲ Side setting triangles   ◣ Corner setting triangles

Basic Setting Diagram

Cutting							
First Cut		**Second Cut**			**Third Cut**		
Strip Width (in inches)	No. to Cut	Shape	Cut Size (in inches)	No. to Cut	Shape	Total Needed	
Black print							
Side borders	5¼*	2	▬	5¼ × 64⅛	2	—	—
Top and bottom borders	5¼*	2	▬	5¼ × 61	2	—	—
Setting squares	9½†	6	■	9½ × 9½	12	—	—
Assorted olive green prints							
Side setting triangles	13⅞	2	◻	13⅞ × 13⅞	4	⊠	14
Corner setting triangles	7¼‡	1	◻	7¼ × 7¼	2	◩	4

*Cut lengthwise to avoid seams.
†Cut these strips crosswise from the remaining width of fabric after cutting the borders.
‡Cut this strip from the remaining width of fabric after cutting the side setting triangles.

2 If you are using Fox and Geese blocks for your quilt, refer to the **Assembly Diagram**, and sew the blocks, setting squares, and side and corner setting triangles together in diagonal rows. Press the seams toward the setting pieces. Sew the rows together, pressing the seams toward the top of the quilt.

ACCURATE and Easy To avoid bulkiness in the seams, press toward the setting squares. If your setting square fabric is a light color, the seam allowances may show through as a shadow line. To avoid this, either press the seams toward the pieced blocks, or trim the seam of the pieced block so that it's narrower than the seam of the setting square.

Assembly Diagram

Borders

1 Referring to the **Assembly Diagram**, sew the side borders to the quilt. Press the seams toward the borders.

2 Sew the top and bottom borders to the quilt. Press the seams toward the borders.

Finishing Touches

1 Read "Finishing" on page 224 for details on assembling and finishing the quilt.

2 Mark quilting designs on the quilt top, referring to the **Quilting Diagram** for ideas. The pieced blocks were also quilted in the ditch.

Quilting Diagram

3 Cut the backing fabric in half crosswise to make two 2¼-yard lengths. Cut a 34-inch strip from each length and trim the selvages. Sew these lengths together along one long edge to create a backing with a vertical seam. Press the seam open.

4 Layer the quilt top, batting, and backing. Baste to secure the layers. Quilt by hand or machine.

5 Cut 279 inches of 1½-inch bias strips for single-fold binding. Sew the strips together to form one continuous binding strip. Sew the binding to the quilt top.

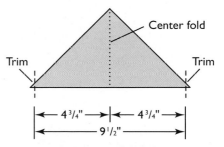

Trimming Points on Setting Triangles

When you're assembling a diagonal row of blocks and setting triangles, it's easy to misalign the edges, often leaving little or no seam allowance on one end. Avoid the dreaded seam ripper by trimming the points on the setting triangles before you sew. For side setting triangles, measure 9½ inches from the 90 degree corner on each short side of the triangle, then trim the point, as shown in the **Side Triangle Trimming Diagram**. This will make the short sides of the side triangle fit perfectly with the 9½-inch block.

For corner setting triangles, find the center line of the patch by folding it in half. From the folded center line, measure 4¾ inches toward each point and trim, as shown in the **Corner Triangle Trimming Diagram**. This will make the long side of the corner triangle fit perfectly with the 9½-inch blocks.

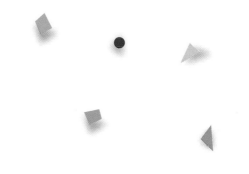

Side Triangle Trimming Diagram

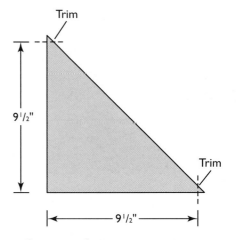

Corner Triangle Trimming Diagram

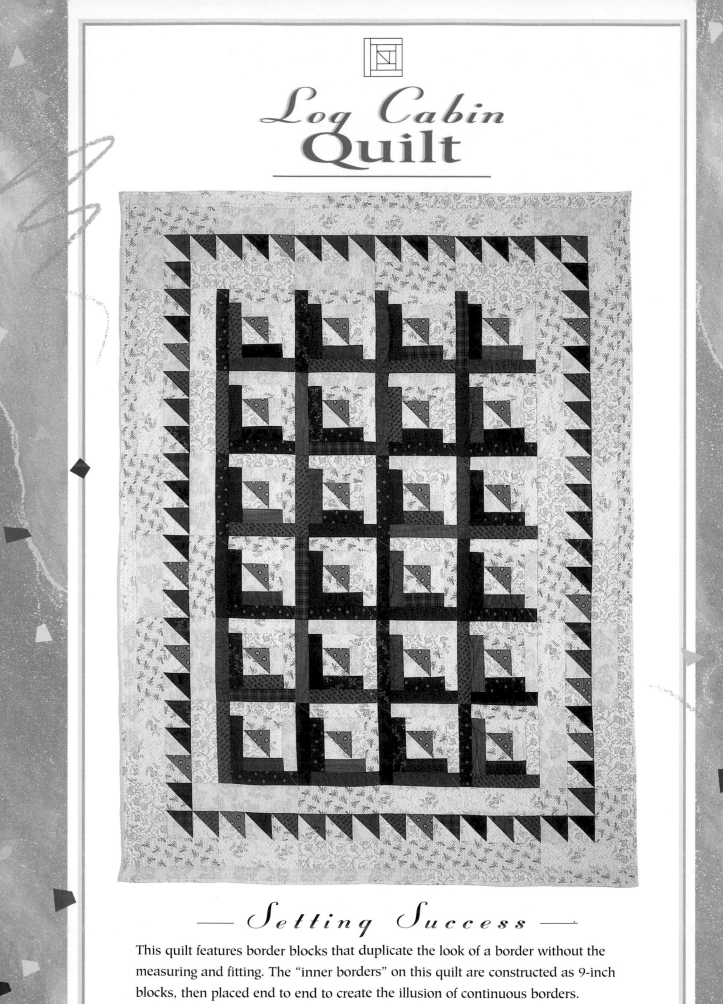

Log Cabin Quilt

— Setting Success —

This quilt features border blocks that duplicate the look of a border without the measuring and fitting. The "inner borders" on this quilt are constructed as 9-inch blocks, then placed end to end to create the illusion of continuous borders.

24

pieced blocks

choosing **blocks** to use

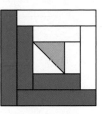

Log Cabin

This quilt features the Log Cabin block (page 68). It also features Sawtooth border blocks made with triangles the same size as the center of the Log Cabin; the directions for these Sawtooth border blocks are given within this project. Refer to the **Basic Setting Diagram** on page 198 to see the setting used in the quilt. The Log Cabin blocks are set side by side and have a strong diagonal coloration. Other blocks that look good in this kind of setting are Jacob's Ladder, Log Cabin with a Chain, Lost Ship, Ocean Waves, and Woodland Path. The Sawtooth border blocks form a bold border and could easily be paired with any number of blocks that contain similar large triangles like Air Castle, Perpetual Motion, and Whirligig.

Project Basics

Finished Size: 57½ × 75½
Finished Block: 9 inches
Number of Blocks: 24 Log Cabin and 24 Sawtooth border blocks used in the setting
Setting Highlights: Straight side-by-side set surrounded by easy-to-make border blocks that mimic the look of time-consuming pieced borders

Fabric and Supplies

Log Cabin Blocks

⅜ yard *each*	four assorted teal-on-cream prints (light)
⅜ yard	medium teal print (medium)
¼ yard *each*	five assorted dark teal prints (dark)

Setting

| ½ yard *each* | four assorted teal-on-cream prints for border blocks and outer border |
| ⅛ yard *each* | six assorted medium and dark teal prints for border blocks |

Finishing

4¾ yards	backing fabric
¾ yard	binding fabric
65 × 83-inch	quilt batting

Cutting

All measurements include ¼-inch seam allowances. Cut all strips on the crosswise grain.

Blocks

Refer to the cutting chart on page 68 for the Log Cabin block. The fabric values listed in the parentheses in the Fabric and Supplies list correspond to the fabric values in the cutting chart on the block page. Cut the widest strips in each value first, even if they're not the first alphabetical letter. Often you can cut the narrower strips out of the fabric left over from the widest strips.

Setting

Refer to the cutting chart on page 199 to cut the fabric for the Sawtooth border blocks and the outer borders.

Making the Quilt

This quilt consists of 24 pieced blocks in the center of the quilt, 24 Sawtooth border blocks, and narrow, randomly pieced outer borders in a variety of scrap fabrics. See the **Basic Setting Diagram** on page 198.

Blocks

Refer to page 68 to make 24 Log Cabin blocks. Or, cut and piece the block or blocks of your choice.

Border Blocks

Referring to the **Border Blocks Assembly Diagrams** on page 198, make 12 side border blocks, 8 top and bottom border blocks, and 4 corner blocks. Be sure to follow color placement in each of the blocks carefully. Press seams in the direction indicated by the pressing arrows in the diagrams.

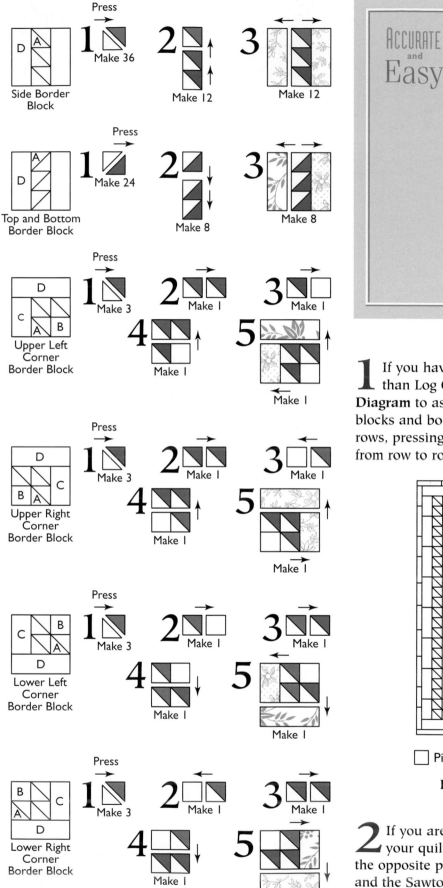

Border Blocks Assembly Diagrams

ACCURATE and Easy

You can increase your fabric choices when making the Sawtooth border blocks by using the wrong side of some of the dark fabrics for the half-square triangles. Many dark fabrics make good medium fabrics when flipped over. Since the border contains an assortment of mediums and darks, using the wrong side of a few darks will add to the scrappy flavor of the border.

Assembly

1 If you have selected a block or blocks other than Log Cabin, refer to the **Basic Setting Diagram** to assemble the quilt. Sew the pieced blocks and border blocks together in horizontal rows, pressing the seams in opposite directions from row to row. Sew the rows together.

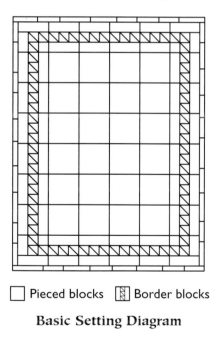

☐ Pieced blocks ▨ Border blocks

Basic Setting Diagram

2 If you are using the Log Cabin blocks for your quilt, refer to the **Assembly Diagram** on the opposite page, and sew the Log Cabin blocks and the Sawtooth border blocks together in horizontal rows. Press the seams in opposite directions from row to row. Sew the rows together.

Cutting for 24 Sawtooth Border Blocks

Fabric	Block Basics			Rotary Cutting				Templates	Yardage
	Patch	Shape	Total Needed	Strip Width (in inches)	Squares to Cut	Cut Size (in inches)	Next Cut	Template	Strip Length Needed (in inches)
Teal-on-cream prints	A	◸	72	3⅞	36	3⅞ × 3⅞	◩	T12	139½
	B	☐	4	3½	4	3½ × 3½	—	S13	14
	C	▭	4	3½	4 rectangles	3½ × 6½	—	—	26
	D	▭	44	3½	44 rectangles	3½ × 9½	—	—	418
Medium and dark teal prints	A	◢	72	3⅞	36	3⅞ × 3⅞	◪	T12	139½

Cutting for the Outer Borders

Fabric	Used for	Strip Width (in inches)	Strip Length Needed (in inches)	Total Length Needed (in inches)				
Teal-on-cream prints	Outer borders	2	Random lengths from 6½–9½	290	—	—	—	—

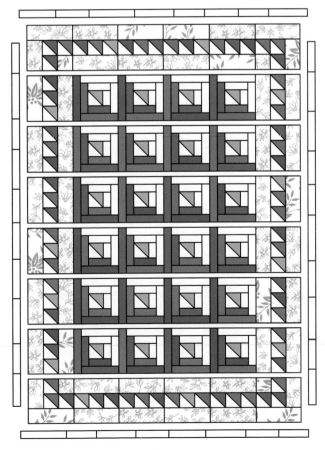

Assembly Diagram

Borders

1 The outer borders are pieced together from random lengths of 2-inch-wide strips sewn end to end. Cut random-length strips, ranging from 6½ to 9½ inches long. Sew these strips together along their short sides to create two 2 × 72½-inch outer borders for the sides of the quilt and two 2 × 57½-inch outer borders for the top and bottom of the quilt.

2 Referring to the **Basic Setting Diagram** on the opposite page, sew the side outer borders to the quilt. Press seams toward the outer borders.

3 Sew the top and bottom outer borders to the quilt. Press seams toward the outer borders.

Finishing Touches

1 Read "Finishing" on page 224 for details on assembling and finishing the quilt.

2 Mark quilting designs on the quilt top, referring to the **Quilting Diagram** on page 200 for ideas. The pieced blocks and the pieced area of the border blocks were also quilted in the ditch.

Log Cabin Quilt   199

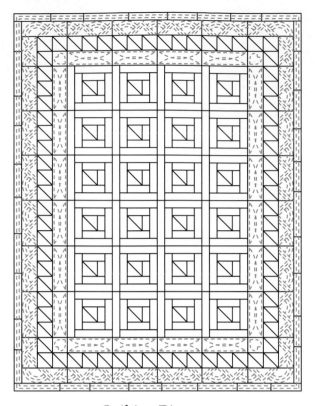

Quilting Diagram

3 Cut the backing fabric in half crosswise to make two 2⅜-yard lengths. Cut two 13-inch-wide strips from one of the lengths. Trim all selvages. Sew one narrow strip to each side of the full-width piece to create a backing with vertical seams. Press the seams open.

4 Layer the quilt top, batting, and backing. Baste to secure the layers. Quilt by hand or machine.

5 Cut 276 inches of 1½-inch bias strips for single-fold binding. Sew the strips together to form one continuous binding strip. Sew the binding to the quilt top.

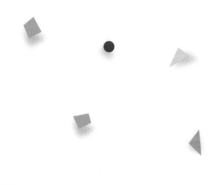

Discovering the History behind the Log Cabin Quilt

Abraham Lincoln's presidential campaign in the 1860s sparked Log Cabin fever. As the nation celebrated its rural history and the ideals behind the simple lifestyle of log cabin inhabitants, a quilt block called Log Cabin became an instant favorite of late nineteenth-century quiltmakers. The Log Cabin block pattern was named because it closely resembled the construction of a log home—the layering of log after log—rather than for its resemblance to an actual log cabin.

American quiltmakers embraced the Log Cabin block and used it to embody their pioneer spirit. A red center in a Log Cabin block symbolized the hearth of the home, while a bright yellow center was the fabric equivalent of a lantern placed in the window to welcome guests. During the Civil War, slaves headed north on the Underground Railroad knew to look for Log Cabin quilts on clotheslines—if the quilt had a black center square, the house was considered a safe haven.

Traditional Log Cabin blocks have one light half and one dark half to represent the sunlight and shadows that fill a home. The symbolism of the setting names themselves lend credence to the notion that country life and simplicity were foremost in the minds of Log Cabin quiltmakers. Barn Raising, Sunshine and Shadow, Streak of Lightening, Straight Furrows, Zigzag, Courthouse Steps, and Windmill are just a few of the names given to the placement of light and dark in a Log Cabin quilt.

Rosebud Quilt

─ *Setting Success* ─

This strippy setting was aptly named because it contains long strips of fabric. Strippy sets were very popular in the early 1800s and often featured elegant striped fabrics in the wide sashing. Here, pieced blocks are turned on point, then sewn together diagonally with setting triangles to create vertical block rows. Borders are added only to the sides of the quilt to keep the vertical orientation of the quilt intact.

24 choosing **blocks** to use

pieced blocks

This quilt features the Rosebud block (page 94). Refer to the **Basic Setting Diagram** on the opposite page to see the setting used in the quilt. The pieced blocks are set diagonally in a strippy set. Strippy sets are characterized by blocks set diagonally in vertical rows with side triangles completing each vertical column. Vertical strips of fabric are traditionally used to separate the rows.

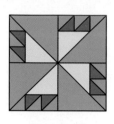

Rosebud

Choose blocks that look good when set on point and that can stand up well on their own, such as Duck Paddle, Ohio Star (a traditional favorite for this setting), Road Home, and Scrap Basket. You may want to consider blocks that have a diagonal center division that becomes vertical when the block is set on point, such as Log Cabin with a Chain, Lost Ship, Ocean Waves, and Star Stairway. For the sashing strips between the vertical block rows, try choosing a striped or linear fabric that includes all the colors in the quilt design.

Project Basics

Finished Size: 77 × 82 inches
Finished Block: 9 inches
Number of Blocks: 24
Setting Highlights: Vertical rows with blocks set on point, setting triangles, vertical sashing, and triple side borders, including pieced Dogtooth borders

Fabric and Supplies

Rosebud Blocks

⅝ yard	assorted light green prints (light)
2 yards	assorted medium blue prints (medium)
⅝ yard	assorted dark red-orange and red prints (dark)

Setting

2½ yards	assorted light yellow and gold prints for setting triangles
½ yard	assorted light yellow and gold prints for Dogtooth borders
½ yard	medium blue prints for Dogtooth borders
2¼ yards	light yellow plaid for sashing and inner and outer borders

Finishing

7½ yards	backing fabric
¾ yard	binding fabric
85 × 90-inch	quilt batting

Cutting

All measurements include ¼-inch seam allowances. Cut all strips on the crosswise grain, unless otherwise indicated.

Blocks

Refer to the cutting chart on page 94 for the Rosebud block. The fabric values listed in the parentheses in the Fabric and Supplies list correspond to the fabric values in the cutting chart on the block page. Cut the widest strips in each value first, even if they're not the first alphabetical letter. Often you can cut the narrower strips out of the fabric left over from the wider strips.

Setting

Refer to the cutting chart on the opposite page to cut the remaining fabric for the quilt top.

Making the Quilt

This quilt consists of 24 pieced blocks, side and corner triangles, and sashing between the rows. Narrow inner borders, Dogtooth borders, and wider outer borders are added to the sides of the quilt top. See the **Basic Setting Diagram** on the opposite page.

Cutting						
First Cut		**Second Cut**			**Third Cut**	
Strip Width (in inches)	No. to Cut	Shape	Cut Size (in inches)	No. to Cut	Shape	Total Needed
Assorted light yellow and gold prints						
Side setting triangles	$13\frac{7}{8}$	5	◻	$13\frac{7}{8} \times 13\frac{7}{8}$	10	⊠	40
Corner setting triangles	$7\frac{1}{4}$	2	◻	$7\frac{1}{4} \times 7\frac{1}{4}$	8	◺	16
Dogtooth borders	$5\frac{1}{2}$	2	◻	$5\frac{1}{2} \times 5\frac{1}{2}$	9	⊠	34
Dogtooth borders	3	1	◻	3×3	2	◺	4
Assorted medium blue prints						
Dogtooth borders	$5\frac{1}{2}$	2	◼	$5\frac{1}{2} \times 5\frac{1}{2}$	9	⊠	36
Light yellow plaid						
Inner borders*	$2\frac{5}{8}$	2	▭	$2\frac{5}{8} \times 77$	2	—	—
Sashing and outer borders*	5	5	▭	5×77	5	—	—

*Cut on the lengthwise grain.

Blocks

Refer to page 94 to make 24 Rosebud blocks. Or, cut and piece the block or blocks of your choice.

Assembly

1 If you have selected a block or blocks other than Rosebud, refer to the **Basic Setting Diagram** to assemble the quilt. Sew the blocks and setting triangles together in diagonal rows. Press the seams toward the triangles. Sew the block rows and sashing strips together in vertical rows.

2 If you are using Rosebud blocks for your quilt, refer to the **Assembly Diagram** and sew the pieced blocks and setting triangles together in diagonal rows, then sew the diagonal rows into vertical columns. Press the seams toward the setting triangles. Finally, sew the vertical columns and sashing strips together to make the quilt top.

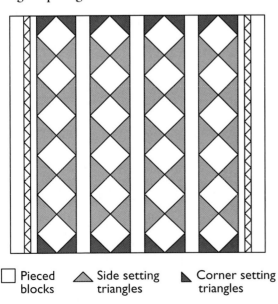

☐ Pieced blocks ◣ Side setting triangles ◥ Corner setting triangles

Basic Setting Diagram

Assembly Diagram

ACCURATE
and
Easy

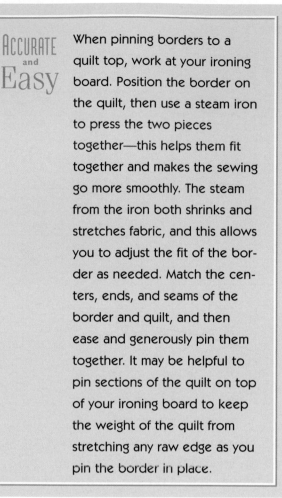

When pinning borders to a quilt top, work at your ironing board. Position the border on the quilt, then use a steam iron to press the two pieces together—this helps them fit together and makes the sewing go more smoothly. The steam from the iron both shrinks and stretches fabric, and this allows you to adjust the fit of the border as needed. Match the centers, ends, and seams of the border and quilt, and then ease and generously pin them together. It may be helpful to pin sections of the quilt on top of your ironing board to keep the weight of the quilt from stretching any raw edge as you pin the border in place.

Borders

1 Sew one inner border to each side of the quilt. Press the seams toward the borders.

2 Referring to the **Dogtooth Borders Diagram**, make two Dogtooth borders. Press the seams as indicated by the arrows. Sew one to each side of the quilt, positioning the dark triangles nearest the block rows. Press the seams toward the inner border.

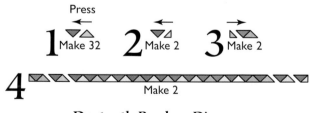

Dogtooth Borders Diagram

3 Sew one outer border to each side of quilt. Press the seams toward the borders.

Finishing Touches

1 Read "Finishing" on page 224 for details on assembling and finishing the quilt.

2 Mark quilting designs on the quilt top, referring to the **Quilting Diagram** for ideas. The pieced blocks were also quilted in the ditch.

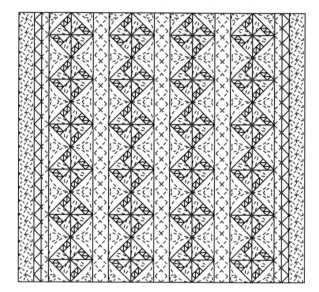

Quilting Diagram

3 Cut the backing fabric into three 2½-yard pieces. From the length of two of the pieces, cut a 23-inch-wide piece. Sew one narrow piece to each side of the full-width piece to create a backing with vertical seams. Press the seams open.

4 Layer the quilt top, batting, and backing. Baste to secure the layers. Quilt by hand or machine.

5 Cut 328 inches of 1½-inch bias strips for single-fold binding. Sew the strips together to form one continuous binding strip. Sew the binding to the quilt top.

Giving Your Quilt Zing with a Zigzag Set

With only two alterations, you can turn this strippy set into a zigzag set. First, you'll need to eliminate the long sashing strips between the rows, and second, you'll need to offset the block rows by half a block. Look for blocks that can be featured on point and can be cut in half without disrupting the pattern. Half-blocks are featured in alternating rows. Good block choices for this set include Birds in the Air, Double Windmill, Job's Troubles, and Kansas Troubles.

If you decide to create a zigzag set, you will need to decide how many blocks and rows you would like in your quilt. An odd number of rows actually works best because it creates a symmetrical design. The quilt shown in the **Zigzag Set Diagram** has three rows of four blocks each (the middle row has three whole blocks and two half-blocks). It finishes at 43¾ × 56½ inches, including the borders. The directions given here are for this quilt setting and size. A larger zigzag set may include five rows of five blocks each.

Zigzag Set Diagram

If you've selected the Rosebud block for your zigzag set, refer to page 94 to cut enough fabric for 12 blocks. Make 11 Rosebud blocks, referring to "How to Assemble" on page 94. Make two half-blocks, referring to the **Half-Block Diagram**. Or, cut and piece 11 full blocks and two half-blocks of your choice.

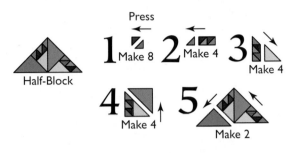

Half-Block Diagram

Consider using just one fabric for the corner and side setting triangles so that your zigzag pattern is very unified. A print fabric will disguise the vertical seams even more. Cut setting triangles for this quilt size and setting as follows: Cut four 7¼-inch squares for the corner setting triangles; cut each square in half once diagonally. You will need a total of eight corner triangles. Cut five 13⅞-inch squares for the side setting triangles; cut each square in half twice diagonally. You will need a total of 20 side setting triangles.

Piece the two other block rows in the same manner as in the **Assembly Diagram** on page 203. For the middle row, simply begin and end with a half-block, omitting the corner triangles. Press your seams toward the setting triangles.

Cut two 3 × 51½-inch side borders and two 3 × 43¾-inch borders for the top and bottom. Add the side borders to the quilt top and press the seams toward the borders. Add the top and bottom borders and press the seams toward the borders.

Finish the quilt, following the directions under "Finishing" on page 224. You will need to cut 210 inches of 1½-inch bias strips for single-fold bias binding.

Jericho Stars Quilt

— Setting Success —

A simple side-by-side setting can become the picture of elegance when you carefully choose blocks that interact with each other, then plan your fabric placement to highlight the interaction. Here, the large triangles surrounding the nine patch centers in the first featured block are cut from matching fabric, then placed so they surround Star blocks to create larger, more dominant star patterns. The addition of a third block into the quilt—a simply pieced, low-contrast Nine Patch—lends excitement to an area that would otherwise be a plain alternate block.

choosing **blocks** to use

This quilt features the Crossroads to Jericho block (page 26) and the Sawtooth Star block (page 96). It also features pieced Nine Patch blocks as interesting alternate blocks. The directions for the Nine Patch blocks are given on page 209 of this project. Refer to the **Basic Setting Diagram** on page 209 to see the setting used in the quilt. An interesting feature of this quilt is the careful fabric selection and placement in the Crossroads to Jericho blocks (block one), allowing a secondary star pattern to emerge around another pieced block—in this case a Sawtooth Star block (block two). There are several slightly more complex star blocks that could be substituted for Sawtooth Star in this setting, including Judy's Star, Missouri Star, and Rising Star. Two other blocks that would have the same "star within a star" effect as Crossroads to Jericho are Road Home and Square within a Square. Pair either of these two blocks with any 4 × 4-grid star block for stellar results.

Note: While the piecing and assembly for this quilt can be achieved by a beginner, the fabric placement and cutting directions are somewhat complex. Read through all directions *completely and carefully* before beginning this project.

Crossroads to Jericho

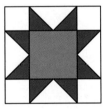

Sawtooth Star

Project Basics

Finished Size: 81½ × 81½ inches
Finished Block: 9 inches
Number of Blocks: 24 Crossroads to Jericho and 9 Sawtooth Star blocks, plus 16 Nine Patch blocks used in the setting
Setting Highlights: Two different blocks set side by side, with specific fabric placement creating a larger, secondary design where the blocks intersect; pieced alternate blocks for added interest; wide inner borders; and scrappy-pieced outer borders

Fabric and Supplies

Crossroads to Jericho Blocks

⅜ yard	very light cream print*
¾ yard	light cream print (light)
¾ yard	assorted medium tan prints (medium)
¼ yard *each*	nine assorted dark blue and brown prints (dark)

Sawtooth Star Blocks

⅝ yard	light cream print (light)
⅜ yard	medium tan floral print (medium)
⅜ yard	assorted dark blue and brown prints (dark)†

Setting

¾ yard	very light cream print for Nine Patch alternate blocks
⅞ yard	light cream print for Nine Patch alternate blocks
2⅜ yards	medium brown floral print for inner borders
¾ yard	assorted medium and dark blue prints for outer borders

Finishing

7½ yards	backing fabric
¾ yard	binding fabric
90 × 90-inch	quilt batting

*This is an additional fabric for this block that is not listed in the cutting chart for the Crossroads to Jericho block. The color placement in this quilt is very specific, and this fabric is used for the outer triangles in the blocks placed around the edge of the quilt center. See Step 2 on page 209.
†Or use nine different scraps, each at least 7 inches square.

Cutting

All measurements include ¼-inch seam allowances. Cut all strips on the crosswise grain, unless otherwise indicated.

Cutting					
	First Cut		**Second Cut**		
	Strip Width (in inches)	No. to Cut	Shape	Cut Size (in inches)	No. to Cut
Very light cream print					
Nine Patch alternate blocks	3½	7	—	—	—
Light cream print					
Nine Patch alternate blocks	3½	8	—	—	—
Medium brown floral print					
Side inner borders	7¼*	2	▬	7¼ × 63½	2
Top and bottom inner borders	7¼*	2	▬	7¼ × 77	2

Cutting for the Outer Borders				
Fabric	Used for	Strip Width (in inches)	Strip Length (in inches)	Total Length Needed (in inches)
Assorted medium and dark blue prints	Outer borders	2¾	Random lengths between 11–34 inches*	346†

*Cut from the lengthwise grain.

†See Step 2 under "Borders" to piece together the random lengths. From the pieced strips, cut border strips as directed in Step 2.

Blocks

Refer to the cutting chart on page 96 for the Sawtooth Star block. The fabric values listed in the parentheses in the Fabric and Supplies list correspond to the fabric values in the cutting chart on the block page. Cut the widest strips in each value first, even if they're not the first alphabetical letter. Often you can cut the narrower strips out of the fabric left over from the wider strips.

Refer to page 26 to cut the fabric for 24 Crossroads to Jericho blocks, using fabrics as noted below:

- Patch A: Cut 24 sets of 4 matching-fabric patches from the light cream print, for a total of 96 squares.
- Patch B: Cut 24 sets of 5 matching-fabric patches from the assorted medium tan prints, for a total of 120 squares.
- Patch C: Cut 24 triangles from the very light cream print. Cut 9 sets of 8 matching-fabric patches from the assorted dark blue and brown prints, for a total of 72 triangles.

Setting

Refer to the cutting chart above to cut the remaining fabric for the quilt top, including the fabric for the Nine Patch alternate blocks and the inner and outer borders.

Making the Quilt

This quilt consists of 33 pieced blocks (24 of one block and 9 of another) that interact to create a larger, secondary star pattern on the quilt top. There are also 16 pieced alternate blocks, wide inner borders, and scrappy-pieced outer borders. See the **Basic Setting Diagram** on page 209.

Blocks

1 If you have chosen not to use the Crossroads to Jericho and Sawtooth Star blocks, cut and piece the block or blocks of your choice.

2 Follow Steps 1 and 2 on the opposite page to make the Nine Patch centers for the Crossroads to Jericho blocks. Wait until all the other blocks are pieced to add the C triangles to these blocks.

3 Refer to page 96 to make nine Sawtooth Star blocks.

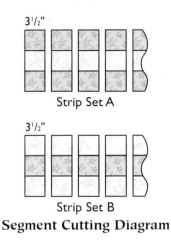

3½"

Strip Set A

3½"

Strip Set B

Segment Cutting Diagram

Accurate and Easy

Check the block sizes as you work! When using more than one block design, it is really important that the blocks be the same size in order for the seams to match when you assemble the quilt. Sew a sample of each block you'll be using to check its size—these pieced blocks should measure 9½ inches with seam allowances. If any of your sample blocks do not measure 9½ inches, adjust your seam allowances accordingly and sew a second sample.

3 To make each Nine Patch, sew a strip set A segment to the top and bottom of a strip set B segment. Press the seams toward the A segments. You will need to make a total of 16 Nine Patch blocks.

Assembly

1 If you have selected a block or blocks other than Crossroads to Jericho and Sawtooth Star, refer to the **Basic Setting Diagram** to assemble the quilt. Sew the pieced blocks and pieced Nine Patch alternate blocks together in horizontal rows. Press the seams in opposite directions from row to row. Sew the rows together.

Alternate Blocks

1 The Nine Patch alternate blocks are strip-pieced from two different strip sets. There are two strip set A segments and one strip set B segment in each block, as shown in the **Strip Set Diagram**. To make strip set A, sew one light cream strip to each side of a very light cream strip, as shown. Press the seams toward the light cream strips. To make strip set B, sew one very light cream strip to each side of a light cream strip, pressing the seams toward the light cream strip.

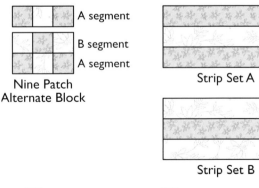

A segment

B segment

A segment

Nine Patch Alternate Block

Strip Set A

Strip Set B

☐ Light cream print   ☐ Very light cream print

Strip Set Diagram

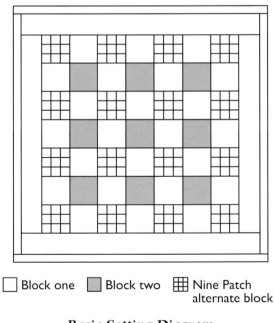

☐ Block one   ■ Block two   ⊞ Nine Patch alternate block

Basic Setting Diagram

2 Square up one end of each strip set. Cut 3½-inch segments from each set; see the **Segment Cutting Diagram**. You will need a total of 32 segments of strip set A and 16 segments of strip set B.

2 If you are using Crossroads to Jericho and Sawtooth Star blocks for your quilt, you will need to lay out the completed Nine Patch centers of the Crossroads to Jericho blocks, the Sawtooth Star blocks, and the pieced Nine Patch alternate blocks in horizontal rows. Referring to the **Assembly Diagram**, place each set of eight dark blue or brown print C patch triangles around a Sawtooth Star block to form a larger, secondary star pattern. (The quilt shown on page 206 alternates dark blue and brown fabrics for every other secondary star pattern.) Place the very light cream C patch triangles along the outer edge of the Crossroads to Jericho blocks. When you have the fabrics arranged to your liking, sew the C patch triangles to the Crossroads to Jericho blocks, as shown on page 26.

Assembly Diagram

3 Sew the blocks together in horizontal rows, pressing the seams in opposite directions from row to row. Sew the rows together.

Borders

1 Referring to the **Basic Setting Diagram** on page 209, sew one side inner border to each side of the quilt top. Press the seams toward the borders. Sew one inner border to the top and bottom of the quilt top, pressing the seams toward the borders.

2 The outer borders are pieced together from random lengths of 2¾-inch-wide strips sewn end to end. Cut random-length strips, ranging from 11 to 34 inches long. The "Total Length Needed" measurement in the cutting chart is generous and allows for seam allowances and adjustments. (You may want to trim or replace a length if a seam falls too close to the end of a border strip.) Sew these random-length strips together along their short

sides to create two 2¾ × 77-inch outer borders for the sides of the quilt and two 2¾ × 82-inch outer borders for the top and bottom of the quilt.

3 Sew the side outer borders to the quilt. Press seams toward the outer borders. Sew the top and bottom outer borders to the quilt. Press seams toward the outer borders.

Finishing Touches

1 Read "Finishing" on page 224 for details on assembling and finishing the quilt.

2 Mark quilting designs on the quilt top, referring to the **Quilting Diagram** for ideas. The Sawtooth Star blocks were also quilted in the ditch.

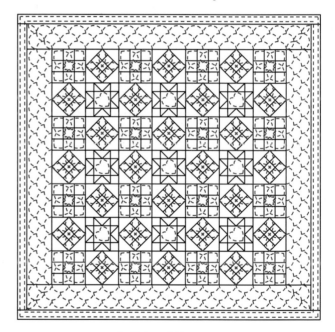

Quilting Diagram

3 Cut the backing fabric into three 2½-yard pieces. From two of the pieces, cut a 25-inch-wide piece. Sew one narrow piece to each side of the full-width piece to create a backing with vertical seams. Press the seams open.

4 Layer the quilt top, batting, and backing. Baste to secure the layers. Quilt by hand or machine.

5 Cut 336 inches of 1½-inch bias strips for single-fold binding. Sew the strips together to form one continuous binding strip. Sew the binding to the quilt top.

Cross-Country Quilt

Setting Success

An easy way to approach designing two-block quilts is to choose one fancy block and one plain block. When selecting a plain block, it's important to find one that supports and enhances the fancy block without fighting or overpowering it. Combining a plain and a fancy block often creates a dynamic interaction that can, at first glance, leave you guessing where the block seams are, and can make a simple side-by-side setting look quite dramatic.

50 choosing **blocks** to use

pieced blocks This quilt features the Cross-Country (page 25) and Variable Star II (page 115) blocks. Refer to the **Basic Setting Diagram** on page 214 to see the setting used for this quilt. Variable Star II is the fancier block to the plainer Cross-Country. The long strip on the outside edge of Cross-Country allows you to combine it with almost any block without matching seams. Other plain alternate blocks you could consider are Art Square, Crossroads to Jericho, Double Four Patch, Puss in the Corner, Shoofly, and Stepping Stones. You could creatively pair any of these plain blocks with a fancy block like Centennial, Grape Basket, Judy's Star, or Scrap Basket. Or you could make a variety of star blocks (like Combination Star, Dolley Madison's Star, and Eliza's Nine Patch), and sprinkle them here and there around the Cross-Country block to create a visual surprise.

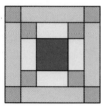 

Cross-Country   **Variable Star II**

Project Basics

Finished Size: 75 × 88 inches
Finished Block: 9 inches
Number of Blocks: 30 Cross-Country, 20 Variable Star II
Setting Highlights: Diagonal side-by-side set and setting triangles

Fabric and Supplies

Cross-Country Blocks

¾ yard	assorted light cream prints (light 1)
½ yard *each*	four assorted cream prints (light 2)
⅞ yard	medium tan print (medium)
½ yard	large-scale dark rust print (dark)

Variable Star II Blocks

⅜ yard *each*	four assorted light cream prints (light)
⅝ yard	large-scale medium rust print (medium)
¾ yard	dark red print (dark)

Setting

| 2½ yards | large-scale cream print for side and corner setting triangles and borders |

Finishing

7⅞ yards	backing fabric
¾ yard	binding fabric
83 × 96-inch	quilt batting

Cutting

All measurements include ¼-inch seam allowances. Cut all strips on the crosswise grain, unless otherwise indicated.

Blocks

Refer to the cutting chart on page 25 for the Cross-Country block and page 115 for the Variable Star II block. The fabric values listed in the parentheses in the Fabric and Supplies list correspond to the fabric values in the cutting chart on the block pages. Cut the widest strips in each value first, even if they're not the first alphabetical letter. Often you can cut the narrower strips out of fabric left over from the wider strip.

Note: The quilt in the photograph features a number of different star blocks for the fancy blocks. However, the directions for this project have been simplified and call for all 20 fancy blocks to be Variable Star II blocks.

Setting

Refer to the cutting chart on the opposite page to cut the remaining fabric for the quilt.

| Cutting | | | | | | |
| First Cut | | Second Cut | | | Third Cut | |
Strip Width (in inches)	No. to Cut	Shape	Cut Size (in inches)	No. to Cut	Shape	Total Needed
Large-scale cream print						
Side borders	6*	2	▭	6 × 76⅞	2	—	—
Top and bottom borders	6*	2	▭	6 × 75¼	2	—	—
Side setting triangles	13⅞†	5	□	13⅞ × 13⅞	5	⊠	18
Corner setting triangles	7¼†	1	□	7¼ × 7¼	2	◻	4

*Cut lengthwise to avoid seams.
†Cut these pieces from the remaining width of fabric after cutting the borders.

Making the Quilt

This quilt contains 50 pieced blocks—30 plain blocks and 20 fancy blocks. The quilt is assembled in diagonal rows. Wide borders finish the quilt. See the **Basic Setting Diagram** on page 214.

Blocks

Refer to page 25 to make 30 Cross-Country blocks and page 115 to make 20 Variable Star II blocks.

Or cut and piece the block or blocks of your choice.

Assembly

1 If you have selected blocks other than Cross-Country and Variable Star II, refer to the **Basic Setting Diagram** on page 214 to assemble the quilt. Sew the plain blocks, fancy blocks, side setting triangles, and corner setting triangles together in diagonal rows, pressing the seams in opposite directions from row to row. Sew the rows together.

Cutting Patches on Grain

Fabric's two types of grain (straight and bias) play a part in how you cut patches. Bias grain is stretchy, while straight grain is more stable, so cut patches so the straight grain is along the outer edges. This applies to units within a block, as well as along the outside edge of the finished block itself. In the block shown in the **Straight Grain Diagram,** all the triangles finish at the same size, but you actually cut two different types of triangles. The outer cream triangles are *quarter-square* triangles, made by cutting a square in half diagonally *twice*. This keeps the straight grain on the outside of the block. The burgundy inner triangles are *half-square* triangles, made by cutting a square in half only *once* diagonally. The bias edges of the patches are sewn to the straight grain of the corner squares, stabilizing the triangle's bias edge.

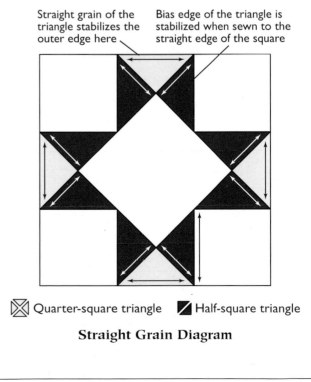

Straight grain of the triangle stabilizes the outer edge here

Bias edge of the triangle is stabilized when sewn to the straight edge of the square

⊠ Quarter-square triangle ◩ Half-square triangle

Straight Grain Diagram

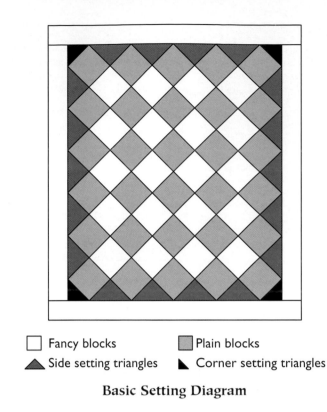

☐ Fancy blocks   ☐ Plain blocks
▲ Side setting triangles   ◣ Corner setting triangles

Basic Setting Diagram

2 If you are using the Cross-Country and Variable Star II blocks for your quilt, refer to the **Assembly Diagram** and sew the blocks, side setting triangles, and corner setting triangles together in diagonal rows, pressing the seams toward the Cross-Country blocks. Sew the rows together.

Assembly Diagram

Borders

1 Referring to the **Assembly Diagram**, sew the side borders to the quilt. Press seams toward the borders.

2 Sew the top and bottom borders to the quilt. Press seams toward the borders.

Finishing Touches

1 Read "Finishing" on page 224 for details on assembling and finishing the quilt.

2 Mark quilting designs on the quilt top, referring to the **Quilting Diagram** for ideas. The pieced blocks were also quilted in the ditch.

Quilting Diagram

3 Cut the backing fabric crosswise into three 2⅝-yard pieces. From two of the pieces, cut a 22-inch-wide strip. Trim the selvages on all pieces. Sew one narrow piece to each side of the full-width piece to create a backing with vertical seams. Press the seams open.

4 Layer the quilt top, batting, and backing. Baste to secure the layers. Quilt by hand or machine.

5 Cut 336 inches of 1½-inch bias strips for binding. Sew the strips together to form one continuous binding strip. Sew the binding to the quilt top.

Changing the Quilt's Size

The greatest benefit of a mix-and-match approach to blocks and settings is that all the blocks featured in this book fit in each setting, making it easy to use your favorite block in your favorite setting. This setting is perfect if you want to try pairing two different blocks, or if you want to try using one block in two different values (see page 130 for details). If you want to make this two-block, diagonally set quilt in another size, use the chart below to get started. Refer to the **Size Variation Diagrams** for block placement and layout.

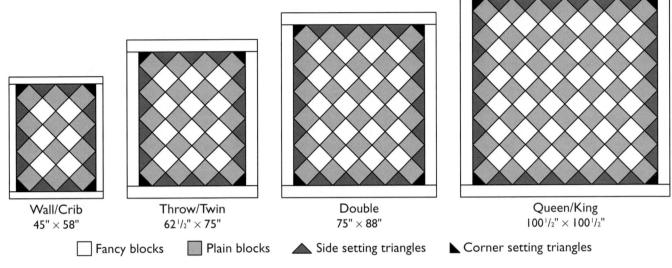

| Wall/Crib | Throw/Twin | Double | Queen/King |
| 45" × 58" | 62¹⁄₂" × 75" | 75" × 88" | 100¹⁄₂" × 100¹⁄₂" |

□ Fancy blocks   ▪ Plain blocks   ▲ Side setting triangles   ◣ Corner setting triangles

Size Variation Diagrams

Size Variations for a Two-Block Diagonal Setting

Quilt Size	No. of Fancy & Plain Blocks	Side Setting Triangles				Corner Setting Triangles			
		Cut Size (in inches)	No. to Cut	Next Cut	Total Needed	Cut Size (in inches)	No. to Cut	Next Cut	Total Needed
Wall/Crib	6 and 12	13⅞ × 13⅞	3	⊠	10	7¼ × 7¼	2	◨	4
Throw/Twin	12 and 20	13⅞ × 13⅞	4	⊠	14	7¼ × 7¼	2	◨	4
Double	20 and 30	13⅞ × 13⅞	5	⊠	18	7¼ × 7¼	2	◨	4
Queen/King	36 and 49	13⅞ × 13⅞	6	⊠	24	7¼ × 7¼	2	◨	4

Cutting for the Borders

Quilt Size	Side Borders		Top/Bottom Borders	
	Cut Size (in inches)	No. to Cut	Cut Size (in inches)	No. to Cut
Wall/Crib	3¾ × 51½	2	3¾ × 45⅛	2
Throw/Twin	6 × 64¼	2	6 × 62½	2
Double	6 × 76⅞	2	6 × 75⅛	2
Queen/King	6 × 89⅝	2	6 × 100⅝	2

Quiltmaking Basics

Even if you've been quilting for years, you may find it helpful to browse through this section of quiltmaking techniques. From rotary cutting to finishing, the methods described here are ones I use to make my cutting, piecing, and quilting more accurate and efficient.

Highlights at a Glance

Clear Steps

The description of each method or technique is written for all skill levels.

When matching diagonal or multiple seams, it may be helpful to use a positioning pin. The match point may have several stitching lines coming through it, but it's at this point—¼ inch below the raw edges—that the seam intersections need to match. Push a pin vertically through the point of the top patch, then the bottom patch, where you want them to match, as shown in **Diagram 20**. Keep this pin standing upright in the fabrics to avoid shifting the patches. Pin on either side of the first pin to hold the fabric together firmly, as shown. Sew the seam, holding the stabbed pin steady to keep it vertical and removing each pin as it nears the needle.

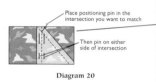

Place positioning pin in the intersection you want to match

Then pin on either side of intersection

Diagram 20

Helpful Diagrams

Detailed diagrams help to illustrate the technique or method being described.

Rotary-Cut Patches at a Glance

Shape Name

Describes the shape of the patch.

How to Cut the Shape

Follow the directions here to rotary cut the shape accurately and easily.

What It Looks Like

Simple drawings show you what the finished shape looks like.

Detailed Diagrams

Illustrations show at a glance how to cut the shape.

(Inset pages 218–219: "Cutting Shapes" — Squares and Rectangles, Half-Square Triangles, Long Triangles, Quarter-Square Triangles, Isosceles Triangles, Trapezoids, Octagons, Kites, 45 Degree Diamonds, Parallelograms, with Diagrams 3–13.)

I can't imagine life without my rotary cutter, but I know that there are quilters who still enjoy using traditional templates. To offer the best of both worlds, I've provided templates *and* rotary-cutting directions for all the shapes used in the 120 blocks.

Rotary Cutting

Posture and table height are important factors in accurate rotary cutting. Stand, don't sit, because you'll have more control over your rotary ruler, and center your head and body in front of the cutting area. You may be more comfortable if your cutting table is higher than a normal sewing table.

Reviewing the Basic Motion

When making cuts, place the fabric to your right and the ruler on the left edge of the fabric. (If you are left-handed, reverse the directions.) Firmly press on the ruler with your left hand, keeping the ruler accurately positioned on the fabric edge. Using even pressure, cut away from you, keeping in constant contact with the right edge of the ruler.

Cutting Strips

Yardage in this book is based on 40-inch-wide fabric. You can cut strips on the crosswise grain (perpendicular to the selvages) or lengthwise grain (parallel to the selvages). The crosswise grain is easy to use because fabric is already folded correctly for these cuts, but you may find the length-

wise grain offers a more stable grain line for patches and borders. For crosswise-grain strips, fold the fabric selvage to selvage. Place the folded edge of the fabric closest to you. To square up the edge, align a square plastic cutting ruler with the fold and place a long ruler to the left of the square ruler. See **Diagram 1**. Remove the square ruler and cut along the right side of the long ruler. Then align the cut edge with the desired measurement on the long ruler, and cut fabric strips as needed.

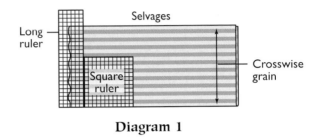

Diagram 1

To cut lengthwise strips, fold the fabric so that the fold is perpendicular to the selvages. Trim away the selvage on one end. Referring to **Diagram 2**, align the cut edge with the desired measurement on the long ruler, and cut fabric strips as needed.

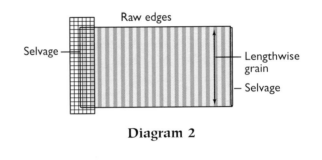

Diagram 2

What Does "+" Mean after a Rotary Measurement?

Most cutting dimensions in the cutting charts are given to the nearest eighth of an inch. There are a few patches, however, that need to be cut to the nearest sixteenth of an inch to fit properly in the block, especially when there are patches set on point. In the charts, this extra $\frac{1}{16}$ inch is indicated by a "+" after the patch measurement. Unfortunately, most rotary rulers are marked in eighths, not in sixteenths. But because a sixteenth is half of an eighth, it's pretty easy to "eyeball" the sixteenth measurement—just find the eighth on the ruler (given in the chart with

the "+" after it) and cut halfway between that eighth number and the next eighth marking. For example, the cutting dimension 3⅝+ inches is actually 3¹¹⁄₁₆ inches, halfway between 3⅝ inches and 3¾ inches. To cut it, find 3⅝ inches on the ruler, then move up half a space, as shown in the **"+" Measurement Diagram.**

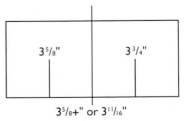

3⅝"   3¾"

3⅝+" or 3¹¹⁄₁₆"

"+" Measurement Diagram

Cutting Shapes

Squares and Rectangles

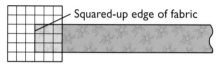

For large quantities of squares or rectangles, cut fabric strips the desired width, then square up one end. Position the strip so the squared-up end is to your left. Line up the edge of the strip with the correct measurement marking on a ruler, and cut your shape. Align a horizontal marking with the lower edge of the strip to keep the patch square, as shown in **Diagram 3**. Cut rectangles in the same manner, cutting strips the width of the rectangle, then cutting to the proper length.

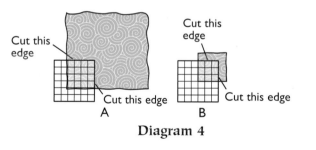

Squared-up edge of fabric

Diagram 3

You can also cut patches one at a time. Position a square ruler on a fabric corner and cut an oversize square. Make two cuts along the right and top edges of the ruler to separate the square from the yardage, as shown in **Diagram 4A**. Turn the cut square 180 degrees so the cut edges are on the left and bottom. Position the ruler to cut a patch to the size you need, and cut the remaining edges, as shown in **4B**.

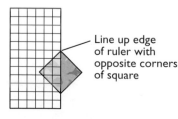

Cut this edge

Cut this edge

Cut this edge

Cut this edge

A   B

Diagram 4

Half-Square Triangles

For right triangles with two sides on the straight grain, cut half-square triangles. Cut a square, then cut it in half diagonally once, as shown in **Diagram 5**. To trim points for easy matching, see page 221.

Line up edge of ruler with opposite corners of square

Diagram 5

Quarter-Square Triangles

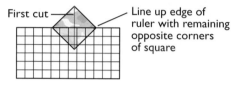

For right triangles with the straight grain on the long side, cut quarter-square triangles. Cut a square in half diagonally. Without moving the triangles, make a second diagonal cut in the opposite direction, as shown in **Diagram 6**. To trim points for easy matching, see page 221.

First cut

Line up edge of ruler with remaining opposite corners of square

Diagram 6

Long Triangles

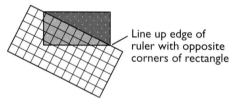

Long triangles are right triangles with one long and one short leg. Cut strips the width of the triangle's short leg, including seam allowances. From these strips, cut rectangles the length of the longer leg of the right angle (including seam allowances). Cut the rectangles in half once diagonally to yield two identical long triangles, as shown in **Diagram 7**. To get reversed long triangles, cut the next rectangle diagonally in the opposite direction. To trim points for easy matching, see page 221.

Line up edge of ruler with opposite corners of rectangle

Diagram 7

Isosceles Triangles

Isosceles triangles are triangles with two equal sides. They are easily cut with the help of a paper template (see page 220). Place the paper template underneath your ruler, aligning the base of the triangle with the edge of the ruler. Measure from the triangle's base to its tip. This is the width you will need to cut your strips. If this measurement does not correspond to a line on your ruler, use Post-it notes to mark the measurement in at least two places along your ruler, and line up the edge of your fabric with them. Then use your ruler as a straight edge and the paper template as a guide to cut your triangles from the strip, turning the template upside down for every other triangle, as shown in **Diagram 8** on the opposite page.

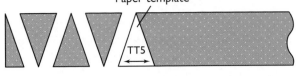

Paper template

TT5

Diagram 8

Trapezoids

Some blocks feature trapezoids, which are cut from triangles or squares and then have corner triangles trimmed away. Trimming templates are included for all shapes that have cutaway triangles. To cut a trapezoid, cut a square the size specified in the block's cutting chart. Then cut the square into triangles: If the straight grain (indicated by the arrow on the template) is on the *short* side of the trapezoid, cut a half-square triangle. If the straight grain is on the *long* edge of the trapezoid, cut a quarter-square triangle. After cutting the triangle, make a paper template (see page 221) of the cutaway triangle and tape it to the underside of your ruler. Using the paper template as a guide, trim the cutaway triangle from the larger triangle, as shown in **Diagram 9**.

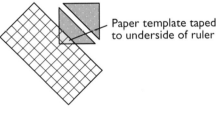

Paper template taped to underside of ruler

Diagram 9

Octagons

Some blocks feature octagons. These are cut from squares, then have the corner triangles trimmed away. To cut an octagon, cut a square the size specified in the block's cutting chart. Make a paper template (page 220) of the cutaway triangle, and tape it to the underside of your ruler. Using the paper template as a guide, trim four cutaway triangles from the square, as shown in **Diagram 10**.

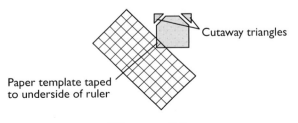

Cutaway triangles

Paper template taped to underside of ruler

Diagram 10

Kites

A kite has two long sides of equal length and two short sides of equal length. Cut a square the length of the long side of the kite. Cut the square in half once diagonally. Using the cut size of the original square as a measurement, start at one cut point and place the ruler along the triangle's long side. Find the line on your ruler that matches the size of the original square, as shown in **Diagram 11**, and cut off the triangular tip that extends beyond the ruler.

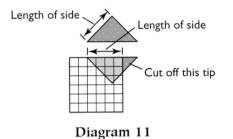

Length of side
Length of side
Cut off this tip

Diagram 11

45 Degree Diamonds

A diamond has equal sides and equal opposite angles. Cut a fabric strip the width required, then make a 45 degree cut at one end. Using the strip width measurement as a cutting measurement, cut parallel to the first cut, as shown in **Diagram 12**.

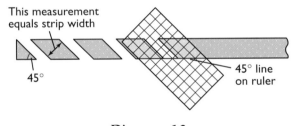

This measurement equals strip width

45°

45° line on ruler

Diagram 12

Parallelograms

A parallelogram has two long sides and two short sides. Cut a fabric strip the width required. Make a 45 degree cut at one end. Referring to **Diagram 13**, make cuts parallel to the first cut, using the dimension given in the cutting chart. This measurement will be either larger or smaller than the strip width.

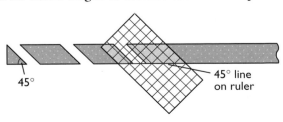

45°

45° line on ruler

Diagram 13

Quiltmaking Basics   **219**

Templates

In patchwork, pattern pieces are called templates. You'll find templates on pages 226–240 for all of the blocks in this book. The templates are arranged by shape (square, diamonds, and triangles, for example) and are identified by the letter-and-number combination (S4 means square 4, and R7 means rectangle 7). Each block cutting chart in "The Block Library" lists the templates that correspond to the rotary-cut shapes used in the block.

Using Templates

The templates in this book can be used to cut patches the traditional way if you prefer not to rotary cut, or you can use the templates to check your rotary-cut patches for accuracy. The outer solid lines on each template are cutting lines; the inner dashed lines are sewing lines. Trimming lines are indicated on the templates. (See "Trimming Points for Easy Matching" on the opposite page.) Odd-shape templates include grain line arrows as guides.

Rotary Cutting with Templates

When you're rotary cutting, you can use paper templates for shapes that don't match measurements on your ruler—like a square that measures $3\frac{13}{16}$ inches, or shapes like diamonds and parallelograms. To make a paper template, trace the needed shape (including seam allowances) onto paper. Label the paper template with its size or letter, include any grain markings, then cut it out with scissors. Using removable tape, tape your paper template to the underside of your ruler with one edge flush with the edge of the ruler. Line up the other edge of the template with the fabric edge to cut a strip the correct width, as shown in **Diagram 14A**, then with the strip to cut the shape, as shown in **14B**.

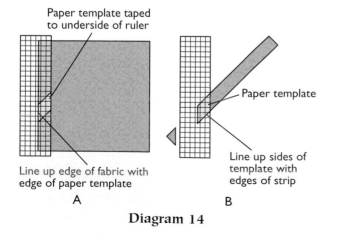

Paper template taped to underside of ruler

Paper template

Line up edge of fabric with edge of paper template

Line up sides of template with edges of strip

A　　　　　　　　B

Diagram 14

Making Durable Templates

If you choose not to use a rotary cutter, you can make traditional templates by tracing the templates in this book. To make a template you will need tracing paper, a glue stick, and a stiff material like lightweight cardboard, card stock, or transparent plastic. Carefully trace the template from the book onto the tracing paper (or directly onto the transparent plastic), transferring all grain line arrows and markings, as shown in **Diagram 15**. If you use tracing paper, cut out the pieces just outside the cutting line, and glue them to the cardboard. Cut your plastic or cardboard durable templates out just inside the cutting line. Make a template for each shape in the design. Use these templates over and over again to mark and cut your fabric.

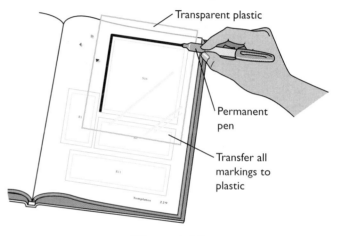

Transparent plastic

Permanent pen

Transfer all markings to plastic

Diagram 15

To use templates in the traditional way, position them on the fabric so the arrows match the straight grain of the fabric. With a sharp pencil (white for dark fabrics, regular pencil for light ones), trace around the template onto the fabric; this is your cutting line. Using sharp fabric scissors, cut just inside this line to most accurately duplicate the template.

If using templates to check the accuracy of your rotary-cut pieces, simply place your cut fabric patch on top of the corresponding template in the book. If your patch doesn't match the template size, you may want to analyze your cutting method and check your ruler for accuracy, then recut the patch. Always remember that the more accurate your cutting is, the more accurate your finished block size will be. *Note:* You may notice that some of the rotary-cutting dimensions in the block cutting charts have been rounded off slightly to the nearest $\frac{1}{8}$ or $\frac{1}{16}$ inch for ease of cutting. This variance is very minimal and will not affect the accuracy of your piecing.

Trimming Points for Easy Matching

Trimming points from triangles and other shapes takes the guesswork out of matching cut patches before sewing them together. Once you've trimmed the points, the patches will fit flush with one another when correctly aligned. It may take some practice if you've never trimmed points before, but it will improve your machine piecing in a number of ways.

First, trimming eliminates bulk in seams and prevents show-through of dark fabrics to light fabrics. Most quilters trim points before they quilt anyway, so why not trim them before the seams are sewn? Second, points create extra length on patches and sometimes cause the patches to drag through the sewing machine, preventing accurate piecing. Last, trimming points allows you to easily match one patch to another, eliminating the guessing, pinning, and matching of patch centers.

The templates in this book have trimming lines indicated. Points have been left on to make measuring for rotary cutting easier. When trimming triangle points, it's important to remember that points can be trimmed in two different ways: perpendicular to the short sides, or perpendicular to the long side. The direction of the trim line will depend on how the triangle is to be sewn to the next shape, but the amount you trim will *always* be ⅜ inch on 45 degree angles.

If you are sewing the short side of a triangle to another shape, trim the points perpendicular to the short side of the triangle, as shown in **Trimming Quarter-Square Triangles.**

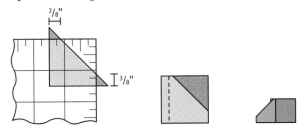

Trimming Quarter-Square Triangles

If you are sewing the long side of a triangle to another shape, trim the points perpendicular to the long side of the triangle, as shown in **Trimming Half-Square Triangles.** This method is perfect for trimming quarter-square triangles that are being sewn to a square for a Square within a Square block, as shown. It helps prevent the long bias tip from stretching your patches out of shape. This method is also perfect for trimming half-square triangles.

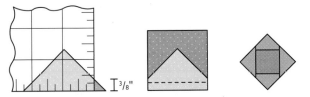

Trimming Half-Square Triangles

Machine Piecing

The standard quiltmaking seam allowance is ¼ inch, and the standard stitch length is 10 stitches per inch. When piecing, place patches right sides together, then sew from raw edge to raw edge unless directions specify otherwise.

Finding an Accurate ¼ Inch

Many machines have presser feet that measure a perfect ¼ inch; on other machines you can use the edge of the presser foot as a sewing guide and just adjust the needle position for a perfect ¼ inch. To test your seam allowance, cut three 1½-inch squares. Sew them into a row, using the ¼-inch seam allowance you've identified. Press the seams to one side, then measure the resulting three-block strip; it should measure exactly 3½ inches long. If it's too long, adjust your machine to sew a slightly wider seam allowance. If it's too short, try a slightly narrower seam allowance. Once you've found it, write down the machine settings so you'll have them in the future!

If this method isn't working for you, find an exact ¼-inch seam allowance on your sewing machine this way: Place a piece of ¼-inch graph paper (or a paper template with a marked ¼-inch seam allowance) under the presser foot. Gently lower the needle onto the ¼-inch line, as shown in **Diagram 16**. The distance from the needle to the edge of the paper is exactly ¼ inch.

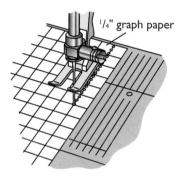

Diagram 16

Once you've found the perfect ¼ inch, create a seam guide by laying a piece of masking tape to the right of the ¼-inch seam allowance you've identified on your machine's throatplate, as shown in **Diagram 17**.

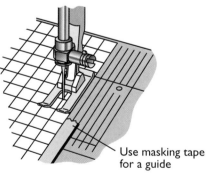

Use masking tape for a guide

Diagram 17

Speeding Up Your Piecing

When piecing a block, sew the smallest pieces together first to form units. Join smaller units to form larger ones, and continue until the block is complete. Each block in this book contains a "How to Assemble" section that leads you through the block construction step by step.

Try chain piecing to save both time and thread. With chain piecing, you sew many pairs of patches together one right after another without lifting the presser foot, clipping the threads, or removing the pieces from the sewing machine. Begin by sewing the seam on a pair of patches, then feed the next set of patches right after the previous set, being careful not to overlap them. Sew the seam of the new patches. There will be a little twist of thread between the two pieces. Chain piece in this manner, as shown in **Diagram 18**, until you reach a natural stopping point, then remove sewn patches from the machine and clip them apart. Clip the end threads at the same time—threads left hanging from the ends of seams get in the way and can be a real nuisance.

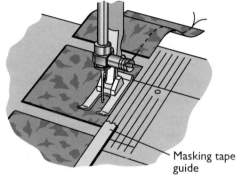

Masking tape guide

Diagram 18

Pinning

The general rule for pinning is that if you don't have to, don't do it. But if matching is involved, if your seams are longer than 4 inches, or if you are unsure, then pin. Pin points of matching (where seam lines or points meet) first. Once these important points are firmly in place, pin the rest of the seam, easing if necessary. Keep pins away from seam lines, as sewing over them tends to damage the needle and makes it hard to be accurate in tight places.

Pressing

Some machine piecers press every seam after it is sewn, and others only finger press during sewing and save pressing with an iron for later, when the block or whole quilt is complete. I press with an iron at some places and finger press at others. It just depends on the situation, and experience will teach you what works best. Generally, press seams to one side so the stress is on the fabric instead of the stitches. Press toward the darker fabric whenever possible to prevent the darker fabric from showing through the lighter fabric. The two main exceptions to this rule are when seams are pressed open to distribute bulk and when, for matching purposes, seams are pressed in opposite directions.

Be careful not to overpress because this can stretch and distort fabric pieces and often creates shiny spots in bulky seams. Press first from the top when pressing to the side, taking care to press the whole seam; don't leave little pleats at the ends. If you have a particularly bulky spot in your piecing, like where eight points of a pinwheel come together, consider pressing the final seam open to distribute the bulk, and press from the wrong side to avoid creating a shiny spot at the seam join.

Matching and Sewing

When sewing one unit to another, press seam allowances that will butt against each other in opposite directions. Hold the two units together, snugging the seam allowances together until you feel that the seams have nested against each other. Pin on either side of a seam intersection if you wish, placing the pins perpendicular to the patch edge, as shown in **Diagram 19**. Remove each pin as it nears the needle.

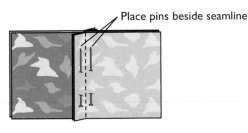

Place pins beside seamline

Diagram 19

When matching diagonal or multiple seams, it may be helpful to use a positioning pin. The match point may have several stitching lines coming through it, but it's at this point—¼ inch below the raw edges—that the seam intersections need to match. Push a pin vertically through the point of the top patch, then the bottom patch, where you want them to match, as shown in **Diagram 20**. Keep this pin standing upright in the fabrics to avoid shifting the patches. Pin on either side of the first pin to hold the fabric together firmly, as shown. Sew the seam, holding the stabbed pin steady to keep it vertical and removing each pin as it nears the needle.

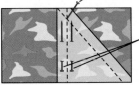

Place positioning pin in the intersection you want to match

Then pin on either side of intersection

Diagram 20

When triangles are pieced, stitches form an X at the next seam line. To create crisp points, use this X as a sewing guide. Place two units right sides together, positioning the units so the sewn X is on top. Sew the seam, sewing right through the center of the X, as shown in **Diagram 21**.

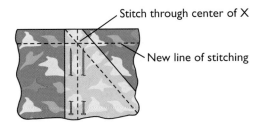

Stitch through center of X

New line of stitching

Diagram 21

If you find that the two patches you are ready to sew together are slightly different lengths, pin them together at the matching points (seam lines or points). Sew the seam with the shorter patch on top; the feed dogs will ease in the fullness of the bottom patch.

Set-in seams are found where three patches come together. The seam construction looks like the capital letter Y. The example shown in **Diagram 22** on page 224 is a Y-seam unit of two diamonds and a triangle. To begin, sew a diamond to a triangle, as shown in **22A**. With the triangle on top, begin sewing at the ¼-inch seam line. (You may want to mark this point lightly with a pencil beforehand.) Backtack, taking care not to stitch into the seam allowance. Sew the remainder of the seam, ending at the cut edge of the fabric.

To add the second diamond, position the pieces with the triangle on top. Sew as shown in **22B**, beginning at the outside edge of the fabric and ending with a backtack at the ¼-inch seam line. Fold the triangle out of the way and match the points of the two diamonds, as shown in **22C**. Stitch the diamonds together, beginning with a backtack at the inner ¼-inch seam line, and ending at the cut edge of the fabric.

To finish your set-in seam, gently press the center seam open, as shown in **22D**. Press the other two seams toward the diamonds.

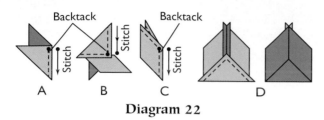

Diagram 22

Finishing

Once your quilt top is done, follow these guidelines for putting your quilt together. These are the methods that I use and that have worked well for me.

Quilting Designs

Quilting suggestions are included with each project. Mark your quilting designs before layering your quilt. Use a silver or white pencil, chalk marker, or a 0.5 mm mechanical lead pencil. For light fabrics, place the pattern under the quilt top, and trace the quilting design directly onto the fabric, marking a very thin line. For dark fabrics, mark on the right side of the fabric, tracing your quilting pattern.

Layering and Basting

To layer, fold the quilt backing in half lengthwise and press to form a center line. Place the back, wrong side up, on the basting table. Fold the batting in half lengthwise and lay it on the quilt backing, aligning the center lines. Open out and smooth the batting. Fold the quilt top in half lengthwise, right sides together, and lay it on the batting, aligning the fold with the center of the batting. Unfold the top and smooth it out.

If you are hand quilting, use a darning needle and white thread to baste the layers together, making lines of basting 3 inches apart. Baste from the center out, or make a grid of horizontal and vertical lines of basting. If you plan to machine quilt, use safety pins to secure the layers together, pinning approximately every 3 inches from the center out.

Hand Quilting

Use a hoop or frame to hold the quilt layers taut. Work with one hand on top of the quilt and the other hand underneath. Use short quilting needles, called betweens, in either size 9 or 10. To start, thread a needle with quilting thread and single

knot the end. Insert the needle through the quilt top and batting about 1 inch away from where you will begin stitching. Bring the needle to the surface to make the first stitch. Tug on the thread to pop the knot through the quilt top and bury it in the batting, as shown in **Diagram 23**.

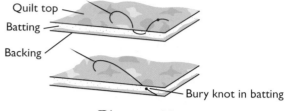

Diagram 23

To make quilting stitches, insert the needle through all layers. When you feel the needle's tip with your underneath finger, guide it back up through the quilt. When the needle comes through the quilt top, press your thimble on the eye to guide it down again through the quilt layers, as shown in **Diagram 24**. Continue to quilt in this manner, taking two or three small running stitches at a time.

Diagram 24

To end stitching, bring the needle to the quilt top, just past the last stitch. Referring to **Diagram 25**, make a knot at the surface by bringing the needle under the thread where it comes out of the fabric and up through the loop of thread it creates. Repeat this knot and insert the needle into the hole where the thread comes out. Run the needle inside the batting for an inch and bring it back to the surface. Tug gently on the thread to pop the knot through the quilt top and into the batting layer. Clip the thread.

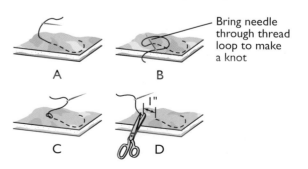

Diagram 25

Machine Quilting

To secure the thread at the beginning and end of a design, adjust your machine's stitch length to make several very short stitches. When machine-guided quilting, use a walking foot for straight lines. Keep the feed dogs up and move all three layers smoothly under the needle. Machine-guided quilting is ideal for quilting in the ditch and creating grids.

For free-motion quilting, use a darning or machine embroidery foot and disengage the feed dogs. For best results, choose continuous-line quilting designs so you won't have to begin and end threads frequently. Guide the marked design under the needle with both hands, working at a steady pace.

Binding

Rotary cut 1½-inch bias strips for binding. To join the cut strips, place right sides together and offset the ends, as shown in **Diagram 26**. Sew the strips together using a ¼-inch seam, then trim the points. Press the seams open to distribute bulk.

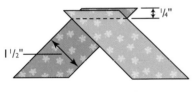

Diagram 26

To attach the binding, trim the batting and backing even with the quilt top. Or, to make a firm, filled binding, leave ¼ inch extending past the quilt top. Beginning in the middle of a side, place the binding strip right sides together with the quilt top, align the raw edges, and pin if desired. Leaving 2 to 3 inches of binding unsewn at the beginning, sew the binding to the quilt top using a ¼-inch seam, as shown in **Diagram 27**.

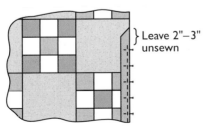

Diagram 27

As you approach a corner, stop stitching ¼ inch from the raw edge of the corner, as shown in **Diagram 28A**. Backstitch two or three stitches and

remove the quilt from the machine. Fold the binding strip up at a 45 degree angle, as shown in **28B**. Fold the strip back down so there is a fold at the upper edge, as shown in **28C**. Pin the binding and begin sewing at the top edge of the quilt, as shown, stopping ¼ inch from the next corner.

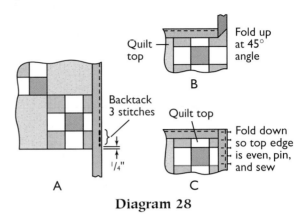

Diagram 28

When you are within 4 inches of your starting point, backtack and remove the quilt from the machine. Fold one binding end over the other end and finger-press to mark the point where the ends meet. Baste the binding ends together at the pressed mark, then check the fit on the quilt top, adjusting the seam line if necessary. Sew the seam, then trim the excess fabric, as shown in **Diagram 29**.

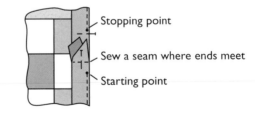

Diagram 29

Turn the binding to the back of the quilt. Starting at the center of any side, turn under the raw edge ¼ inch, lightly press it, then hand sew in place. Sew until you are ¼ inch from the corner, as shown in **Diagram 30A**. At the corner, fold in the unsewn binding to form a miter, then tack with a few stitches, as shown in **30B**. Continue sewing the binding in place around the entire quilt.

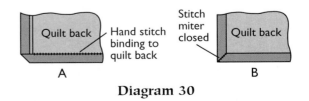

Diagram 30

Templates

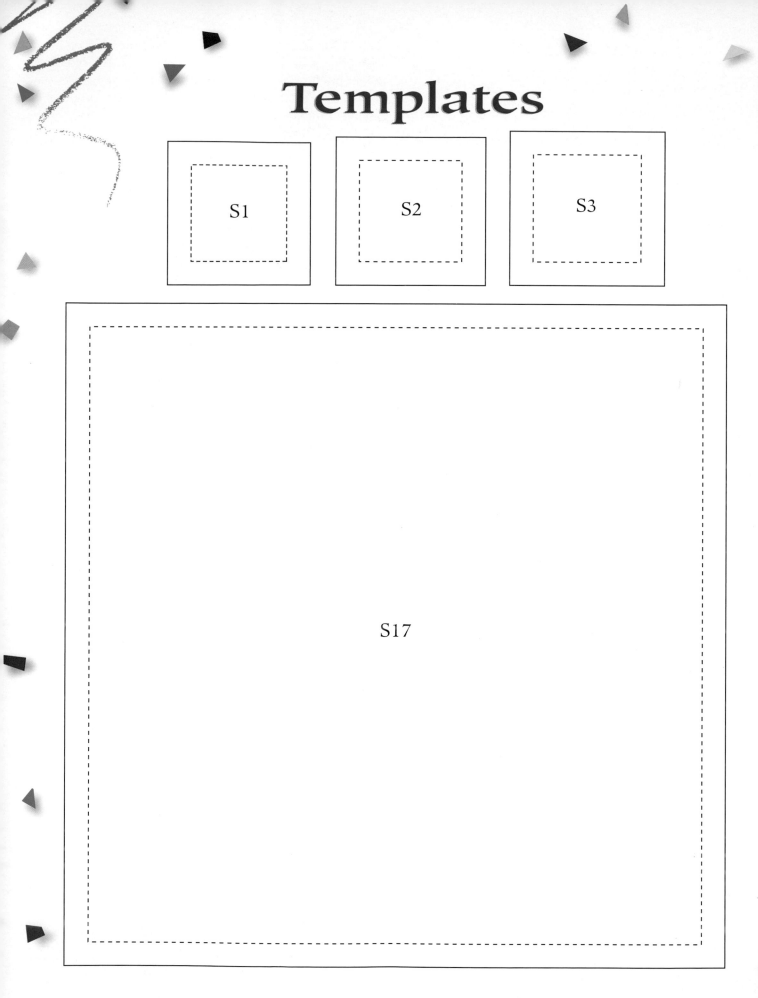

S1

S2

S3

S17

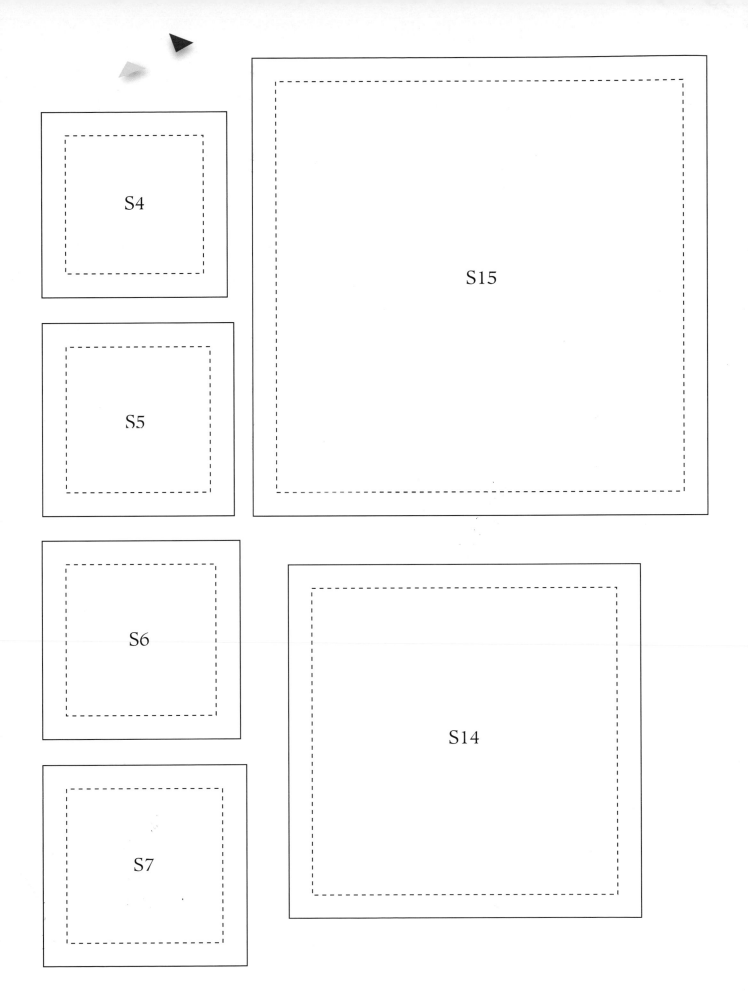

S4

S5

S6

S7

S15

S14

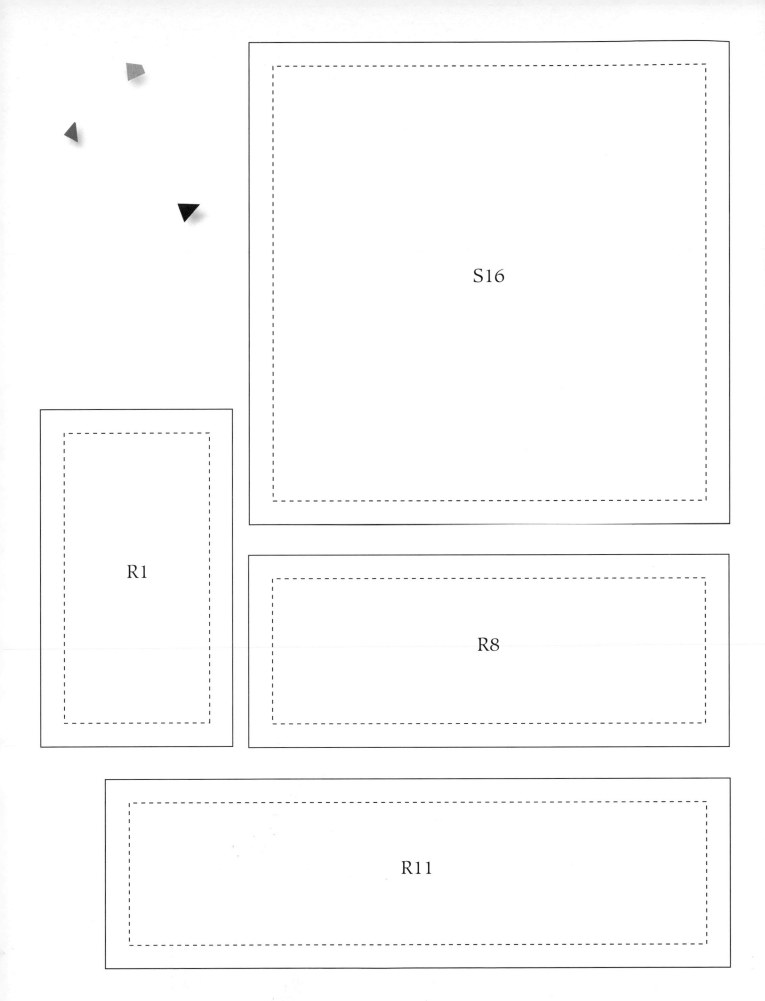

S16

R1

R8

R11

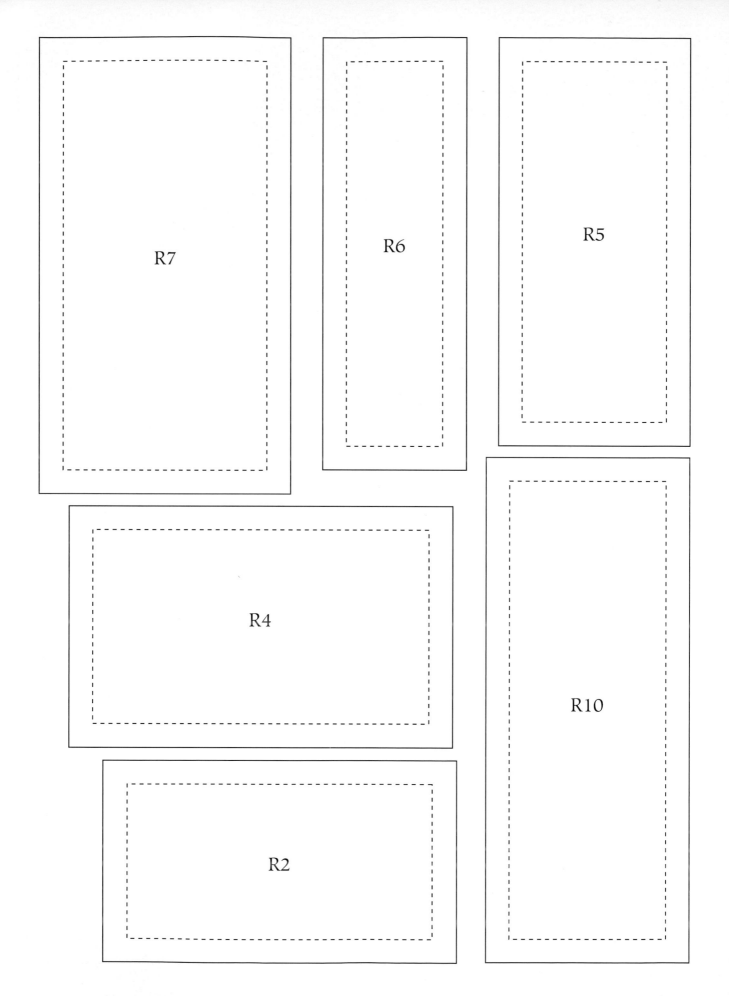

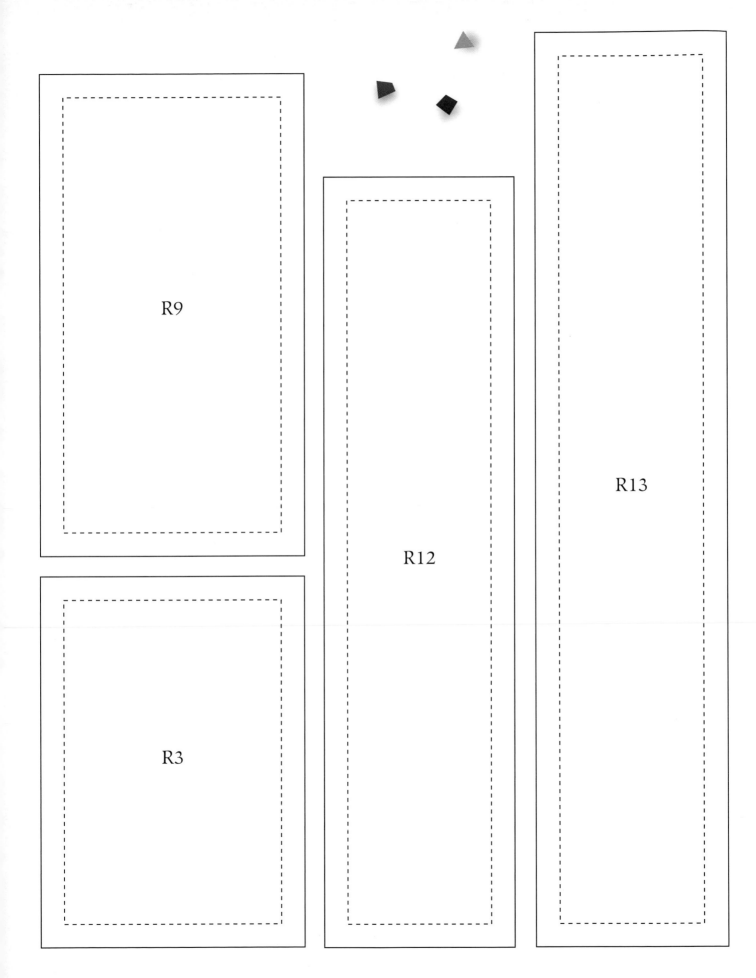

R9

R3

R12

R13

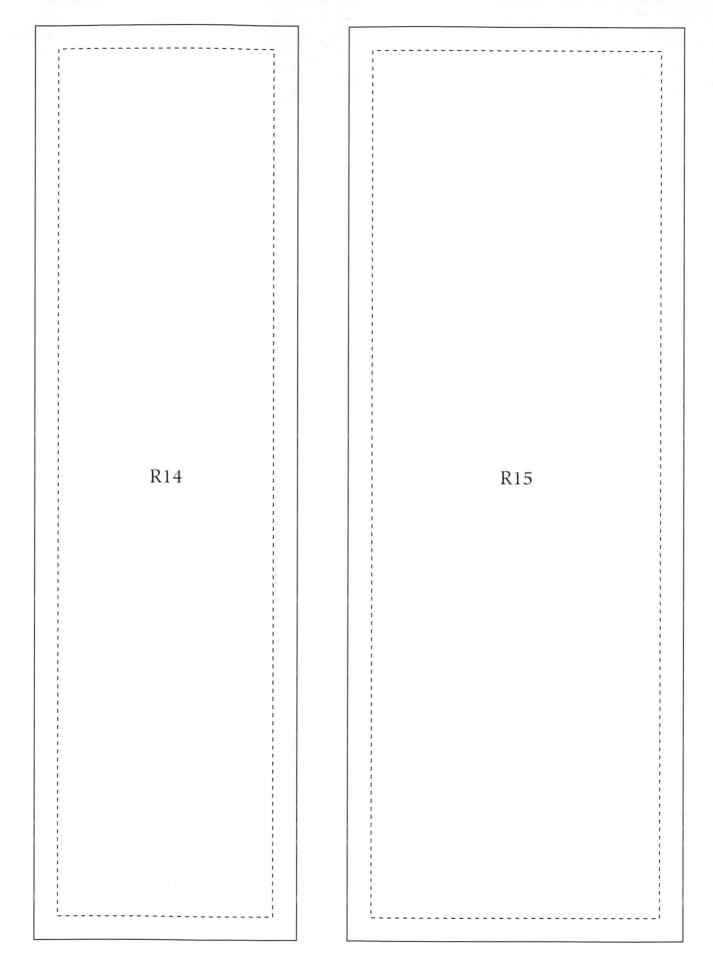

R14

R15

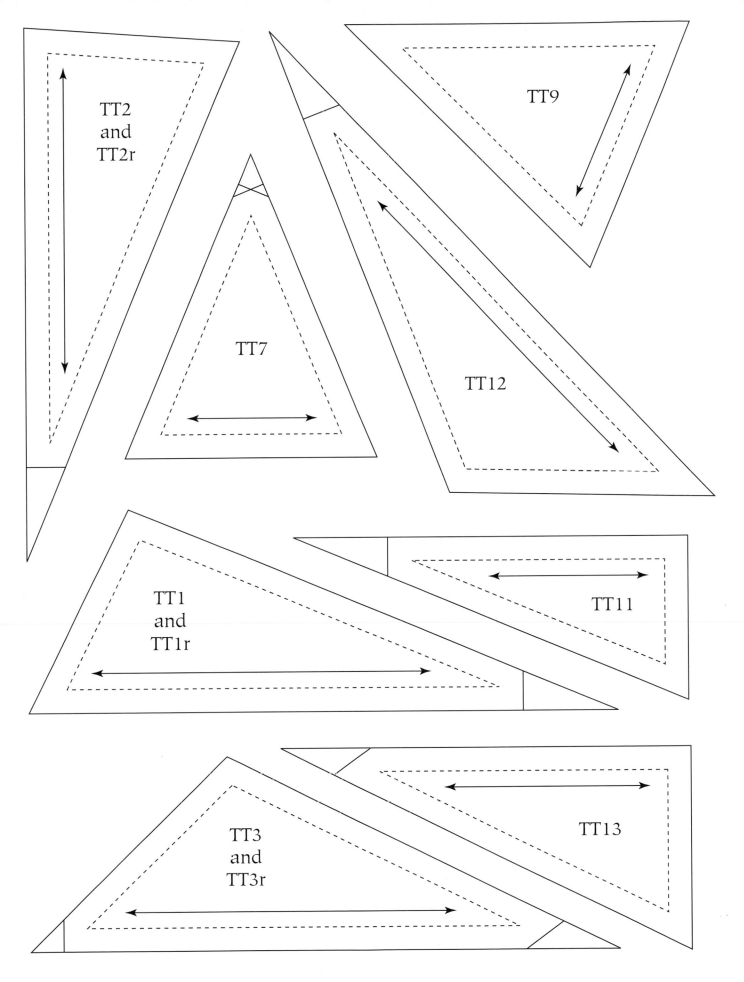

TT2
and
TT2r

TT9

TT7

TT12

TT1
and
TT1r

TT11

TT3
and
TT3r

TT13

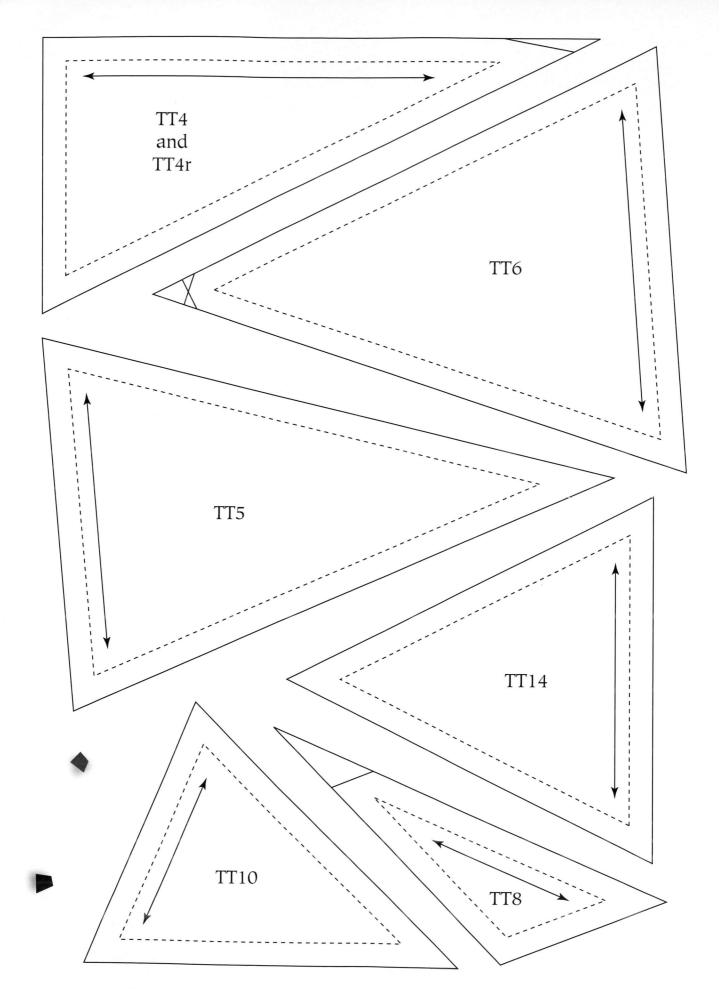

TT4
and
TT4r

TT6

TT5

TT14

TT10

TT8

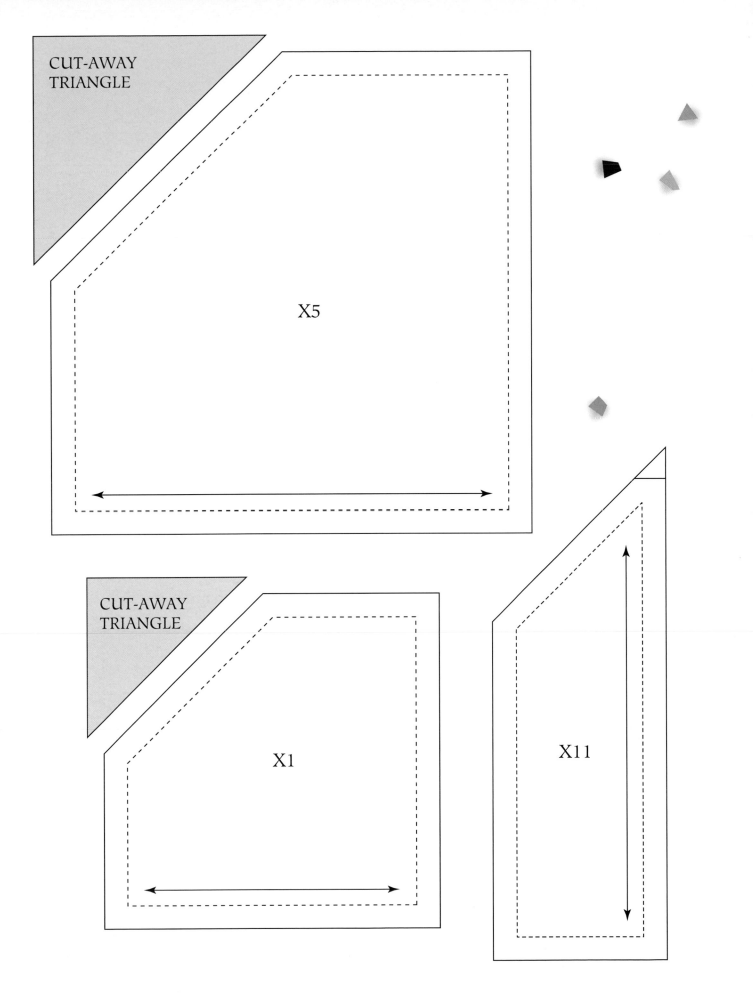

CUT-AWAY
TRIANGLE

X5

CUT-AWAY
TRIANGLE

X1

X11

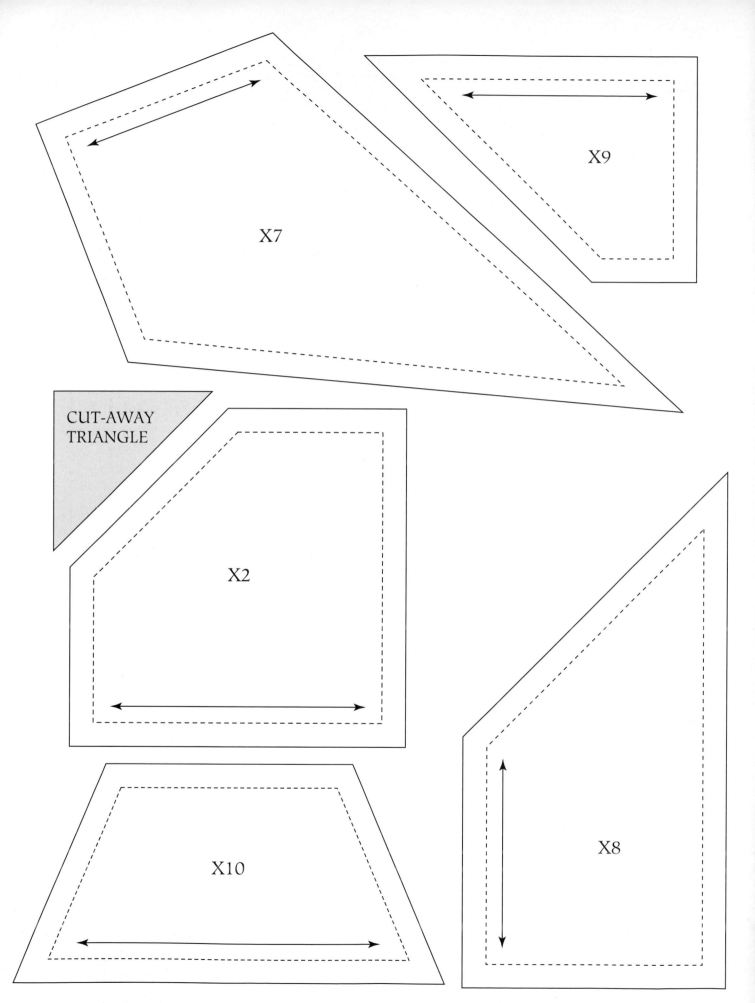

X9

X7

CUT-AWAY
TRIANGLE

X2

X8

X10

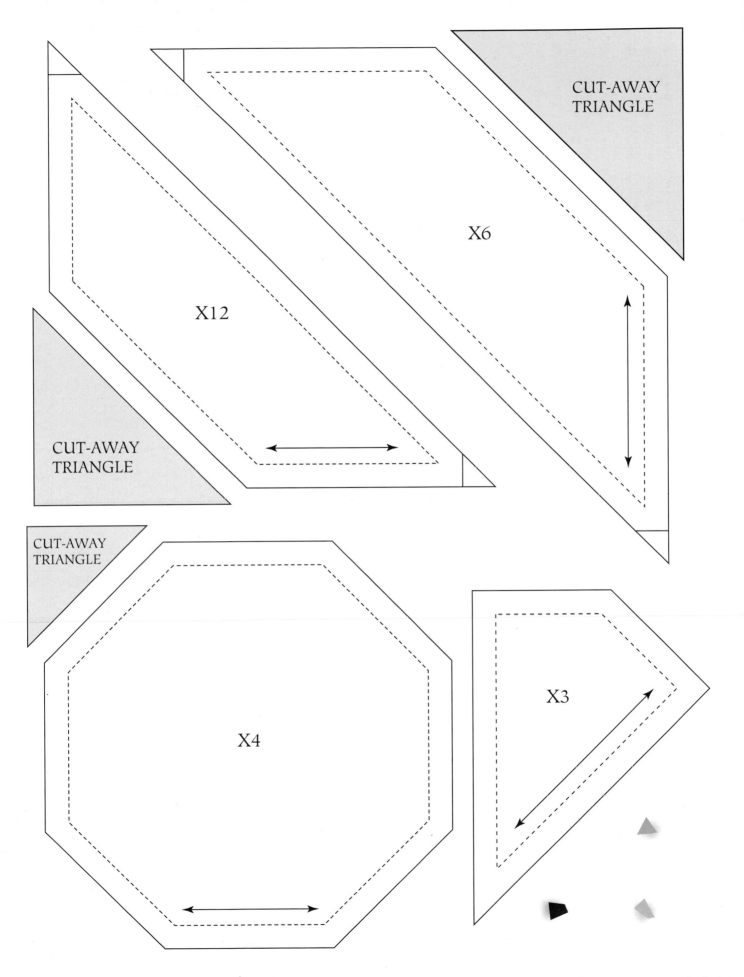

CUT-AWAY TRIANGLE

X6

X12

CUT-AWAY TRIANGLE

CUT-AWAY TRIANGLE

X4

X3

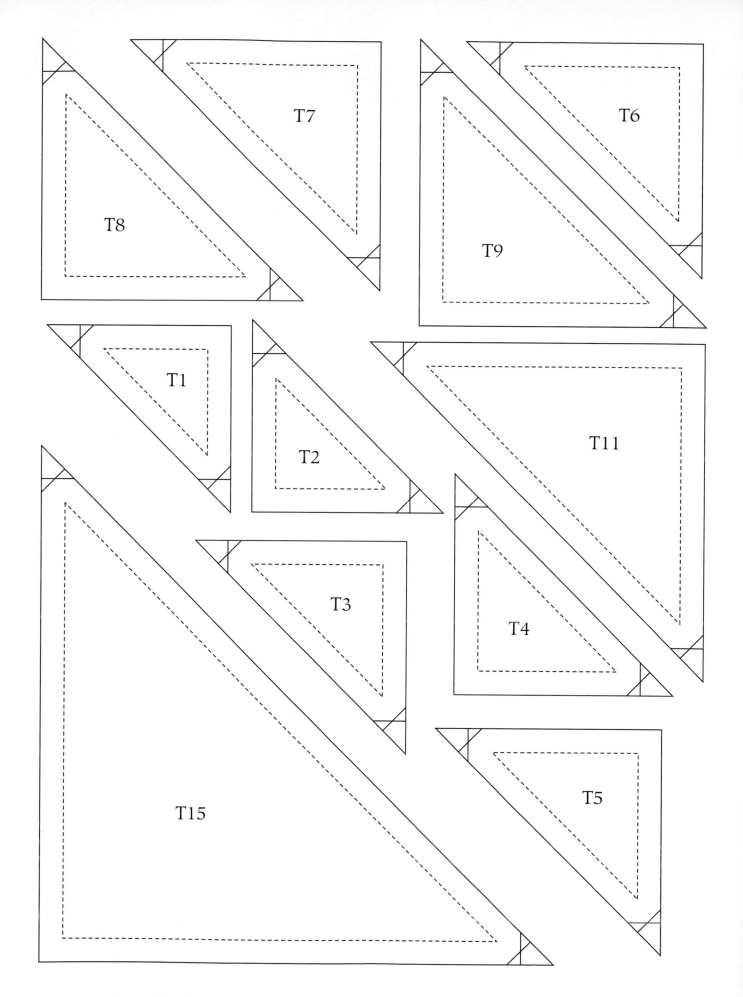

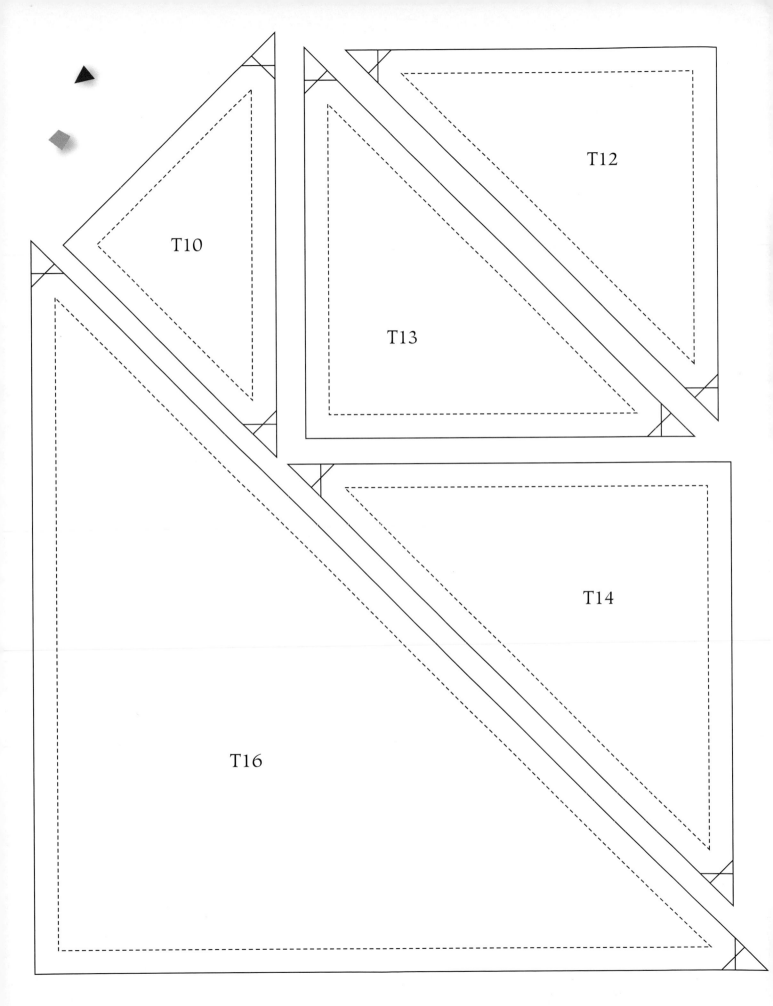

T12

T10

T13

T14

T16

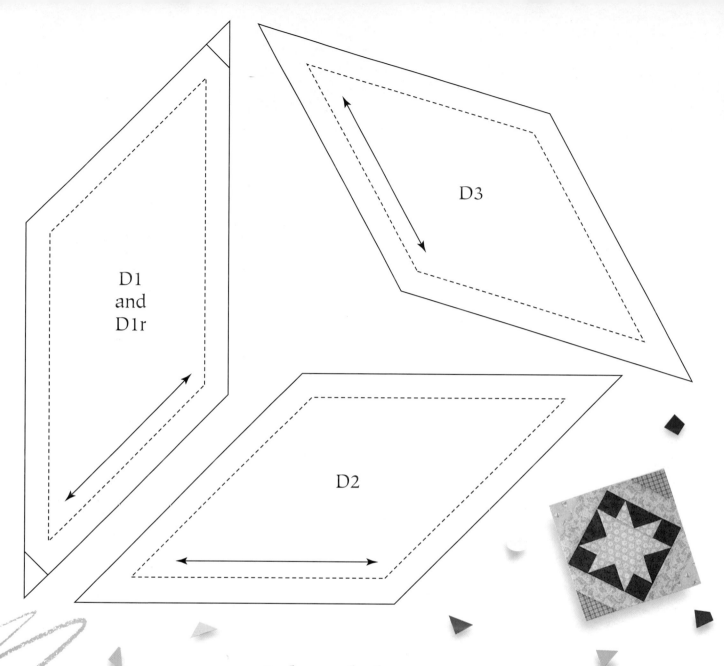

D1
and
D1r

D3

D2

Acknowledgments

My thanks to **Wendy Slotboom**, my assistant, who designed Wendy's Gift Bags and who helped me immeasurably with proofreading and moral support; **Cleo Nollette**, who pieced many of the 9-inch blocks, made the Cross-Country blocks in the Cross-Country Quilt, and pieced the Log Cabin Quilt; **Joan Dawson**, who designed and made Joan's Quilt Bag; and **Judy Pollard**, who designed and made the Bear's Paw Wallhanging.

I'd also like to thank **Terri Shinn**, who took my black-and-white drawings of the Rosebud Quilt top and made it sing with her wonderful colors; **Barbara Ford**, who machine quilted the Cross-Country Quilt, Flying Geese Table Topper, Four-Block Sampler, Jericho Stars Quilt, Log Cabin Quilt, Patchwork Pillows, and Rosebud Quilt; **Jenny Biwer**, who machine quilted the Fox and Geese Quilt and Sampler Medallion Quilt, the Star Tile Baby Quilt, and the Three Block Table Runner; **Pepper Cory**, who lent expert advice on quilting designs and stencils; **David Peha** at Fabric Sales Company, for encouraging me to design the Staples line of background fabrics that I used in most of the quilts in this book; and **Glendora Hutson**, for teaching me to properly pipe a pillow 20 years ago.

My appreciation to **Bernina of America**, for loaning a sewing machine for photography; **Olfa**, for sending a generous supply of rotary cutters and blades; and **Omnigrid**, for donating rotary cutting mats and rulers in every size imaginable.

Block Index

Note: Subjects are indexed on pages 243–44

Air Castle
2, 158

Antique Star
3, 162

Art Square
4, 133

Aunt Vina's Favorite
5

Beacon Lights
6

Bear's Paw
7, 172

Berkeley
8

Big T
9

Birds in the Air
10

Blazing Star
11

Broken Star
12, 162

By Chance
13, 133

Cake Stand
14, 143

Candlelight
15

Capital T
16

Castles in Spain
17

Cat's Cradle
18

Centennial
19

Chain of Squares
20

Clay's Choice
21

Combination Star
22

Corn and Beans
23

Courthouse Steps
24

Cross-Country
25, 133, 212

Crossroads to Jericho
26, 207

Darting Minnows
27

Dolley Madison's Star
28, 135

Double Dutch
29, 177

Double Four Patch
30

Double Windmill
31

Double X
32

Duck Paddle
33

Ducks and Ducklings
34

Dutchman's Puzzle
35

Eddystone Light
36

Eight-Pointed Star
37

Eliza's Nine Patch
38

Evening Star with Pinwheel
39, 162

Fifty-Four Forty
40

Flying Geese
41, 177, 183, 185

Flying Pinwheel
42

Flying Star
43

Flying X
44

Fox and Geese
45, 193

Free Trade
46

Friendship Block
47

Gentleman's Fancy
48

Goose Tracks
49

Grandmother's Favorite
50

Grandmother's Pride
51

Grape Basket
52

Grecian Square
53

Handy Andy
54

Hourglass
55

Hovering Hawks
56

241

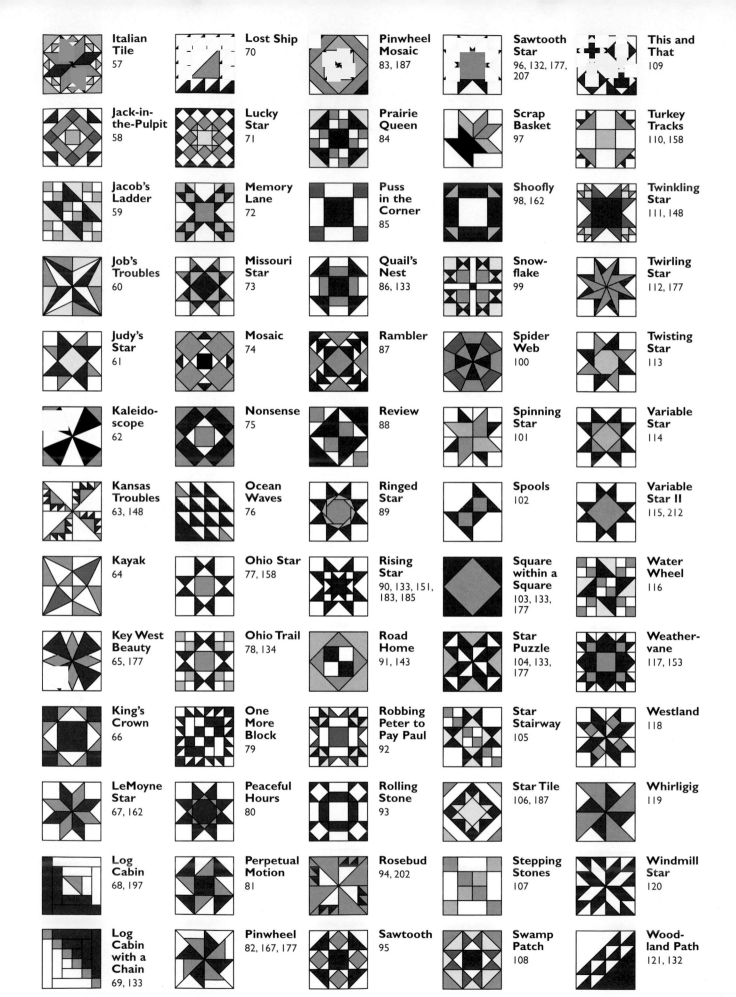

Italian Tile 57	**Lost Ship** 70	**Pinwheel Mosaic** 83, 187	**Sawtooth Star** 96, 132, 177, 207	**This and That** 109
Jack-in-the-Pulpit 58	**Lucky Star** 71	**Prairie Queen** 84	**Scrap Basket** 97	**Turkey Tracks** 110, 158
Jacob's Ladder 59	**Memory Lane** 72	**Puss in the Corner** 85	**Shoofly** 98, 162	**Twinkling Star** 111, 148
Job's Troubles 60	**Missouri Star** 73	**Quail's Nest** 86, 133	**Snow-flake** 99	**Twirling Star** 112, 177
Judy's Star 61	**Mosaic** 74	**Rambler** 87	**Spider Web** 100	**Twisting Star** 113
Kaleido-scope 62	**Nonsense** 75	**Review** 88	**Spinning Star** 101	**Variable Star** 114
Kansas Troubles 63, 148	**Ocean Waves** 76	**Ringed Star** 89	**Spools** 102	**Variable Star II** 115, 212
Kayak 64	**Ohio Star** 77, 158	**Rising Star** 90, 133, 151, 183, 185	**Square within a Square** 103, 133, 177	**Water Wheel** 116
Key West Beauty 65, 177	**Ohio Trail** 78, 134	**Road Home** 91, 143	**Star Puzzle** 104, 133, 177	**Weather-vane** 117, 153
King's Crown 66	**One More Block** 79	**Robbing Peter to Pay Paul** 92	**Star Stairway** 105	**Westland** 118
LeMoyne Star 67, 162	**Peaceful Hours** 80	**Rolling Stone** 93	**Star Tile** 106, 187	**Whirligig** 119
Log Cabin 68, 197	**Perpetual Motion** 81	**Rosebud** 94, 202	**Stepping Stones** 107	**Windmill Star** 120
Log Cabin with a Chain 69, 133	**Pinwheel** 82, 167, 177	**Sawtooth** 95	**Swamp Patch** 108	**Wood-land Path** 121, 132

Index

Note: Blocks are indexed on pages 241–42

METRIC EQUIVALENCY CHART

mm=millimeters
cm=centimeters

Yards to Meters

YARDS	METERS	YARDS	METERS	YARDS	METERS	YARDS	METERS	YARDS	METERS
1/8	0.11	2 1/8	1.94	4 1/8	3.77	6 1/8	5.60	8 1/8	7.43
1/4	0.23	2 1/4	2.06	4 1/4	3.89	6 1/4	5.72	8 1/4	7.54
3/8	0.34	2 3/8	2.17	4 3/8	4.00	6 3/8	5.83	8 3/8	7.66
1/2	0.46	2 1/2	2.29	4 1/2	4.11	6 1/2	5.94	8 1/2	7.77
5/8	0.57	2 5/8	2.40	4 5/8	4.23	6 5/8	6.06	8 5/8	7.89
3/4	0.69	2 3/4	2.51	4 3/4	4.34	6 3/4	6.17	8 3/4	8.00
7/8	0.80	2 7/8	2.63	4 7/8	4.46	6 7/8	6.29	8 7/8	8.12
1	0.91	3	2.74	5	4.57	7	6.40	9	8.23
1 1/8	1.03	3 1/8	2.86	5 1/8	4.69	7 1/8	6.52	9 1/8	8.34
1 1/4	1.14	3 1/4	2.97	5 1/4	4.80	7 1/4	6.63	9 1/4	8.46
1 3/8	1.26	3 3/8	3.09	5 3/8	4.91	7 3/8	6.74	9 3/8	8.57
1 1/2	1.37	3 1/2	3.20	5 1/2	5.03	7 1/2	6.86	9 1/2	8.69
1 5/8	1.49	3 5/8	3.31	5 5/8	5.14	7 5/8	6.97	9 5/8	8.80
1 3/4	1.60	3 3/4	3.43	5 3/4	5.26	7 3/4	7.09	9 3/4	8.92
1 7/8	1.71	3 7/8	3.54	5 7/8	5.37	7 7/8	7.20	9 7/8	9.03
2	1.83	4	3.66	6	5.49	8	7.32	10	9.14

Inches to Millimeters and Centimeters

INCHES	MM	CM	INCHES	CM	INCHES	CM
1/8	3	0.3	9	22.9	30	76.2
1/4	6	0.6	10	25.4	31	78.7
3/8	10	1.0	11	27.9	32	81.3
1/2	13	1.3	12	30.5	33	83.8
5/8	16	1.6	13	33.0	34	86.4
3/4	19	1.9	14	35.6	35	88.9
7/8	22	2.2	15	38.1	36	91.4
1	25	2.5	16	40.6	37	94.0
1 1/4	32	3.2	17	43.2	38	96.5
1 1/2	38	3.8	18	45.7	39	99.1
1 3/4	44	4.4	19	48.3	40	101.6
2	51	5.1	20	50.8	41	104.1
2 1/2	64	6.4	21	53.3	42	106.7
3	76	7.6	22	55.9	43	109.2
3 1/2	89	8.9	23	58.4	44	111.8
4	102	10.2	24	61.0	45	114.3
4 1/2	114	11.4	25	63.5	46	116.8
5	127	12.7	26	66.0	47	119.4
6	152	15.2	27	68.6	48	121.9
7	178	17.8	28	71.1	49	124.5
8	203	20.3	29	73.7	50	127.0